Brief Separations

Brief Separations

Christoph M. Heinicke, Ph.D.

and

Ilse J. Westheimer, A. A. P. S. W.

with the assistance of

ELIZABETH WOLPERT

INTERNATIONAL UNIVERSITIES PRESS, INC.

New York   New York

Manufactured in the United States of America

Contents

Foreword

In medical research a major shift of perspective occurs whenever a causative agent is recognized. Whereas up to that point the focus of attention is on a pathological condition and the path of the investigator still leads backward to possible causes, once a causative agent is identified (or is thought to be identified) the focus shifts. Thenceforward, the path leads forward from the cause to the effects on the organism. In the study of maternal deprivation such a shift occurred rather more than a decade ago.

By the early 1950's it was already clear from retrospective research that disruptions of the young child's relationship to his mother could have an adverse effect on his emotional development and mental health. The more closely the problem was studied, however, the more complex it was seen to be. On the one hand, outcome seemed to be very diverse: not only did some children seem very gravely damaged whereas others seemed to come through little affected, but the damage itself appeared to take protean forms. On the other hand, the events that come under the umbrella of "deprivation of maternal care" were recognized to be heterogeneous: some children have practically no mothering at all, others are mothered but by an assortment of women none of whom the children can call their own, others again are passed at intervals from one mother-figure to another. When to this are added the variables arising from age and health and from the different kinds of environment in which a child may be living, it becomes clear that we are faced with a very tangled skein indeed. The problem then is to decide how best to start the process of unraveling it.

Inevitably, a clinician's bias is to continue with retrospective studies, examining cases that appear to illustrate outcome in the hope that good historical data will throw light on the variables. But this strategy has great limitations. First, the clinician is likely to be seeing only a very special sample of outcomes and, secondly, historical data are always inadequate and often inaccurate. To make progress, a shift of attention from outcome to cause is required.

Reflecting on these problems a decade or so ago, my colleagues and I decided that the most productive strategy was likely to be the direct study of how young children respond to situations of separation and deprivation at the time they occur. In adopting this course we were much encouraged by the illuminating data obtained by James Robertson, a member of the group, who had a good knowledge of the earlier observations made by Dorothy Burlingham and Anna Freud in the Hampstead Nurseries during the war. Naturalistic observations made by him on children of different ages from different sorts of homes and placed in different kinds of situations had led us to believe there were certain predictable sequences of response that occurred both during and after an event of this kind. What was now wanted, we believed, was a planned and controlled study. It was at this point that Dr. Heinicke signified his wish to join us, and he received a warm welcome.

In a field such as this it is very much easier to conceive a planned study than to conceive one that is practicable. In an armchair, samples of children can be specified, the events to which they will be exposed can be selected, procedures for observation can be laid down. In actuality, children of the samples specified may be found not to exist, or to be exceedingly rare; the events to which they are subjected turn out to be very different from what had been expected; the observations that can be made may fall far short of those desired. Instead of being controlled by the investigators, the experiment of opportunity tends to control them.

Nonetheless, in this inquiry the investigators, with much experience of their own and others behind them, were able to carry through their plan without major change. As a result, their report presents the most systematic and reliable data yet available of how children in their second and third years respond to a short period away from home in a residential nursery. Moreover, by studying children of a contrast group, reasonably well-matched for relevant variables, who remained in their own homes over a comparable period, the extent to which the behavior of the separated children is due to change of environment is thrown into relief. The very different way that children of the two groups responded to the visit of the investigator four months later is of particular interest.

Though much further work is required before we have a clear understanding of the effect on the responses of the many variables that may influence them, this inquiry adds something to our growing sum of knowledge. Among other things, it confirms that the responses become more pronounced the longer the child is separated, and also that the responses are much diminished by the presence of a sibling.

The study reported here belongs to the class we have termed short longitudinal. In this class of study the aim is to observe subjects before, during and after they are exposed to events that are believed to have significance for behavior and future development. Since there is pressing interest in what long-term effects (if any) such events may have, arguments for continuing the follow-up over a long period always seem strong. The authors of this study, however, have limited its scope; and in my view have been wise to do so. Even a short longitudinal study is a major undertaking, and not until we have a much clearer understanding of the nature of the responses under study and how they may be expected to be detected in the long run, will the time be ripe to extend a follow-up from a few months to a few years. To be productive research must usually move forward from one modest step to another; only gradually will the central strongholds of ignorance fall.

While all research must be inspired and guided by theory, it is desirable, in the exposition of data, that theory be reduced to a minimum. In this the authors of the present study have been meticulous. Only in the final chapter, written by the senior author, does one of them give an account of how, in terms of one theoretical schema, their findings might be interpreted. By proceeding in this way they have made it easy for readers of different theoretical persuasion (of whom I am one) to consider the data and, if they have good reason, to interpret them in other ways. Only thus can the great debate of science productively proceed.

It is unfortunate that all too often in the field of personality development and psychopathology, debate over theory has been sterile because reliable and relevant data have been lacking. It is therefore a source of much satisfaction to me, in regard to issues concerned with maternal deprivation, that this deficiency is now being made good. As a notable addition to this process, the present study is greatly to be welcomed.

JOHN BOWLBY

Acknowledgments

This project was undertaken as part of the work of the Child Development Research Unit of the Tavistock Institute of Human Relations and the Tavistock Clinic and has received support from the following bodies: The Josiah Macy Junior Foundation, The Foundations' Fund for Research in Psychiatry, the Ford Foundation and the Paddington Group Hospital Management Committee of the National Health Service.

We are much indebted to the following for permission to work in the nurseries under their jurisdiction and for assistance in finding the sample of nonseparated children: The London County Council, the Thomas Coram Foundation for Children and the Wellgarth Nursery Training College. Without this permission and the co-operation of their staffs, this study could not have been undertaken.

We are particularly grateful to Dr. John Bowlby, Director of the Child Development Research Unit, for his stimulus and consistent support. His help was invaluable in the planning and execution of the study and in the presentation of our findings.

We also wish to thank the other members of the team and especially Mrs. Elizabeth Wolpert for her help in collecting and analyzing the data; Mr. James Robertson for giving us throughout the benefit of his extensive experience and for much help in revising the manuscript; Miss Janice Edmunds for her assistance in all phases of data and manuscript preparation; and Miss Audrey Sanders for her editorial and administrative assistance.

We also wish to thank Mrs. Beatrice Soles and Mr. Eric Rump for their help in analyzing the data; Mrs. Elise Greenhouse for her editorial assistance; and Mrs. Rosemary McVey, Mrs. Diana Hager and Mrs. Roselyn Katz for their help in preparing the manuscript.

Finally, we have benefited greatly from the careful reading and constructive criticism of our manuscript by Mary D. Ainsworth, Pauline S. Sears, and Merton M. Gill.

The senior author's year at the Center for Advanced Study in the Behavioral Sciences did much to further the successful completion of the project.

The Background and
Aims of the Study

1 ## I. The Background of the Study

Many previous studies have pointed to the importance of the separation of the mother and child as an event affecting both the immediate and future development of the child. While most of these have concentrated on the later effects of institutionalization occurring early in the child's life (see Bowlby, J., 1951, and Yarrow, L. J., 1961, for reviews), there have also been some studies of the immediate effects of separating a young child from his parents for a brief period of time. The study to be reported here deals with brief separations such as these.

Most immediately influential in planning the present study was a pilot study begun by Heinicke in 1953.[1] This pilot study in turn was based on previous work reported by others. Particularly important in guiding us were the writings of Freud, A. (1951) and Freud, A. and Burlingham (1943, 1944). Equally influential were papers by Bowlby (1951, 1953, 1954), Robertson (1953a, 1953b, 1953c), Robertson and Bowlby (1952) and Ainsworth and Bowlby (1954).

These as well as other studies to be cited later were helpful in mapping out both the types of reactions likely to be observed in the separation situation and the variables that would influence these reactions. They served as a guide both in choosing our methods of observation and in designing the study. For example, all observers agreed that when a 2-year-old child is separated from his parents, he frets. Moreover, it had become clear that the forms of fretting ranged from temper-like crying for the parents to quietly watching for their appearance at a window. The example reported by Robertson (1953a) well illustrates the latter. Laura had been watching a steamroller working below the ward window. As it disappeared she insisted: "I want

---

[1] The main findings of this earlier study (Heinicke, 1956) are summarized at the end of this section.

to see the steam roller. I want to see the steam roller. I want to see my MUMMY. I want to see the steam roller" (p. 383).

The previous work also suggested a variety of factors which might well influence the child's reactions to separation: (1) What was the nature of the child's previous development and what in particular was his relationship to his parents? (2) Under what circumstances did the separation occur? For example, was the separation gradual or abrupt? (3) What was the age of the child and, more important, what was the developmental status of the child? Of central importance here was the question of whether or not the parents had acquired a distinctive significance for the child. (4) For how long a period was the child separated, and could he expect to return to his parents? (5) How much contact with his family could he maintain? How frequently did the parents visit, and was the child accompanied by a sibling? (6) Finally, once in the new environment, what was the potential for forming substitute relationships?

Though most informative, the early studies, as one might expect, were also deficient in certain respects. The observations were not always undertaken in a systematic manner and were seldom part of a planned design. The samples of children were not homogeneous and several factors other than the separation were likely to influence the child's reaction. Some children were observed in a hospital setting where illness and medical treatment, including being confined in a cot, provided additional disturbing experiences. In other studies the possibility of the child returning to his parents was uncertain. In still others the child was placed in a series of institutions.

The pilot study (hereafter referred to as the first study) was planned to meet some of the above difficulties. The sample of children observed was homogeneous and more systematic procedures were used to gather the data. Since all the children returned to their parents, it was possible to add to the information on the nature of children's reactions when reunited with their parents. Furthermore, a design including the use of contrast groups gave one greater confidence in determining what factors were likely to be of most importance in affecting a child.

II.   The Aims of the Study

Given both the positive values and the deficiencies of the previous work, and given the areas of further investigation suggested by the first study, the present study was planned with two broad aims in mind: (1) to describe further through the use of a more refined methodology the reactions of 2-year-old children to separation and the factors which most influence these reactions, and (2) to make a contribution to the knowledge of how young children respond to a traumatic event.

A. The Substantiation and Extension of the Findings on Separation

Although the findings of our first study had substantiated much of the earlier work, they were themselves based on small samples. Further and very similar work was indicated.

Since the inclusion of a contrast group had proven of value in this pilot work, such a group was again included as part of the design. This time we compared a group of separated children with a matched group of childen living in their own homes. Many of the findings generated by comparing a completely separated group (residential nursery children) and a partially separated group (day nursery children) could be checked in this manner. If by comparison with the day nursery children the children in the residential nursery were characterized by severe hostility, would a replication, this time comparing them with children living at home, result in a similar finding?

The actual sample of residential children chosen for the study reflected the experience of others as well as that gathered from our first study. Since the child's reactions before, during and especially after the separation had not always been covered systematically, we studied those families in which there was considerable likelihood that the child and parents would be reunited after a relatively brief period. The periods of separation in fact ranged from two to twenty weeks and were thought of as brief only by contrast to separations which last for six months or more. As will be seen, from the child's and mother's point of view, a twenty-weeks' separation is by no means brief.

That the periods of separation in fact varied also allowed us to study further the influence of a variable that had been emphasized by previous investigators—namely, the length of separation.

If the above represents the major areas for the testing and extension of findings on separation, the choice of sample and nature of design also made it possible to investigate further the influence of certain background factors and variations in the conditions of the separation. In regard to background factors we could consider the effect of previous separations, the sex and age of the child and the nature of the relationship to the mother. Among the variations in conditions considered were the different reasons for the separation, the amount of contact with the parents and siblings, the quality and quantity of substitute care and the extent of change in the child's environment when he moves from his home to the nursery.

B. The Developmental Study of Reactions to a Traumatic Event

The studies of other investigators as well as our own work had left no doubt that for the normal 2-year-old child, being placed into a residential nursery, even only temporarily, is very likely to be experienced as a traumatic event. Further questions could then be raised: what aspects of this event are particularly stressful to the child, how is the stress evidenced and how does he respond to it? How does his initial mode of responding differ from subsequent attempts to adapt as the separation continues? Most important, once the traumatic event ceases and the parent and child are reunited, what processes of readjustment occur before the previous family equilibrium is restored or a new equilibrium is achieved? Finally, how does the child's behavior during the separation relate to the quality of the readjustment that occurs after the child and parents have been reunited? Although the questions had previously been posed by other investigators, few answers had been systematically derived. In an effort to answer them, care was taken to include assessments of changes in members of the family other than the child. For example, how do changes in the mother's feelings affect the family equilibrium achieved at a given moment during the period of reunion?

It is clear that the answers to these questions will vary depending on the developmental status of the child, on the course of his previous development and particularly on the nature of his attachment to his parents. By confining our sample to children of an age range varying around 2 years, and after actual study of the children before and at the beginning of separation, it was possible to state the following about them: they had all reached a point in their development at which the parents and possibly other figures had acquired a distinctive significance for them and had become the focus of both positive and negative affects; all children could walk independently and most could already run; their control of sphincters and speech varied, but in each case some degree of control had been acquired.

Thus, one of the aims of this study was the investigation of the reactions of 2-year-old children to the temporary loss of significant persons. The interpretation of these reactions, however, is complicated by the fact that the children not only lost significant persons but also were transferred to a new environment. The latter in turn involves not only the loss of the familiar environment, but also changes in the quality and quantity of the child's interaction with people in this new environment. The exact contribution of these factors could not be determined in this study. Yet our choice of age group and developmental status made it possible to make certain assumptions about their relative importance. As formulated recently by Yarrow (1961):

After the point of fixation of positive feelings on the mother, new elements enter into the child's reactions to a loss or a change in mothers. At this point, sensory deprivation and environmental change may be secondary, the loss of a significant person becomes of primary significance. This experience cannot occur until the infant reaches a developmental point at which he is able to conceptualize the existence of an "object" outside of himself [p. 486].

C. The Aims of the Study and the Theoretical Frame of Reference

Ideally one might carefully have examined the previous findings in relation to the aims stated above, derived specific hypotheses from a theoretical interpretation of the data and then proceeded systematically to test these hypotheses. Though we had certain general hypotheses in mind, we did not feel that the area of research was sufficiently advanced to formulate these hypotheses in a precise and detailed manner. In planning future research we hope to be able to take this step.

Although our findings have been presented in a manner making it possible for readers of different theoretical persuasion to interpret them as they see fit, both the choice of problem and the collection and analysis of the data were guided by a psychoanalytic framework. This is not the place to defend the value of this theoretical body for the study of early development. Yet it may help the reader's orientation to have an initial view of what aspects of the theory we have emphasized in relation to the study to be reported here.

The emphasis on the early relationship to significant figures, the differentiation of the stages in the development of such relationships, the importance of early traumatic experiences and the importance for later development of the particular solutions adopted to deal with the conflicts associated with a traumatic event—all have guided the planning and execution of this study.

The developmental approach—or genetic point of view—implied above, was, however, not the only one which guided our thinking. Other points of view and the empirical considerations related to them were of equal influence. These points of view—dynamic, economic, structural and adaptive—have been summarized by Rapaport and Gill (1959). To illustrate the influence of each of these points of view we were among other things interested in the following: the quality of the affects stimulated by the trauma of separation; the intensity as well as the form of the aggressive derivatives that were expressed; the persisting structures whose functioning could be observed in relation to efforts to resolve the conflicts generated; and the adaptive value of such resolutions.

But most important, perhaps, we share the conviction that all the points of view should be considered in understanding a given phenomenon and the underlying psychological processes that are inferred.

D. The Aims of the Study and the Methods Chosen

The methods used in this study will be given in greater detail in Chapter 2. Some indication of how the aims of the work influenced the choice of these methods is given here.

The interest in giving the details of the children's development suggested that intensive and frequent observations would be necessary to follow that development.

To be able to infer the underlying psychological processes, not only frequent but also diversified types of observation seemed desirable. Though we did not anticipate that the behavior of the 2-year-old child would be strikingly different in different situations, some facets of behavior might for example be seen in the private Doll-Play Setting that would add to the picture derived from other settings. Particularly important in providing a complete picture were the observations of the child and family made in the home.

Further, to facilitate the inference about underlying psychological processes, we not only recorded the details of certain behavioral sequences but also noted our clinical impressions of the child's functioning. Similarly, the data on the family included both behavioral descriptions and inferences about the personality and interactions involved.

While the aim of being able to follow underlying psychological processes developmentally was thus of importance in choosing our methods, considerations of substantiating and extending the findings were equally influential in the final choice. We included methods (for example, the category observations) which yielded quantifiable data, and others where the data were at least potentially quantifiable. The careful design of observations often facilitated the latter. Thus, we introduced certain observers at certain points in the child's experience and carefully studied his reactions to this "standard situation."

III. A Preview of What Was Done

Before giving the details of the design of the study and the procedures for obtaining the data, a general description of the steps taken is given below.

The main sample consisted of ten children in the second and third year of life. They were visited at home by the psychiatric caseworker before they were placed in a residential nursery. The reasons for placement implied no rejection of the child or break-up of the family and led to the expectation that the separation would be a brief one. While in the nursery they were observed at regular intervals by each of two observers. During the observation periods the behavior was recorded systematically and in sequence using a coding system particularly suited to recording interpersonal interaction, but including the child's interaction with nonhuman objects as well. This recording system lent itself readily to scoring the child's behavior by classifying it into categories and determining the frequency of each class of behavior. Although this method of recording behavior facilitated quantitative comparisons between behavior at one time and behavior at other times, and hence an objective assessment of behavioral changes, it necessarily omitted descriptive nuances and global impressions which might be expected to be of clinical significance. Consequently, the coded record was supplemented by descriptive accounts of the child's behavior during the observation period, which were written immediately afterward. We refer to the observations made during these regular periods as observations made in the Everyday Nursery Setting. To supplement these observations of everyday behavior, we observed the child in at least two sessions of doll play—on the third and eleventh day of separation. The doll-play behavior was recorded both in code and in terms of clinically relevant descriptions. As a further supplement to these observations, the information given by the nurses was also recorded regularly.

The matched contrast group of nonseparated children were visited at home by a psychiatric caseworker who immediately after the visit recorded her observations of the child's behavior, as well as the mother's behavior and information given by her in interview. Inferences arising out of the material were also recorded but were kept separate from the behavioral descriptions. The psychiatric caseworker was unable to utilize the coding system for recording during the visit, because this would have interfered with her relationship with the mother.

At least two doll-play sessions were undertaken with each of the nonseparated children. The timing of these sessions and the observations recorded corresponded to that of the separated children.

Particular care was taken to observe the moment of reunion of the separated child and his parents. Following this, each family was visited by the caseworker at least once a week for a minimum period of twenty consecutive weeks. The method of observation and recording were the same as for the contrast group of nonseparated children. Furthermore, similar contacts were maintained with the nonseparated group for comparable periods of time. Finally, both the separated and nonseparated children were again observed in the standard Doll-Play Setting six and sixteen weeks after the day they had first been reunited with their parents. For the nonseparated children the "day of reunion" was designated as indicated below.

IV.   The Specific Goals of the Study: An Outline of the Design

Figure 1 gives a graphic picture of the design. It includes a representation of the length of the separation in terms of the length of the lines and indicates the major types of data analysis that it is possible to execute within the design. We briefly discuss each of these in the approximate order in which they appear in the book.

Figure 1. *Showing Outline of Design of Study*

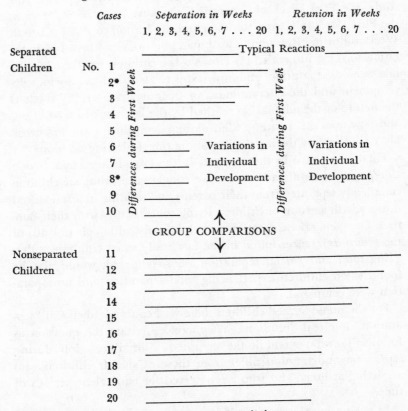

* These children are subjects of the *Case Descriptions*.

First we present full descriptions of two cases showing not only the individual child's development during separation and reunion, but also the nature of his background and relationships within his family. These *Case Descriptions* were chosen not only to show the data for each of the two children and his family in detail, but also to illustrate certain of the group findings.

All further analyses concern groups of children. The first of them is a characterization of *Typical Reactions*. Here we draw together such statements as can be made about the development of all or nearly all children during a specified period of time—for example, the typical reactions of the children during the first three days of separation.

Secondly, we can study the *Individual Differences in the Development* of the children. Four time spans were chosen to pursue this study: the First Week of Separation, the Last Week of Separation, the First Week following Reunion and the Second to the Twentieth Weeks following Reunion. Two broad questions can be asked in relation to these intervals: (1) How do the children react during the first week of separation, and how is this related to their previous development and the circumstances of their separation? (2) What is the nature of the adaptation reached by the last week of separation, and how does this relate to their development during the first week after reunion and during the rest of the time following reunion?

Finally, we have in this study as in the last made certain *Group Comparisons*. As already stated, we compared a group of children completely separated from their parents and residing in a residential nursery with a group of children living continuously with their families. Our general expectation was that many, although not all, of the *group differences* found in the first study when children undergoing *total* and *partial* separation were compared, would also be found when children experiencing total separation and no separation were compared.

For the nonseparated children there is of course neither real "separation" nor real "reunion." We therefore restate the question as follows: To what extent do the separated children's reactions during separation and reunion differ from those of similar children who are living at home and who are observed for equivalent periods of time?

In evaluating the results of these group comparisons, it is necessary to determine whether or not the children and their families differ in relevant respects before the separation occurs, and the extent to which observed differences of behavior could be accounted for by differences in family relations. In Chapter 4 as well as throughout the rest of the book we shall be considering this problem.

V. The Design of the Study: Sequence of Procedures for Obtaining Data

Figure 2 shows the procedures used for obtaining data. They are listed down the page in chronological order.

Figure 2. *Showing Planned Sequence of Procedures Applied to the Separated and Nonseparated Groups*

		Separated	Nonseparated
Preseparation	1.	Visits paid to home by IW*	Visits paid to home by IW
Separation	2.	Actual separation observed by IW, CH* or EW*	
	3.	Observations of child in Everyday Nursery Setting throughout separation by CH and EW	Continuing visits by IW that include observations of child
	4.	First doll play on third day of separation by CH or EW	First doll play in home on comparable third day by CH or EW
	5.	Child visited by IW in nursery on seventh day of separation	Continuing visits by IW that include observation of child
	6.	Child's mother visited by IW in the hospital or elsewhere at least once	
	7.	Child visited by father or other relative in nursery, observed by CH or EW	
	8.	Second doll play on eleventh day of separation by CH or EW	Second doll play in home on comparable eleventh day by CH or EW
	9.	Child visited by IW in nursery on fourteenth day of separation	
	10.	Further doll plays to fit child's length of stay by CH or EW	Third doll play in home on twenty-first day by CH or EW
Reunion	11.	Observation of actual reunion by IW	
	12.	Continuing visits until at least twentieth week after reunion by IW that include observation of child	Continuing visits by IW that include observations of child
	13.	First doll play during sixth week after reunion by IW	First doll play during sixth week after reunion by IW
	14.	Second doll play during sixteenth week after reunion by IW	Second doll play during sixteenth week after reunion by IW
	15.	Visit to home by CH or EW during sixteenth week after reunion	Visit to home by CH or EW during sixteenth week after reunion

* IW stands for **Ilse Westheimer, CH for Christoph Heinicke and EW for Elizabeth Wolpert.**

Since the nonseparated children were never away from home, a criterion was needed for deciding at what point in time their notional separation should be deemed to have begun. Because in the case of the separated children the first doll play usually took place on the third day of separation, the day of notional separation for the nonseparated children was taken as two days before the administration of the first doll play in the home of the child in question. For example, Margaret stayed in the residential nursery for seventeen days, and, following reunion, was observed for the required period of twenty weeks. Her match in the nonseparated group is Helen. The comparable period of time used for analysis of data equivalent to separation data was from the two days before until fourteen days after the administration of the first doll play. The time equivalent to the period after the reunion was the twenty weeks directly after the seventeen-day period equivalent to the separation. Observations made by Westheimer before the period equivalent to separation were regarded as the equivalent of the preseparation period.

In the next chapter we describe the various methods that have been listed in Figure 2.

Methods of Observation
and Recording

2 We have previously indicated that a variety of
considerations governed our choice of methods of observation. Prominent among them was a desire both to demonstrate some of the behavioral changes using quantitative indices and to infer the salient
psychological processes. With these considerations in mind, two main
types of observation and recordings were made: (1) category or
coded observations of the child in either an Everyday or Doll-Play
Setting, and (2) clinical descriptions pertaining to the child or family members in either an Everyday or Doll-Play Setting.

To indicate what was and was not available for separated and nonseparated children respectively we present Figure 3.

Figure 3. *Showing the Type of Observation Available in
Various Settings*

Type of Observation	Period of Separation		Period of Reunion	
	Everyday Nursery	*Doll Play*	*Everyday Home*	*Doll Play*
Category Observations	Available	Available	Not available	Available
Clinical Descriptions	Available	Available	Available	Available

It can be seen that coded or category observations were not made
in the Everyday Home Setting; it was felt that this would not be feasible because it would impair the relationship to the family. The
other observations are available, however, and are discussed in the
sections below.

I. Observations of the Child: The
Categorization of Behavior

A. *The Categories: A Definition*

Our first major source of data consists of the categorization of behavior. The categories used in this study are the same as those employed in the first study (Heinicke, 1956, pp. 112-117). Briefly, to record the sequence of a child's behavior we employed what Wright (1960) has called a field-unit analysis category system of a general interaction type. As defined by this author, the field-unit analysis has two phases: "1) A behavior sequence is divided into consecutive units 'in the field' on the basis of explicit rules; and 2) Descriptive categories are applied to the phenomena of each unit." (p. 108)

This approach is further defined by Wright through a contrast with other observational methods: diary description, specimen description, time sampling, event sampling and trait rating.

In the type of field-unit analysis employed in this study, for each unit of behavior we noted the following: the agent of the action, the recipient (object) of the action, the nature of the relation to object, the mode of relating and, in certain cases, the intensity of the action. For example, if a child—say Ronald—punches another child—Peter —so hard that he falls over and cries, it is scored as follows:

Agent	Object	Relation	Mode	Intensity
R	Peter	Hostile	Push	Severe

More extensive examples giving a series of such categorizations can be found in an earlier study (Heinicke, 1956, pp. 113-117), but certain features of it will be emphasized here. The categories focus not only on a child but also on the objects (human or otherwise) with whom he interacts. Thus, if a nurse gives him affection, this too is scored and she becomes the agent. Furthermore, the scoring is continuous, so that a particular scoring is seen in the context of those that go both before and after it. Clearly the most important part of any score is the nature of the relation to the object. Some may prefer to think of this as the aim or the motif of the behavior sequence. Moreover, how one conceives the motivational aspect will influence the way the categories are defined.

In this and previous studies we have concentrated on certain general categories and have defined specific subcategories in relation to each. They deal primarily with motives or intents in an interpersonal context. The categories are:

1. *Nurturance.* The primary motive of the agent is to satisfy the needs of the object.

      a. Agent *gives attention* to object.

      b. Agent *gives affection* to object.

2. *Succorance.* The primary motive of the agent is to seek satisfaction from the object.

      a. Agent *watches object.*

      b. Agent *seeks to be near object.*

      c. Agent *follows object visually.*

      d. Agent *seeks attention from object.*

      e. Agent *seeks affection from object.*

      f. Agent *seeks to regain object.*

      g. Agent *sucks object.*

      h. Agent *rubs object.*

      i. Agent *messes object.*

3. *Restrictive Demands.* The primary motive of the agent is to restrict the need-satisfaction attempts of the object.

4. *Achievement Demands.* The primary motive of the agent is to channel the way in which the object will satisfy his needs.

5. *Hostility.* The primary motive of the agent is to actively injure the object.

6. *Avoidance.* The primary motive of the agent is to avoid relating to the object.

7. *No Inferable Relation.* In those instances in which it is not possible to score one of the above general relations, the observer simply noted whether the child was active or inactive.

B. *The Use of the Categories in the Everyday Nursery Setting*

1. *The Nature of the Everyday Nursery Setting.* The sample of residential children was drawn from three residential nurseries; thus, it is important to note, we are not studying the effects on children of being in any one particular nursery. While two of the nurseries were the same as those used in the first study, the third was not. Though different in some respects, the general atmosphere and organization of these three nurseries was similar. Apart from the usual routines of feeding, toileting and rest (usually near the middle of the day), the children had ample opportunity for free play either in large rooms or outdoors in a garden. Each child belonged to a defined

group of children and was cared for mostly by one or two nurses. There was thus an opportunity for each child to form attachments both to the nurses and to the children in his own particular group.

In a later section of this chapter we describe how initial contacts were made with the families of children going into the nursery, as well as how the children of the nonseparated group were obtained.

2. *The Relation of Observers to the Child.* As might be expected, making notations in the presence of a child raises questions about the observer's relation to that child. An effort was made to maintain a role that was neither so objective that it might be felt by the children as a rejection nor so close that it would have led, in the case of these separated deprived children, to attachments whose implicit promise the observer would not fulfill. Thus, in the earliest pilot work prior to the first study when such attachment was encouraged, both child and observer found it extremely difficult to deal with the observer's inevitable departure. Under such conditions, moreover, all systematic observation and recording became impossible.

The role of Observers Heinicke and Wolpert can be further defined by contrast to that of the nurses and also of Observer Westheimer. Since each of the nurses had a limited number of children in her care, she attempted actively to develop a relationship with the children and of course tried to comfort them when needed. Westheimer visited each child once a week and though she did not actively attempt to engage the child to interact with her, she did respond to all of his initiations. The following excerpts from observations made by Westheimer on Katie on her fifteenth day of separation illustrate the kind of role she adopted:

Katie was grizzling even before she saw me, but soon after I entered she stopped. When she saw me a moment later she smiled, stretched out her arms, but did not actually advance toward me.

At this point Westheimer did not pick Katie up although she might easily have done so. The report continues:

At various times she looked in my direction, smiled, but other than this she paid no attention to me at this point. She seemed particularly cheerful when Nurse K. picked her up, put her beside her and gave her attention.

When Katie actively initiated a request Westheimer did respond:

A little later Katie trotted up to me, showed me her book and wanted to sit beside me. Since there was no room because of other children sitting there, I put her on my lap and she sat there very happily looking at her book, pointing at different objects in the book and looking at me from time to time with a smile.

Observers Heinicke and Wolpert also responded to the affection-seeking of the child; not to have done so would have been artificial. Wolpert recorded the following on the thirteenth day of Katie's separation:

When I came in this afternoon Katie approached me very affectionately, wanted to hold my hand and walked with me along the corridor.

But holding Katie's hand at such a moment leads to a different relationship from the one that follows picking her up every time she asks for it.

There was, however, one moment during each of the observation periods when Observers Heinicke and Wolpert actively though cautiously approached each child to see how he would react. Such reactions to a standard stimulus situation facilitated later comparison of the children. Similarly, in a study of separation the child's response to the observer's entrance and departure became of special interest.

3. The Nursery Observer's Relations with the Parents. During the period of separation the child's relations with an observer and the nature of the behavior he exhibits are likely to be influenced by the relation he perceives between the observer and his parents. There were three types of occasion when the child was confronted simultaneously by his parents and an observer. First, the child experienced the simultaneous presence of both observer and parent in his *home* before the separation. Since Westheimer was the only one to visit the home before separation, it was only in regard to her that the child experienced this particular link.

Secondly, by design, at least one of the three observers observed the actual physical *separation* of parent from child in the nursery. Each of the two observers, Heinicke and Wolpert, who made most of the observations in the nursery, covered an equal number of these events. It might have been anticipated that the observer's presence at the moment of separation would affect the child's subsequent feelings about him. Case presentations will reveal, however, that, while the children clearly associated both observers with the parents in some manner, whether or not a particular observer was actually present at the separation has little influence on a child's later behavior toward him.

Thirdly, one of the two observers was always present during a *visit* by the father. For this and practical reasons Observers Heinicke and Wolpert took turns covering these visits. The case presentations indicate the way in which these visits influenced the child's behavior in relation to the particular observer who had been present.

4. The Length of Observation, the Time of Day and the Sex of the Observer. Further details of the use of the categories in the Everyday Nursery Setting can be found in the first study (Heinicke, 1956, p. 118), and a few are repeated here.

During the first study we had tried to make observations during as many parts of the day as possible. While this had ensured that various kinds of behavior associated with particular times of day and activities were covered, the greater heterogeneity introduced problems in quantitative comparisons. Since in the second study we were confident that the behavior we wished to observe was likely to occur during the morning from 10:30 A.M. to 12:30 P.M. and during the afternoon from 2:00 to 5:00 P.M. (perhaps as well as at other parts of the day), and though an effort was made to observe the child every day, we decided that if each observer observed for *at least* thirty minutes during one of these times in each of the sample periods into which the week was broken, the coverage would be sufficient. The week was arbitrarily divided into three sample periods: Monday and Tuesday; Wednesday and Thursday; and Friday, Saturday and Sunday. The range in the time of day that the observations were made as well as the duration of observation was tested statistically by comparing the length of observation of the six residential children of the first study with that of the twelve residential children of this study. The mean length of observation for the first group (stated in minutes of observation) was significantly greater than for the children of this study (.01 level) in both the first and the second week of separation. Study of differences in length of observation and the correlated greater coverage revealed that the most important consequence of this greater coverage was a greater variability in the behavior observed. In any comparison involving both groups, therefore, care has to be taken that differences found cannot be accounted for by this difference.

In view of our interest in the child's relation to the observer, the fact that we had both a male and a female observer seemed an advantage. Although certain children showed different aspects of themselves depending on which observer they were being observed by, systematic examination of the data indicated that the similarities in the reactions to the observers were far greater than the differences. (Such differences as were found could of course be attributable to differences in the observers' personalities and modes of relating to a child rather than to a difference of sex.)

5. *The Reliability of the Categories As Used in the Everyday Nursery Setting.* As in the previous study, we made sure that every child was observed by each observer for an equal amount of time. Although this does not remove sources of systematic bias on the part of either observer, it gives assurance that the total observations on each child are affected in a similar way.

Although it would have been desirable to have repeated the reliability test made during the first study, the results of that test (except for the category of "Watching") had been such that we could conclude that the categories were being applied similarly by the two observers.

C. The Use of the Categories in the Doll-Play Settings

1. *The Nature of the Doll-Play Procedure.* Descriptions of the doll-play equipment and the procedure of administering it are given in the previous publication (see Heinicke, 1956, pp. 121-123). On certain days, (the third, eleventh and a day near the end of the separation—see outline of design), the child was asked if he would like to play with some "dollies." The moment for attempting this was carefully chosen and prepared for. Once in another room, where the doll equipment had already been set out, the child was asked to identify the dolls as a way of interesting him in the material. Although further encouragement was sometimes necessary, usually the child immediately began to play and the observer sat a little apart in order to record the sequence of behavior for about twenty minutes. As in the Everyday Nursery Setting, the observer, although responding to the child, did so usually in only a minimal way; thus he did not participate actively in the child's play.

The mode of coded recording was similar to that used in the

Everyday Nursery Setting. Thus the play was seen as a sequence of interactions, even though in almost all cases the child himself was the agent (not some doll as might occur in the play of older children). In order to cover, even at a minimal level, the various activities seen, certain categories had to be added. These were: (1) taking things in and out of objects, (2) opening and closing certain pieces of furniture, (3) examining certain objects, and (4) shaking certain objects (see Heinicke, 1956, pp. 123-124 for examples).

Our first study suggested that the behavioral classifications we had used for coding doll-play behavior were not wholly adequate to cover some of the aspects of the play which we considered significant. We retained the previous method, however, so that our records of behavior in this study would be comparable to those in the first study and relied upon the subsequently recorded clinical descriptive account to cover the aspects lost in the coding.

2. *The Frequency of Observation and the Sex of the Observer.* In the more intimate situation of the doll play, the sex of the observer in relationship to the sex of the child being observed is likely to be of greater importance than in the group setting of the nursery. Because of this the number of children of each sex given doll-play sessions by each observer in each group was the same for both groups (see Table 1).

Table 1. *Showing the Number of Children of Each Sex Given Doll-Play Sessions by Each Observer in Each Group*

| | Observer | | | | |
| | Heinicke | | Wolpert | | |
Group	Male	Female	Male	Female	Total
Separated	3	3	1	3	10
Nonseparated	3	3	1	3	10

3. *The Reliability of the Categories As Used in the Doll-Play Setting.* As we indicated in the first study (Heinicke, 1956, p. 124), at least two major kinds of safeguard with respect to reliability are possible. First we can ensure that the results are not unduly influenced by the doll-play protocols of any one observer. As can be seen in Table 1, Heinicke undertook twelve of the twenty doll plays as op-

posed to the ten which would have been the ideal number. Since he contributed the same number, namely six, to each of the two groups, however, the error due to this deviation is not serious.

More serious is the fact that a lack of time and facilities prevented us from checking the reliability through scorings made simultaneously by the two observers. It would have been ideal if all three doll-play observers (CH, EW and IW) could have recorded and scored a series of doll plays using a one-way screen.

Heinicke did take part in a reliability study conducted by P. S. Sears at Harvard University. Ten observers observed and scored simultaneously by means of a one-way screen a series of children in the doll-play situation. It was thus possible to compute correlation coefficients on such matters as Agent, Object and Type of Relation scored. The coefficients derived were judged to be adequate and are reported by Heinicke (1953).

One other check of reliability was possible. Westheimer recorded all her doll-play observations in extenso instead of in terms of the categories described above, which gave Heinicke and Wolpert the opportunity later to score them independently. When each had done three of Westheimer's doll-play protocols, it was found that their scoring was practically identical. One or the other therefore scored the rest of Westheimer's doll-play reports. A disadvantage of such a procedure is that some of the cues for making the score are likely to be missing. On the other hand, Westheimer's records were less likely to be influenced at the moment of scoring by previous experience of the first study and by ideas about what to expect.

D. Suggestions for the Revision of the System of Categories Used

It is not our intention to explore extensively the various methodological issues raised by the choice of methods employed. Use of the categories did lead to suggestions which may be of interest to others who contemplate using such a system of observing and recording in future research. The most important change envisaged would be an attempt to subdivide and redefine certain of the categories in order to make their meaning more specific. While the further distinctions would be governed partly by the experience derived from studying separation and partly by theoretical considerations, the value of keeping the categories at the level of description need not be sacrificed. For example, whether the child wants to be attended to in the sense of wanting to be waited on or wants attention because he wants an achievement recognized, makes a great deal of difference theoretically and clinically, but the resulting categories of seeking to be waited on and seeking recognition retain their descriptive value.

Since Wright (1960) has discussed the categories used here (see his pages 125-127) as part of his general critique of observational methods, it is relevant to relate our suggestions to his concepts. Posing the problem of which of an infinite number of possible categories to use, he proposes that any given system can be characterized in terms of three dimensions: literal objectivity, psychological specificity, and theoretical integration. He cites categories from a study by Arrington (1932) which reflect the choice of both staying close to the literal meaning of a word and yet doing little to indicate what is specifically involved psychologically. Contacts with material things, verbal contacts with persons (i.e., talking), physical contacts with persons, are examples. Nor were these categories in any way tied to existing conceptual schemes.

By contrast Wright characterizes the categories used here as low in literal objectivity, high in psychological specificity and very high in theoretical integration. On the basis of our experience, our inclination would be to increase the psychological specificity even further. Nor would we hesitate to make such revisions or additions as are suggested by the greater theoretical clarification achieved and/or by the needs of testing new hypotheses. Again in Wright's terms, we would if anything increase the theoretical integration of the categories. To repeat, this does not mean that the "everyday core meaning" of the description need be sacrificed. That is, it is possible that an observer of different theoretical persuasion could take the resulting data and interpret them differently.

While the categorizations turned out to be of considerable value, further use of other observational techniques is suggested by our experience. The more extensive recording of clinical impressions would add to the efficiency of the procedure. As indicated below, such events as sleeping disturbances and sphincter lapses were observed not only as part of the categorization, but also at times when the observer was for some reason not recording. These types of observations could usefully be expanded and could be supplemented by the reports of the staff.

II. Observations of the Child: Clinical Descriptions

A. Clinical Descriptions of Behavior in the Everyday Nursery Setting

Our second major source of data was the clinical descriptions. Following each period of observation in the Everyday Nursery Setting and using the category observations as a guide and reminder, we recorded our clinical impressions of the total period of observation. The purpose of this record was to add emphasis, to draw the observations together and to confirm or disconfirm from a larger base of observations those inferences (i.e., categorizations) made on the basis of the immediate and smaller context of the child's behavior. The questions we asked ourselves were: what aspects of the child's behavior seemed outstanding, how were the various elements linked together and how did they relate to certain events in the child's life? The answers to these questions would help us to go beyond the first level meaning of the descriptive observations.

It is important to note, however, that all such clinical descriptions and inferences were based on and accompanied by notations of the behavioral sequences involved. The following illustrates how the inference that Katie would gain comfort from playing in the kitchen is based on observations which were also recorded:

When we got to the upstairs part of the nursery today, it was quite interesting to note that the children were all in the kitchen and Katie then seemed to become quite happy; she took the pans and spoons out of the kitchen and started to mix as though she had done this with her mother. Though absorbed and seemingly happy for some time, after she had tea she once again started rubbing her eyes and crying for her mother. She stopped for a while but my leaving again set off her cries for "mummy."

No attempt was made systematically to cover given areas of behavior, but a general outline of them was kept in mind while making a record of a particular observation session. One of the areas covered was how the child interacted with the people in his environment and especially with the observer. As we have indicated, we made a special note of the child's reactions to the observer's entrance and exit, and also of how he reacted when the observer gently approached him and then tried to pick him up.

Another major emphasis in the descriptive account was a statement in general terms of how the child was eating, sleeping, controlling his sphincters and speaking, and whether or not he was ill. Here we supplemented our own observations of these events by obtaining reports from staff members and copies of the nursery records.

Thirdly, we tried to give some indication of what appeared to be the child's main defenses, motivational trends, fantasy expressions, activities and signs of identification or guilt. To repeat, this was not systematically covered each time but depended on what was in fact striking on that day. Repeated observations on a fairly strict sampling basis by two observers ensured that the coverage would capture the main trends.

Finally, in these impressions we tried to record not only the individual expressions of each child, but also how individual patterns changed. This will be illustrated in our detailed presentation of the two cases.

B. Clinical Descriptions of Behavior in the Doll-Play Setting

Following each doll-play session, the observer made a record of his over-all impressions of the play. Although no particular set of headings or categories was used, the observer tried to note what was outstanding about the play and what seemed likely to be the meaning of it to the child.

C. The Reliability of the Clinical Descriptions As Used in the Everyday Nursery and Doll-Play Settings

No attempts were made to assess the reliability of the clinical descriptions in either setting. The fact that at least two observers contributed to the pool of data for each child provided some check on the bias of any one observer. Also, the process of drawing further inferences from these observations made in the Everyday Nursery Setting was checked for reliability (as reported in the next chapter).

Although the observations made by Westheimer are methodologically similar to the descriptive observations of the child, they are discussed in a separate section below.

III.   Interview and Observation of the
Child and His Family

Since this part of the inquiry was carried out by a psychiatric caseworker, it is relevant to state briefly some of the fundamental concepts and principles inherent in this professional discipline because they influenced the attitude of the worker, her method of approaching the families and her manner of interviewing. (For elaboration see Hamilton, 1940, and Hollis, 1939.)

A first principle is respect for the client as a person and for his right to choose his way of conducting his life. It includes warmth and understanding on the worker's part, a responsive and uncritical way of listening and a capacity to empathize, and a real care and concern about what happens to his particular client.

A second is understanding of the structure and functioning of personality and of appropriate casework techniques.

A third is a professionally acquired self-awareness and insight.[1] This enables the recognition of transference and countertransference phenomena to become important aspects of the interview process and is a necessary qualification for a reasonable degree of objectivity to be attained.

A. Method of Approach

In the light of these principles the attitude underlying the approach to the families of the observed children can be understood. Although we tried to give the parents clear ideas about the requirements of the investigation, we also let it be known that we had a concern for the family and the child and that we would be ready to help in areas of personal relationships if such help was wanted. (Initially it was not envisaged that we might also be called upon by a few of the families to support them in dealing with external social pressures.) The varied use the families made of this contact will be described later; here it suffices to state that each time a family or a member of it asked for and received personal help, our understanding of the family, its interaction and the effects on the observed child was deepened and the research data accordingly enriched.

1. Method of Approach to the Mothers of the Separated Children.

Information of the forthcoming separation of the child was given by the matron of the nursery when it was a private placement by the

---

[1] Gordon Hamilton (1940) writes: "In any of the professions aiming to help people knowledge of the self is essential for the conscious use of the relationship. If one is to use the self, then one must be aware how the self operates. Not only should the caseworker know something of his motivation for choosing this profession, but he must also surmount another hurdle by recognizing his own subjectivity, prejudices and biases" (p. 41).

parents, and by the Children's Officer when the child was being taken
into temporary care by the Local Authority. Although we had hoped
to get several days' advance notice, this was given in a few cases only.
In the others we received such short warning that we had to be content with one or two preseparation visits instead of the planned number of three.

All the interviews were conducted in the child's home. The first
preseparation visit followed a letter or telephone call and had three
purposes:

1. To inform the parents of why we were interested in the behavior of the child during the forthcoming separation and to gain
their permission and co-operation. The relative length of the study
and its requirement of regular visiting were emphasized.

2. The second purpose of the preseparation interview (s) was to
obtain data for the inquiry. Observations of the behavior of the child
and mother, and of the interaction between them, were made from
the moment of entry into the family and led to an initial assessment
of the mother-child relationship. Reports and information were obtained from the parents about current behavior and relationships as
well as those of the past. The amount so obtained depended both
on the mother's own feelings and on the period of time available before the separation occurred.

3. The psychiatric caseworker (hereafter referred to as the fieldworker) sought to convey that her interest might be of help to the
parents and the child during the period of separation and perhaps
beyond it. The fact that she had a knowledge of the nursery where
their child would spend his days and nights was useful.

Most mothers had had no opportunity to discuss the forthcoming
separation with anyone and were eager to use the visit of the fieldworker to do so. Some liked to ponder what the child's reaction
might be to being away from mother and home. Some wanted a lead
as to the benefits of visits to the nursery by the father; others raised
the question of the child taking familiar toys, feeding bottles or pacifiers as comforters from home to the new environment. Some mothers acquainted the fieldworker with the child's special vocabulary
and other idiosyncrasies and asked that the information be passed
on to the nursery staff; one mother wanted the fieldworker's help in
arranging a preliminary visit to the nursery so that the child might
feel less strange in the new surroundings.

Some mothers discussed more domestic matters, wanting to make sure that they had selected the right garments to be taken, that the child would be warm enough and would be looked after with care. One mother felt much reassured when she learned that she could send a safety strap to the nursery.

Most mothers were appreciative of this unforeseen opportunity to discuss their concerns with a friendly and interested person. The worker's attentive listening, her recognition and acceptance of a mother's unease and difficulty, coupled with her readiness to clarify practical procedures, engendered in most mothers a feeling of being understood. As a result the fieldworker's suggestion that she visit the mother in the hospital was usually welcomed, and many saw this as a useful link between themselves in the hospital and the child in the nursery. Some expressed the belief that they might learn more from the fieldworker on how the child was faring in the nursery than from the father after his visits there.

2. *Methods of Approach to the Mothers of Nonseparated Children.* Access to a group of children who did not undergo a separation and who matched the age of the separated children was obtained through the help of a health visitor. In these cases the health visitor had a preliminary talk with the mother, during which she gave information regarding the investigation and discussed her readiness to partake in it. When the mother showed willingness and interest, the health visitor took the fieldworker to the home and introduced her. The fieldworker then explained the nature of the project further and clarified the requirements. If, after hearing the details, the mother wished to decline to participate, she had the opportunity to do so. If, on the other hand, she wanted to take part, a regular, convenient visiting time was arranged. As it happened none of the mothers withdrew at this point, though two mothers whose anxiety was aroused by the research requirements did so three weeks later by not being at home at the time of the arranged visits.

The introduction of the fieldworker by the health visitor, whom the mothers liked and trusted, was extremely helpful in establishing initial contact. Unlike the mothers of children to be separated, those in this group had no immediate needs so that the help the fieldworker might possibly extend was not obvious. Their initial readiness to participate depended to a large degree on good will. Nevertheless the fieldworker explained the kind of return the mothers might get from her understanding of family relationships, in particular of mother-child interaction, and from her knowledge of children and their development.

B. The Nature of the Interview

All the interviewing was done during regular visits to the home of the observed child. Although these interviews were relatively unstructured so that special attention could be given to the current situation and to the needs of the mother and of her special way of relating, particular foci were borne in mind; toward these the interview was steered when needed research data had not been volunteered. The duration of these interviews varied between one and two and a half hours. Procedure was the same in the two groups.

The fact that all observations were carried out by visits to the home allowed for extensive and varied observations. Whereas in some homes the observations always took place in the sitting room, in others the setting might change from one interview to the next, from sitting room to kitchen to the garden. What at first seemed like limitations or interruptions, the fieldworker learned to use constructively. For example, much could be learned about the personality of a mother by discussing her cleaning procedures while she was occupied in scrubbing the draining board. Similarly much could be understood about her way of interacting with the child by taking note of her response when the child made demands or otherwise interrupted conversation during the visit.

For parents to participate in an inquiry which demands regular weekly visiting over a period of six months with a minimum of twenty-eight visits to the home, they must be strongly motivated. Good will and a certain amount of interest would hardly have been sufficient. The main factor making for real co-operation, it is believed, was the parents' awareness from the beginning that they were not just being used for the purpose of research, but that they themselves might gain from the procedure through the worker's response to their interests and needs.

As might be expected, the initial interview was critical in determining whether the family concluded that co-operation in the inquiry would be worth their while. Even so, if co-operation was to be maintained the family had continuously to feel that they were being considered or helped. The nature of the help given varied a great deal and will be described later.

1. The First Interview. As already indicated the mother usually decided during the first interview whether or not she was going to participate. This decision was based to a large extent on the fieldworker's first approach.[2] This is illustrated by one mother who stated her feelings very frankly. When told by the matron about the inquiry, she had decided to "put off" the fieldworker. "You see," she explained, "it was just one more thing." She had, however, reversed her decision during the course of the initial telephone conversation during which, she said, she had judged the fieldworker to be "an understanding sort of person," and this impression had been confirmed for her during the first interview by the fieldworker's response and interest. In this interview, the mother had been given a description of the nursery to which her boy was going, which had relieved her of some uncertainties. She had also been enabled to express her concern over the separation and to voice her anxieties about her own ill health and the prospect of an operation. The fieldworker's appreciation of this mother's need to discuss, and her readiness to listen and share in her concerns at a critical time, established her as a supportive person to whom the mother could turn in moments of crisis. This role was maintained throughout the total span of research time. In this, as in other cases, the approach proved helpful not only to the mother but also to the research. The material obtained was richer and revealed aspects of her personality which otherwise might not have emerged so clearly. Further, it called forth the co-operative and positive elements in an otherwise controlling and not altogether easy woman.

In the case of a mother of a nonseparated child, the first visit to the home also proved to be of significance and also laid the foundation for effective research. While expressing her willingness to participate in the project, Andrew's mother voiced a doubt as to whether her child would be a suitable subject: "I don't think that he is

---

[2] Mary Richmond (1917) many years ago drew attention to the importance of the first interview when she said: "I am more and more convinced . . . that the finished skill of a good social worker is most shown in this first visit or interview. No knowledge of general principles, no cleverness in gaining co-operation, no virtues in the worker and no committee, however wise, can make up for want of skill in gaining quickly the confidence of the family and getting the foundation for all good work to follow." (p. 104).

really a happy child—you see he is sandwiched in between two other children." Instead of reassuring her of the child's suitability, the fieldworker inquired further about the child's unhappiness. In this way, she was able to offer the kind of help that the mother needed and that might lead her to want to continue the relationship. The picture which emerged was of a whiny and easily frustrated child who was intensely jealous of his 4½-year-old sister, and of a mother who was deeply disturbed by this jealousy and much involved in the problem. (For a more detailed account of this child and family, see appendix to this chapter.)

The therapeutic climate characteristic of the subsequent interviews was an outcome of the worker's approach during this first interview when she had responded to the mother's anxiety about the child.

C. The Varied Use Made of the Fieldworker by the Mothers and Their Families

The casework help given was as varied as were the requests of the families. Since, as in the above case, the relationship between the mother and the fieldworker was sometimes essentially a therapeutic one, the worker employed techniques similar to those practiced by a psychiatric caseworker in a child-guidance setting: a combination of psychological support, clarification and insight giving (Hollis, 1939). The interpretations were largely confined to linking significant bits of material, thus showing the interrelatedness of current feelings with earlier experiences.

Nevertheless, a situation where mother and child are for much of the time together with the fieldworker, provides special opportunities. In such a situation the mother's current feelings are expressed as much by her attitude and behavior toward the child as by what she says about them. Thus, when the relationship between mother and worker is a secure one, there are occasions when the mother can use well-timed clarifications in terms of feelings she has just experienced and of behavior she has just demonstrated in the presence of the child and the worker.

Thus the child's presence and sometimes that of siblings make it possible to discuss a mother's way of handling her children in the immediate situation and how she is feeling about the child's behavior. Later on in a contact it sometimes became clear that as a result a mother was adopting a different way of handling the children. Such modifications were effected by a variety of casework techniques. An illustration is given in the appendix to this chapter.

In other cases the relationship was of a more supportive nature with an occasional request for environmental help. For all but a few cases, however, no one aspect of casework was dominant. During a period of time circumstances change and with them a client's needs. Further, the way in which environmental help is asked for and received can in itself make for greater understanding of particular clients.

Home visiting, during which the mother and her family are seen in the real day-to-day situation, brings the fieldworker into contact with many unforeseen situations and crises. This is particularly true of mothers with young children. For example, the sudden illness or accident of a child can cause temporary disorganization and a mother may be glad of the fieldworker's practical help as well as of her moral support. Often when the particular crisis has passed, a discussion brings useful information to light. Two contrasting examples follow.

A mother was trying to cope simultaneously with a hungry, howling baby and with an obviously ill and feverish 2-year-old child, pathetically whimpering and in much need of her mother's attention. By taking over the feeding of the baby, the fieldworker freed the mother to give her undivided attention to the ailing child whom she was then able to rock to sleep in her arms. In the discussion that followed, more understanding was acquired of the mother's anxieties about the 2-year-old child under study and of her feelings of being an incompetent and perhaps even a damaging mother.

On a visit to Dennis's mother, the fieldworker was confronted with a different kind of situation. A loud bang at the front door was followed by the booming voice of the rent collector who stated in uncompromising terms that an eviction order would be issued unless the arrears were paid within the next few days. The mother returned to the room, her face ashen, her whole body shaking; going down upon her bended knees she implored the fieldworker to help. She expressed her inability to tell her husband about this crisis and how terrified she was of his reaction. For the first time she discussed her fear of her somewhat authoritarian husband and her reluctance to reveal to him how helpless she felt. This was in contrast to previous interviews when she had always described him as a kind and clever man, toward whom she felt only affection and respect. She was now able to admit other, more negative, feelings toward him and to confess her shame in relation to this incident and her other feelings of inadequacy. As a result much better understanding was gained of the relationship between the parents and of the mother's doubts concerning her own worth, while for her a number of issues began to be clarified. With the support of the fieldworker the mother was able to deal with the rent situation herself; after having applied for and obtained an extension of time for the payment she was eventually able to discuss the problem with her husband. The parents then dealt jointly with the matter. This shared experience, furthered by a constructive casework approach, strengthened the relationship between the mother and the worker.

In the case of another family, active support over a housing problem was not only of use to the parents but told us much about the functioning of the family, their attitude toward the world and their way of dealing with pressures.

In another instance the therapeutic handling of a mother who was feeling depressed and discussion about her condition with the medical social worker resulted in an effective plan for easing conditions on her return home from the hospital.

In these situations casework skill is essential. Frequently, a quick assessment has to be made of the most useful way of meeting a client's demands. This requires a flexible but responsible approach; common sense and a preparedness to deal with practical situations is quite as necessary as is the professional understanding of people.

There were also mothers who did not ask for any specific help but who seemed glad, nevertheless, of the opportunity to talk, to reflect and to confide. To be listened to attentively was a novel experience for many. They liked to discuss day-to-day events or difficulties, talk about relatives and friends, misunderstandings with neighbors and relationships with husbands. But, above all, they liked to talk about their children. They sought discussion of the developmental phases of childhood and enjoyed relating to the worker the funny episodes and statements of their offspring. Frequently time was used in discussing questions of handling and management, in the course of which many a mother gained a better understanding of her own attitude and way of behaving and insight into the complexities of relationships. Many saw that this had been a rewarding experience and showed their disappointment when the inquiry came to an end.[3] Only one mother seemed to find the requirements of the research tiresome. On a number of occasions she was out when she knew the fieldworker would be calling, and once or twice questioned the motives of the worker over the regularity of the visits by expressing doubts as to whether the visits were perhaps arranged to ensure that the child was being well cared for. It must be recognized, even so, that this mother had many demands being made on her and that these could have explained to some degree her spasmodic co-operation.

Much has been said about the enrichment of the research material through casework methods. There was by contrast one case in which it seemed to be in the interest of the mother to prevent her from revealing too much. This was the case of a heavily defended mother who, late in the research contact, had reached a stage when she seemed close to revealing her ambivalent feelings toward her husband. Since there were to be only one or two more visits, the fieldworker judged that excessive guilt might be generated which in the brief space of time available could not adequately be worked through.

While attempting to meet the needs of the parents, the fieldworker restricted herself to those they made explicit. She did not attempt to deal with any others.

D. Collection of Data

The data obtained during the course of the interviews were of three kinds: 1) Direct observations of the behavior of child, mother and other members of the family, 2) Information reported by mother or father, or other members of the family, and 3) Inferences drawn from the way information is given.

Extensive observations were made of the child's behavior and responses. In order to comprehend each mother-child relationship and to make possible a comparison of a number of such relationships, particular attention was paid to the interaction of child with mother.

[3] Even after the research contact had ended, the worker was on occasion called into a home during a family crisis—for example to support and advise parents during a marital dispute; when an older child had to appear in court; following the death and funeral of the baby which left the parents apprehensive about the safety of the other children.

Further, whenever possible, we observed the child's interactions with his father and with other members of the family. Many of the fathers became well-known to the fieldworker. Out of twenty fathers, three were seen twenty times or more, two fourteen times and seven others three times or more; six were seen once or twice. Only two fathers were never seen. One of the latter was seen, however, by one of the observers in the nursery.

It will be apparent that the interview was not a structured one. Due to minor changes in household routine and the presence or absence of other family members, the setting was never quite the same from one week to another. This provided opportunity for varied observation and made it possible to witness over a period of time their natural spontaneous behavior with one another.

Nevertheless, the fieldworker made sure that certain basic observations were made. In addition to the picture of relationships in the family, firsthand observations of the following were sought: eating, toileting, language, illness, autoerotic habits, use of toys, signs of identification and such specific reactions to the separation experience as fear of being separated again.

These observations were recorded immediately after the fieldworker left the home. The records were made in great detail, often with quotations from the participants. No inferences were made without reference to the behavior or episode that led to them. Anyone reading the material was thus enabled to make independent deductions.

Reported information obtained for all cases consisted, among other things, of a developmental history of the observed child. Special attention was again paid to certain areas, such as the child's relationships and his eating, sleeping, toilet training, language development and health. In all cases too, reports by members of the family of the current behavior and responses of the child were gathered, and special note taken of the child's way of relating to people. Accounts both of current family relationships and also of the parents' earlier relationships and background were always obtained. The greater amount of information was in all cases given by the mother, but usually useful additional material was provided by the father. These data complemented those of firsthand observation. The reports were recorded in great detail immediately after the interview. Occasionally historical data, when given as a straightforward factual account, were noted in the presence of the mother, but this was done sparingly and only when there seemed little emotional involvement.

E.   Evaluation of the Method of Interviewing Used

Once more we stress that we are not attempting to deal with all the methodological issues that are raised by the method of interviewing used here. Only some of the assets and limitations will be discussed.

In an investigation such as this the continuous co-operation of participants is essential. Whether the wholehearted co-operation on the part of almost all mothers could have been obtained by an approach that did not show respect and concern for the participants and a preparedness to help in the many diverse ways described is very doubtful. A participant does not give so readily unless she is also receiving.

This two-way process, in which the fieldworker is available and ready to help with matters of concern to the client in return for an opportunity to conduct the study, provides a framework in which both can feel comfortable, each aware of her special contribution. The guilt reaction of fieldworkers when the research design excludes service to the participants has been noted by social investigators. For example, Sofer (1956), in describing the methodology of a collaborative research project and the advantages of making the service to the client part of the research object, writes:

The guilt which the social investigator commonly experiences about watching or disturbing others becomes reduced because he has his responsibility for helping them and is not observing them for some secret or frivolous reason or one which they do not share.

Nevertheless, there are social scientists who question this method of study and who argue that to avoid contamination of the data a research worker should remain a neutral observer, with only minimal interaction. But against this others have pointed out that, when studies are conducted under rigorously controlled conditions, the findings may be relevant only to the research situation and not to the complex settings of real life, because the behavior of participants is widely influenced by their role as research subjects.

In addition to ready co-operation, the method of interviewing employed allowed us to assume that the data collected, especially observations of the child and of his relationship to his mother, were a valid sample of the events in the family. We stress this because, al-

though other types of inquiry may be of equal value, we think that
the one employed here was best suited for gathering information on
the mother-child relationship over a period of time. Periodic visits
by mother and child to a clinic would have the great advantage of
making it possible to have more than one person observe their interaction. But this is no substitute for observation of the whole family
in its natural setting. To have more than one worker visit the family was also plausible, but if done intensively might well have been
confusing both to the workers and to the family members.

It often happens that the type of unstructured interview used here
results in certain areas not being covered for certain cases or in an
uneven coverage. As has already been indicated, however, when certain information was not obtained spontaneously during the interview, it was specially sought—the moment for doing so always being
carefully considered. Even so there remained one or two areas which
were not uniformly covered and in which the data analysis eventually had to be limited. These will be indicated in subsequent chapters.

In any study in which the investigator is part of the interview
process, the questions of observer error and selective perception must
be given special attention. It is difficult for one fieldworker to maintain the same degree of alertness to all the significant happenings,
and in the resulting selective perception, important aspects of the
very thing in which we are interested can be missed. There were,
for example, moments when a conflict existed between the necessity
for detailed observation required for research and the demand of
the mother for the worker's attention. On each such occasion a decision of priority had to be made. Furthermore, since it is not easy
to make detailed observations of a child while engaged in an intensive interview with a mother, the observational record for such a
session was often sparse. Nevertheless, because the fieldworker spent
long periods with mother and child, even after such a session the
record might contain a good deal of useful material.

A further question not adequately dealt with in this project is the
reliability of the recording itself. The fieldworker may well have forgotten certain things and distorted others. To some extent the latter
was countered by the fieldworker recording her observations in detail and by keeping separate any deductions she made. In this way inferences drawn from the observations could be checked for reliability. Without being able to show systematic proof, we believe that the

very length and frequency of the contact with the family provided certain safeguards. It allowed for opportunities to recognize discrepancies between early and later accounts of behavior, made for constant reflection on newly obtained material, and necessitated assessments about current interactions and relationships. There was thus a continuous checking of observations. Some further check was provided by the contact which Heinicke and Wolpert also had with the families.

Whatever may be the disadvantages of this kind of interview, there exists as yet no other method that can provide these kinds and levels of data regarding the child and his family undergoing separation. As a result the richness of the data made it possible to answer many of the questions posed at the beginning of this study. Despite apparent shortcomings, the experience gained in this project of this method of interviewing encourages us to use it again.

Appendix to Chapter 2

Additional Details of Andrew's Family and Further Discussion on the Nature of Casework with His Mother

Andrew was aged 2. He had an older sister, Carol, aged 4½, and a baby brother. Both parents were intelligent and cultured and were interested in their children, but father saw little of them because of professional commitments. Certain features of the family relationships were outstanding: Andrew was an easily frustrated little boy whose unhappy state was evident in his facial expression and behavior. Andrew and Carol were extremely jealous of one another; mother was unable to say "no" to any of the children and found it especially difficult to do so with Andrew; and she was obviously distressed by the children's jealousy.

Mother described how she came from a comfortable middle-class home and was the elder of two children. Until the age of 3 she had been both the only child and the only grandchild, and much attention had been centered on her. When her brother was born she had felt displaced. She recalled how intense her feelings of jealousy and hatred toward him had been and how on certain occasions she had wished he would die. Therefore, when he was drowned at the age of 10, she had felt "as though it were in answer to my prayers."

At the time of the accident mother had been at boarding school, and she described how, on her return home, she had found her mother depressed and self-absorbed and her father quiet and brooding. She continued her boarding-school education and a few years later went on to a university. Thenceforward she did not visit her parents very often, but instead spent the greater part of her holidays in the home of one of her friends. She was popular and sought after. She also participated in such various adventurous activities as gliding and motor racing, and described how she enjoyed being in situations where death was almost round the corner.

She married soon after leaving the university, and a couple of years later Carol was born. She had been an easy baby who presented no difficulty. Two years later mother again found herself pregnant. Her own mother then asked that the baby, if it were a boy, be named after the boy who had died, but after worrying a good deal about it, mother refused this request. She began, however, to feel restless and depressed at times and to anticipate difficulties with the baby, and she felt sure that Carol would feel jealous of it. Though usually thoughtful in such matters, she gave Carol no preparation for the new arrival. Finally her fears were realized when Carol, on first seeing the baby, ran out of the room crying and shouting that she did not want him.

As the children grew older, the jealousy grew too; and on the occasions when Carol shouted that she wished Andrew were dead, mother became acutely distressed.

In the interviews this mother was able to discuss her current anxieties and in so doing seemed to gain much relief. She also recalled and re-experienced events and feelings from her past. By linking and comparing current events and anxieties with those of the past she came gradually to differentiate between them. For example, mother's pain and depression whenever Carol expressed her wish for Andrew to be gone, was linked with mother's earlier wishes that her own younger brother die and the strong feelings of guilt she had suffered when he was drowned.

In the course of time, mother's anxiety about the children's jealousy decreased considerably, and she became better able to deal with it; she also became altogether more confident in her capabilities as a mother. (Because of mother's needs, regular visiting in this case continued beyond the period required by the research design; in all, thirty-five visits were paid instead of the usual number.)

An even greater change seemed to occur in the boy himself. He became independent and self-reliant and able to fight his own battles with his sister without appealing to his mother. He also looked much happier.

In the course of regular visiting, the data of current interaction gained significance as these became complemented by data obtained in a therapeutically oriented interview. Observation showed that this mother, ever patient and giving, was trying to accede to Andrew's every wish and demand and was wearing herself out by carrying, fetching and doing; the casework data showed how this behavior stemmed from her need to make vicarious reparation to Andrew because of an association between him and her dead brother. Observation recorded mother's distress and helplessness when confronted with the children's jealousy of one another; interview data clarified why.

Methods of Analysis of Data

3 There are several types of data available in this study: the coded records of behavior of the child in the Everyday Nursery and the Doll-Play Settings, the clinical descriptions of his behavior in the same two settings, and the descriptive record of the interviews and observations of the behavior of the child and his family yielded by home visits.

Since the coded records of behavior were already in a form readily leading to quantitative treatment, little further needs to be said about them. The descriptive records, however, required a great deal of preliminary analysis before they could be used for statistical comparisons. The rich volume of data available on each child and family had to be reduced into relatively few manipulatable dimensions, without losing too much that was significant and without distorting the unique qualities of each child's development.

Our attempts to organize the descriptive material of the child are of two kinds. First, the daily records on the child were organized into periods of development. Second, we distinguished a number of dimensions in terms of which behavior varied from one child to another, and we made our quantitative comparisons in terms of these dimensions.

Similarly, following certain preliminary analyses, we developed a series of dimensions making comparison of the mothers possible.

I.   Data from the Categorization of the Child's Behavior in the Everyday Nursery and Doll-Play Settings

In the case of the observations of the behavior sequences of the child both in the Everyday Nursery Setting and in the special Doll-Play Setting, the coded recording can be used without any further processing except selective tabulation. First, we can simply count for each child the incidence of behavior in each category in each sample period, e.g., the first two days of separation. We can then determine

41

what percentage of the total behavior recorded for the child is comprised, for example, of hostile behavior, of severely hostile behavior, etc.; or, taking hostility as the base, what percentage of these hostile acts are directed to one object or another. Both the total units and the units per minute scored during the observation periods of the first two weeks of separation were sufficiently constant to make such percentage computations feasible. Nevertheless, we carefully scrutinized each trend to determine if they could be simply a function of changes in the base of the percentages.

Since observations in the home of nonseparated children were not recorded by means of the coding system, group comparisons are not possible. We can, however, using the coded data, compare the present sample of separated children with the two samples of the pilot study. Furthermore, concentrating on the present sample of separated children alone, we can tabulate the mean incidence of a given category, or we can rank them in order of incidence of each category of behavior in any given time span; for example, the first week of separation or the last week of separation. Especially interesting here is the change in score of a child from the first to the last week of separation.

Turning to the doll play, many of the above considerations apply. The tabulation, calculation of percentages, and all the types of comparisons mentioned above are possible. For example, by comparing the incidence of certain behavior categories in the separated children from data obtained in the first and last doll-play sessions, we can again record the change from the first week to a time near the end of separation.

Because the doll play was administered to the nonseparated as well as to the separated children, group comparisons within the present study, as well as with the two samples of the pilot study, are also possible.

II.   Data from the Clinical Descriptions of the Child in the Everyday Nursery Setting

A. Grouping the Observations in Terms of Aspects of Behavior and Periods of Development

Confronted with a large number of clinical reports covering the period of separation of each child, some way of abstracting the most relevant features from the mass of data had to be devised so that the children could be compared. Both the form of the behavior and periods of time had to be taken into account.

That we would wish to consider the various aspects of behavior independently as well as in context does not need justification. A child does not develop evenly in all aspects. The particular aspects of behavior chosen can be related to the aims and theoretical considerations outlined in Chapter 1.

Behavior in each of these aspects passes through a succession of periods during each of which it is fairly stable. This means that it is possible to find for each child periods of time during which his behavior relating to a particular aspect differs from what it is in the preceding and succeeding period. We wished in fact to derive these periods empirically by studying the development characterizing *each* of the aspects of the child's total behavior.

The first step was to go through every record for each child and to classify the material under a series of headings. These headings were divided into: relations with people; modes of coping with the stress of separation; development of certain basic functions like eating, toileting, sleeping; sickness; speech; and the fantasy development of the child. Under "Relations with People" we included relations with the visiting father, the observers, the nurse, siblings if any, and the other children in the nursery. Under "Modes of Coping" we included the use of specific defense mechanisms and also such things as the use made of the favorite possession from home. Under "Fantasy" we did not develop any subheadings but noted behavior which we thought indicated the presence of fantasy.

Having extracted all the material suitable for classification under each of the headings or subheadings and having recorded it chronologically, we were ready for the second step, which was to group it into time periods. In defining periods, data relating to each heading were treated independently, but our knowledge of the rest of the data on the case inevitably influenced us to some extent in delineating the periods. No arbitrary limits were set to the length of a period, some of which were as short as one day and others as long as a month. An attempt was made to define the main characteristic of each period in a short paragraph headed by the dates of the period. Special effort was made to define why certain days had been demarcated as a second period, for example, rather than included in the first. The emphasis thus was on the characterization of the main trends, say, of the child's relation to the observer—at what points in the relationship changes occurred and how these were expressed. We did not assume linear development, but did attempt in a final paragraph to summarize the over-all picture. The results of this formulation of time periods could be used both to describe the development of an individual child (see Chapter 5) and also to characterize the typical development of a group of children (see Chapters 6 and 8).

The procedure described above for the grouping of descriptions of development of the child during separation was also applied to the material on the child recorded by Westheimer during the first twenty weeks after reunion. Clearly some of the headings had become redundant, e.g., "Relation with Nurse," while others, such as "Relation with Mother," were added.

1. Reliability of Grouping the Descriptions into Time Periods. Using their combined records for the separation period and the records of Westheimer for the reunion period, the above grouping into time periods was carried out for each of the areas of behavior on each of the ten separated children by Heinicke and Wolpert independently. When comparing any two specific sets of time periods that resulted, we first assessed the degree of agreement; next the differences were discussed, and in this way an agreed set of periods was arrived at.

In assessing the degree of agreement between Heinicke and Wolpert we made four distinctions: an *agreement* was scored if both the dates and the main content of the period abstracted were identical in both sets of analysis; a *disagreement on subdivision* was scored when there was agreement on the content and on the dates of a period, say December 1–14, but one observer had thought that the period could better be subdivided—for example, December 1–6 and 7–14; an *omission* was scored when one observer had formulated a period but the other for some reason had not; finally, a *disagreement* was scored either when the observers differed by a day or more over the dates of a period, or when they differed on the content of a period. In Table 2 we present the percentage of total ratings characterized by each of the above degrees of agreement on the time periods for each of the subheadings (aspects of behavior) during separation and reunion. The subheadings listed are the ones we will be dealing with in later analysis. The percentages of omissions and disagreements are highest for relation to siblings and sickness during both separation and reunion. The former arose from inadequate information and the latter from poor definition. The over-all picture, however, is an encouraging one. In only 5 per cent of the total of the five hundred and thirty-six periods formulated was there either an omission or a disagreement.

The assessment of agreement on the extraction of information on when the children showed either a spurt in identification with the parents or a spurt in language during reunion was not included in the initial reliability study. Examination of the period analysis of the two raters revealed that they agreed perfectly on whether or not such a spurt occurred, and when it occurred.

B. Ranking the Children in Terms of Behavioral Dimensions: The General Procedure

While the comparisons of behavior from one time period to another are sufficient for purposes of individual case presentation and for the elucidation of developmental trends, to compare the separated children with each other a further analysis of the data was necessary. Examination of the conclusions about development agreed upon by both observers revealed not only that children differed from one another right from the beginning, but also that their later development differed. To capture both kinds of difference we ranked the children in terms of a number of dimensions for each of four time spans.

The procedure was first to define a dimension appropriate to the aspect of behavior and time span. It should be noted that these time intervals are not the same as the empirically derived time periods. This dimension was then further defined and points along it demarcated by a series of verbal descriptions or subheadings. Each child was first assigned to one of these subheadings and finally the total sample of ten children was rank-ordered in terms of the dimension. In this way we derived the advantages of ranking (such as maximizing the quantitative spread of a sample) and yet could specify in detail the manner in which the ranking was achieved.

Using this procedure, dimensions for the first and for the last weeks of separation and for the first and for the second to twentieth weeks after reunion were formulated and used for ranking. (The reasons for choosing these time intervals and why in particular the last time interval was such a long one will be explained later.) To enable us to make group comparisons the nonseparated children were ranked according to the same behavioral dimensions.

Table 2. *Showing Degree of Agreement between Heinicke and Wolpert in Assessing Periods of Development*

Development during Separation

Relation with People	Agreement	Disagreement on Subdivision	Disagreement and Omission
Relation with Heinicke	68.0	29.9	2.1
Relation with Wolpert	81.5	13.9	4.6
Relation with Father	63.3	31.5	5.2
Relation with Nurse	80.7	16.1	3.2
Relation with Westheimer	100.0	.0	.0
Relation with Siblings	80.0	10.0	10.0
Relation with Children	80.0	20.0	.0
Major Functions			
Eating	73.4	20.0	6.6
Toileting	86.7	13.3	.0
Sleep	95.5	.0	4.5
Sickness	73.9	.0	26.1
Modes of Coping			
Favorite Object from Home	86.7	13.3	.0
Over-All Assessment	79.3	15.2	5.5

Development during Reunion

Relation with People			
Relation with Mother	88.3	7.8	3.9
Relation with Father	63.7	31.8	4.5
Relation with Westheimer	84.7	10.8	4.5
Relation with Siblings	65.0	21.0	14.0
Major Functions			
Eating	89.6	5.2	5.2
Toileting	94.7	5.3	.0
Sleep	85.0	10.0	5.0
Sickness	84.6	.0	15.4
Over-All Assessment	84.9	9.9	5.2

1. Behavior Seen during First Week of Separation. Dimensions in terms of which we describe the child's reaction to the first week of separation provide a useful summary of these reactions. The results were then also used for systematic comparison with dimensions describing the preseparation picture.

As an example we give the way we used the dimension: *the child's affectionate relationship to the nurses* during the first week of separation.[1] We were interested in the extent to which the child turns to

---

[1] The other dimensions will be described in detail in Chapters 7 and 9 as part of the presentation of results.

the nurse for comfort and especially the extent of attachment made to a particular nurse. For this dimension there are six subheadings:

A. Children who resist the nurse initially, never show their affection and develop no clear-cut preference for any nurse

1. Margaret

B. Children whose resistance is fleeting and who then make some contact, but who do not establish intense involvement with any one nurse

2. Dennis
3. Elizabeth
4. Georgy
5. Dawn

C. Children who resist the nurses in the beginning, then cling to many of them and then show some preference though not a clear-cut one

6. Owen
7. Jimmy
8. Josephine

D. Children who resist the nurses actively or passively in the beginning, and then begin to develop an affectionate relationship with specific nurses

9. Gillian

E. Children whose predominant response is to cling to all the nurses from the beginning and who then begin to develop an affectionate preference for one or maybe two nurses

10. Katie

We shall explain later why we thought this dimension was valuable. It may be noted that, even when dealing with a period as short as a week, we take account of changes over time and incorporate them in our ratings. It is, however, the child's dominant response during the whole time interval that determines his place on the dimension. The numbers refer to the rank order and are assigned after the children have been placed under the headings.

Using the same method, the children were rated and ranked in terms of the extent to which they manifested the following behavior during the first week of separation: lack of affectionate contact with the father, avoidance of Observers Heinicke and Wolpert, avoidance of Observer Westheimer, greed for food and sphincter control.

2. *Behavior Seen during Last Week of Separation.* Even a cursory examination of the results revealed that the behavior at the end of separation differed strikingly from one child to another. In order to compare this behavior both with the children's initial reaction to separation and with their behavior later during reunion, we distinguished a set of behavioral dimensions pertinent to a description of their terminal status. Because, in order to evaluate the terminal status, the development of the child during the whole separation experience needs to be taken into account, we also studied this development before assessing it.

The children were ranked in terms of the extent to which they showed lack of affectionate contact with the father, affectionate involvement with the nurses, ambivalence toward Observers Heinicke and Wolpert, greed for food and concern over a lapse in sphincter control.

3. *Behavior Seen during the First Week after Reunion.* The procedure used here is identical with that used for the first week of separation. The behavioral dimensions are lack of affectionate contact with the mother and Westheimer and reluctance to eat.

4. *Behavior Seen during the Second to Twentieth Weeks after Reunion.* In contrast to the above dimensions which focus either on the first or the last week of a period, those designed for reunion beyond the first week cover a much longer time interval. To have made it strictly comparable to the dimensions abstracted for the separation, the time interval involved should have been the last week of reunion. There is, however, no last week of reunion. Since examination of the material suggested that the most significant events occurred over a span of time and could not be captured by focusing on one cross section, we decided to conceptualize dimensions relating to the most general question of whether a certain development such as, for example, the emergence of ambivalence, did or did not occur and, if so, what course it took. Thus we are concerned not merely with the extent to which each child manifested a certain

type of behavior, but also with the length of the latent period before this type of behavior emerges or with the length of time that elapses before it disappears. Because the children were observed for at least twenty weeks after reunion, statements covering the interval from the second to the twentieth week after reunion were chosen.

The procedure was otherwise the same and the children were ranked according to the following: ambivalence toward the mother, ambivalence toward Westheimer, progress toward complete sphincter control (and this includes judgments of when the child reached the level of control seen before reunion), the extent of sleep disturbance, and the length of time in weeks after reunion before an acceleration in speech and before a marked increase of behavior indicative of identification with parents occurred. Attempts were made to develop a dimension describing the child's relation to the father, but the reactions did not vary sufficiently to permit this.

5. The Reliability of the Rankings. We have already stated that the rankings of the ten children originally undertaken by one observer were repeated by the other. In Table 3 we give the results of comparing the two sets in terms of Spearman rank-order coefficients (Siegel, 1956).

Formal reliability assessments were not made for three dimensions, those characterizing the length of time that sleep disturbances persisted, and the lengths of time before spurts in speech and in identification occurred. The previous analysis of these areas of behavior and their development in terms of time periods had already indicated the reliability of the information extracted from the descriptive material. That is, the ordering of the length of time involved for each of the children on each of the dimensions did not involve an additional judgment.

C. Comparing the Development of the Separated and Nonseparated Children

So far we have been concerned only with ways of describing the development of the separated children. At many points, however, conclusions drawn can be strikingly amplified when the development of the separated children is compared with that of the nonseparated ones.

Table 3. *Correlation of Rankings of Dimensions Made*
Independently by Heinicke and Wolpert

Description of Dimensions	Spearman Coefficient
Behavior during First Week of Separation	
The Child's Lack of Affectionate Response to the Father	.95**
The Child's Affectionate Relationship with the Nurses	.77**
The Child's Avoidance of Observers Heinicke and Wolpert	.79**
The Child's Avoidance of Observer Westheimer	.89**
The Child's Greed for Food	.92**
The Child's Sphincter Control	.73*
Behavior during Last Week of Separation	
The Child's Lack of Affectionate Response to the Father	.87**
The Child's Affectionate Relationship with the Nurses	.89**
The Ambivalence Expressed by the Child toward Observers Heinicke and Wolpert	.94**
The Child's Greed for Food	.70*
The Child's Concern Over a Lapse in Sphincter Control	1.00**
Behavior during the First Week after Reunion	
The Child's Lack of Affectionate Response to the Mother	.78**
The Child's Lack of Affectionate Response to Westheimer	.95**
The Child's Reluctance to Eat	.70*
Behavior during the Second to the Twentieth Week after Reunion	
The Ambivalence Expressed by the Child toward the Mother	.94**
The Ambivalence Expressed by the Child toward Westheimer	1.00**
The Child's Progress toward Complete Sphincter Control	.86**

  * Significant at the .05 level
**Significant at the .01 level

To make this possible we first ordered the material in terms of the same areas of behavior used for the separated children (e.g., relation to observer) and then grouped the material on each child in each area of behavior into a series of time periods.

The next step was to devise a series of dimensions which would enable the children to be ranked. To facilitate comparison between the two groups of children, wherever possible we used the rating scales already developed for the separated children but extended them to include points appropriate to the behavior of the nonseparated.

This extension of the ratings could have been applied to each of the time spans equivalent to the ones used for the separated children: the first weeks respectively of separation and of reunion, the last week of separation, and the second to the twentieth weeks after reunion. Dimensions were developed, however, only for intervals of time equivalent to the last week of separation and to the second to the twentieth week after reunion. The two main reasons for this restriction were that the most significant findings on the separated children were obtained for these time spans and the changes in the nonseparated children were not as great as those for the separated, so that too fine a time differentiation was not warranted.

A limitation on the value of comparing the material for separated and nonseparated children must be noted. Material for the separated children was gathered by Heinicke and Wolpert observing the child at least three times a week while that for the nonseparated was recorded by Westheimer on the basis of weekly visits.

1. Reliability of Rank-Ordering of Nonseparated Children. Rank-ordering on one dimension was checked and a near perfect agreement found. Since we used these rankings exclusively for group comparison and since the differences found are very large, there seemed less need to check the remainder.

III. Data from the Clinical Observations of the Child in the Doll-Play Setting

Although the clinical impressions recorded after each doll-play session were important in formulating hypotheses and in guiding our analyses of the categorizations, few systematic analyses of these impressions themselves were done. In examining them, however, it was noted that both Heinicke and Wolpert had frequently included in their records a detailed account of the hostility directed by the child toward one of the family dolls.

Using the protocols both of the categorization and the clinical observations, Heinicke and Wolpert independently determined whether or not they saw clear evidence in a given doll-play session of hostility directed toward one of the family dolls. Only where both assessments agreed that a sequence was present was it included in the analyses of the data (see Chapter 10). The analysis is thus based on a simple present-absent count and does not deal with frequency counts.

IV.   Data from the Interviews with the Child and His Family

A.   Introduction

As we show in Chapter 5, the extensive qualitative description of the members of the family and their interaction provided a rich source for the study of the development of the child as well as being of interest in its own right.

In order to do certain systematic and quantitative analyses, we rated and ranked the cases on various aspects of the mother-child relationship. Several difficulties arose. In singling out a dimension, one runs the risk of losing the context of a given communication. The affection given by one mother may be descriptively similar to that of another mother and yet occur in a different context and thus have a different meaning. Although single dimensions were defined, a great variety of evidence pertaining to each was used, and the context of the evidence was taken into account. We are also aware, when rating, that only the gross components can be demonstrated while the more delicate shades of feeling cannot always be utilized.

Despite these limitations, three kinds of dimensions of the mother-child relationship were formulated: (1) those describing certain broad aspects of the mother-child relationship drawing on material obtained during the *total period* of study; these were applied to both separated and nonseparated children, (2) those describing the attitudes of the mothers during the period *before reunion,* and (3) those describing their attitudes during the period *after reunion.* The second and third were applied to the separated children only.

While the first of these types of dimension was formulated primarily to enable us to make a comparison of the separated and the nonseparated children based on the largest body of information available, this very comparison is complicated by the fact that while one group was experiencing a special event (separation), the other was not. Since for the separated group most of our data was gathered during the reunion period when the mother was at times struggling with her own and the child's difficulties, the assessment of such things as the amount of affection shown is complicated. Comparison with the nonseparated group must therefore be made with caution.

Although ideally we might have undertaken rankings for the period before separation, the material was not sufficient to warrant it. It was possible however to assess the cases on the material obtained during the whole of the period *before reunion* had occurred. By so doing, such complications as are introduced by changes that may occur in the child during separation, and which may then affect the mother's attitude, are minimized. In addition, it is possible to develop a dimension which makes use only of the data on the mother's reaction during the period *after reunion*. Since these dimensions were in most instances specifically formulated in relation to the events of the separation, and since the relative lack of change in the attitudes of the mothers of the nonseparated children did not in their case warrant defining dimensions for each of the time periods, they were applied only to the separated families.

B. Dimensions Describing the Mother-Child Relationship for Both Separated and Nonseparated Children during the Total Period of Study

Confronted with a wealth of detailed data some preparatory analyses were necessary before relevant dimensions could be formulated.

Since the family is a dynamic social system, it can be understood only through a study both of the functioning of the component individuals and of how this functioning is influenced by, and expressed in, the characteristic patterns of family interaction.

While keeping the total family interaction in mind, therefore, the first grouping of the data was done in terms of two very broad categories: (1) descriptions of the personality functioning of each individual (e.g., the father) and his development, and (2) a description of the relationships that existed between particular individuals. The results of these two types of description can be found in Chapter 5 as part of the case illustrations.

Even though these preparatory analyses had suggested many other possibilities, since the prime interest of our study is the child and since the child's relationship with his mother is of great importance in his development, this relationship was the logical one on which to focus. On the basis of two main criteria, eight dimensions of the mother-child relationship were formulated. The criteria were (a) that each dimension should deal with an important part of the mother-child relationship, and (b) that sufficient material be available to rate all the families. The twenty families were then ranked in terms of each dimension.

1. The Definition of Dimensions Concerning the Mother-Child Relationship. Since for reasons to be described only two of the dimensions were ultimately used in the analyses to be presented in later chapters, only these will be defined and illustrated here. The remaining six are simply listed; they are defined and illustrated in Appendix A of this chapter. The two selected dimensions are:

The Mother's Affection for and Pleasure in the Company of the Child. This dimension describes the extent to which a mother loves her child, expresses this affection and enjoys the company of her child. The affection is frequently expressed in the form of kissing and hugging but can also be communicated in other more subtle ways. Also important in making this rating is the extent to which the mother's affection is expressed spontaneously and naturally. At one extreme of this dimension we have *Margaret's mother* whose spontaneous cuddles were rare and whose enjoyment of her daughter was limited to an occasional expression of amusement when Margaret said, "I love you with all my heart"; and at the other extreme we have *Jean's mother* who was consistently warm and affectionate and who even during sleepless nights with the child could find pleasure in taking care of her.

The Mother's Ability Consistently to Set Limits. This dimension describes the extent to which the mother effectively and consistently limits the child when this is conducive to his good and does not arise from the mother's own needs to cut short or restrict. More weight is given to consistency than to mere frequency. Those mothers who set many limits yet did not carry them out were given a low ranking. Under consistency of limit setting we not only considered the termination of an activity, but also the manner in which it was terminated. Mothers did this in a variety of ways: by stopping the activity physically, by a firm statement, by distracting the child's attention or by finding another outlet. For example, one mother set a limit to the boy hitting his sister by suggesting he hit a drum instead. At one extreme of this dimension we have *Dennis's mother* who threatened all kinds of things and imposed limits but could seldom effectively keep her child within them, and at the other extreme we have *Jean's mother* who set a given number of limits which she maintained and who usually at the moment of limit setting also managed to turn her child toward other activities.

The remaining six dimensions concerning the mother-child relationship are:

> *The Mother's Interest in the Child*
>
> *The Mother's Ability to Understand the Child's Communications*
>
> *The Mother's Sympathy in Meeting the Child's Wishes*
>
> *The Mother's Tendency to Perceive the Child as a Threat*
>
> *The Mother's Tendency to Use the Child for Her Own Unconscious Purposes*
>
> *The Mother's Tendency to React toward the Child's Misbehavior Hostilely*

2. Intercorrelation of Dimensions concerning Mother-Child Relationship. In Tables 4 and 5 we give the rank-order intercorrelations for the eight dimensions concerning the mother-child relationship. Table 4 is based on the rankings of all twenty separated and nonseparated children; each of the Spearman coefficients in this table reaches at least the .01 level of significance.

Since we found, however, that the two groups of children differed on some of these dimensions (see Chapter 4), the intercorrelations were recomputed on the rankings of the separated children only. The results are given in Table 5 and indicate that the general intercorrelation of the first seven dimensions is maintained. The minimal statement one can make is that all the dimensions except the one describing *The mother's ability to set limits* correlate significantly with the first one, *The mother's affection for and pleasure in the company of the child,* to the extent of .56 or more. (For an N of 10 it takes a coefficient of .56 to reach the .05 level, and .75 to reach the .01 level of significance.)

We are not in a position to determine whether this high intercorrelation of seven of the dimensions is the product of some special characteristics of this sample, represents a true concomitance of maternal characteristics or was produced by the operation of a halo effect. In regard to the latter, a concept of the good, affectionate, understanding mother might be guiding all the rankings.

Without wishing to underestimate the many qualitative distinctions, the results of the statistical analysis suggested that in further

Table 4. *Showing Intercorrelation of Mother-Child Relationship Dimensions for Separated and Nonseparated Children during the Total Period of Study (N Equals 20)*

Mother-Child Dimensions	1	2	3	4	5	6	7	8
1. Affection for and Pleasure in the Company of the Child	——							
2. Interest in the Child	.94**	——						
3. Ability to Understand the Child's Communications	.97**	.96**	——					
4. Sympathy in Meeting the Child's Wishes	.96**	.96**	.98**	——				
5. Tendency to Perceive Child as a Threat	−.91**	−.79**	−.88**	−.87**	——			
6. Tendency to Use Child for Her Own Unconscious Purposes	−.86**	−.76**	−.80**	−.82**	.89**	——		
7. Tendency to React toward the Child's Misbehavior Hostilely	−.81**	−.75**	−.82**	−.85**	.91**	.73**	——	
8. Ability Consistently to Set Limits	.64**	.74**	.71**	.72**	−.56**	−.60**	−.56**	——

*Significant at the .05 level
**Significant at the .01 level

data analysis we confine our efforts to two of the dimensions—that describing the mother's affection and that describing her ability to set limits.

It is of interest that these two dimensions can easily be related to the two dimensions isolated by Schaeffer and Bayley (1963) as a result of their extensive analysis of maternal behavior data—love versus hostility and autonomy versus control.

3. The Reliability of the Mother-Child Relationship Dimensions.
Although the reliability of all the above dimensions might have been
checked, in view of both the pattern of interrelation and the use to

Table 5. *Showing Intercorrelation of Mother-Child Relationship*
Dimensions for the Separated Children during the Total
Period of Study (N Equals 10)

Mother-Child Dimensions	1	2	3	4	5	6	7	8
1. Affection for and Pleasure in the Company of the Child	——							
2. Interest in the Child	.89**	——						
3. Ability to Understand the Child's Communications	.94**	.95**	——					
4. Sympathy in Meeting the Child's Wishes	.91**	.94**	.99**	——				
5. Tendency to Perceive Child as a Threat	−.73**	−.30	−.57*	−.52	——			
6. Tendency to Use Child for Her Own Unconscious Purposes	−.89**	−.72*	−.77**	−.81**	.72*	——		
7. Tendency to React toward the Child's Misbehavior Hostilely	−.56*	−.39	−.54	−.54	.82**	.39	——	
8. Ability Consistently to Set Limits	.06	.32	.05	.36	−.28	−.07	−.03	——

* Significant at the .05 level
** Significant at the .01 level

which the dimensions are put, it seemed sufficient to check only the
two selected dimensions.

To do this a second psychiatric social worker, Soles, read the complete material on the mothers gathered by Westheimer. After studying the definition of the dimension, she ranked the mother-child relationships of the ten separated children in terms of *The mother's affection for and pleasure in the company of the child.* A Spearman
rank-order correlation coefficient of .85 (significant at the .01 level)
describes the extent of the relation between this ranking and that
made by Westheimer.

For reasons beyond our control, Soles was unable to rank the families on the dimension describing the mother's ability to set limits consistently. Heinicke therefore repeated the rankings of the separated and nonseparated children on this dimension. Rank-order correlation coefficients of .91 and .96 describe the extent to which his rankings agreed with those of Westheimer. The first coefficient was computed for rankings on all twenty children (separated and nonseparated) and the second for the separated children only; both are significant at the .01 level.

We conclude therefore that both these dimensions, *The mother's affection for and pleasure in the company of the child* and *The mother's ability to set limits,* are ranked reliably. We believe it of special value that a person not otherwise engaged in this project took part in these assessments of reliability.

C. Dimensions Describing the Mother's Attitude toward the Separated Child during the Period before Reunion

These dimensions were originally defined to enable us to evaluate the mother-child relationship before the event of reunion. The likely effect of the reunion experience was thus eliminated. Dimensions referring to the mother's attitudes at the beginning of the separation could be correlated with the child's behavior at that time. Similarly, dimensions referring to the mother's attitudes toward the end of the separation (but before reunion) could be correlated with the child's behavior at that point or on the day of reunion (see Chapters 7 and 9).

The dimensions formulated below have the further advantage that they are based on variations in reaction to specific problems which all mothers of the separated children had to face: what are likely to be the effects on the child of the separation; what preparations can be made to ameliorate these effects; and how soon should the child return home?

1. Definition of Dimensions Describing the Mother's Attitude toward the Separated Child during the Period before Reunion. The Mother's Concern about and Sensitivity to the Welfare of Her Child at the Beginning of Separation. The dimensions numbered 9, 13 and 16 in Table 6 attempt to show the sensitivity, concern and thoughtful attitude expressed in the mother's thinking, feeling and acting in relation to the child at the beginning and at the end of separation. Thus, in making the ranking for the beginning of the separation, her capacity to observe and the use she made of her observations have been taken into account; for example, Elizabeth's mother understood her daughter's sudden wetting in terms of her anxiety about the forthcoming separation. These dimensions also considered

Table 6. *Showing Intercorrelation of Dimensions Describing the Mother-Child Relationship during the Period before Reunion (N Equals 10)*

Mother-Child Dimensions	9	10	11	12	13	14	15	16
9. Concern at the Beginning of Separation	—							
10. Specific Concern about the Effects of Separation	.72*	—						
11. Extent of Missing the Child	.80**	.49	—					
12. Extent of Planning for the Separation	.77**	.88**	.42	—				
13. Concern at the End of Separation	.83**	.57*	.54	.55	—			
14. Eagerness to Have the Child Home	.77**	.52	.60*	.64*	.75*	—		
15. Extent of Planning for the Reunion	.87**	.72*	.63*	.78**	.84**	.73*	—	
16. Change in Concern from the Beginning to End	-.60*	-.52	-.28	-.39	-.78**	-.79**	-.73*	—

*Significant at the .05 level
**Significant at the .01 level

the effectiveness of the mother's planning in relation to the needs of the child. For example, if she thought a prolonged separation was likely to harm the child, what did she do in order to make it as brief as possible? The dimension describing the mother's concern at the beginning of the separation ranged from *Margaret's mother,* who did little to prepare for the separation and did not seem concerned about the possible effects, to *Georgy's mother,* who from the beginning was concerned about the effects of the separation and constantly thought about him.

The Mother's Concern about and Sensitivity to the Welfare of her Child at the End of Separation. The considerations in ranking the children on this dimension are the same as those defined above for the beginning of separation. At one extreme there is *Katie's mother,* who had become remote from her child, no longer understood her needs and showed reluctance to have her back. At the other extreme there is *Georgy's mother,* who did everything to have Georgy and his sister back as soon as possible.

The Extent of Change during Separation of the Mother's Concern about and Sensitivity to the Welfare of her Child.   Having rated the mothers in terms of their general concern both at the beginning and at the end of separation, we could also rank them in terms of the degree of *change* in this concern and of sensitivity that had taken place during separation. At one extreme of this dimension is *Georgy's mother* who was concerned about her children throughout the separation and thus showed no change. At the other extreme is *Katie's mother* who was at the beginning of the separation very distressed about losing her child but at the end showed reluctance to have her back.

The remaining five dimensions describing the mother-child relationship of the separated children during the whole period before reunion are given below. They are defined and illustrated in Appendix B of this chapter, and as it turned out were in fact not used in later analyses.

The Mother's Specific Concern about the Effects of the Separation and What She Did to Ameliorate These Effects

The Extent to Which the Mother Missed the Child

The Extent to Which the Mother Planned Adequately for the Separation

The Mother's Eagerness to Have the Child Home Again

The Extent to Which the Mother Adequately Planned for the Reunion

2. The Intercorrelation of the Dimensions Describing the Mother's Attitude to the Separated Children during the Period before Reunion. In Table 6 we present the rank-order intercorrelation coefficients for the dimensions describing the mother's attitude to the separated children during the period *before reunion.* Once again intercorrelations are high. This one would expect since some of the dimensions are components of the others. Thus, the mother's specific concern about the effects of separation, the extent of planning for the separation and the extent of missing the child probably influenced the ranking of the mothers on the dimension of the degree of concern seen at the beginning of the separation. Similarly, the eagerness to have the child home and the planning the mother did for the reunion were no doubt influential in determining the ranking of degree of concern at the end of separation.

The evidence of Table 6 also suggests, however, that we are dealing with a general dimension which might be termed *The mother's concern about and sensitivity to the welfare of the child as seen during the period before reunion*. With few exceptions the mothers who were most concerned before the separation tended to be the same mothers who were most concerned about their child at the end of the separation. That is, even though some of them decreased in their level of concern they maintained their relative position vis-à-vis the other mothers. It will not be surprising, therefore, that the dimensions describing the mother's concern at the beginning and at the end each correlate quite highly with the even more general but similar dimension described previously: *The mother's affection for and pleasure in the company of the child* (the Spearman rank-order correlation coefficients are respectively .94 and .80).

3. The Reliability of the Dimensions Describing the Mother's Attitude toward the Separated Child during the Period before Reunion. Since the dimensions describing the mother's concern at the beginning and at the end, as well as the change in her concern, emerged as central to the cluster given in Table 6 and were the ones to be used in later parts of the book, it is these that were checked for reliability by Heinicke. The correlation coefficients between his and Westheimer's rankings are .91 for concern at the beginning of separation, .88 for concern at the end of separation, and .96 for the degree of change in concern.

In addition, Soles ranked the dimension describing the mother's concern at the beginning of separation; her rankings correlate with those of Westheimer to the extent of .86. The particular advantage in having Soles do the reliability ratings on this dimension lies in the fact that she did not read any of the material on the child's development during the separation. This is of importance since in Chapter 9 we explore the relationship between the mother's concern and the child's reaction during the first week after reunion.

From the evidence above we conclude that the rankings of the mother's concern about and sensitivity to the welfare of her child were done sufficiently reliably to be used in further analyses.

D. A Dimension on Describing the Mother-Child Relationship of the Separated Children during the Period after Reunion

Since we had observed that the mother's attitude toward her child often changed again considerably after they were reunited, it was necessary to develop a dimension to describe her attitude during the reunion period.

Again, many facets of the relationship could have been abstracted. Study of the reunion material revealed one dimension of central importance. This was *The mother's capacity to adapt herself to a disturbed child and her sensitivity in meeting his needs.* How did she deal with the problem of re-establishing an affectionate relationship with the child? How insistent was she when the child was not able or ready to comply with her wishes? Given the increased hostile and demanding behavior, could she understand and deal with it, or was she likely to reciprocate in a negative manner? The dimension ranges from *Margaret's mother,* who could not adapt herself to the needs of her child and easily became exasperated with her, to *Georgy's mother,* who understood what her children needed and despite a variety of external difficulties could meet their demanding behavior.

1. The Reliability of the Dimension Describing the Mother's Capacity to Adapt Herself to a Disturbed Child. To assess the reliability of the above dimension, Heinicke repeated the ranking procedure independently. A rank-order correlation coefficient of .89 describes the extent to which these rankings agree with those made by Westheimer.

Appendix A to Chapter 3

Definition of Dimensions Concerning the Mother–Child Relationship

Below we give the definitions of the six dimensions concerning the mother-child relationship previously mentioned in this chapter.

The Mother's Interest in the Child. This dimension describes the degree of consistent and constant interest that the mother takes in her child. Some mothers take a permanent interest in the whole child, while others demonstrate an interest in only certain aspects of the child's personality; for example, it may be the child's developmental skills, such as vocabulary, his manipulative ability or his good looks and general popularity with others. Some mothers are erratic in the degree of interest shown at any one time, while others are fairly consistent. Still others reveal a minimal interest, expressed by an attitude of ignoring the child's presence and by behavior which takes no note of his interests and demands.

The mothers who show a consistent and constant interest have a readiness to perceive his needs and to respond to his interest of the moment. They are able to encourage by their interest and to stimulate the child toward further explorations. They help him in his attempts and then enjoy together with him his simple achievements.

Those mothers who demonstrate a minimal interest are lacking in the capacity to respond and to share what is of interest to the child. One mother who was unable to play with her child in any way limited herself to surrounding him with toys. Another showed no interest in her child whom she found disappointing and wanting; on rare occasions, however, her interest might be briefly stimulated by some activity of her child that she considered clever, and then in turn she could become somewhat more encouraging and interested, instead of stifling. The dimension ranges from *Anne's mother,* who usually behaved as though the child was not present, who rarely played with her and hardly ever cuddled her, who when serving everyone else omitted to give her a drink, and who was never observed to respond to the mood or the need of the child, to *Colin's mother,* who showed a consistent and constant interest in Colin as an individual, was very encouraging and responsive, and played with him and enjoyed his experiences. At his exclamation "Smell" she would repeatedly lift him to smell the flowers because of his obvious enjoyment and interest. Even when busy and not able to respond to him immediately, she never became disinterested.

The Mother's Ability to Understand the Child's Communications. This dimension describes the mother's capacity to pick up and respond to the child's communications. Such communications can be conveyed by the child to the mother by means of gesture, action or verbal comment. The mother's response to the communication can be expressed by touch, gesture or verbal comment.

The mothers most able to respond to the child's communications are those whose own personal needs do not obtrude and who have only a minimum of preconceived ideas. Thus they are able to consider the child as an individual and are interested in his expression of individuality. They want to listen and to understand and enjoy the flow of communication between him and them.

The mothers poorest in the ability to respond to the child's communications are those whose preoccupations with their own concerns prevent them from effective listening, or those who do not consider the child as an individual with his own needs but regard him as an extension of themselves. The dimension ranges from *Sally's mother,* who was much preoccupied with her own problems and never seemed to pick up Sally's communications, who would not listen to Sally's entreaties for her mother's love and did not understand the child's need to tell herself what the mother did not tell her: "Let her have the cup, let her have the cup, let her have some milk," to *Sandra's mother,* whose own needs never obtruded, who invariably picked up and responded appropriately to the child's communication and who was outstanding in terms of her sensitivity and affection which were constantly available to the child.

The Mother's Sympathy in Meeting the Child's Wishes. This dimension describes the degree of sympathy that the mother has in relation to the child's wishes. Both recognition of these wishes and an understanding of them are essential in this process.

Mothers varied from those who are mostly in sympathy with the child's wishes—though this does not necessarily mean they will concede them—to those who can be in sympathy with such wishes of the child as are in tune with their own but not with others, to those who either did not recognize the child's wishes (largely because of their lack of interest in the child's feeling life) or felt threatened by the child's wishes, which were felt to be in conflict with their own wishes and needs. At one extreme of the dimension is *Margaret's mother,* who was rarely able to meet Margaret's wishes because of her own obtruding needs; rather, she would expect the child to meet her wishes and would become extremely irritable and impatient if this did not occur; Margaret's wishes were either not understood or were seen as a threat and therefore had to be curbed. At the other extreme was *Rosemary's mother,* who was mostly in sympathy with Rosemary's wishes though she could not always accede to them (e.g., she understood Rosemary's wish to have her oldest sister's workbasket and subsequently understood her frustration over the refusal).

The Mother's Tendency to Perceive the Child as a Threat. This dimension describes the extent to which the mother tends to perceive certain aspects of her child's personality as a threat.

The mothers who experience the child as a threat are those who have not come to terms with certain aspects of their own personality so that the child's presence or behavior can stimulate these areas of conflict. For example, the child's wish for dependence or independence calls forth conflicting feelings in some mothers, just as negative responses from the child often mobilize feelings of hostility in those mothers who have not come to terms with their own aggressive feelings. Again mothers who could not be sure of their love relationship with their husbands or their status in the home would on occasion view the child as a rival. The dimension ranges from *Jean's mother,* to whose mature personality Jean presented no threat and who considered the minor eye injury caused by Jean as a mere accident, to *Dawn's mother,* who considered the child as a rival for father's affections, a "snatcher" of possessions, and who regarded her as a being who could cause much damage. When this mother injured her wrist she blamed Dawn's kicks for the accident. Many of her statements expressed her belief that Dawn did damage; for example, *"Stop pushing that pram, you have done enough damage."*

The Mother's Tendency to Use the Child for Her Own Unconscious Purposes. This dimension describes the extent to which the mother uses her child for her own unconscious purposes. It takes into account the extent to which the mother has to live through the child, or to act out currently and in relation to the child, some unconscious part of herself (mostly with roots in the past) not directly relevant, and frequently harmful to the child. The dimension ranges from *Ewan's mother,* who never showed any tendency to relate in an inappropriate or irrelevant way to her child, to *Andrew's mother,* who attempted to make amends for her past destructive wishes against her own brother by being too permissive and indulgent as well as overprotective toward this boy.

The Mother's Tendency to React toward the Child's Misbehavior Hostilely. This dimension describes the extent to which the mother reacts in a hostile manner toward the child's misbehavior. Many mothers have means other than hostility for dealing with their child's misbehavior; for example, by means of diverting the child's attention or by consistently setting limits. These mothers are able to view the child's misbehavior with understanding and sympathy and thus can assist the child in dealing with his negativism. The dimension ranges from *Gillian's mother,* who would deal with Gillian's misbehavior by distracting her attention and interesting her in some other activity or sometimes by telling her in a calm but firm manner, "Don't be cheeky," to *Margaret's mother,* who reacted to mild misbehavior with extreme hostility. For example, she dealt with Margaret's reluctance to be washed by rubbing Margaret's face so hard that the child burst into heart-rending sobs.

Appendix B to Chapter 3

Definition of Dimensions Describing the Mother's Attitude to the Separated Child during the Period before Reunion

Below we give definitions of the five dimensions describing the mother's attitude toward the separated children before the period of reunion previously listed in this chapter.

The Mother's Specific Concern about the Effects of the Separation and What She Did to Ameliorate These Effects. This dimension describes the mother's concern about what the separation will mean for the child and *how troubled she is about this* as reflected by her attitude and statements. It further concerns itself with the efforts the mother makes to minimize the effects of separation prior to the event, for example, by letting the child have familiar objects in a strange environment or by acquainting the strange nursery staff with the child's idiosyncrasies. The dimension ranges from *Jimmy's mother,* who gave the matter little thought and supposed the nursery would have plenty of toys, to *Owen's mother* who wondered whether she had made the right decision, wanted the nursery to know Owen's vocabulary and did a variety of other things to ensure his comfort.

The Extent to Which the Mother Missed the Child. This dimension classifies the mothers in terms of how much they are aware of and feel the absence of the child. While the evidence for this dimension was relatively easy to assess, a reservation about the rankings is introduced by the fact that five of the mothers remained in their homes for a few days after the child had left and might thus have been made more aware of the absence of the child than those mothers who went almost immediately into the hospital. The dimension ranges from *Margaret's mother,* who did not seem to miss the children, to *Georgy's mother,* who missed them greatly both when she was still at home, after they had left and later when she was in the hospital.

The Extent to Which the Mother Planned Adequately for the Separation. With this dimension we assess the extent to which the mother adequately plans for the separation. Planning here refers to the various arrangements that could or had to be made in relation to the separation and is considered in terms of how it is or is not to the advantage of the child. To plan effectively a mother must have knowledge of the facilities available (e.g., private or public nurseries) and must have a certain confidence in putting her points across and making what to her are necessary requests. Both the knowledge of facilities and the degree of confidence varied with different mothers. This dimension ranges from *Jimmy's mother,* who did not even know exactly which nursery the child was going into, to *Josephine's mother,* who made all her own arrangements and who visited the nursery with her child before the separation.

The Mother's Eagerness to Have the Child Home Again. With this dimension we describe the mother's eagerness to have the child home again and especially what she does to make a quick reunion possible. Evidence of longing for the child as well as indications of ambivalence are included. For example, *Owen's mother* expressed a desire to have the child home as soon as possible but was much relieved when she found reasons for postponing it. The dimension ranges from *Dennis's mother,* who continually postponed the homecoming of her two children by bringing up practical difficulties, to *Georgy's mother,* who discharged herself from the hospital in order to be reunited with her children.

The Extent to Which the Mother Adequately Planned for the Reunion. Here we assess the extent to which the mother adequately plans for reunion with her child. We consider how aware she is of what the separation experience might have meant to the child and how she arranges the reunion in order to take account of the child's needs effectively. The dimension ranges from *Margaret's mother,* who had made no plans and left things to the father, to *Dawn's mother,* who planned things to the point where she told the father to hold the new baby while she greeted Dawn.

Description of the Samples

4 In this chapter we describe in greater detail the characteristics of the separated and nonseparated children and their families.

An important question that arises is whether the two samples differ in any significant respect other than the fact of separation and placement in a residential nursery. Ideally, they would be so constituted that it would be reasonable to attribute any differences in their behavior to the effect of a single independent variable, i.e., separation. In Sections II and III of this chapter we examine this question by comparing the two groups in terms of a number of variables other than the separation—including those related to the family background and the nature of the mother-child relationship.

I.   The Characteristics of the Children

A. Criteria for Obtaining the Two Samples

In selecting the separated children it was originally intended to use the five criteria used in the first study, namely: (1) that the child had had no previous separations of more than three days, (2) that he fell within the age limits of 15 to 30 months, (3) that he did not enter the nursery with a sibling, (4) that he was living with both his mother and father at the time, and (5) that there was no evidence that being placed in a nursery indicated a rejection by his parents. Because of the difficulty of obtaining cases, however, these criteria had to be modified to allow greater latitude.

Although most children had had either none or only very brief separations previous to the one being studied, in one case the length of previous separation was four weeks and in two it was three weeks (see Table 8). The age range was slightly extended and ran from 13 to 32 months, instead of from 15 to 30 months. But the most marked departure from the previous criteria was that four of the children entered the residential nursery in the company of a sibling; in three cases this was a 4-year-old sibling and in one case the sibling was younger. The remaining two criteria remained unmodified; each of the children was living with both mother and father at the time of separation, and there were no indications that he was being rejected by the parents by being placed in the nursery.

B. Sex and Age of the Children in the Two Samples

While a modification of the criteria for including a separated child in the sample made for greater variation, increased control was introduced by a closer matching of the children in the two samples for age and sex. The results are given in Table 7. Although the matching for age is not perfect, the median age falls at approximately 2 years for each group, with a similar range up and down the scale.

Table 7. *Showing Age and Sex of Separated and Nonseparated Groups of Children*

Separated			Nonseparated		
Name	*Age*	*Sex*	*Name*	*Age*	*Sex*
Georgy	1–1	M	Ewan	1–5	M
Gillian	1–4	F	Jean	1–4	F
Dawn	1–5	F	Anne	1–6	F
Katie	1–6	F	Sandra	2–0	F
Jimmy	1–9	M	Colin	1–9	M
Josephine	2–0	F	Sally	2–2	F
Margaret	2–1	F	Helen	2–3	F
Owen	2–2	M	Ian	2–0	M
Dennis	2–7	M	Andrew	2–5	M
Elizabeth	2–8	F	Rosemary	2–7	F
Median age:	22 months		Median age:	24 months	

Most of the comparisons between the two groups deal with the above ten pairs. For a limited number of comparisons concerning behavior during the first two weeks of separation, we shall add two further pairs. They are the following: Lucille, 2 years 2 months matched by Janet, 1 year 4 months; and Ronald, 1 year 7 months matched by Irwin, 1 year 11 months. Although in these pairs matching for age is much less adequate than for the main sample of ten pairs, the median age for the separated children is not affected and that of the nonseparated children is changed by only half a month, from 24 to 23.5 months.

A complication is introduced by the fact that no data on the doll-play sessions during the reunion period are available for one of the separated children, Jimmy. This means that it is necessary to reduce the sample to nine pairs whenever we analyze the data of the reunion doll plays. The median age for the nine nonseparated children remains at 24 months while that for the nine separated children changes from 22 months to 24 months, which makes them identical.

In the above we have described certain characteristics of both the samples, the separated children and the nonseparated. Below we describe only the sample of ten separated children.

C. Reasons Why the Children Were Placed in a Residential Nursery

In seven out of the ten cases that constitute our main sample the mother was going to the hospital to have a baby. In another case— Jimmy—the mother was also pregnant, but she went to the hospital only to be observed, which meant that on his return home Jimmy did not find a baby. Owen's mother went to the hospital to be treated for a back injury. In the remaining case, Katie, the family was homeless and for this reason had to take their child to a residential nursery.

D. Length of Time the Children Were Separated

Since we were interested in brief separations, we chose cases which were not expected to remain in the nursery long. In the event, six children remained less than three weeks, two between five and seven weeks and the remaining two considerably longer. There is thus a considerable variation in the length of separation; the length in days is given in Column 1 of Table 8. The two additional cases, Lucille and Ronald, are not included because they were not utilized in analyses relating to length of separation.

E. The Presence of a Sibling

Table 8 gives the sex and age of the sibling who accompanied the child to the residential nursery. A blank indicates that the child was not accompanied by a sibling. Three of the children, Georgy, Margaret and Dennis, were accompanied by a sibling 1½ to 2 years older than themselves, while Elizabeth was in the nursery with her brother, Georgy, 1 year 7 months younger. Though not part of the main sample, Lucille and Ronald were also accompanied by a sibling: Lucille had a sister 2 years older and Ronald a brother 2 years older.

Table 8. *The Length of Separation, the Presence of a Sibling and the Nature of the Previous Separation*

Name of Child	Length of Separation in Days	Age and Sex of Sibling if Present	Length of Previous Separation	Age at Previous Separation
Jimmy	12		None	
Josephine	13		1 week	Unknown
Dawn	15		None	
Georgy*	15	2 years 8 months; F	5 days	6 months
Elizabeth*	15	1 year 1 month; M	3 weeks	29 months
Margaret	17	4 years 1 month; F	1 week	12 months
Dennis	49	4 years 5 months; M	1 week	18 months
Gillian	72		4 weeks	11 months
Owen	81		10 days	3 months
Katie	148		3 weeks	7 months

* These children were brother and sister.

F. The Nature of Previous Separations

In Table 8 we present certain further facts about the children. It can be seen that eight of the ten children had experienced previous separations. They range in length of time from five days to four weeks with the median length approximately eight days.

The circumstances of the separations were as follows: Elizabeth, Georgy and Katie had been in a hospital, and Gillian and Dennis in a residential nursery. Gillian's separation had occurred because the mother had been ill. Owen was looked after by friends at the time of his mother's hospitalization, and Josephine was looked after by her maternal grandmother; Margaret was cared for by her father at home when her mother was confined with another baby.

II. The Family and Social Backgrounds of the Children

In this section facts regarding the parents and siblings, their socio-economic status and their relation to relatives, friends and neighbors are presented. As before, comparisons of the two samples are made.

A. Parents and Siblings

In Tables 9 and 10 we give the data for the two samples on the age of the father and mother and the age and sex of the older and younger siblings.

Table 9. *Showing Nature of Family Constellation for Separated Children*

Name of Child	Age of Father	Age of Mother	Sex and Age of Older Sibling	Sex and Age of Younger Sibling
Elizabeth	26	23	None	M, 1–1; F, Newborn
Georgy	26	23	F, 2–8	F, Newborn
Owen	Early 40's	Early 40's	F, 8 years plus	None
Dawn	43	30	M, 6–6 (half-brother)	F, Newborn
Margaret	Unknown	38	F, 4–1 F, 17 years (half-sister)	F, 1–1; M, Newborn
Katie	Early 40's	Mid-30's	M, 14½ years (half-brother)	None
Josephine	Early 30's	27	None	M, Newborn
Jimmy	Early 30's	27	None	None
Gillian	Unknown	38	13, 9 & 4 years (unknown to Gillian)	Twins, F, Newborn
Dennis	58	35	M, 4–5	F, Newborn

Table 10. *Showing Nature of Family Constellation for Nonseparated Children*

Name of Child	Age of Father	Age of Mother	Sex and Age of Older Sibling	Sex and Age of Younger Sibling
Andrew	37	Early 30's	F, 4 years	M, 7 months
Rosemary	38	40	M, 8 years F, 6 years F, 5 years M, 3 years	M, a few months
Sally	Unknown	Late 30's	M, 18 years (half-brother)	None
Colin	Mid-30's	Mid-30's	F, 5 years	None
Sandra	35	32	F, 7 years	None
Ian	40	32	M, 8½ years	F, 9 months
Helen	34	32	M, 12 years F, 10 years M, 7 years M, 4 years	None
Jean	Mid-30's	Mid-30's	M, 4 years F, 6 years	None
Ewan	28	27	F, 3 years	None
Anne	32	32	None	None

Because in some cases the ages of the parents had to be estimated, it is not possible to assign exact median values for the ages in the two groups.

It is plain, however, that there are no gross differences in the ages of the parents. The median age of the fathers of both groups falls in the late 30's while that for the mothers falls in the early 30's.

Similarly, there are no gross differences in the number of older siblings in the two groups of children. The median figure for both samples is one older sibling. It should be noted, however, that the only two children who have four older siblings both fall into the non-separated sample.

When the samples are compared for the number of younger siblings, results vary according to whether or not the child born at separation is included in the count. When it is, there is a noticeable difference between the two samples: the separated children more frequently have one or more younger siblings. When it is not, the two samples are similar; most of the children did not have a younger sibling.

B. The Socio-Economic Status of the Families

In Table 11 we present the information on the socio-economic status of the family. The occupation of the father is described and is then classified in terms of the social class categories used by the United Kingdom General Register Office, 1960. These are:

  I. Professional, etc. occupations
  II. Intermediate occupations
  III. Skilled occupations
  IV. Partly skilled occupations
  V. Unskilled occupations

The frequency with which the separated and nonseparated families fall into each of the social-class categories is given in Table 12. Examination of Table 12 reveals that the nonseparated children come from homes of rather higher socio-economic status. Statistical analysis, however, shows that this difference may well have occurred by chance.

Thus, when the nature of the family constellations and the socio-

Table 11. *Showing Information on the Socio-Economic Status of the Families*

Separated Families	Occupation of the Father	Social Class
Elizabeth's family	Factory worker	V
Georgy's family	Factory worker	V
Owen's family	Civil servant	III
Dawn's family	Construction laborer	IV
Margaret's family	Restaurant waiter	IV
Katie's family	Butcher	III
Josephine's family	Engineer in charge of men	I
Jimmy's family	Plumber	III
Gillian's family	Furniture mover	V
Dennis's family	Civil Service clerk	III
Nonseparated Families		
Andrew's family	Theater producer	II
Rosemary's family	Factory worker	IV
Sally's family	Owner of firm	II
Colin's family	Accountant-employed	III
Sandra's family	Factory worker	IV
Ian's family	Dispatch manager in factory	II
Helen's family	Postman	IV
Jean's family	Clerk in export firm	III
Ewan's family	Regular Army man	IV
Anne's family	Physiologist	I

Table 12. *Showing Comparisons of Separated and Nonseparated Families in Terms of Socio-Economic Status*

Social Class Categories	Separated	Nonseparated
I	1	1
II	0	3
III	4	2
IV	2	4
V	3	0

economic status are considered, the two samples do not differ appreciably. In the sections below we deal with variations in the family and social backgrounds of the two groups of children for which we had some reason to expect that differences between the two samples other than those due to chance might be found.

C. The Family's Relationship to Close Relatives

The way a family functions, and therefore the experiences a child has within it, is much influenced by the quality and quantity of contacts the family has with relatives, friends and neighbors. In the next two sections these are compared for the two samples. It is evident that the findings for the separated group go some way to explain why

Figure 4. *Example of Family Contacts with Relatives*

Ewan's Family (Nonseparated Sample)

Type of Relative	Alive or Dead	Location	Type of Contact	Mutual Attitudes
Paternal Grandparents	Alive	10 miles away	Family visited grandparents every two weeks.	Happy, friendly relationship
Maternal Grandparents	Alive	160 miles away	Family spent all their holidays with grandparents, who looked after family when mother was confined and in general were ready to assist.	Warm, happy relationship including a readiness to help
Maternal Aunt	Alive	160 miles away	Seen on visit to maternal grandparents.	Friendly relationship

Dennis's Family (Separated Sample)

Type of Relative	Alive or Dead	Location	Type of Contact	Mutual Attitudes
Paternal Grandparents	Dead			
Maternal Grandparents	Dead			
Maternal Step Grandmother	Alive	50 miles away	Maintained contact until two years before present study, when she had a misunderstanding with Dennis's father.	Mother felt she should re-establish contact with her stepmother but did not do so. She felt her stepmother had been a good mother even though her attitude was now detached.

alternative methods of care could not be found for these children and why they therefore had to be placed in a residential nursery.

To study the quality and quantity of contact that the separated and the nonseparated families respectively had with their relatives, information was arranged in terms of the following categories: relative; whether the relative is alive or dead; geographical distance from family; the nature and frequency of contact with the family; and the nature of the mutual attitudes. For purposes of illustration and contrast the family contacts of two children, one separated and one not separated, are summarized in Figure 4.

Examination of the data on all twenty families shows that they vary in several important respects—whether the relationship to their relatives is continuous, whether the relationship is supportive and the number of relatives alive. In order to consider systematically whether the absence of a supportive and continuous relationship more frequently characterized the families of the separated when compared with the nonseparated children, all the families are placed into one of the set of categories shown in Table 13. If the relationship with one set of grandparents is supportive and continuous, the family is placed into Category A. Although such ratings do scant justice to individual variations and complexities, to effect a comparison some simplification is necessary.

The categorizations given in Table 13 were made by Westheimer and repeated independently by Heinicke. Out of the twenty judg-

Table 13. *Showing Families in Terms of Their*
Relationship to Relatives

Relationship Characterized as:	Separated		Nonseparated	
	Most Relatives Alive	Most Relatives Dead	Most Relatives Alive	Most Relatives Dead
A. Continuous and supportive	0	1	6	1
B. Continuous but of limited helpfulness	2	1	1	0
C. Neither continuous nor supportive	3	3	1	1

ments made, they disagreed on only two. Table 13 can be statistically analyzed in various ways. There is one relevant question in the context of the present discussion: When the relatives are alive, is the relationship to them continuous and supportive or neither? Applying Fischer's Exact Text to Categories A and C, and Columns 1 and 3 of Table 13, we obtain a P value of approximately .05. Other analyses support the conclusion that the fact that the nonseparated families more frequently had a continuous and supportive relationship to their relatives is unlikely to be due to chance factors.

D. The Family's Contacts with Friends and Neighbors

In making the ratings presented in Table 14, the total pattern of social contacts of the family has been considered. This includes friendships, neighborliness and other forms of social interaction.

There are two major difficulties in studying a family's contact with friends and neighbors. One results from the unevenness of the data; because we had not originally envisaged the inclusion of material on social patterns, the data on some families is incomplete. A second is due to the fact that crisis situations are especially likely to call forth responses of sympathy from neighbors and friends, so that assessments differ depending on whether a crisis occurs and response to it is observed.

In Table 14 we give the frequency with which the two groups of families were placed in each of the five categories describing the nature of the relationship to friends and neighbors.

Table 14. *Showing Nature of Families in Terms of Their Relationship to Friends and Neighbors*

Type of Relationship to Friends and Neighbors	Frequency among Separated Families	Frequency among Nonseparated Families
A. High degree of mutually supportive relationship	3	3
B. Moderate degree of mutually supportive relationship	2	1
C. Regular social interchange by means of mutual entertainment	1	2
D. Some social interchange	1	3
E. No planned social contact and minimal contact with neighbors	3	1

Category A comprises contacts with much "give and take," mutual concern and a readiness to help. Category B has similar components though of lesser intensity. Contacts in Category C reflect the wish for planned social interchange and the sharing of interests without the making of demands. Category D comprises social relationships of a more casual nature—not usually planned nor sought after, yet as a rule appreciated when they happen. Category E indicates that contacts are confined to the superficial and casual, and often amount to no more than a greeting to a neighbor.

The ratings were made independently by Westheimer and Heinicke. They agreed perfectly except in one case where a family was placed by one in Category A and by the other in Category B.

Examination of Table 14 reveals that the two samples of families, separated and nonseparated, do not differ markedly in terms of the nature of their contacts to friends and neighbors. It seems, therefore, that although the separated families lack a supportive relationship with relatives, at least five of them are able to form supportive relationships with friends and neighbors.

E. Conclusions

During the course of this study we have frequently pondered the question of alternative care for the separated child. What examination of the data on the families of the ten separated children shows is that alternative care of the child was not possible either because the relatives were dead or because a continuous and supportive relationship with them was lacking. In the latter cases the lack of support was often due to the families' inability to maintain constructive contacts with relatives. It was usually not due to geographical distance. When a tie existed, grandparents or other relatives would travel many miles to give support.

One implication of these findings is that the families of the separated children had to carry their own responsibilities and difficulties and rarely got relief or help. Nor did they have the comfort of knowing there was support in the background. The mere knowledge that support and help are available is often sufficient to enable an individual or family unit to deal more effectively with crises. In its absence responsibility is sometimes felt to be too great and so outside help is called for.

The question of alternative care of the child by friends is a more difficult one. Five of the families of the separated children had mutually supportive relationships with friends, in three of which it was of high degree. Why then was there no offer by friends and neighbors of alternative care?

One reason is that help of this nature comes more readily from relatives than from friends and neighbors. A second is that, if there is more than one child to be cared for (as there was in six of the families), neighbors are usually unwilling or unable to help. A third reason is that when a neighbor does help, she expects it to be reciprocal and, for different reasons, the families of the separated children were unable to consider making such return.

III.   The Nature of the Mother-Child Relationship

Ideally, the two groups of families should be described and compared in terms of a series of dimensions dealing not only with the personality characteristics of each individual member but also with all the many inter-relationships between them. Only certain relationships can be so treated; the two cases described at length in the next chapter give some indication of the complexity and extensiveness of the material.

A. Comparison of the Two Groups on Dimensions Concerning the Mother-Child Relationship

Our interest in the mother-child relationship is clear from the many dimensions formulated to describe it. Central to this cluster of dimensions and correlating highly with all but one of them is the one describing *The mother's affection for and pleasure in the company of her child.* Only the one entitled *The mother's ability to set limits consistently* does not correlate with the cluster. In Table 15, therefore, the ranking for the two groups treated together are given for each of these two dimensions. (Italicizing of a name indicates that the child belongs to the nonseparated sample.) Applying the Mann-Whitney Test we found that the mothers of the nonseparated children tend to be more affectionate than are those of the separated children (significant at the .05 level, two-tailed). When ratings of *The mother's ability to set limits* are compared, no significant difference is found between the two groups. There is, however, a tendency for the mothers of nonseparated children to set limits more consistently.

In Chapter 3 we noted that any comparison between the two

groups of families should be made with caution because the families of one group were experiencing a crisis, while those of the other group were not. It is very likely that the anxieties associated with the separation, and particularly the difficulties encountered during the period of reunion, would affect the behavior of the mothers of the separated children and thus the rating they received on the dimension describing the degree of affection. Some mothers would be strained by the experience and become less affectionate; others would become more affectionate to meet the needs of the child. It is therefore difficult to be certain whether the lesser affection shown by the mothers of the separated children reflects a permanent attitude or is a result of the crisis of separation and thus more or less temporary. In reporting comparative findings on the children in the two groups (see Chapter 10), we consider whether or not such differences of behavior as are found can be explained by the difference between them in the mother-child relationship.

Table 15. *Showing Rankings for Separated and Nonseparated Children on the Mother's Affection for and Pleasure in the Company of the Child and The Mother's Ability to Set Limits Consistently*

The Mother's Affection for and Pleasure in the Company of the Child	*The Mother's Ability to Set Limits Consistently*
1. Margaret's mother	1. Dennis's mother
2. Gillian's mother	2. Jimmy's mother
3. *Anne's* mother	3. Georgy's mother
4. Dennis's mother	4. *Sally's* mother
5. *Sally's* mother	5. Margaret's mother
6. Jimmy's mother	6. *Anne's* mother
7. Owen's mother	7. *Ian's* mother
8. Katie's mother	8. Josephine's mother
9. Dawn's mother	9. Katie's mother
10. Josephine's mother	10. Dawn's mother
11. *Helen's* mother	11. *Sandra's* mother
12. *Ian's* mother	12. *Andrew's* mother
13. Elizabeth's mother	13. Elizabeth's mother
14. Georgy's mother	14. Owen's mother
15. *Sandra's* mother	15. Gillian's mother
16. *Andrew's* mother	16. *Helen's* mother
17. *Ewan's* mother	17. *Ewan's* mother
18. *Rosemary's* mother	18. *Rosemary's* mother
19. *Colin's* mother	19. *Colin's* mother
20. *Jean's* mother	20. *Jean's* mother

IV.   Summary of the Description of the Samples

We have shown in this chapter that in the following respects the two samples, separated and nonseparated, did not differ: age and sex of child, age of mother and father, the sibling constellation before separation, the socio-economic status of the families, the nature of the relationship to friends and neighbors and the mother's ability to set limits for her child. By contrast, the nonseparated families more frequently had a supportive and continuous relationship to their relatives, and the mothers were more affectionate than were the mothers of the separated children.

Of the differences found, those relating to the mother's affection for her child have the greatest potential for influencing the various types of child behavior to be examined in later chapters. To anticipate the discussion in Chapter 10, in order to check whether the greater frequency of a more affectionate mother-child relationship in the nonseparated group could account for our findings, cases falling at the extremes on the dimension *mother's affection for child* were eliminated. Then, using as the dependent variables certain key dimensions of the child's behavior, the two groups were again compared. From the comparison we can conclude that it is unlikely that the differences of behavior of the separated and nonseparated children were a function of differences in the mother-child relationship.

Two Children and Their Families

5 I. Introduction

In this chapter we describe the behavior during separation and reunion of two different children viewed against the background of their families. There are several reasons for doing so.

First, we wish the reader to have a detailed and concrete picture of the phenomena we observed.

Secondly, a thorough examination of a single case in all its complexity adds an essential perspective, namely, the context in which a given piece of behavior occurs.

Thirdly, the two cases were chosen to illustrate the different courses of development during separation and reunion that are typical of different lengths of separation and that are highlighted in later chapters of the book. Once reunited with her parents after only fifteen days of separation, Dawn returned more quickly to the kind of behavior she had shown previous to separation than did Owen, whose separation lasted eighty-one days.

Certain features of the presentation are the same for both cases. As part of an introductory statement, we first give certain basic facts about the family, including the events leading up to the separation. Still as part of the introduction, we indicate at what points and how frequently the family and child were observed. Since most of the material on the family was gathered by Westheimer, her relation to the family is sketched. Continuing the presentation, the description of the mother's personality, her background, the nature of the marital and other family relationships and especially the mother's relation with the child and his background provide the context within which the behavior of the child during separation and reunion can be considered.

The descriptions of the child's stay in the nursery and his readjustment to his home are based mainly on the qualitative descriptions made by the various observers. As reported in Chapter 3, these observations are organized in terms of certain relationships to significant people (e.g., to the observers) and functions (such as eating). The development of *each* of these relationships and functions was then conceptualized in terms of a series of time periods. Finally, for each of the two cases to be reported we first noted at which points in time several, if not all, relationships and/or functions changed their character, and then used these dividing points to break the total span of separation and reunion into a series of general time periods or phases. For example, for Dawn we identified three such phases within the fifteen days of her separation. That six phases were formulated for Owen's separation reflects the greater number of changes that took place in his behavior during his much longer stay in the nursery.

II.   Dawn and Her Family

A. Introduction to the Case

1. Family Constellation and Reason for Separation. Dawn, aged 16 months and the younger child in a lower working-class family, was in the residential nursery for fifteen days while her mother was in the hospital for the birth of baby Mary Rose. Dawn's half-brother, Ralph, aged 6½ years, the illegitimate child of mother, was cared for during mother's absence and for three weeks afterward by the maternal grandparents. Father fended for himself.

2. Observations Made on Dawn and Her Family. The case presentation to follow is based on the direct observations and interviewing by all three observers: Westheimer, Heinicke and Wolpert.

Westheimer made the following contacts with Dawn and her family:

a. *Dawn,* aged 16 months, was seen twenty times within the period prescribed by the research design—(one preseparation visit, twice during the separation and seventeen times at fairly regular weekly intervals for twenty weeks after her return).

b. *Mother,* aged 30, was seen nineteen times during this period—(one preseparation with Dawn, once alone in hospital and seventeen times afterward with Dawn).

c. *Father,* aged 43, was seen four times in this period—on the day of reunion and on three further occasions after Dawn's return home.

d. *Ralph,* aged 6½, was present during nine visits.
e. *Additional Home Visits* numbering five were made after the series prescribed by the research design had been completed. Two of these additional visits were made during the next six months, one fourteen months after, another eighteen months after, and the last twenty-two months after Dawn had returned home.
f. *Each Home Visit* lasted from one-and-a-half to two-and-a-half hours.
g. *Telephone Conversations with Mother,* five during separation, of which four were initiated by mother and one after reunion.

Heinicke and Wolpert observed Dawn during her stay in the nursery, in accordance with the procedures outlined in Chapters 1 and 2. Coded observations in the Everyday Nursery Setting, data from doll-play sessions, extensive clinical comments on her behavior and observations by the staff are all available on Dawn.

3. Mother's Relationship with the Fieldworker. We were notified of Dawn's admission to the nursery only one day prior to the event. Thus there was no time to send a letter asking if the fieldworker might call; there was only just time for her to call at home and there to explain her interest and role as well as to discuss the mutual advantages of collaboration in this research project.

Although mother was not prepared for this visit, she was friendly and co-operative. Indeed, once she had understood its purpose and also how it might be useful to her, she welcomed the opportunity wholeheartedly and from the very beginning regarded the fieldworker as a supportive and helpful person. She utilized this, the first visit, in two different ways; first, to consider what the forthcoming separation would mean for Dawn and other family members and, secondly, to communicate some of the complexities of the family relationships and her feelings about them.

Mother wanted to learn about nursery conditions and to assure herself that the child would be well looked after. She inquired about taking familiar toys and garments to the strange setting and was concerned that Dawn should have to undergo the experience. But her concern was not only for her child but also for her husband. Because she could foresee how distressed he would be when visiting his little girl, she hoped he would not visit, even though she realized that visits would be of advantage to the child.

In this first interview mother talked about many concerns and anxieties. She dwelled at some length on Ralph's position in the family (he was illegitimate) and the differing repercussions of it on the family members. It seemed almost as though she had been waiting for an opportunity to talk things over and that she experienced relief when she found herself understood.

It is of interest that mother herself made every effort, following this single preseparation visit, to keep in touch with the fieldworker by telephone and saw to it that she was kept informed of what was happening. During the fifteen days of separation she initiated four telephone calls; on two occasions she herself was able to telephone and on two others she asked the ward sister to communicate on her behalf.

Mother was eager for the fieldworker to visit her in the hospital and again made good use of the time available. She wanted to know how Dawn was faring in the nursery and had already assured father, who found visiting at the nursery distressing, that "Miss Westheimer will tell me how she is." She used the visit to make constructive plans about Dawn's return and voiced mixed feelings about father's devotion to the child.

Once Dawn had returned home, mother continued to look to the fieldworker for support. As in the case of Owen, the fieldworker was often able to clarify the meaning of the child's responses. For instance, she helped mother to understand that the reason Dawn clamored for her attention whenever she was occupied with the baby, or insisted on being a baby, was due to her fear of losing mother's love. As a result mother could then be tolerant and even sympathetic, whereas previously she had been irritated.

During subsequent weeks, mother continued to discuss her feelings and reactions; she became increasingly able to recognize her feelings of rivalry with Dawn. The fieldworker's acceptance of mother encouraged her to become more accepting of herself and of Dawn.

At times when mother had to deal with both children simultaneously, she was pleased to entrust care of the baby to the fieldworker— as she might have done to her own mother. Mother looked forward to the visits and, in anticipation of the fieldworker's arrival, would often leave the front door open. Even after a visit had lasted two-and-a-half hours, mother still wanted to prolong it. She described how she had never been able to make such demands on her own mother. She had always felt that she must not burden her mother with her own worries and so had been unable to ask for help or advice.

From time to time during the contacts, mother commented on the novel and helpful nature of these interviews. Even when visits became less regular the relationship remained unaltered and mother continued to utilize them.

B. Mother—Her Personality and Background

Mother was a big, stout woman with straggly hair, a poor complexion and pimples round her chin, looking older than her 30 years. Her manner was forthright and direct but not aggressive. She always wore garments with short sleeves and considered this practical for working purposes.

Although the two-room working-class apartment was sparsely furnished, it was always clean and orderly. The recent ironing was meticulously arranged on the clotheshorse for airing; the dishes were neatly stacked on the draining board. Mother ran the home competently and could deal with chores and children, and with the restrictions of the confined space, without becoming ruffled. She managed her small housekeeping allowance economically, seeing to it that father and children got meat each day with their main meal. Frequently she herself had to go without because the money would not stretch far enough, but on this she made no comment and it usually went unnoticed. All her time and energy went into the care of home and family. She had no outside interests or friends. She was on speaking terms with neighbors but had no wish for closer relationships with them.

Her competence extended to the outside world. Poor though she was, she could stand her ground with officials of the local authority. And although her motivation, as will be shown, in having Dawn cared for in the residential nursery was complex, she was one of the few mothers in the study who made early and adequate arrangements.

But although mother dealt with her environment in a sure and competent way she was subject to many anxieties. With each pregnancy she had strong fears of not being able to produce a healthy baby; this linked with fantasies about being damaged and about her ability to do damage.

Although not obsessional, she was rather rigid about matters of cleanliness and unduly concerned about her children's bodily functions. The messy 2-year-old stage gave her discomfort, and she was sometimes in conflict between her need for cleanliness and her sensitive concern for her children's happiness. She was overly preoccupied with her own minor ailments.

Mother was one of five children. Her parents' marriage was not considered a happy one; mother remembered much quarreling as a child, which she had found distressing. The maternal grandmother, who was still alive, was remembered as a very busy woman who must not be troubled or burdened. Hence mother would never ask for help and was always pathetically grateful for any assistance she got from her.

The maternal grandfather was said to be a man with strong convictions who would tolerate no differences of opinion. He had been a strict father and had used the belt on his children. Even so mother admired him, and his good opinion was still important to her.

The attitude of Dawn's father, who did not care much for mother's family, made regular visiting difficult, though mother always maintained contact.

C. Marriage and Family Relationships

The parents had been married for two years and at this point, when aged respectively 43 and 30, their marriage was strained. Father was from Ireland and Roman Catholic, an uneducated man with a limited vocabulary and an awkward, unsure manner. As an unskilled laborer, his small wage could only provide a meager home without comforts and was barely sufficient to sustain his family of five. Prior to marriage he had had a variety of unskilled jobs and, in his own words, had been a "rolling stone." Married to a different kind of woman he might well have continued in that pattern and become the father of a "problem" family. With the support of his wife he remained in his job and earned a wage which, although small, was regular.

On the other hand, although she supported him in many ways, for instance by reasoning with him when he wished to give up a job impulsively because of some misunderstanding, she also undermined him by her underlying disapproval of his being unskilled and never bothering to train himself for something and get on. She commented disparagingly to the fieldworker that "a lot of these Irish are feckless like him."

They had first met when they were both working in a hotel; they had become "good pals." Mother left the hotel when she became pregnant by a married man and went to a hostel for unmarried mothers, where in due course she gave birth to Ralph. Two years later, and after many ups and downs during which she kept to her decision not to part with Ralph, she returned to work in the same hotel—largely because "Patrick" (father) was still there. Though he warned her, "Don't take me serious, I'm only a rolling stone," she embarked on a relationship with him and in due course conceived once again—this time with Dawn. They decided to get married.

Mother's illegitimate son, Ralph, was then aged 4. Father knew of Ralph's existence and agreed that he should become a member of the family. But after the birth of Dawn, he made it increasingly clear that he had no use for Ralph.

Mother had always doubted whether father would have married her had she not become pregnant, and it did nothing to reassure her, in contrast to his disregard for Ralph, that he became intensely attached to Dawn. At times it seemed that he almost contrived situations to show her that Dawn meant more to him than she did. For instance, one evening when Dawn could not get to sleep, father put her to bed and himself went to bed in the same room to keep her company—leaving mother to continue with her chores in solitude and with pent-up feelings. Mother resented it very much that father would willingly take Dawn for a walk but refuse to take the new baby. At times she commented bitterly on the length of time father and Dawn had been out together.

Mother found it hard to tolerate the close relationship that existed between these two and these incidents strengthened her fear that he considered her only second best.

Father, on the other hand, appeared equally uncertain of mother's feelings for him. Despite her assurances to the contrary, he insisted that she was still attached to Ralph's father. Ralph's presence was a constant reminder of her first attachment and provided the basis of father's feelings of rivalry and hostility.

After the birth of Dawn, father's rejection of Ralph had become so complete that he denied all responsibility for him, did not count

him as coming within the housekeeping budget, ignored him and refused to answer his questions. He forbade the children to play together and not uncommonly would give a sweet to Dawn but not to
Ralph. When strangers commented on Ralph, father would brusque-
ly deny paternity. Mother's reaction to all this was to be specially
understanding of Ralph and more tolerant and permissive toward
him than to the much younger Dawn. Whenever he was slightly unwell or she sensed he was upset, she would keep him away from
school and give him her unstinting attention.

When really angry with father over his treatment of Ralph,
mother would threaten not to bear him any more children, though
in actual fact she did not refuse sexual relations despite her lack of
satisfaction. The performance of the sexual act she considered her
duty and father's right, and she submitted herself for these reasons.
She also felt reluctant to "take over his faith" while he treated Ralph
so badly, though she thought it advisable for the sake of the other
children to share the same religion as father.

However, there were times when father could be helpful and con-
siderate to mother; particularly when she was tired or unwell he
would do the chores ungrudgingly and deal with the children in a
patient and competent way. Such stability as he had came largely
from her support and from her greater initiative and responsibility.
But in this marriage hurting each other played a large part. Both
parents tended to perceive their children as allies or rivals and to
use them accordingly. At times they had to belittle and undermine
one another, each claiming that he or she could carry out more satisfactorily the task of the other. Thus they tended to be unduly critical
of each other and so to lack tolerance. Yet, despite all, father and
mother had a need of each other, and although in crisis there were
threats of parting, this never seemed a serious possibility.

After the completion of the prescribed research contact but during
the period of additional home visits, another agency arranged for
Ralph to be placed in a residential school. This represented a concession by mother which at some emotional cost to her removed a
source of friction from the home.

D. Dawn's History and Mother-Child Relationship

Dawn was born in the hospital and weighed 8 pounds 8 ounces. She
was an easy feeder, and when breast milk gave out at 1 month, she

transferred to dried milk without difficulty. Mother ascribed the loss of her milk to the general rushing around but expressed only mild regret at ending breast feeding.

From the first mother was overanxious about the child and apprehensive of the harm that might befall her. Already when pregnant, she had feared damage to the fetus. This appeared to link with a fantasy of herself as a damaging person, responsible for any upsets that might occur. Thus she recalled how, while still in the maternity hospital, she had over-reacted to a minor stomach upset the baby had had and how she had given much anxious thought to the things she had been eating and she supposed must have passed on to the baby. She had felt so distressed and responsible that she had been unable to mention the setback to father and had asked a nurse to tell him about it. She also recalled how, when Dawn was a few months old, she would often wake in a panic and anxiously look for the baby, convinced that she was under the bedclothes and in danger of being smothered. The relief on finding the baby peacefully asleep in the cot was enormous. On other occasions she had pushed father over to the other side of the bed and had accused him of lying on the child. She felt she had always been nervous about the care of Dawn and gave as reason that "If anything happened to the child her father would blame me." The fieldworker had many opportunities to note mother's anxiety about the dangers besetting a young child and her special concern to protect her from them. Whenever Dawn fell over or developed a slight temperature, mother showed undue anxiety. Yet this was only one aspect of the relationship. The anxiety was coupled with a good deal of common sense, competent and, at times, sensitive handling.

This may explain why, despite mother's feelings, Dawn was not a particularly fearful or anxious child. When seen on the day before the separation began, the fieldworker recorded:

A big, bouncy, round-faced, happy-looking girl of 16 months. She had reddish cheeks, straight brown hair, rather plain features, but a slow and rather endearing smile. She was very lively and occupied herself actively with toys. From time to time she was eager to share her achievements with her mother, and mother responded appropriately. At a later stage, when mother and I had been talking together for a longish time, Dawn began to be bored and disgruntled. Mother then gave her full attention and interested her in a new activity; at once Dawn's mood brightened. Restored by her mother's attention, she hopped around anew in a gay and lively manner.

This record continues:

Initially Dawn viewed me with a somewhat cautious air, but seemed more friendly after a few minutes and smiled at me; a little later she handed me some toys and showed eagerness to establish contact with me. When I left she shouted a bright "bye-bye."

Mother considered Dawn unusually independent for one so young, and related how once when Dawn had made a mess, she had also on her own initiative fetched a bucket and cloth and made the place tidy again. This action had pleased mother. Yet on another occasion when Dawn had spilled a lot of milk and she had become distressed, mother had been able to forget her demands for cleanliness and had comforted the child. Yet there were many instances when mother seemed inflexible and insisted on Dawn's compliance to strict standards.

When Dawn was unwell her mother knew how to relieve her discomfort despite very poor facilities. She would nurse Dawn to sleep on her lap, then place her gently into a cozy bed improvised from a stroller. There was ample evidence of affectionate mothering.

However, there also was evidence of negative feeling to Dawn, which was provoked by father's preference for Dawn and neglect of Ralph. His rejection of Ralph mother felt as a rejection of herself. Of Dawn she would say bitterly: "He puts her before me," and "He is all for Dawn." It went against the grain to feel jealous of a child to whom she was in most ways a good mother, but she told of occasions when she had shouted angrily at father, "You can make me hate this child, the way you behave"—in these words acknowledging both her ambivalence toward Dawn and her recognition of how much it derived from father's attitude and behavior. She feared to smack Dawn lest she do damage to her.

Mother's jealousy of Dawn's being alone with father no doubt played some part in accounting for her insistence that Dawn go to a residential nursery instead of being looked after in part by him. Also important was mother's concern that her daughter be well taken care of. A foster home had previously been turned down by both parents because they were not convinced that Dawn would be sufficiently supervised. Hence Dawn went to the nursery accompanied by her safety strap, a reassuring symbol to the mother that the child would be protected during the period of separation.

On the dimensions, Dawn's mother was rated and ranked within the sample of ten separated children as follows: *The mother's affection for and pleasure in the company of the child*—(7th); *The mother's ability to set limits consistently*—(7th); *The mother's concern about and sensitivity to her child at the beginning of separation*—(7th); *The mother's capacity to adapt herself to a disturbed child*—(4th). A rank of 10 would have meant that she was highest on the quality.

E. Dawn's Development during the Days of Separation

1. The First Day of Separation. Dawn arrived at the nursery in the late morning with her father and was soon running around looking into all the rooms, thoroughly exploring the new environment. After a while when father said "Ta, ta," and even though he repeated it three times, Dawn still just looked at him, said nothing and did not seem to register that he was leaving her. She was quite willing to have her coat taken off and then amused herself in an active way by pushing a high chair around. Toward the other children she was friendly and, when a little boy cried, she went up to him and comforted him with affection and some whispered words.

Although at first she did not like being put in the high chair and preferred running around, she readily sat in the chair for lunch and fed herself. She was equally willing to sit on the pot, pass urine and let herself be changed.

Her first sign of resistance did not appear until the noontime nap during which she kept saying "Up, up," and refused to lie down. When Wolpert said "Bye-bye," Dawn began to cry softly for her mother. This soon stopped, however, and in the afternoon she was again active. Even when her father returned with her favorite teddy bear, she only cried for a few minutes and then went on playing actively.

At the end of the day resistance to going to bed was again evident. Only much attention from a nurse and a bottle of milk could finally persuade her to lie down.

Thus, on the first day Dawn was active, complied with all routines and seemed unaware of the situation. Only when activity was precluded, as at bedtime, and when it became clear that someone else was dealing with her, did any sign of unease appear.

2. The Second to the Ninth Day of Separation. By the second day Dawn had changed. During the morning she cried a great deal and in a desperate and appealing way. She stood near the door through which her father had left, crying "Mummy, Daddy"; and continued to do so even though the door often gave her a heavy jolt.

Initially Dawn neither sought nor gained much comfort from the adults in the nursery. While she let the nurses wipe her nose which was constantly running, during the first three days of this phase mostly she stood apart and cried. When certain routine caretaking became necessary and the nurse dealt with her more quickly than she was probably used to, she cried even louder. Her sobbing was extreme when she was placed on the toilet. Once she turned to the male observer with "Daddy, up, up," but she gained little comfort from his attentions and continued her pathetic crying. Throughout this day she would not let the female observer even approach her. As if to keep her at a distance, Dawn threw down her favorite teddy bear, then picked him up and hugged him, and later repeated the sequence.

During the next few days Dawn allowed both Wolpert and West-heimer to pick her up. But, as when the nurses picked her up, she was soon ready to be put down again. Often she then returned to the door to continue her fretting in an inconsolable way.

Episodes of active resistance continued to occur. On the second day of separation she objected to being fed and bathed. Throughout the first four days being put to bed and especially being placed on the pot aroused her opposition and provoked her to loud crying.

When her father visited on the fifth day of separation, Dawn immediately recognized him and tried to struggle out of the high chair in which she was sitting. At first she was rather subdued. She ate greedily the sweets he had brought, but he was upset that she refused, despite coaxing from the nurses, to say "Ta." She clung to him and did not want to be put down. The first time he tried to do so she whined "Mm, mm" (which sounded like "Mum mum") and clambered back into his lap. The second time she allowed it and then suddenly began to speak, using a vocabulary and a clarity of speech not previously heard in the nursery. Impulsively she took candy from another child and cried bitterly when father told her she was "a naughty little girl."

When Dawn sensed that her father was leaving, she again whined "Mm, mm, mm," and as he got up she broke into a loud cry and clutched him around the neck. Father became upset, put her down and tried to console her. Dawn then threw herself in a temper on the floor and screamed for her father. As he was departing through the door, she almost knocked her head on the floor. When the nurse picked her up, she continued to scream but later comforted herself by sucking her finger and some candy.

In view of her reactions to father's visit, those to the male observer the next morning (the sixth) are of special interest. When he entered, she was again sitting in a high chair. She tried actively to get out of it, in the same way as when she had greeted her father, and then talked in the same rapid way as she had during father's visit. The nurse remarked that Dawn had not cried at all that morning. She ate a great deal of lunch, crying for "More, more," did not resist the pot, although she did not perform, and was even willing to go to rest. However, when the observer left, she began to cry in an extreme fashion and continued to do so for some time.

Throughout her separation Dawn sucked various objects; from the second through the fourth day she intensively sucked her pacifier and interrupted only to cry for "Daddy." The nurses quickly discovered that a bottle of milk made it possible to put Dawn to bed. After a fleeting resistance to food, by the sixth day she became noticeably greedy. She clamored for "More, more," even though her mouth was still full of pudding.

Dawn clung to her favorite object, a teddy bear, and expressed her feelings toward it. Often it was difficult to know whether she was talking about her "Teddy" or her "Daddy." Most frequently she would hug the teddy bear, but suddenly she would throw him away as if rejecting him and would ignore him for some time, only to search urgently for him again.

Turning a passive experience into an active one was also evidenced in Dawn's constant "Bye-bye." On the fifth day of separation when she and the children were all watching television Dawn got up, stood at the door and kept anxiously saying "Bye-bye" to one of the nurses in the room.

As on the first day, Dawn continued at times to be extremely active. She especially liked pushing high chairs and baby carriages around. Still another form of activity can best be described as wandering. Often on these occasions one had the impression she was looking for something.

We have seen both how Dawn tried to maintain a relation to her parents and also how she tried to cope with the obvious fact of their absence. Later, signs of deterioration in control began to appear. Such sphincter control as she had achieved at home turned first into anxious resistance and, by the seventh day, into a complete lapse. Control of aggression also began to weaken.

Since the reason for the separation was her mother's confinement, it is perhaps not surprising that much of Dawn's activity and especially hostile activity involved the "Baba." She took a keen interest in the babies to be seen in the nursery, pointing them out to people as if they couldn't see them, and telling them—the babies—to "Sshh" whenever they cried.

The doll-play session on the fourth day gave clear indication of latent hostility. Dawn readily came to the room where the dolls were set out, but then needed a little encouragement. After the male observer had looked at the toys and shown some interest in them, Dawn picked up the baby doll and handed it to him. She examined a few other toys and then, apparently by accident, sat on the father doll so that he protruded between her legs. She smiled and clearly was delighted. She then began to masturbate and next hit herself slightly in the genital area. This was quickly followed by her picking up the mother doll and examining her between her legs; then after opening the large wardrobe she threw it down with such force that it almost broke. Two minutes later she picked up the baby doll, examined it between the legs, and in a severe manner first hit it and then swept it away. Similarly, there was little doubt about her intentions as she singled out the mother doll and deliberately stepped on it. Later in the session she placed the toy bathroom sink, a rather elongated object, between her legs, started to move her upper legs back and forth as if rubbing against it, and again laughed and enjoyed it very much.

In attempting to interpret these sequences, it should be noted that both father and mother had very openly expressed their wish that the baby be a boy. Furthermore, Dawn had a close relation to Ralph, her 6½ year-old half-brother. Not seen here but equally clear was the very determined way she tried to remove or destroy the eyes of her teddy bear and other dolls.

3. The Tenth to the Fifteenth Day of Separation. On the eighth day of separation a good friend of the family had visited Dawn; he had done so instead of father, because father felt he would get too upset. It is possible that the arrival and departure of a person closely associated with her mother and father precipitated certain changes in Dawn. When the friend left, Dawn screamed frantically but soon regained control and fell asleep. Next day she was at times very quiet, stared into space and then sat with her eyes half-closed. Both observers used the word depressed in describing her and noticed that she was now biting her finger. On the tenth day, she seemed very sad and forlorn, but this was now for the first time interrupted by sudden outbursts of laughter which gave a manic impression.

The most obvious change seen during the last five days of Dawn's separation—avoiding the female observers—occurred for the first time also on the tenth day of separation. Although some tendency to avoid her had been evident since the second day of separation, when on the tenth day Wolpert tried to approach her, Dawn made it clear that she wanted her to keep her distance; and she began the same anxious whine, "Mm, mm, mm" that had been heard as her father began to leave her at the end of his visit. Only when Wolpert left did Dawn show any positive affect—a cheerful "Bye-bye." When on the thirteenth day of separation Westheimer visited, Dawn reacted to her in an identical manner, including the cheerful "Bye-bye" at the end. It was therefore unexpected that, according to the nurses' report, Dawn cried for Westheimer after she had left.

On the eleventh day Dawn greeted Wolpert with "Daddy come today." A little later she turned to her with "Bye-bye, bye-bye." When Wolpert tried to pick her up, Dawn avoided her and once more started her whine, "Mm, mm, mm"; as before this often sounded like "Mummy." When informed that her father would not be coming, she was not visibly upset but soon afterward she began to cry; and when the mother of another little girl arrived, Dawn's crying became uncontrollable. Wolpert tried to comfort her, but Dawn again reacted with the "Mm" and avoidance. A woman friend who accompanied this mother and who was a complete stranger to Dawn managed, however, to comfort Dawn, who then stopped crying. Each time she spotted Wolpert, however, Dawn started to cry again. During the next days this reaction to Wolpert became extreme.

Wolpert's record for the 13th day of separation runs as follows:

Dawn had been playing quite cheerfully as I could see through the glass window of the playroom. The minute she spotted me she started crying for her mother and then masturbated. She looked away and rubbed her eyes as if she could not bear to see me. She then sucked her finger alternating this with crying and masturbating. After I had been there for some time I approached her affectionately but she gave a loud cry, backed away as if I was going to hit her and then again masturbated. When momentarily left alone with me in the room she screamed and stood frozen in one spot until the nurse returned.

It should be noted that during these days Dawn's relation to the male observer continued to be friendly. For example, on the thirteenth day of separation the minute he entered, she cried, "Up, up, Daddy," indicating she wanted to be picked up. Sometimes she ran away from him only to search for and find him again. She liked being picked up by him and left him with a cheery "Bye-bye," when put down. When he left the room, however, she cried bitterly.

The reactions to the two observers were thus strikingly different. That the two reactions were dynamically related to each other is suggested by the observations made by Wolpert on the following day, the fourteenth of Dawn's separation.

On this day Dawn took one look at Wolpert and said "Bye-bye." She did not cry and was eating a sweet. However, she then became preoccupied with attempting to get Wolpert to follow her. She would run into one room, wait until the observer caught up with her and then run off again. During this time she lost her teddy bear and quite happily accepted it when Wolpert returned it.

A little while later, however, one of our colleagues, a male research worker, arrived, and Dawn met him in the hall. She had not seen this man before, but it is possible that his physical features reminded her of the male observer, Heinicke. She insisted on standing by him, began to cry and tried to follow him. All this time she still actively avoided Wolpert. When the latter returned to the nursery in the afternoon, Dawn again began screaming the minute she saw her.

Although by this time occasionally cheerful, Dawn generally cried a great deal and had a sad expression on her face; this picture was compounded by a continually running nose and by a tendency to interact little with her environment. Often she looked unwell, and on the fourteenth day of separation her temperature was above normal. At times she could be comforted by the nurses, but she never sought their affection as some of the other children did. Nor did it seem to make much difference to her which nurse handled her.

Among other sorts of behavior, it was observed that signs of greed increased, as if Dawn sought substitute gratification from food. In a characteristic way, she would shift suddenly from muttering "Mama" to "More, more" as she cried for second helpings of pudding. She also continued to suck her thumb, and during this phase, the frequency of masturbation increased. While she did not abandon her teddy bear, she no longer had it with her as often as during the previous period. Soiling was even more frequent and Dawn showed little concern when the nurses had to change her cot completely on several occasions.

That Dawn turned the passively experienced separation into one that she initiated has already been suggested. The "bye-byes" were actively initiated by her on many different occasions. New was the rapidity with which a sad expression was replaced. On the fifteenth day of separation, Dawn was sitting on her pot crying in a miserable way, when the male observer entered. The crying continued for some time only to be interrupted suddenly by a storm of laughter. She then began to masturbate and became very interested in the birds sitting on the window sill, saying "Birdie, birdie." But after another burst of laughter her attention shifted to "baba's" and then, as if a mother herself, she said "Sshh."

It was soon after this that the third doll play was administered. As if setting the theme for the session, she picked up the baby doll, showed it to the male observer and several times said "Gone." She now took the baby, threw it away and then very deliberately first stepped on it three different times and then stepped on the mother and father doll. A later sequence relating to the baby is of special interest. After opening and closing the large wardrobe and suddenly dropping it so that it crashed to the floor, she opened and closed the small wardrobe, carefully examined its inside and then let it also crash to the ground. "Shssh" she said to the observer and then explained herself by picking the wardrobe up, showing the observer the inside of it and saying "Baby." Immediately after this she went to the door, waved good-bye, seemed very happy and said "Bye-bye."

F. Changes in the Family during Separation

The newborn baby, Mary Rose, took Dawn's place as youngest in the family. Ralph, who had been sent to the maternal grandparents while mother was in the hospital, did not return home until two-and-a-half weeks after Dawn's return.

In contrast to the changes seen in Owen's mother (see next section), Dawn's mother maintained her sensitivity and concern about Dawn's welfare. Dawn's return was brought about as soon as possible and arrangements for it carefully planned.[1]

G. Dawn's Behavior and Family Relationships during the Period of Reunion

Mother planned the reunion in the same way as she had made arrangements for the residential nursery, with plenty of forethought and consideration for Dawn's feelings. By giving thought to easing the reunion for Dawn, she also allayed some of her own anxiety about their coming together again.

Since how best to arrange the reunion troubled her so much, she discussed the matter in detail with the ward sister and again with the fieldworker during her visit to the hospital. Her final plan was that Dawn and father should come to the hospital so that Dawn would first see the baby there, and that the whole family should then go home together. Ralph was not included in the plan since, to save the peace, he was to stay for a further two-and-a-half weeks with the maternal grandparents.

1. The Day of Reunion. When father arrived at the nursery, Dawn began to cry and her crying became louder as he talked to her. She had not seen him for ten days as he had visited her only once. She stretched out her arms to be picked up, and shortly after he had put her on his arm her crying stopped; her finger was in her mouth. When he put her down for a moment, she cried again and again quieted when back on his arm.

Within a very short time her expression had brightened and, held securely by her father, she pointed to the babies' room and said "Baba." Her bearing had become more animated and confident; she sought to be put down so that she could eat a few sweets in comfort, and on leaving shortly afterward, she waved a bright good-bye to the matron.

But this was a precarious recovery. When father put her gently into the back of the fieldworker's car, she was momentarily alone

[1] Within the sample of ten separated children, Dawn's mother was given a rank of 3 on the dimension: *Change in the mother's concern about and sensitivity to the welfare of the child.* Since the rank of 1 indicates the least change a rank of 3 represents relatively little change.

and instantly began a fearful crying which continued for some minutes even after she was on father's knee and he was comforting and soothing her. She clung to him as if afraid to lose him again, while he gave her his sole attention.

Arrived at the hospital, Dawn was reluctant to leave the car, but after father had explained that they were going to fetch mummy and the baby, she left the car without protest. She went upstairs on her father's arm and, during a brief period of waiting, looked around her with interest.

Suddenly mother was there. She rushed toward Dawn and, snatching her from father, clutched her to her and hugged her in a fierce, desperate grip which made it impossible for Dawn to look at her mother's face. Unlike the other children observed during this study, Dawn was given no time by her mother in which to register non-recognition, bewilderment or indifference.

Later mother said that initially Dawn had tried to push away from her; but in the circumstances it had been impossible for the fieldworker to see the gesture. Dawn began to cry, perhaps as much because of the suddenness of her mother's appearance and the fright of her desperate embrace as for any other reason. Mother too began to cry, but was soon busy drying Dawn's tears and her own at the same time. Although Dawn stopped crying, mother continued to give her her total attention—completely ignoring father and Westheimer.

A nurse arrived with the baby and, in accordance with mother's plan, gave it directly to father. Father hesitated momentarily to accept the baby, as if preferring to regain charge of Dawn; but he took over as required. Dawn pointed to the baby and said brightly, "Baba."

The party then left the hospital, mother carrying Dawn, father carrying the baby and the fieldworker carrying the parcels. The record continues:

In the car mother quickly arranged herself in the back seat with Dawn, so that father had no option but to sit in front with the baby. It was quite clear from his bearing that he would have preferred to have been the one sitting in the back with Dawn. A short time before, when alone in the nursery with father, Dawn had been restless and uninterested in her teddy bear; but now after an initial mild whimpering she sat quietly on her mother's lap, held the teddy bear to her and occasionally gave him a special hug. During the latter part of the journey she remarked on things seen through the car window—"Horsey! Bus!"—but most of the time she sat quietly on her mother's lap.

Arrived at the house, Dawn walked upstairs unaided to the family's apartment. She stood in the doorway of the living room and looked around; then she walked over to the cooker [oven], opened the door, and mother said, "I wondered when you would do that." She allowed her outdoor clothes to be removed without fuss and, after eating a pear with relish, set about rediscovering the familiar setting. She touched various items of furniture, then called for her toys and a jar of smaller treasures and played intently with them on the floor. After a time she asked to be put back into her high chair, as if she had now accepted that she had come home. During this time mother had been preparing tea, and father had waited in close attendance on his favorite child.

The apathy and inactivity seen in the nursery had gone, and Dawn was again active, animated and busy with her interests; the sad look that she wore in the nursery had disappeared during the course of one morning with her mother and father. Compared with Owen, the readiness with which she returned to her old ways and re-established contact with her mother after the first few doubtful minutes was most striking.

2. *The Second and Third Day after Reunion.* These two days are differentiated from the first day and from later ones because during this time Dawn anxiously stayed close to her mother. On the first of them mother remarked how Dawn tended to cling to her and wanted to stay close by her when they went out together. In the familiar corner shop mother had placed Dawn on the counter, as she had many times before, but as she moved away a little to make a purchase Dawn had looked anxious, then stretched out her arms to her mother. In the street and elsewhere she had frequently insisted, "Up, up," as if to escape from some danger into her mother's arms.

Insecurity showed also in Dawn's difficulty in getting to *sleep* on her own. She would go to sleep in the sitting room with her parents present but cried bitterly if taken to the bedroom. On the first evening she woke and cried frantically each time father tried to lower her gently into her cot; in the end she fell asleep from sheer exhaustion. On the second afternoon she allowed herself to be put down, whimpered a little, but was not nearly as upset as on the first evening. On the fifth day (which belongs to the next phase of development) she was still reluctant to be put down and, with an uncertain expression, would point to the trees and shadows to be seen through the window. During the first days in the residential nursery she had also had trouble going to sleep, though before separation there had been no difficulties.

Another way in which difficulties arose during the first days was over *toilet training*. Prior to separation Dawn had not objected to being sat on the pot, though she did not always use it, and had not resisted having a diaper put on. But two days after reunion mother reported that Dawn was reluctant to sit on the pot and never performed. She also resisted having a diaper on, and invariably wet herself a few minutes later.

3. *From the Fourth Day through the Fourth Week after Reunion.* On the third day of reunion Dawn had her first temper tantrum. They continued throughout the next phase and were accompanied by hostile behavior to both mother and baby. Mother found it all very difficult to handle. She had felt utterly worn out: "What with the baby crying and Dawn screaming, it is not funny."

Before the separation Dawn had had minor outbursts of temper appropriate to her age and their cause had been easily understood—usually when something she wanted had been withheld. But since her return she threw full *temper tantrums* on the slightest provocation, and sometimes for no reason that mother could detect. The slightest frustration set her screaming and kicking. This greatly distressed mother, not least because it aroused her own ambivalence toward Dawn due to her favored place in the family. Dawn was always wanting things, and when father was around she tended to get them. Most of Dawn's tantrums, mother said, occurred when she was feeding the baby; they caused her to put the baby aside because she found she could not continue until Dawn had been placated. During the baby's feeding time Dawn would demand "Popo quick," though when given it she would not use it.

When Westheimer arrived on the sixth day after reunion, Dawn cried. Mother, who was just feeding the baby, comforted Dawn, but when Dawn looked up at Westheimer she almost began to cry again. For thirty minutes Dawn continued to look rather pathetic. Then she began to make contact with Westheimer by pointing to the baby's shoes and calling "Shoe shoe." She asked for some sugar and became interested in a coffee cup and spoon. When she spilled a little of the coffee, she said "Dirty, dirty." At this point Dawn's mother was telling a story of a cousin whom she despised because he was always playing with a sticky jam spoon. Later, when Dawn wanted to help herself to the malt and mother insisted on controlling the spoon, Dawn began to stamp her feet. It was easy for mother to distract her from crying, however, and Dawn then climbed over her lap in an affectionate way. Mother gladly put up with this until Dawn, for no apparent reason, smacked her. Then mother, very annoyed, scolded Dawn and threatened to smack her back if she did it a second time.

On the thirteenth day Dawn was hurting mother by kicking and treading on her. Father took notice and smacked Dawn who, taken aback by her father's unusual displeasure, was very upset and "brokenhearted." But this incident did not alter the basic situation which was that father continued to dote on Dawn and treat her as his favorite child. Toward him Dawn showed no hostility—all her negative behavior was directed at mother.

When father smacked Dawn, mother's remark that he was "learning some sense" reflected both her long-standing criticism of him for his indulgence of Dawn and her feeling that he undervalued her and the other children. This long-standing grievance flared up around the naming of the new baby. Mother insisted that he was not interested in the baby and that he did none of the things for her that he had done for Dawn when she was a baby. The question whether the baby should have one Christian name or two became an issue charged with mother's suspicion of neglect. Father thought that one name—Mary—was sufficient for "a working man's child," but mother wanted to call her Mary Rose. Why, she demanded, had Dawn been given *two* names—Dawn Anne? When in the end mother won the battle, it gave her immense satisfaction that she had compelled father to equalize things between the children.

Beside all the hostility, however, Dawn during this period showed increasing affection for her mother. While during the first days after reunion she never said "Mummy," by the sixth day with prompting she was again saying it. Before the separation Dawn had said it much more frequently. There were also other signs of increasing affection such as crawling into mother's lap.

The same mixture of hostility and affection was present during this period in Dawn's attitude to the baby, suggesting a connection between the two. Although during the first three days Dawn had been affectionate with the baby, now she tended to push Mary Rose away as soon as she was shown to her, especially when she began to cry, and at times she tried to hit her. This was very similar to the way she poked at the eyes of her teddy bear while she was in the residential nursery. Nevertheless, when during the third week after reunion, Ralph returned home, Dawn was eager to show him the baby. She dragged him upstairs saying "Baba baba."

Dawn was also hostile toward both her mother and Mary Rose in less direct ways. Although her father attended to Dawn a great deal, he refused to deal with diapers, especially when dirty. As if sensing this, Dawn during the third and fourth week after reunion was still waiting until the baby's evening feed began and then demanding, "Popo quick." If not attended to immediately she threw a temper. As already indicated, mother had to stop feeding the baby to sit Dawn on the pot. Soon Dawn would announce "All finished," but the minute the diaper had been put on she wet herself. Actually putting the diaper on was also difficult. On one such occasion mother had to hold Dawn very tightly in order to control her own anger.

4. From the Fifth to the Twelfth Week after Reunion. Problems over toileting continued during this phase, but the number of difficulties and the intensity of the provocation was clearly less, particularly when compared with her behavior during the first three days after reunion. Dawn now asked for and used the "popo" more often, even though she also still wet herself. This exasperated mother, not only because of the wetting, but also because father tended to imply she was incompetent in allowing it to continue.

In other respects there were also changes. While on occasion still ready to punch the baby in the nose, Dawn now tried to deal with her conflicting feelings regarding the baby by often wanting to be the baby. Already during the first three weeks it had been noted that whenever the baby was being fed, Dawn not only demanded "Popo quick," but also wanted to eat. Mother eased this situation by giving Dawn a bottle. Frequently when mother lifted the sleeping baby to place it on her lap, it was a signal for Dawn to spread a diaper on the floor and herself lie on it muttering "Bye-bye" or "Night-night." Then, getting up from the floor, she tried desperately to put on first the baby's cardigan, next its dress and finally she struggled to get her feet into the booties. When mother had finished washing the baby, Dawn acquired the wash bowl as well. At other times Dawn would climb into the baby's perambulator and sit there clutching a rattle, all smiles at her success.

Temper tantrums were now rare, but battles between mother and daughter still occurred, especially over cleanliness about which mother adhered to rigid standards. For example, when during the eighth week after reunion mother tried to put a diaper on Dawn she protested, wriggled and kicked. Mother complained: "You are hurting my arm." When mother gave up battling with Dawn and began to coax her, however, Dawn co-operated. During the same visit mother refused to let Dawn drink milk from a plate and, after a prolonged tussle, finally took the plate away. As if to justify her action, mother remarked that father blamed her for all of Dawn's recent misbehavior. She then went on to tell the fieldworker a revealing story of a few weeks earlier. At the end of a trying day, when the baby was unwell and crying and Dawn was being generally awkward, Dawn had upset a bucket of water. At that moment father had walked in and, in a tone which she felt implied criticism, had demanded his evening meal. Overcome with rage against both father and Dawn, mother had shrieked: "For goodness sake take her away or I'll kill her! I'll kill her!"

The two themes of the baby and cleanliness are reflected in Dawn's behavior during the doll play administered by Westheimer six weeks after reunion. Of all the play, 38 per cent and 31 per cent involved the baby and the toilet respectively. Again and again she would pick up the baby doll and exclaim "Dolly." Or she would pick up the lavatory, open the lid, shut the lid, and say "Bang." Although in form the play was repetitive and guarded, she was clearly interested.

At the end of this phase Westheimer observed that Dawn, now aged 20 months, was a bright, robust little girl, with a confident manner, very different from the whiny despondent resident in the nursery.

5. *The Twelfth to the Twenty-Second Week after Reunion.* The most striking change during this phase was in *toilet training.* Dawn no longer resisted and with tactful handling usually performed in the pot.

Her relationship to the baby also underwent change. As a rule she no longer sought to be the baby. Instead she made sympathetic remarks and tried to be helpful, thereby obtaining attention and approval for herself.

A tremendous spurt in Dawn's vocabulary was observed. In addition she could now be left by her mother without protesting.

The exchange of affection between mother and daughter predominated and the former battles were now rare; one was, however, observed during this period. Dawn was wriggling about making it difficult for mother to dress her. When by chance she kicked mother fairly hard, the instantaneous reaction was: "If you hurt me any more, I'll have to have you put away." Earlier during the same interview, mother had told how some time ago Dawn had given her a painful, swollen wrist—"This too from a kick." She added uncertainly that she did not think Dawn had meant to hurt her. Less sympathetic feelings emerged a few minutes later, however, when she stopped Dawn from pushing the baby's perambulator and demanded in a rough voice: "Stop pushing that pram, can't you! You've done enough damage." And when Dawn made to go onto the small balcony, mother hauled her back with the sinister pronouncement: "One of these days you'll disappear down there."

The fact that by the next visit the atmosphere was again harmonious was consistent with later developments but also shows how mother alternated in attitude.

All in all this was a loving mother, concerned to do what was best for Dawn, and uncomfortably aware that she was coping with angry feelings against the child for the privileged place she occupied in relation to father and the other children. Despite mother's concern and competence, she was not fully in control of her feelings. She varied from permissiveness to severity and sometimes even to temporary rejection.

6. *Relationship of Dawn to the Fieldworker during the First Twenty-Two Weeks after Reunion.* As in the case of Owen, Dawn's relationship to Westheimer serves as an illustration of her behavior during reunion. Whereas in the nursery Dawn had cried and avoided the fieldworker, on the first day after reunion, after having been in father's arms for some time, she began to show some positive responses. Throughout the first three weeks, however, she usually watched anxiously. From the fourth to the eleventh weeks she became more friendly, but slight signs of anxiety remained. Finally, from the twelfth week onward Dawn treated the fieldworker with confidence. Some illustrations follow.

On the day Dawn was to return home, Westheimer arrived at the nursery some time before father:

Dawn was sitting quietly watching other children at play. The moment she saw me, as on the occasion of my previous visit, she began to weep quietly and to whimper "Mmmm, mmmm." She refused to take the teddy bear when I offered it to her. A familiar nurse then picked her up and she quietened immediately. But when a few minutes later the nurse had to put her down, Dawn again began to cry—and as she cried she kept looking fearfully at me. Since my presence was so disturbing to her, I withdrew until her father arrived.

Some time later the same nurse came in my direction with Dawn on her arm and, as though afraid she might get too close to me, Dawn made a warding-off gesture with both arms. The nurse put her on a swing, and I left the room to find a place from which I could watch her unnoticed.

In my absence she sat quietly watching the other children, but when I re-entered the room some minutes later she instantly saw me and burst into tears. I therefore left the room once more, and she regained her composure. But when she became aware that I was looking at her through the glass panel, she again began to cry. Since my presence was so disturbing to her, I retired until her father came.

Once on her father's arm she no longer seemed to mind my presence, and by the time we had reached home and she was safely with both her parents, she turned toward me to establish contact—just as she had done on our first meeting before she went into the nursery. My leaving was of no consequence to her now that she was together again with both her parents.

The ready acceptance of Westheimer, however, did not continue. Five days later the following was recorded:

As I entered the room, Dawn sat very quietly in her high chair and looked at me in a puzzled manner. She had lost all interest in eating her breakfast. She watched as mother and I talked together. Then, after about ten minutes of complete inactivity, her eyebrows went up, her face puckered, she looked bewildered and burst into tears. Mother's remark, "I thought you were thinking things out," was apt.

Mother took Dawn out of the high chair and, placing the child close to her, put an arm around her. It was some minutes before the desperate crying ceased, and Dawn could respond to the attention and caressing of her mother. When her crying had stopped, she stood with finger in mouth looking at me uncertainly, and now and again would whimper if I glanced in her direction. Each time her mother's comforting arm reassured her. Only after thirty minutes did she begin to make tentative contact with me, a pathetic little figure with tear-stained cheeks and running nose.

Yet during the latter part of this two-hour visit, Dawn began to feel more comfortable. She sought to gain my attention by peering into my face saying "bee-bo" with a smile. Later when her shoe needed fastening, she allowed me to lift her on my lap in order to attend to it. She was now at ease. When I left, a smiling Dawn waved to me from the balcony.

The same type of intent watching still appeared during the third week after reunion. After that week, however, the doubtful, searching look was there no longer. Her relationship with the fieldworker rapidly became friendly and cheerful, especially after the fourth reunion visit when Dawn, after several times calling the fieldworker "Mummy, Mummy, Mummy," spontaneously kissed her as she left the house. Henceforward, Dawn allowed Westheimer to do things for her, for instance to change her diaper, and would happily sit on her lap to play with the jewelry she was wearing, pronouncing it to be "Pretty, pretty." There was, however, still behavior which could be interpreted as an effect of separation. For example, in the eleventh week a game developed at Dawn's initiative. She repeatedly said "Up, up," but in response to Westheimer's outstretched arms laughed and exclaimed, "No, no." She could approach her but then suddenly had to leave her.

Starting with the twelfth week, Dawn's confidence in the fieldworker became firmly established, so that at the end of the twenty-two weeks of reunion she was content to be left at home with Westheimer when mother went out shopping. The conclusion that Dawn got over the effects of the separation more quickly than did Owen is supported by the friendly way she behaved toward Heinicke when he visited.

7. *A Visit by Heinicke to Dawn's Home during the Sixteenth Week of Reunion.* Dawn was the only child in the sample who did not actively avoid the male observer when he visited; she let herself be picked up and seemed quite pleased to see him. When he left, she even tried hard to get out of her mother's arms in order to go with him.

8. *The Two Years following Reunion.* Although the twenty-second week concluded the period of observation prescribed by the research design, the fieldworker maintained some contact with the family thereafter and brief reference to subsequent history may be of interest.

Ten months after reunion, when Dawn was 2 years 3 months, the family moved into a Council house. A few days later Dawn fell and sustained a greenstick fracture. Her leg was put into a plaster cast in the outpatient department of a hospital, and she was brought home the same day by ambulance. Though her reactions to the episode are reminiscent of the way she behaved after her nursery stay, we are in no position to assess what role the previous separation may have played in them. When seen by the fieldworker three weeks after the accident, Dawn was still clinging to her mother and constantly waiting to be picked up.

She had become afraid of many things. Planes flying overhead were after her, and a harmless black cat was feared to be chasing her. She had constant need to assure herself of her mother's whereabouts. Her many fears appeared to have the common element of being pursued and feeling helpless. It is possible that her anxieties were in some measure reactive to her experience at the outpatient department on the day of the accident. There is no information on how she was treated there; but it was father who accompanied her and not mother. Mother had felt guilty about the accident, although she had not been in the least to blame.

Mother reported that following the accident Dawn had gone off her food for several days and had not passed a bowel movement for five days, and only then with the help of a laxative. She refused for a while to go to the lavatory and, although formerly clean and dry, was still wetting herself when Westheimer visited three weeks later. She would not go to sleep in her cot upstairs but would do so in the sitting room. Mother considered her to be more touchy and easily upset. During the meal Dawn accidentally spilled some soup and at once dissolved into tears; mother's gentleness soon restored her equilibrium. Temper tantrums had returned in full force, two occurring in response to minor frustrations during the fieldworker's visit.

Dawn's attitude to Westheimer was initially fearful, as indeed mother said it was to the baker and to any other caller. With quivering lips she mumbled "Mummy, Mummy"; she stayed close by her mother and frequently insisted on being picked up. Gradually she began to talk to the fieldworker from the safety of her mother's arms, but it was an hour before she brightened sufficiently to show interest in the doll-play material that Westheimer had brought with her. Then she allowed the fieldworker to comfort her after a tantrum.

Seven months later Dawn was 2 years 11 months old, and mother was in the last stages of another pregnancy. Dawn remembered the fieldworker and was instantly friendly, asking eagerly for the "dollies" (doll-play material). She had a good vocabulary, spoke freely and with no signs of anxiety, and willingly came on to Westheimer's lap to look at a picture book.

The parents thought, nevertheless, that Dawn was unhappy; possibly, they thought, because father's head was bandaged following an eye injury; possibly because of mother's pregnancy and her recent obstetric examination, which Dawn had witnessed. Mother then added that recently she had encouraged Dawn to throw away her pacifier, which mother had always disliked as a "dirty" thing. Dawn had agreed, had thrown the pacifier away herself, but had been restless and tearful thereafter and unable to get to sleep. A habit of picking the skin of her fingers, observed by Westheimer, was said to have started at that time. When soon afterward she had developed a temperature, the doctor had linked it to the loss of the pacifier, and a new one was provided. The new pacifier was much in use during the fieldworker's visit. From time to time Dawn looked searchingly at her and said: "Big girls don't suck pacifiers." She smiled when assured that even big girls sometimes liked sucking pacifiers.

On Westheimer's final home visit four months later, almost two years after reunion, Dawn was confident, trusting and friendly. At the same time, as on the previous visit, mild symptoms of anxiety were to be observed. These troubled the parents, who offered various possible reasons for them yet did not mention the most obvious one—tension between the parents intensified by the fourth pregnancy. Furthermore, Ralph's removal from home had been decided upon and he himself was greatly distressed by the thought of a residential school. Mother's feelings were mixed. At this point in time the atmosphere was tense and explosive, and Dawn must have been aware of it.

* * * * * * * * *

To help the reader link details of Dawn's behavior with generalizations derived from the comparison of groups of children, salient aspects of her behavior at the end of separation and after reunion with her parents are compared with Owen's development to be described next. Unlike Owen, at the end of her separation Dawn was still fretting for her parents, still clung to her teddy bear (instead of completely abandoning him), showed little attachment to the nurses and showed no open ambivalence toward the observers.

Dawn's behavior during reunion can also be compared with Owen's. The absence of affectionate contact with mother during the first day and week after reunion was not observed. Instead, she clung to her mother as well as to her father. As this diminished, she hit her mother as well as seeking her affection, but the onset of this was sooner than for Owen (by the first week after reunion) and continued for a briefer time. Though mutual ambivalence could be seen as late as the twelfth week after reunion in the form of battles (for example over cleanliness), they decreased and were rarely seen after this time. By contrast, as will be seen, Owen did not show open hostility toward his mother until the ninth week, and the climax of his temper outbursts was not reached until the fifteenth week after reunion.

III.   Owen and His Family

A.   Introduction to the Case

1. Family Constellation and Reason for Separation. Owen, aged 2 years 2 months and the younger child in a middle-class family, was admitted to the care of the residential nursery while his mother went into the hospital for treatment of a back injury sustained while in the Service eleven years earlier. His father, with the help of friends, coped with Owen's 8-year-old sister, Sheila.

It was expected that the separation would be short, but it became extended to eighty-one days, forty days longer than his mother's stay in hospital.

2. Observations Made on Owen and His Family. The case presentation to follow is based on the direct observations and interviewing by all three observers: Westheimer, Heinicke and Wolpert.

Westheimer made the following contacts with Owen and his family:

a. *Owen* was seen twenty-nine times. (On one preseparation visit, nine times during separation, once at reunion and on nineteen occasions at regular weekly intervals after his return home.)

b. *Mother* was seen twenty-nine times. (Nine times by herself, four of them in hospital, five at home before Owen's return, once at reunion and nineteen times with Owen after his return.)

c. *Father* was seen twenty times. (Once on the day of separation, again on the day of return and on eighteen out of the nineteen post-reunion visits to the home.)

d. *Telephone Conversations* with the parents numbered fourteen.

e. *Additional Home Visits* numbering four were made after the series of post-reunion visits prescribed by the research design had been completed. These additional visits were made at intervals of two months, three-and-one-half months, six months and one year and two months respectively. Each of the visits usually lasted from two to three hours, half of the time in discussion with mother alone.

Heinicke and Wolpert observed Owen during his stay in the nursery in accordance with the procedures outlined in Chapters 1 and 2. Category observations in the Everyday Nursery Setting, Doll-Play Sessions, extensive clinical comments on his development and observations by staff are all available on Owen and are drawn upon in the account which follows.

3. Mother's Relationship with the Fieldworker. Owen's mother was given only three days notice of her admission to the hospital and had to make hurried arrangements for his care. It was not surprising, therefore, that she was initially reluctant to co-operate in the research. But, after a telephone conversation in which the fieldworker expressed understanding of her difficult situation and showed how collaboration could be mutually advantageous, she agreed to take part.

From the first contact, which took place the day before Owen was admitted to the nursery and two days before she herself went into the hospital, this mother regarded the fieldworker as a support— a helpful person from whom she could learn about nursery conditions and Owen's well-being while there, and through whom she could convey to the nursery staff the idiosyncrasies of her son. She also sought understanding of the meaning to Owen of separation from her, and of the extent to which, by continuous and regular visiting, the father might soften the separation experience. She was ready to adjust her thinking in the light of these discussions.

Once Owen had returned home after the separation, the fieldworker frequently acted as interpreter to the mother of certain of Owen's reactions and responses, and thus was able to ease the situation by furthering understanding. Similarly, when in the early days after reunion the mother had difficulty in communicating to Owen her positive feelings, the fieldworker again acted as an interpreter. The mother was able to learn from the fieldworker by means of identification, example and discussion.

It soon became clear that this mother could readily have become overdependent, and the fieldworker had to make an early decision on the limits of her function. Working in the unusual degree of social intimacy which this type of study requires, and with a mother basically unsure of herself and wishful that the fieldworker should make decisions on her behalf, it was difficult to maintain a positive yet limited role—namely to help clarify issues without taking responsibility for decision. For instance, while in the hospital mother was anxious about Owen's well-being and about her own health, discontented by the results of treatment, and in a mood of hopelessness, she rejected the medical social worker's offer to find household help. In despair, she then turned to the fieldworker who was able to help her sort out her feelings and clarify the situation, with the result that the medical social worker could be approached afresh and realistic arrangements made for mother's return home. The fieldworker was thus under constant pressure to give direct advice and to make decisions about Owen; the position was complicated both by mother's ambivalent feelings toward the boy and by her tendency to feel worthless and incompetent.

Indeed, throughout the association the mother insisted on long discussions about her own concerns and worries before allowing the research interest in Owen to have its place. Sending father and Owen out for long walks so that the discussions should not be interrupted, she sought to monopolize the fieldworker. Any member of the family returning before the appointed time had to bear the full brunt of mother's frustration and disappointment. She behaved then as if something good had been taken away from her prematurely.

By the end of the extended period of research contact, the consistently supportive approach of the fieldworker seemed to have helped this mother to a greater acceptance of herself and of Owen, and so to an ability to cope with him better.

B. The Mother—Her Personality and Background

When Owen was due to go into the residential nursery, his mother was in her late 30's, a fair-haired woman of medium height who was always well-groomed and dressed with care. In a cultured voice she conversed easily and gave an immediate impression of being relaxed and self-assured, with a friendly interest in other people. With neighbors and shopkeepers she was invariably pleasant and equable. People she met for the first time were quickly made to feel at ease, indeed to feel as if they were acquaintances of longer standing. In consequence she was popular with people who met her at this casual level of acquaintance at parties and in other social situations, and admired and liked her for her qualities of serenity and easy friendliness.

Characteristically, the fieldworker was accepted by the mother on the first acquaintance with a friendliness and confidence suggesting an established relationship. But it was soon apparent that her relationships, although easy and entertaining, were also superficial. Her apparent self-assurance and outgoing interest in other people masked deep uncertainty about her personal worth and competence. She doubted her ability to cook or be a good housewife, and also her adequacy as a sexual partner in marriage.

Her account of her early life was consistent with the fieldworker's view of her as someone insecure and specially dependent on the affections of others. The fourth child of a middle-class family, she was born at a time when the maternal grandmother, then in her late 40's, was leading an active social life, was always at bridge parties and spared little time for the children, who were left mostly in charge of a nurse. Described as self-indulgent and inaccessible, the maternal grandmother was a constant disappointment.

As the youngest child, and a late arrival, mother was at a special disadvantage compared to her older brother and sisters; this became intensified when the family's financial situation deteriorated and the maid had to go. At 10 years of age mother found herself required to do housework which her sisters had been spared and prevented from going on to boarding school as they had done. Thus, to the initial disadvantages of being an afterthought and of suffering the inadequate care of her mother, was added the change of family fortune which deprived her of the material advantages in education and other experiences that her older siblings had enjoyed. She felt that "Whenever it was my turn, there was never enough."

Her childhood memories were of being underprivileged and neglected in the essentials of loving concern. Even a birthday had gone uncelebrated. Late adolescence was a round of parties and outings with groups of young people. As a disguise against loneliness, a superficial ease and good humor won her popularity among her own age group and more acceptance than she felt she ever had had from her parents, of whom she saw little. When she got home they were usually asleep.

These character traits she carried into adult life, into the Women's Service in which she had served during the war and into the hospital when she was ill. In such group situations she was popular. But she had no close friends. Her relationships were superficial, the motive underlying her poise and engaging good humor being to secure the regard and affectionate consideration of others—and to conceal from them her doubts about her personal worth.

Despite some intellectual understanding of the vicissitudes of her early life, and in particular the deterioration in family standards which had had such an effect on her, she continued to feel the underprivileged and inferior member of the family. Her sisters, who had enjoyed all the advantages deriving from the family's early affluence, had retained their privileges by making good marriages. She believed also that in consequence of their better early experience they had the ease and self-assurance which she herself lacked—although to the world these were the very qualities she seemed to display.

Her doubts regarding her capacities she camouflaged by a definite and controlling manner, so that outsiders would gauge little, if anything, of her feelings of inadequacy. On occasions when she felt least in control, her control became most marked; for example, when on the day of reunion she felt bewildered by Owen's changed behavior and helpless, she became dictatorial. In this way her uncertainty frequently made her feel it necessary to win battles with the children and her point in an argument with others. When doubtful whether she had anything good to give, she tended to withhold. Not until the very end of the fieldworker's contact could this woman, either at the right moment or without some accompanying disparaging remark, offer the good homemade cakes she had made. Although at times with characteristic defensive humor she sought to make light of these feelings, they weighed heavily upon her.

It was a novel experience for this highly defended mother to reveal her feelings of helplessness and inadequacy as she did to the fieldworker and to find herself nevertheless accepted and valued. It was inevitable that she should seek to convert the fieldworker into a wise and loving mother-figure who would solve her problems and make decisions for her; someone whom she, who had never gotten close to her real mother, could monopolize and enjoy.

By helping this mother discover unacknowledged qualities as well as face more realistically her inadequacies, the fieldworker brought a limited therapeutic component to the interviews.

Although her illness was incapacitating, it had as compensation that she could obtain some of the consideration and privilege which she felt she had lacked when a child. In the hospital she got special pleasure from the nursing, especially the tending of her body. This is perhaps linked to the care she bestowed upon herself—in marked contrast to the relatively casual interest she took in her home which lacked care, color and comfort. She had never in fact accepted the restricted life of a fully committed mother and housewife, which was too like the underprivileged status of her childhood as she recalled it. She also resented the privileged position of men, as she had earlier that of her brother who had been exempted from household chores; at times she competed with them.

As subsequent sections will show, the prolonged stay of Owen in the residential nursery was partly due to his mother's hesitation in resuming the burden of responsibility for him. Admittedly, she was still unfit, but it appears likely that factors mentioned above, culminating in a decline of concern and sensitivity to the welfare of her child, had their part—fear of incompetence, a reluctance to be bound as a mother, identification with her own self-indulgent mother and a readiness to leave Owen in the care of others.

C. Marriage and Family Relationships

Significant features in father's early life were strikingly like those in mother's and undoubtedly had a bearing on the quality of relationship between them. He too had known little of family life when young. The paternal grandparents had lived abroad, where the grandfather was an army officer of high rank, and father and his brother had been sent early to boarding school. Holidays were spent with an aunt.

The paternal grandparents had opposed the marriage and did not attend the ceremony. They maintained little contact with their grandchildren. There was thus a parallel between the lack of family life experienced by each parent and the lack of affection each had for their own parents.

Father's personality appeared to have been affected by his early experiences. He is a civil servant—conscientious and steady in his work—a tall man of good appearance, apparently always calm and unruffled, never out of temper. The fieldworker's relationship to him was not close enough to discover what other feelings may have lain behind the placid demeanor, but the absence of complaint or retaliation were unusual. In all situations he displayed remarkable qualities of patience and limitless forbearance toward mother and children.

Although to the outside world mother was an easy, equable person, within the home she domineered over father and children with nagging and inconsistent criticism and excessive control. Toward father she was exacting and critical, and during the period of reunion her anger toward Owen was frequently displaced on to him. She knew that he would never seriously oppose her—no matter how excessive her demands and no matter how controlling her behavior. Although from her nagging it might have appeared that she despised him, in fact she leaned heavily upon him. When she did not feel well enough to do the shopping, he would do it for her—even to the extent of bringing home skirts and dresses for her selection; when she was unfit for the housework he calmly got on with the things that had to be done; when she was too preoccupied by her ill health or by other matters to give enough attention to the children, he became a competent mother to them—more intuitively understanding of their needs than she was. Without complaint he would accept interruption to whatever he might be doing.

His calmness was a very necessary anchor for mother and the wonder was that he so rarely reacted with resentment to the inconsistencies she showed. Before the vagaries of her behavior he was resilient; to preserve the peace he rarely resisted and was usually accommodating. It seemed likely that this pattern had first been fostered in father's early years by his own domineering mother and her "henpecked" husband.

The reactions of Sheila, aged 8, to her mother were very similar to those of her father; but in Sheila the element of cowed submission was more apparent. When scolded sharply and unfairly Sheila would move away quietly and without retort, head bowed. She was instant-

ly conforming and obedient and, without protest, would forego a
play period to meet some whim of her mother's. Under the constant
pressure of her mother's controlling behavior Sheila had already the
features of someone who found greatest security in compliance, just
as her father probably had done many years before.

Father did nothing to protect his daughter. Similarly with Owen;
fond as he was of him he would obediently chastise him when told
to do so. One suspected that during a long childhood without affectionate ties, father had found the lines of least resistance, and
that it was this which did so much to prevent recriminations.

The mother used her poor state of health as a reason for contract-
ing out of some of her wifely and motherly tasks, handing these over
to father without any apparent guilt. Since he was quite prepared to
assume some of them and no conflict arose between them, the pattern seemed to suit them both.

D. Owen's History and Mother-Child Relationship.

Owen was the second child, born when his sister Sheila was 6 years
old. Throughout the pregnancy mother had been continuously unwell with "heartburn"; but, although a specialist had been called in
because of anticipated difficulties with her injured back, the delivery
was easy. The baby weighed 8 pounds 4 ounces.

Breast feeding ceased after only two weeks, said to be because the
milk supply failed. Mother expressed no regret. Thereafter Owen
gained weight steadily but was always discontented. He cried night
and day, and the doctor's change of feeds did not seem to help. When
at 2 months he was looked after by friends for ten days while mother
was in the hospital for a minor operation, they were glad to return
him to her because of the incessant crying. This lessened slightly after
the introduction of solids at 4 months. "A windy baby" was the only
known diagnosis.

The crying became much less at 10 months when he began to crawl
and still less at 12 months when he walked. But until a few months
before he went into the residential nursery, episodes of intense distress were common. These occurred mostly in the evening. After he
had thoroughly enjoyed his bath and allowed his mother to put him
into the crib, when she re-entered his room a few minutes later she
would find him standing up, clinging to the bars while crying desperately. To get some quiet the parents had to alternate in keeping

him company. Toward the end of his second year the mother accepted, with some reluctance, the health visitor's suggestion that he be given a "syrup pacifier" at bedtime. Thenceforward, Owen loved his pacifier and got much comfort from sucking and fondling it. The crying had stopped soon after its introduction, which had also coincided with mother obtaining for him a proper bed, having been aware for some time of his dislike of the bars of his crib.

Mother had no deep-seated antipathy to the pacifier, and she appreciated that it brought Owen consolation. When the time came for him to enter the residential nursery it was she, understanding something of his need, who insisted that his comforter must accompany him.

From the time of their birth, this mother had found it difficult to understand or respond to her children's needs. When Sheila was a baby, she reported she had had no idea how to talk to her and often listened to other mothers with their babies and then imitated their ways. Similarly she felt she did not understand Owen's crying and described how she became helpless and desperate when he did not respond to what she supposed he wanted. As Owen gradually developed a vocabulary, she became better able to understand him; and whenever he could express what was upsetting him and his need of her, she could respond by being gentler and more affectionate. But, when distress was so great that he had no words for it, she was often unable to understand or to help.

Owen was first seen by the fieldworker the day preceding his separation. Her original notes give a vivid picture of the child at this time, when he was 2 years 2 months old.

He was sitting in his stroller outside the garden gate, waiting for his mother to take him to the shops with her; he looked a sturdy little boy with fair hair and red cheeks. When I approached him he looked at me in a rather solemn, questioning way. I accompanied mother and Owen to the shops and while mother attended to her errands, Owen and I remained outside. He continued to sit uncomplainingly in his stroller. He seemed used to this procedure and only once strained to see his mother. He did not talk to me then, but at the same time did not seem to mind my presence.

It was only later on during that visit, and after he had the opportunity of making contact with me in his own home, that he smiled and laughed with me and could be more at ease.

It was by means of his horse that Owen first established contact with the fieldworker: pushing it gradually toward her and having it returned to him seemed to please him greatly. Then he produced his picture book and was eager to acquaint the fieldworker with the pictures while he made appropriate noises of trains, cars and the like. Next he handed the fieldworker some of his toys, eager for her to share in his play. When a little later his mother suggested he should make a sand castle on the back steps, assuring him that for once she would not mind, he readily trotted off to fetch sand in his bucket. Soon he became absorbed in his play; content in what he was doing, he occasionally looked up at mother and fieldworker as though making sure he was still part of the party. At this point mother commented on Owen's ability to amuse himself, which at this age his sister Sheila had not been able to do.

Later, when mealtime came, Owen was ready for his food and tackled it with real enjoyment; he was a clean and enthusiastic eater. Before climbing into his chair, which he did without aid, his mother had asked him if he wanted to use his potty. Only interested in beginning his meal, he shook his head and paid no heed to her warning that he could not go in the middle of his dinner. He had almost finished his first course when he indicated his need for the potty. Although complying with his request, mother was put out and twice repeated, "You're a naughty boy," but Owen remained unaffected. Back at the table he approached his food once more with relish and enjoyment.

During this first visit, although mother commented on Owen's good points, especially his ability to amuse himself, she dwelt longer on his shortcomings. Half-jokingly, she had called him "a little menace" with "a will of his own," so different from his conforming sister. Although on this occasion the mother reflected that Owen was not a child to be pushed and that he responded better to a less forceful approach, she made it plain that when her authority was put in question she could rarely act accordingly. This she illustrated with the account of an episode, which seems to have been the worst of its kind, when Owen had shown fierce and prolonged resistance. Mother had insisted on removing Owen from his pot even though he had declared that he had not yet finished. Being sure that he had, she was determined not to let him sit on it for ages and took him off. At this Owen went into a severe temper tantrum which lasted for more than two hours. Her comment, "I wondered who would win," explained why she had been unable to help him get over it. Finally she had put him into his room and told him that he could come to her when he had quieted down. When in time he did so, he came out subdued and seeking assurance of her love. She had won this battle, she felt.

This short sequence illustrates the main difficulties mother had with Owen. So unsure was she of her ability to cope with Owen that she could hardly make a concession to him and, instead, usually acted as if he were an opponent who must be kept under control. On no account was he to win. She was highly susceptible to his humors. The more positive Owen was to her, the more positive she felt toward him. But to a childish "Don't like you," she would react as to a rebuff. She tended to assume, baby though he was, that he had the capacity to see things her way and was puzzled and angry that he did not. This lack of differentiation was a barrier to her understanding that he was a child with his own needs and wants.

Yet it could not be said that this was a mother who was unkind in intention or who did not care for her child. She did care, was fond of him and wanted him to be happy. In certain situations she could learn about his needs, as for instance about the pacifier, and gleaned from the fieldworker some understanding of the meaning the impending separation would have for him. By contrast she appeared to have little natural sympathy for his vulnerability or for his inability to comprehend verbal assurance. Thus, as we shall see, during the long time he was in the nursery she never once sent a reminder of herself, although she thought much about him. On the other hand, she requested the fieldworker to convey to him in words that she hoped he might understand the reason for his stay in the nursery. Since it had not been in her experience she was relatively unable to empathize with his probable state, though she did want to ease his experience for him.

To enable the reader to link the above material to the ratings and rankings made for Owen's mother, we give the dimensions and her rank within the sample of ten separated children: *The mother's affection for and pleasure in the company of the child*— (5th); *The mother's ability to set limits consistently*— (9th); *The mother's concern about and sensitivity to her child at the beginning of separation*— (6th); and *The mother's capacity to adapt herself to a disturbed child*— (5th). Ten indicates the most of a quality; thus 10 would indicate the mother with the greatest affection for the child and 1 the least.

E. Owen's Development during His Eighty-One Days of Separation

1. The First Day of Separation. As described in the introduction to this chapter, the account of the child's development during separation and reunion is given in terms of phases, during each of which it was fairly stable. For Owen there are five such phases for the eighty-one days of his separation.

Since after the first day Owen's behavior changed in certain ways, the first day is treated separately. On that day his father took him on the train to the nursery where they arrived in the late afternoon. Unlike some children who are already crying when they arrive, and others who don't cry until engaged in such intimate routines as undressing, Owen began to cry bitterly at the moment of being separated. He clung desperately to his father, refused to walk upstairs to the second floor of the nursery and had to be carried. The nurses reported that after the observer had left, Owen cried bitterly the rest of the afternoon and refused to eat anything. This refusal was in striking contrast to his enthusiastic eating seen at home the day before. Once in bed, he went to sleep, but woke up in the middle of the night and called for "Mummy" and "Daddy."

By morning his continuous crying had stopped. The impression he gave was of a child trying desperately to control himself. His facial expression had tightened and contrasted with the rubbing of his eyes as if about to cry. He carefully watched the adults and children, maintained a distance and frequently looked bewildered by all the people around him.

At certain moments, however, his attempts to keep control of himself failed and he dissolved into tears, refusal or anger. When brought downstairs to the nursery school he began to cry, as if this further move was resented. Once in the nursery school he refused to drink his morning milk and then began to bite a small blue racing car which he had brought from home and had been holding most of the time. But the greatest threat to his control of feelings occurred when for the first time in months Owen wet himself; he was very upset and cried until his trousers were changed.

His relationship to the observers was initially friendly but never physically close; later he actively avoided them. Describing his behavior during the early afternoon of the second day, Wolpert recorded the following:

Most of the time he played with his favorite car. He pushed it down the slide making it crash, pulled it back to the starting place and repeated the sequence again and again. He would make sure I was watching and further involved me by getting me to put the tires back on the car when they had come off.

The theme implicit in this play, making something go away and then retrieving it, was seen in many different forms. For example, he at times completely abandoned the car, cried intensively when he realized it was gone and then desperately searched for it.

That Owen could tolerate only a distant type of friendly relationship to Wolpert is indicated by his reaction to her later that afternoon, when she tried to take him to another room to play with some dolls:

When I suggested he might like to play with dollies, he responded by saying "No, no," and turned his back as if to block me out. He just did not want to see me and I tried then to approach him through his car which he had played with all afternoon, but he just pushed it away and would not touch it at all. When I actually showed him some of the dolls he started crying for his daddy very loudly, turned to me saying "No, no" and again turned his back to avoid seeing me. Paradoxically, as I started to leave a little later, he again cried "No, no" as if he didn't want me to go.

2. *From the Second to the Seventh Day of Separation.* Since further changes had taken place by the second day, the remainder of the week constitutes another phase. Two sorts of behavior distinguished these six days. First, Owen avoided *both* observers; secondly, he no longer wet himself by day as he had on the first day. Most of what had been seen on the first day continued, however, especially fretting for his family. Striking was the intense crying that followed his father's visit on the third day; he screamed until his voice became hoarse. When shortly afterward Wolpert entered the room he stamped his feet in anger and shouted "No, no, no." When very tentatively she approached him, he turned his back and closed his eyes. Clutching his blue car he ran to the door through which his father had left and tried hard to open it with a toy key. But while he frequently avoided the observers, and this was accompanied by much feeling, there were other moments when he would hold up his car obviously wanting them to pay attention to him.

While not actively avoiding the nurses his approaches to them were fleeting. He turned to them at times, for example, to have them notice a toy, but he could never really be comforted by them. He still refused his milk and ate very little but did increasingly conform to the nursery routine.

If the involvement either with the nurses or the children was thus not intense, he did continually suck his little blue car, occasionally hit it and also sucked his finger.

Not unexpectedly, the major theme of the doll-play session given during this week centered on his feeling about the separation. A number of toys were used as "choo-choo's," which seemed a likely reference to the train on which he had come to the nursery. He carefully put the father, mother and boy doll side by side and kept saying "Choo-choo" as he did so. Next he threw them violently across the room.

Another set of play sequences impressed us. The first thing he picked up during the doll play was a high chair which had a pot built into its seat. After examining it he began to spank it very hard and to say what he was doing. Furthermore, he spent much time carefully placing the small white kitchen chairs in the brown wardrobe, and then he emptied them out again while saying "Daddy." Finally, the most severe hostility he expressed was toward the toy toilet. This he tried hard to destroy.

The point of transition to the next period occurred on the seventh day when Owen was visited by Westheimer in the morning and by his father in the afternoon. His reaction to Westheimer during her visits was very similar to that toward the nurses. Although he let her pick him up, he was never really comforted; he neither avoided her nor reacted to her departure.

Two new forms of behavior were seen in the hour after this visit. One was to stare into space; this he had not done earlier although he had shown signs of sadness. The second was a curious ambivalent attitude toward milk. As it was served he ran over to it eagerly, but when offered some he refused it and said "Mee, mo," which sounded like a combination of milk, mummy, and me. It may be relevant that Westheimer had been present during Owen's last day with his mother when she was giving him his food.

3. From the Seventh to the Fifteenth Day of Separation. The affectless staring seen after Westheimer's visit was also seen during and after the visit by his father. The visit itself was not observed by one of the observers, but it was reported by the nurse that Owen did not speak a word throughout. Father was very worried. Owen's reactions after the departure of father, however, were observed. After sobbing quietly for a few moments he stopped and then sat, with his mouth slightly open, staring in a detached way at the children and the nurse.

On the next day Wolpert recorded the following:

For the first time when I arrived this afternoon Owen seemed happy. He came running in, suddenly saw me, smiled at me and was warm in his approach. He then ran out again and rushed up to a nurse cheerfully saying "Hello."

Thus on this occasion parting from father led to little overt fretting, and this change was accompanied by other changes; one was that thenceforward crying for his father was observed very rarely. Another involved the observers. The friendliness with which he greeted Wolpert persisted and was also shown at times toward Observer Heinicke. Yet his main reaction to both observers was still to avoid them.

Owen's ambivalent attitude toward milk seen on the seventh day also continued throughout the second week, and in its balance of approach and avoidance resembled his behavior to the observers. As the nurse began to serve the milk, he would run to her crying "Me, me, me" but then refuse to drink it. His attitude toward food was still one of reluctance, but his desire for candy and sweets had by now become intense. Moreover, in addition to biting and sucking his little blue car, he began to bite the nurses. Just as at times he would completely ignore the overtures of the nurses, so at others would he leave his car lying around; but when another child played with it he became distressed. On these occasions he displayed hostile outbursts toward the child in question which increased in severity as the separation continued. Though still not interacting frequently with the other children during this second week of separation, he showed himself able for the first time to effectively stave off the attacks of another child. Nevertheless, there were times when an outburst of rage toward other children could not be understood as a response to previous interaction.

The first thing Owen did during the second doll-play session, given on the eleventh day of separation, was to examine carefully with his finger the toilet in the baby's high chair. He then indicated that he wanted to leave. It seemed to the observer that Owen was terrified of losing control, and that this was made more difficult by the doll play. In this context it should be noted that throughout these seven days, Owen maintained a high level of sphincter control. Because he never really became absorbed in the doll play, the session was a brief one.

Principal features of the second week are that overt fretting diminished greatly, and that several of Owen's reactions contained elements of both approaching and avoiding his environment. Many of the original features remained, however. Thus, while overt crying for father diminished and finally disappeared, indirect signs of wanting him took its place and were seen throughout the remainder of the separation.

A visit by father on the sixteenth day of separation again seemed to be the factor which initiated the transition to the next phase. Though a tendency to detached staring and a measure of cheerfulness were often present after their first appearance on the seventh day of separation, following this visit their frequency increased, and during the next period both were seen in a new context.

4. From the Sixteenth to the Twenty-Third Day of Separation. During this phase, a number of qualitative changes in Owen's behavior occurred. Many of them could be seen during and after father's visit on the sixteenth day of separation. The minute father arrived, Owen exclaimed, "Out, out," to indicate that he wanted to go into the garden. Once seated on the garden bench he rapidly ate the sweets his father had brought. Further observations were as follows:

Owen looked very detached and did not speak to the father at all; the only word he did say was "chocolates." He still did not look at his father and only stared ahead of himself.

Though at times seemingly cheerful and even smiling, Owen showed no affection to his father. The latter was bewildered by this unexpected behavior, since it was clear that he would gladly have been affectionate to Owen.

During this phase, while Owen's reactions to his father's entrance varied between superficial smiles on two occasions to a complete lack of recognition on another, his reactions to father's departure were uniform and dramatic. On the sixteenth day of separation, when father warned "Daddy must go now," Owen's face suddenly became completely blank and he stared ahead of him. It seemed as if he had not heard. When father repeated, "Daddy must go now," Owen looked for a moment as if he were going to cry, but he stopped himself. His father picked him up and kissed him, but Owen refused to look at him and instead stretched out his hand to the nurse. Father was upset; he kept on saying good-bye to Owen, but Owen still behaved as though he did not hear and never once looked at his father. After father had left, Owen appeared on two occasions almost to cry, but each time he quickly controlled himself. Five minutes afterward he was playing cheerfully. This was the first time he had not cried at all after a visit. Less obvious was the fact that Owen was also occasionally biting his finger.

Some of the reactions now seen for the first time in relation to the observers were similar to those seen during the father's visits, while others differed. Owen's determined effort to make the observers sit by his bedside by shouting "Down" is identical with the way he treated his father. Interest in the material things which the observers brought with them, and which Owen claimed as "mine," was also similar. Other examples of making the observers do what he wanted were combined with insistent efforts to turn the passively experienced separation into an event initiated by him. He uttered a loud and cheerful "Bye-bye" whenever the male observer shifted his position. Also new was the following game: Owen would come up to the observer, smile and then run away laughing; next he would turn around, wait for a sign of recognition, and when he had obtained it run back to the observer, avoiding carefully making any contact; then the sequence would begin all over again.

Dissimilar to his relationship to his father was the combination of affectionate and hostile behavior he directed to the observers. On the seventeenth day Owen responded to being picked up by Heinicke both by putting his arms around him and then playfully, though quite vigorously, hitting him in the face. Especially noteworthy is that he showed no avoidance. When Wolpert entered the nursery on the twenty-first day of his separation, Owen did not back away or turn around as he had done previously but greeted her with a big smile and exclaimed "Daddy."

Earlier it was suggested that the detached staring and the cheerfulness appeared in the context of a new pattern of behavior following the visit of Owen's father on the sixteenth day of separation. The various components of this new pattern can now be described: a lack of affectionate response to the visiting father, signs of hostility to himself, a mixture of hostile and affectionate behavior to the observers, and an increasing determination to have his own way and to control the adults. Other changes were an increasing greed for sweets in all situations and not just during his father's visits, a complete neglect of his toy car from home, an increasing tendency to seek affection from the nurses and the usage of a greater number of different words.

The play seen in the third doll-play session, administered on the twenty-second day of separation, links with the toilet sequences recorded previously and anticipates the reactions seen during the next phase. On this occasion much of his play was with the toilet, the wash basin and the bath. The latter was identified as "bah," and the toilet as "wee-wee." He put the toilet in the bath, shook it and then indicated he wanted to leave by saying "Outa, outa." Next he threw the boy and girl doll across the room in a very violent manner and finally turned to the observer and in a half-crying, anxious tone said "Wee-wee." The minute he was outside, however, this quickly changed to "No wee-wee." Both from this sequence and the total play the observer concluded that Owen was afraid of losing his sphincter control and possibly other controls during the doll-play session. This view is supported by observations in the next phase.

Before describing Owen's later behavior, a brief description of the illnesses which he contracted is given. On the twenty-fourth day Owen had both a sore throat and diarrhea. On the twenty-seventh day his morning temperature rose to 101°, and on the thirty-first day the doctor diagnosed a urinary infection. This was treated, and the temperature and infection subsided, so that by the forty-third day Owen was again up and about. On the thirty-seventh day, however, a slight swelling in his right foot was noticed. After observation and X-ray it was diagnosed as otitis media. Starting on the fiftieth day, therefore, Owen was treated with penicillin injections and kept in bed. This regime lasted until the sixty-seventh day. After this time he was again allowed to move freely. It should be added, however, that during the period of the injections he was in fact very active and either sat up or played around the bed. This contrasts with his behavior during the earlier period of illness (from the twenty-seventh to the forty-third day); during the first four of these days he was apathetic, and only gradually did he become more active.

It is difficult to know whether Owen's illness was a result of physical factors only, in which case ego disorganization merely followed, or whether the illness was itself part of a break in the previous level of control. As regards illness, Owen's development was not unique; all but two of the other children fell ill also, though not so seriously. In evaluating the role of the illness it is important to note that most of the behavior seen after its onset had been present beforehand: a lack of affectionate response to the visiting father, hostile and affectionate behavior to the observers, seeking more affection from the nurses, abandoning his favorite car, greed for sweets and a concern about losing sphincter control ("Wee-wee, no wee-wee").

5. *From the Twenty-Fourth to the Thirty-Seventh Day of Separation.* A principal feature of this phase was that Owen again wet his bed, after having been almost completely dry and clean since the first day of separation. Although it is likely that such lapse in control was a result of the onset of illness, in evaluating this lapse it must be remembered that Owen had wet himself as part of the initial reaction to separation and had been most concerned on that occasion, and also that though he had recovered his control in the subsequent days of separation, he had continued to be concerned about the recurrence of a lapse. This concern was now greatly accentuated. Its connection to the wish to retain the observer can be deduced from the following observations recorded by Wolpert on the twenty-seventh day of separation:

When I said good-bye to him he immediately burst out crying very loudly, shook his hands and shouted "Wee-wee, wee-wee." The nurse in the next room heard his crying, came running in with the pot, and after Owen had urinated into it, returned him to his bed. When I again said "Bye-bye," he cried loudly "No, no. Wee-wee, Nanny, wee-wee," but when the nanny offered him the potty, he said "No, no" and then again changed his mind: "Wee-wee."

One explanation of this behavior is that Owen was attempting to control the departing person. In support of this is the fact that he turned many other passive experiences into active ones: the peek-a-boo game now took on a new twist in that sometimes he hit himself hard as he closed his eyes; he would throw things violently out of bed and then demand they be picked up. But the "Wee-wee, no wee-wee" sequence must also be seen against the increasing lapses of sphincter control, his great concern about them, and the fact that the observers were now greeted by two words said almost simultaneously: "Daddy, wee-wee."

A possible connection between departure ("Bye-bye"), ambivalence to his parents (as seen in relation to observer "Daddy"), concern about sphincter control ("Wee-wee") and hostility to an image of himself could be inferred from observations made on the thirty-first day of separation. After first hitting Observer Heinicke and later being affectionate to him and calling him "Daddy," Owen looked in a mirror and said "Bye-bye" to himself. Soon after he began biting the mirror. A little later when the same observer entered, Owen exclaimed "Bye-bye," and "Wee-wee," became quite affectionate with him and began trying to bite him; he then looked at himself in a mirror and said "Wee-wee, Mummy, Daddy."

The lengths to which his attempts to cope with his concern over loss of sphincter control went could be seen just before a visit by father on the thirty-fifth day. A favorite nurse had awakened him by saying: "Get up. Your daddy is coming"; but all Owen did was to turn over as if he wanted to go to sleep again. When the nurse then picked him up, he cried loudly for his father and whimpered plaintively "Wee-wee, wee-wee." She put him on his pot, but he continued crying "Wee-wee" and then refused to get off it. When the nurse attempted to take him off, he cried "No, no, no" and shook his hands. Eventually she took him off screaming and put him on the bed where he struggled in a resistant temper until he hit his head on the back of the bed. Just before his father arrived, he was still lying on the bed crying "Wee-wee." The struggle over remaining on the pot is reminiscent of similar battles with his mother before separation.

When at last father arrived, Owen sat up and immediately stretched his hands out for chocolates. During the whole visit he was interested only in the chocolate father had brought, and the only words one could discern were "More, more." At one stage father put the chocolate on the bed and picked Owen up to put him on his knee. Owen, however, at once struggled off in order to get back to the chocolate as quickly as possible. Then he waved his hands, smiled at his father and looked exuberantly happy. Suddenly he gave a terrible sigh as if some thought had struck him, and his face became sad. At length father said, "Bye-bye, Owen." Owen looked as if he were completely out of touch with his father, but he did reply "Bye-bye." When father repeated "Bye-bye, Owen," Owen gave no answer and refused to look at him. After father's departure Owen started to look at the book which he had on his bed, pointed at all sorts of pictures and called them "Choo-choo." He kept repeating this and then began to tear the book to pieces.

Some of the behavior characteristic of this period had been noted in the previous one, particularly his lack of affectionate response to his father, his greed for sweets, an absence of fretting during and after the visit, his absent gaze on his father's departure and his determination to have his own way. New in this phase were the temper tantrums when he was not allowed to sit on the pot. Also new were the frequency and severity of the hostile outbursts he directed at things like books and other children.

The frequency with which both hostility and affection were shown toward the observers also increased. On the thirty-sixth day of separation Wolpert recorded the following:

When Owen saw me he smiled and responded affectionately to my greeting. But when I came near him, he suddenly and in an aggressive way pushed his hand in my face, laughed and then pulled my arm toward him and bit my jersey.

The same combination of laughing loudly and being affectionate while at the same time pushing his hand in her face was seen also in his reaction to Westheimer; sometimes he would try to bite her hand or pull a button off her dress. A striking example was the end of Westheimer's visit on the thirty-seventh day of separation. When asked for a kiss, Owen readily complied, and he then gave her a second one which turned into a mild bite. The third time was no longer a kiss but a painful bite. When Westheimer asked him what he was up to, he giggled, laughed and wanted to repeat it. This behavior was to be seen again after reunion.

That ambivalence to the observers was linked to the visits of father is shown by Owen not only greeting each observer with "Daddy" and "Wee-wee" but shouting orders of "Down, down," until the observer sat down in the same chair that his father had sat on. Then the sequence of pushing his hand in the observer's face and simultaneously giving affection characteristically emerged.

While similar signs of ambivalence were not shown toward any one nurse, during this period Owen began to develop an affectionate relationship to Nurse R. and a more provocative one to Nurse S. He often cuddled up closely to Nurse R. and received much bodily comfort from her. While he was inclined to anger Nurse S. by getting out of his bed, he did enjoy being tickled by her. The fact that the first of these nurses was very affectionate with the children, while the second was more inclined to restrict them, no doubt contributed to this behavior. Nevertheless, it seems likely that Owen's open expression of both hostility and affection to the observers has much in common with the way he developed an affectionate relationship with one nurse and a provocative one with the other.

6. From the Thirty-Eighth to the Eighty-First Day of Separation. In most respects Owen's mode of adjusting to the separation during this phase continued along the lines described for the previous one. Certain reactions could be seen even more clearly and only a few were altogether new. Owen's greed became even more pronounced. As he sought second helpings, "More, more" became his standard cry; as a result he gained a great deal of weight. Wetting his bed continued and he soiled occasionally; sometimes he seemed very much concerned but at others not to care. Throughout this period he continued to call out "Wee-wee" and to sit endlessly on the pot. His speech was now often distorted. Although he used an increasing number of words, all observers agreed that many of them, for example, "Weedit," were not easy to comprehend. It must not be forgotten, of course, that during the first four of these final six weeks of his separation, Owen was ill. During the last two he was recovered and was up and about.

Nothing impressed the observers more than the increasingly possessive way Owen approached everything. Where possessions were concerned, his frustration tolerance was low and his hostility to other children easily aroused. For example, on one occasion another child happened to pick up a plastic ring with which Owen had been playing. Immediately he screamed "Mine, mine" and attacked the child violently. When this failed he cried desperately: "Mine, mine, my daddy, mine, mine, my daddy."

Similarly, although Owen greeted his father with a cheerful "Daddy," the main interest was always in the material goods and especially the sweets he brought. This greed had been observed before, but his complete failure to recognize his father had not. On the sixty-second day of separation Owen was looking out of the window of the nursery as his father came up the street. Although as a rule he took great interest in the cars and people in the street, when his father came into view, he stared vacantly and seemed not to notice father's wave. When father entered Owen's room, however, he was immediately greeted by "Chocolates, chocolates," and the rest of the time Owen spent stretching for and stuffing down the chocolates his father had brought. On this occasion Owen for the first time called his father "Nanny," though father remonstrated: "I'm your father, not your nanny." When father left, Owen did not cry but turned instead to play with Wolpert's keys to the accompaniment of "Mine, mine."

The above sequence illustrates a possible meaning of Owen's increasing attempt to obtain and play with various of the observer's possessions. Just as the interest in chocolate increasingly replaces the affectionate relation to his father, so the interest shifts to the observer's material goods when the bringer of chocolates is not there or has just left. A similar sequence had occurred on the forty-first day of separation. Soon after his father had left, Owen banged the observer's writing pad and shouted "Mine, mine." He tried to take possession of the whole pad; when given a sheet, he looked at it, said "Wee," and once more banged the observer's pad, exclaiming "Mine," and later "Daddy, weedit, weedit." He was smiling the whole time. When the observer said she must go, he expostulated "No, no," pulled her back and pointed to the chair on which she must sit. Once more he began to pound her writing pad. While his possessiveness and his related attempts to control the observers were thus prominent, the observers continued to be objects of affection and hostility at the same time. If anything, the intensity of the ambivalent behavior became more marked.

Many of Owen's reactions to Westheimer were similar to those to the other two observers. The following observation made during a visit on the fifty-sixth day of separation illustrates Owen's continuing ambivalence to her. At first he was very subdued and passive, but he livened up as he sent a toy engine which his father had brought him toward Westheimer, expecting her to send it back. Gradually, as he first looked into her face and then pushed his hand into it, he began to make more contact. He also took the engine and knocked the observer's knuckles with it. When these games were ended, he wanted to be picked up by her and permitted her to put him down only when he saw another child doing "Wee-wee"; he wanted to do "Wee-wee" too. Signs of possessiveness were also seen as he first greeted her with "Sweety" and "Daddy" and later demanded her "bag." On being given it, he became especially intrigued by the mirror and kept saying "See, see." When Westheimer took it away from him (because of a sharp edge), he became short-tempered.

What impressed Westheimer as being different from previous visits, however, though less evident in relation to the other observers, was Owen's passivity and subdued behavior. Sometimes it appeared as though he did not notice her, though he never actively avoided her; at others he bade her "good-bye" in an unconcerned way. What struck her most was how passive he was while she held him.

Trends seen previously in Owen's relation to the nurses were crystallized even further. By contrast to the lack of affectionate response to his father, he sought more and more affection from the nurses. Of these, his contacts with Nurse R., his favorite "nanny," were the closest. He sought her out and very much enjoyed being held by her. By defiantly getting out of bed, Owen also continued to provoke Nurse S. to chase and tickle him.

Throughout the final six weeks of his stay in the nursery, Owen mentioned his mother only rarely. Every now and then, however, he would voice a quiet "Mummy." The context in which this occurred is seen most clearly before a doll-play session on the forty-third day of separation. On this occasion Owen greeted Wolpert in a very affectionate manner, wanted her keys and sought her attention with "Nanny, nanny." Then he heard a voice down the corridor; he at once turned to Wolpert and exclaimed "Mummy," as though he thought his mother had come at last. When Wolpert suggested that they go to see the dollies she was met with an emphatic "No," which later turned into "Yes."

Once in the playroom Owen immediately became absorbed in the play. He picked up the father doll, said "Dat" and took a drawer out of the dresser and put the mother doll in its place. He then handled the drawer, called it "Dollie," took the mother doll out of the dresser and threw it away in a mildly hostile manner, and again referred to the drawer as "Dollie." He then took the boy doll and put it in the small wardrobe and said "Up, down"; next he closed the small wardrobe and muttered "Baba, babas, babas."

The next sequence was to put the boy doll in the large wardrobe with a "Bye-bye" and to open it again with "Out, dollie, out baby, baby te, baby te." (The observation of many such sequences in Owen and other children suggests that he may have been concerned with the possibility of his mother's having a "baba," that this accounted for the separation, and that in his play he was trying to achieve some control over these events.)

Shortly after that he suddenly cried "Wee-wee, wee-wee," but as it turned out, he had already done a bowel movement. Although not greatly upset by this, his feelings about it were shown in the way he took the toy toilet and spanked the mother doll with it while repeating "Mack, mack."

On this occasion Owen was most reluctant to stop playing. After thirty-four minutes Wolpert suggested that they put the dollies away, but this was met by an emphatic "No." Continuing to play, he picked up the high chair, put his finger in the toilet inside it, shook it and said "Weedit, weedit." Then, as Wolpert started putting the toys in the box, he took the mother doll and tried vigorously to bite off her legs. This was interspersed with loud cries of "Mine, mine" and hitting Wolpert over the head with the mother doll. It was clear that he was both anxious and angry that she was leaving and taking the dolls with her.

Before describing Owen's behavior during and after reunion with his parents, the results of an analysis of his coded behavior during separation are presented and some of the ways his mother changed during it described.

7. *Owen's Behavior as Reflected in the Categorizations Made in the Everyday Nursery Setting.* In Table 16 we present the percentage of total behavioral units scored for Owen in a number of categories. They are given mainly as examples of the type of data used to supplement those derived from our systematic analyses of the clinical descriptions. To facilitate comparison with the qualitative description, we group together for each of the five phases of his separation the data obtained during that phase.

Table 16. *Showing Certain Trends in Categorized Behavior for Owen during the Five Phases of His Separation*

Categories	Days				
	1–7	8–14	15–23	24–37	38–81
Regain Cry Father & Mother*	10.03	.00	1.80	.30	.04
Regain Noncry Father & Mother**	.53	.35	.45	3.24	3.88
Seeks Attention and Affection, and Gives Attention and Affection to Observers	9.48	10.27	15.78	24.09	25.24
Hostility (mild and severe) to Observers	.89	.53	2.03	13.98	9.98
Total Mild Hostility	8.97	6.73	4.06	18.54	13.52
Total Severe Hostility	.71	2.48	.00	5.67	5.64
Seeks Attention and Affection, and Gives Attention and Affection to the Nurses	4.12	8.68	6.09	4.66	6.12
Sucks (all objects)	3.04	2.65	4.51	2.63	3.32

* The crying form of fretting for mother and father
** The noncrying form of fretting for mother and father

In some cases comparison is not possible. Where it is, observations recorded by free description are found to be well supported by the more detailed ones shown in the table. Thus, the high figure during the first week, 10.0 per cent, for Regain Cry Father and Mother (attempting to get the mother and father back by crying for them) confirms this as the period characterized by the crying form of fretting. Subsequently, as the next line of the table indicates, the noncrying form of fretting increases.

The next sections of Table 16 also support a conclusion reached on the basis of general observation: there is an increase of ambivalence, especially the hostile component, shown toward the observers. Strong positive exchanges, categorized as seeking and giving affection and attention, increase, and at the same time hostility toward the observers also increases sharply. Although the categorized observations indicate that signs of ambivalence are present from the beginning, it is not until the third and fourth phase that they become prominent.

The findings for the totals both of mild and of severe forms of hostility parallel the trends for the expression of ambivalence. This is not surprising, since the totals include hostility toward the observers; nevertheless it indicates that the increase in hostility was not confined to the observers, but was a general phenomenon.

The trend of Owen's behavior toward the nurses is difficult to interpret. The obvious conclusion that there was not much change contradicts the finding, reported previously, that Owen became increasingly involved with two of the nurses. One explanation is, since these changes refer to a quality of the relationship, that they are not reflected in gross quantitative changes in the behavior categorized. This conclusion is consistent with reservations about the specificity of the succorance categories expressed in Chapter 2. What is evident, when looked at purely quantitatively, is that during the course of his time in the nursery Owen did not turn more to the nurses; they did not become central figures in Owen's life.

The category reflecting Owen's sucking shows that this also changed little. Other categorizations are available but add little to the results already presented.

F. Changes in Mother's Concern and Sensitivity to Owen's Welfare during Separation

So far only changes occurring in Owen during the separation have been described. To fully understand the nature of the interaction of mother and child when reunited, those observed in his mother must be added. A main finding was that by the end of the separation mother was openly expressing her ambivalent feelings about her son, especially about having him home.

Mother's admission to the hospital had been necessitated by her back ailment but, despite the discomforts of treatment, the hospital proved not too great a hardship for her. Going into the hospital meant going into care, giving herself up to the ministrations of others. The necessity for treatment provided good reason for leaving her family duties to others. In the hospital she was, characteristically, a popular patient—friendly, helpful and outgoing—a patient who almost merged with the staff and who, when up, had easy access to the Sister's office.

The more her own needs were gratified by the concern and attention of the staff the more was she able to think of Owen. She sought to ensure that the separation would be as easy for him as her understanding could contrive. Thus she sent his pacifier with him and asked the fieldworker to inform the nursery staff of details of the limited vocabulary with which he made known his needs. She also asked the fieldworker to explain to Owen in words he could understand what the reason for his stay in the nursery was, namely his mother's illness. Although during the eighty-one days of his absence she did not send him a card or other memento of herself, she was eager and interested to have anecdotes about him from the field-worker.

When she was discharged from the hospital after five weeks and two days, it was because the doctors could suggest no further treatment. Not unnaturally this depressed her with thoughts of continuing incapacity and a fear of becoming increasingly disabled. But it also meant the end of a period of being cosseted and cared for and a return to the problems of being wife and mother. Thrown back upon herself, her concern and sympathy for Owen diminished and for a period she became preoccupied with her own ill health.

The fact that Owen still had to have some medical attention for his otitis media (which the doctor stated could well be done at home) seemed to daunt his mother and to increase her ambivalence about his return. Eventually she decided to delay his homecoming and she found a number of reasons for her decision. To the field-worker it seemed that the reality of the mother's physical disability, coupled with her difficulty in dealing with her feelings of inadequacy and helplessness, heightened by the period of separation during which trained, competent people had taken over the care of her boy, had together made her hesitant to resume her functions as a mother. She seemed afraid to face this strange boy, whom she felt she no longer knew nor understood and with whom she had lost touch.

It may well be that this mother was not unwilling to let others take care of her children, as her mother had done before her. The fact remains, however, that prior to her own hospitalization, and despite some physical disability, she had herself undertaken the sole care of Owen. But now, giving as her reasons her own as well as Owen's illness, she prolonged his stay in the residential nursery and, soon after the reunion, placed him in a day nursery.[2]

G. *Owen's Behavior and Family Relationships during the Reunion Period*

It had been arranged that father would collect Owen at the nursery, and that Westheimer would drive them home, where mother

[2] Within the sample of ten residential children, Owen's mother was given a rank of 8 on the dimension: *The change in the mother's concern about and sensitivity to the welfare of her child,* indicating a relatively large change.

would be waiting. The fieldworker recorded the sequence of events thus:

Owen was still asleep, and the nurse had to rouse him. He sobbed bitterly, could not be comforted even by his favorite nurse, but did cling to her. The crying continued for fifteen minutes. He allowed himself to be dressed without protest and seemed generally docile and submissive. There was a look of sadness about him, and though encouraged, he would not smile. When his nurse left the room briefly, Owen's lips began to quiver, but she returned before he burst into tears—and when he held out his arms she picked him up. When told that Daddy was downstairs waiting to take him home to Mummy, Owen showed no reaction; he continued to look sad. But when I tried to help him carry his belongings, he clung to his bag, shouting "Mine."

He did not respond to his father's greeting, but remained on his nurse's arm still holding the bag with his belongings. He did not move away from his father, nor did he move toward him. But after a little while, when father gently asked, "Do you want to go to Daddy?" he responded with a quiet "Ummm" (Yes). He allowed father to hold him but renewed his insistence on clinging to the bag with his belongings. Keeping hold of his personal belongings was the only active interest he showed during the process of discharge and reunion. He left his favorite nurse with no more than a look.

During the long hour-and-a-half ride from the nursery to his home, Owen was at first very quiet and subdued and simply sat on his father's lap. Father's arms were comfortably around him. After a quarter of an hour during which Owen had been quite still and silent, he showed a faint interest in a "horsey," but not until forty minutes had gone by did he become enthusiastic and begin to name the things we were passing.

Father gave him some chocolate, which Owen promptly stuffed into his mouth. Later father said, "Let me wipe your mouth. Mummy won't like you with a chocolatey mouth."

Toward the end of the journey Owen became more lively and more vocal. He wanted the car window down and took a real interest in what we were passing. When I spoke to him he responded, but otherwise paid no attention to me. Once father said, "We are going home to Mummy now," but Owen behaved as though he had not heard. On passing the familiar railway station, father reminded him how they had looked together at the trains. Owen remembered and responded with enthusiastic nodding, saying "Ummm" (Yes).

When we reached home, mother was standing at a window. Owen did not want to leave the car, and as father lifted him out, he looked bewildered and puzzled. He indicated by an arm gesture that he wanted his father to carry him and, for the third time that day, clutched the bag with his possessions. Thus he returned home eleven-and-a-half weeks after leaving it.

He did not appear to hear his mother's "Hello, Owen" and remained passively on his father's arm—his face dull and expressionless. His mother seemed overwhelmed by his frozen state and said, "He does not seem to recognize this place"—and a moment later, "I have never in all my life seen a child more expressionless than him."

It seemed indeed that all animation had gone out of Owen as he sat motionless on his father's knee, numb and silent. Mother handed him a new toy car and he took it passively—then ignored it. He accepted a biscuit from her and nibbled at it in an uninterested way. Then, after fifteen minutes of similar behavior, mother left the room to make some tea. Only when father tried to place Owen on a chair, did he react in any apparent way—by mildly demonstrating that he wished to be near his father. But without further protest he allowed himself to be placed on the chair, and sat there quite still and expressionless—not even responding when father moved closer and talked to him.

Owen's sister, Sheila, who had been kept out of the way for twenty minutes or so to give him time to readjust, now rushed into the room full of happy anticipation. She called "Hello, Owen" and went to him. But Owen, who had till then been completely still in his chair, turned his head away from her. Passively he accepted her present of a toy bus. Sheila looked unhappy and bewildered. In a puzzled way she reiterated, "It's not Owen's face. It's a different face."

Father, who was the only person to whom Owen had as yet shown any positive response, left the room for a moment, and it seemed that Owen might begin to cry. But father returned almost instantly, saw the quivering lip and bending over Owen said, "Daddy is not going away from you." Owen remained motionless and silent.

After fifty minutes had passed there came the first flicker of animation. Mother produced a book that had been a favorite before separation, and he glanced at it as if with some recognition and mild interest. Following his handling of an old toy car, he brought all his toys and possessions on to his lap and exclaimed "All mine!" When one of them fell to the ground, he called "Mine" and waited for someone to pick it up and return it to him. For the first time he seemed to see the new train that his father had bought for him, and a moment later asked for orange juice, which he drank greedily. He then allowed father to take him to the lavatory.

On re-entering the room he remained standing and gazed at the shiny new train. When a toy car fell to the ground, I said "plonk," just as I had frequently said in the nursery, and Owen looked relieved and threw it down again. At the second "plonk" he laughed his first laugh. More laughs followed further "plonks." At this moment mother verbalized her mixed feelings by saying to him, "Mummy won't be able to pick things up for you like

Miss Westheimer." Ostensibly she referred to her back being in plaster, but the undertone seemed to be the familiar sense of inadequacy.

When some time later father invited him to go to the shops, Owen allowed his mother to put on his suit. He insisted on being carried by father and also on taking an armful of possessions—an old duck and an old car, and the new car mother had given him, as well as a new "bus" that had been Sheila's present. Holding on to his possessions, and in turn being held by father, seemed for the moment to be what Owen wanted and needed.

That evening when put to bed, father had to sit with him for thirty minutes before he fell asleep. At this early stage of reunion, father's was the most reassuring presence.

1. The First Week after Reunion. Throughout the first week after reunion Owen was much more ready to turn to his father for comfort than to his mother; in fact, for the first two days he more or less ignored her.

Owen bumped his knee and seemed about to cry. Mother offered "Hurty, hurty, let Mummy rub it better." But Owen passed her by and went to father for comforting.

This rebuff was unpleasant for mother, since before the separation he had always gone to her for comfort. But, although on the first day home Owen needed his father all the time, by the end of the second day this was lessening, and he made small spontaneous approaches to his mother. He would take a book to her and point to the pictures, would show her a toy or throw his ball to her. But it was only on the fourth day after reunion that he could again allow her to comfort him. He once more walked freely around his home, his bearing strikingly different from what it had been on the day of reunion.

Mother was making a special effort at this time to reach out to Owen with deliberate attempts to meet his needs and to allow him more freedom than formerly. To some extent she succeeded; possibly her contact with the fieldworker had helped toward some modification of her attitude. For the first few days, however, the fact that her back was still in a plaster cast limited such spontaneous behavior as she was capable of. She could not bend, not even to pick up a ball or to get a toy from behind a settee. This she found very frustrating. "I can't play with him," she said. "I can only look at him." For Owen it must also have been frustrating to have a mother who could not respond actively at a time when each was trying to revive the relationship. After five days the plaster cast was exchanged for a belt, and although still handicapped by her physical state, her movements were less restrained.

As part of her attempt to re-establish rapport with Owen, his mother in these first days after reunion not only permitted a ball game in the living room (formerly forbidden) but also joined in the game as well as her plaster cast allowed. Each time that Owen preferred her to father, she noted it with pleasure and reassurance. Because mother was fearful of being left alone with Owen, father had arranged to have five days off from work. Thus, with both parents present, Owen had a choice of whom to approach; as the week went on there were more and more instances when he turned to his mother. By the fourth day mother felt that Owen was becoming more used to her; he had twice asked her to wind up his train engine in preference to father and once had insisted that she take him to the pot. There were, however, other occasions (noted for the first time on the fourth day) when, in the very act of turning toward his mother, Owen turned away from her and instead suddenly seized on a toy he could pick up. This illustrates Owen's conflicting wishes at that time, both wanting to come closer to his mother yet also retreating from her. Mother invariably noticed when he turned away but often missed it when he turned toward her.

Never a patient woman, and always used to being listened to and obeyed, mother had difficulty in dealing with Owen when he disregarded her statements. For example, on the fourth day after reunion, Owen was playing with his train set. When he began to take the clips off the railway lines, his mother told him not to do so as the rails would come apart. Owen looked defiantly at her, replied "Yes" and continued his activity as though she had never spoken at all. Mother was discouraged and irritated and, not knowing what to do next, called him a "little devil" with a "will of his own." During these days mother was quick to feel rebuffed by him and so was apt to react in a negative way, though sometimes she managed to control her response. An example of this occurred that afternoon when Owen handed his engine to Westheimer to have it wound up. When she suggested she should hand it to mummy who would know better how to do it, Owen replied with a mild "No" but made no real protest. Nevertheless, mother was hurt and immediately handed the engine back to him with the curt comment, "Wind it up yourself then." Almost at once, however, she regretted her action, took the engine and wound it up for him.

Mother had always been uncertain of her ability to handle Owen, and the long separation, coupled with his increased negativism, heightened her uncertainty. While she had always felt herself lacking as a mother and had commented on her lack of maternal feeling, there were areas nevertheless in which she had felt competent. She had had no doubts, for instance, about feeding Owen; the child had rewarded her by being a good eater and by enjoying his meals. But on his return from the residential nursery he no longer enjoyed his food. Instead he was cautious, and whereas he had formerly accepted his mother's offerings with relish, he was now hesitant and finicky. Sometimes he refused the main course and ate only the dessert.

Owen's hesitation and lack of pleasure in what she offered him made mother feel helpless, despondent and incompetent in an area where she had formerly had no difficulty. Eager to re-establish a relationship and ready to make allowances for his unsettled state following the separation, she nevertheless found herself at times irritated over his food fads. Readily rebuffed by his refusals, she was quick to feel useless.

It was helpful to mother to be shown by Westheimer that Owen's negative behavior was not always directed toward her but also occurred with other members of the family. A discussion they had of behavior common in children of his age and the effects of separation enabled mother to regard his opposition less as a personal attack and to be more tolerant. As Owen showed increasing need for his mother and a growing wish to include her in his activities, she modified her treatment of him. But there were still occasions when her need to be in control—tested further by episodes of negativistic behavior reactive to separation—came uppermost. This was less marked during the first week after reunion, however, than it became during the following period.

Owen's most severe temper tantrum during this week occurred in the evening of the third day and followed the first bath he had had after his return home. He had apparently enjoyed his bath, but when taken out of it, he began to cry and scream, and refused to have his pajamas put on. This "hysterical" behavior was ended neither by cosseting nor smacking, and finally the child fell asleep in his father's arms, exhausted by his upset. He had a disturbed night. Only belatedly was it discovered that his frantic cries had been for his favorite duck.

There were other consequences of the separation to be noted. For example, when out of doors he looked uncertain and insisted on being carried by his father. Similarly, he became uneasy when on the weekends his mother suggested he accompany her to the shops.

2. *From the Second to the Eighth Week after Reunion.* Father had taken five days off from work in order to help mother, but on the sixth day he had to return to work, and in accordance with a plan devised earlier, Owen began then to attend all day at a day nursery.

On his first attendance both parents took Owen to the day nursery. Mother did not want to be the one to leave him there. When father left to go to work, Owen showed no concern. Shortly afterward mother slipped away unnoticed. The nursery staff reported later that when he discovered she had gone, he sobbed hard for two hours and cried, "Mummy, Daddy, Daddy, Mummy." That evening mother came late to collect him, and all the other children had already gone. She found him looking sad and subdued. Concerned that he should have been so upset, she spoke of keeping him at home if it continued. Nevertheless, the possibility that her lateness was due to ambivalence cannot be ruled out.

From the moment he had returned home from the residential nursery, Owen had used his pot proficiently. On his first day in the day nursery, however, he refused to go to the lavatory. He did not wet himself but instead held himself in all day, and on coming home he announced an urgent "Wee-wee" and nearly filled the pot. Likewise, he refused food and drink at the nursery but ate well on return home. Then after lying quietly in bed for an hour, he called tearfully for his father, who sat with him for twenty minutes until he fell asleep.

Next morning both parents again took him to the day nursery, and when father left, Owen clung to his mother. When she left too, he cried, but for a short time only—at least, so the staff said when he was collected that evening. Thereafter there were indications day by day that he was unhappy to be left in the nursery, but his protests apparently were always muted.

On the twelfth day of reunion, father took him while mother

stayed at home. Although he cried when left, the staff considered that this was the first day on which he had "settled down." He did not cry again during that day, and he ate both dinner and tea. After six weeks he was still saying hopefully at breakfast each morning, "No nursery, Daddy. No nursery," but he complied when told to put his coat on and he no longer cried when left there.

The fact that Owen was placed so soon in a day nursery complicates the interpretation of the likely effects of the long separation he had experienced. It is made even more difficult by lack of first-hand observations of Owen's behavior in the day nursery. Yet, because he best illustrates the sequence of readjustment which was seen in all four of the children who were separated for a long time, including the three who were not placed in a day nursery, we have used his case in this chapter instead of that of one of the other children.

Thus, as in the case of the other children, during the period under discussion, Owen and his mother tried hard to re-establish their relationship. The process was complicated not only by Owen's heightened ambivalence but also by his mother's physical weakness and doubts about her worth as a mother. But it was clear, despite her difficulties in empathizing with her son, that she was eager to understand and do what was best for him.

By the eleventh day it was noticeable that the word "Mummy" had again acquired meaning for Owen. He used it often, as if savoring something that had been lost and found again. He would identify objects as "My mummy's" and, pointing at his mother, would explain to the fieldworker "My mummy"; at times he would be heard murmuring to himself over and over again, "My mummy, my mummy, my mummy." He gradually began to include her in his experiences by pointing things out to her, "Look, Mummy!" and to turn to her for comfort, where formerly he had preferred the nearness of his father. Occasionally he insisted that she and not father should dress him. By the thirtieth day he wanted her to kiss his arm better after he had hurt it, and he kissed her good-bye when asked. On the thirty-seventh day he spontaneously kissed her before leaving the house with his father.

By the forty-fourth day Westheimer observed that Owen several times left off play and moved over to lean on his mother for a moment before resuming his play. At times he would kiss her spontaneously or at her request. The relationship between them once again contained many positive features; there were numerous instances illustrating ease and trust between mother and child—an immense contrast to the emotional barrier seen during the early days after reunion.

With the strong attachment that Owen showed to his mother there were also strong negative feelings. He would be extremely obstinate, his immediate reaction to almost any suggestion or statement being an uncompromising "No." Any mother would have found discouraging and trying the sheer number of his refusals and the frequency of his opposition. This mother, who found it difficult to deal with situations when her authority was put into question, was made to feel particularly helpless by such behavior; but she made great efforts to meet Owen's needs and to tolerate his provocation. Sometimes she succeeded, sometimes not. Sometimes she managed to resolve a tussle without recourse to her "need to win."

For instance, on the eleventh day she told Owen to "sit up straight at table," and he responded with a very definite "No." Mother, after some hesitation, diverted what could have turned into a battle into a compromise by saying, "Have you finished, Owen? Do you want to come down?" Owen *had* finished and the compromise offer suited him as well as it did mother.

Owen's mother recognized that since his separation he was more "touchy." Whereas he could formerly be told not to be silly and would take her rebuke in his stride, a sharp word would now make his lip tremble. Although she tried to handle him more carefully than before, she did not always succeed and sometimes her irritation against him became displaced on to an innocent victim—his sister, Sheila.

During this period Owen was eager to assert his independence; he wanted to do things for himself and in his own way. When mother wanted to demonstrate to Westheimer Owen's new spinning top, he would not allow her to do so; even when he found that he could not work it himself, he insisted, "No, I do it, I do it!"

When he needed his mother's help over getting dressed, he stipulated in what order this had to be done. For example, he would not permit his mother to put on his trousers until she had first taken off his shoes: he could not be persuaded that this was unnecessary. Lengthy explanations had to be given before he would acknowledge that his right arm belonged to the right sleeve and not to the left. These incidents sorely tried mother's patience.

On the forty-fourth day after reunion, Owen chalked on the dining table. On noticing this mother shouted "Owen" and startled him. On this occasion he did not cry but withdrew farther into the corner. Looking sullen and determined, he again used the chalk to draw pictures on the dining table. Mother seemed defeated by this open defiance but with Westheimer's support dealt with the situation by giving Owen his blackboard on which he then proceeded to draw.

Owen continued to need someone to stay with him until he fell asleep; otherwise he would cry until someone came. He also continued to show little interest in food. He used his pot regularly during the day and was mostly dry at night; this pleased his mother, especially as she did not lift him in the night for fear that he would not go off to sleep again.

By the end of the eight-week period Owen was demanding more and more from his mother, and she was beginning to understand something of the stress that the long separation and daily absence in the day nursery meant for him. Although at times she had difficulty in keeping her patience with him, at other times she could be sympathetic to his moods as is shown on the fifty-first day after reunion:

Returning from his walk Owen seemed subdued and unhappy. To her question, "What's the matter, Owen?", the boy responded by turning off the television set and turning it on again a moment later himself. As if appreciative of his mother's understanding, Owen moved closer to her and asked for her help in breaking up his chocolate. When he had spontaneously offered a piece to his mother and also to his father, he seated himself between both parents on the settee, looking relaxed and at ease.

The relationship between Owen and his father was an affectionate one. Throughout the reunion period father showed great understanding of Owen's needs and his sensitive approach was of great help, especially during the critical first stage of readjustment. In many situations father was the more understanding and patient parent. For instance, he could explain calmly that the railway lines would come apart if Owen removed the hinges; and to this the child could listen, though he had refused to do so when his mother had given the same warning earlier.

During his first weeks back Owen was restless whenever father was not at home, but as he began to make tentative approaches to his mother and found them rewarded, the special clinging and dependency on his father lessened. The two still spent a great deal of time together. At weekends father took Owen for walks, and it was he who put him to bed each night—patient and sensitive to his moods. When at home he would play with him and gave the impression of enjoying the company of his small son.

Yet there was a paradox in the situation deriving from the mother's more dominant role in the family. When Owen was particularly obstreperous, and mother, lapsing in her attempts to be forbearing, wanted father to punish him, father would obediently spank his son; he knew, it seemed, of no other way to deal with the highly charged situation.

3. *From the Ninth to the Seventeenth Week after Reunion.* During the ninth week the fieldworker noted:

I found myself thinking that this mother and child had moved more closely together than I would have thought possible earlier.

Owen went over to his mother, and she seemed pleased to see him again; kissing him, she helped him off with his coat. He seated himself next to her to watch television. She had an arm around him, and from time to time she would kiss him unobtrusively. Owen had a very contented expression on his face, and for once these two looked as if they belonged together.

This observation illustrates the new and affectionate relationship typical of the phase. Whenever Owen came home he turned to his mother for attention with a readiness that was absent in the early days of reunion. She willingly did things for him and no longer left father to attend to him. She followed her child's lead; the more affectionate he became, the more she could respond by mothering him.

As Owen's manifest attachment to his mother increased, so too did his ambivalence. A new feature appeared during the ninth week after reunion, when Owen for the first time attempted to bite and hit his mother. For example:

When sitting on his mother's lap, he made as though to bite her hand, but was told by her, "You are not to bite, Owen." A little later Owen said "Bite" and almost immediately tried to bite off the buttons on his mother's cardigan. After a third attempt mother was able to divert his attention.

Since mother could now be more tolerant of verbal expressions of resentment, Owen could also express more freely what he felt.

While earlier in the reunion mother had felt rebuffed by a complaining word from her 2-year-old, she could now deal with a verbal rejection from him and was no longer upset by his pronouncement "Go away." Indeed she related with some amusement how he had shouted this at her when she was telling him off mildly for upsetting the sugar.

A further illustration of Owen's ability to express his feelings toward his mother, which also shows how they fluctuated during a brief span of time, was given during the tenth week of reunion. The fieldworker recorded:

Owen was not feeling well. He called for his mother in a tearful voice, and she attended to him. She mused, "What's the matter, Owen, you usually don't cry for nothing?" Although his father was in the room, Owen followed his mother into the hall and asked her, "Wrap the blanket round me." She tucked the blanket round him, and Owen cuddled up to her, periodically putting his arms round her neck and closing his eyes somewhat sleepily. When asked "Is this what you want?" he replied drowsily, "Shesh." He declined to play but recovered a little when he remembered "Chocolate in Daddy's pocket." He would not permit mother to unwrap it for him but asserted, "No, I wrap it." After giving everyone a piece of his chocolate, he ate some himself. From time to time he placed his head on his mother's chest and cuddled up close to her. But when mother teasingly imitated the noises he was making with his tongue, he hit her and said, "Stop it." Mother gently said, "No, Owen, no," yet once again he hit her and then seemed content. By the time I had to leave, he seemed pretty well asleep.

Mother's ability to deal with Owen had improved, but there were occasions when she was lacking in empathy and her handling of him was motivated by her need to "win." Sometimes her understanding and her own ambivalence were in conflict. Thus when he had a severe cold, Owen had cried until he was taken into his mother's bed. "He clung as if he thought he had got me now and would never let me go," she said. Although she understood that being unwell had heightened both his need of her and his fear of losing her, she resented the loss of sleep caused by his restlessness, remarking, "I haven't enough maternal instinct in me to like children in bed." For three nights she had nevertheless taken him into her bed but the following night had prevented it by going to his bedside and talking to him and staying with him until he fell asleep in his own bed. When Owen woke in the morning, he cried furiously, "Not in Mummy's bed. Not in Mummy's bed." On the fifth night he did not waken and instead slept throughout the night.

Mother's "need to win" was apt to appear in the evening when she was tired and her tolerance lowered; she was then eager to get him off to bed and have some time for herself while Owen, himself tired and irritable, was equally determined to prolong his staying up. Thus, although their relationship had improved in many ways, her "need to win" would still occasionally lead mother to handle the child severely:

Mother related that one evening when Owen seemed very tired, he nevertheless refused to go to bed. Mother allowed him to stay up till his father returned, but even then he resisted his parents' efforts to get him ready for bed and screamed loudly. Mother attempted to deal with Owen herself and finally spanked him when he apparently bit her wrist. Father then took over, but Owen screamed more loudly as father spanked his "bare bottom." Both parents felt pretty helpless, and it was then mother remembered something she had read about the calming effect of cold baths. She soaked a cloth in cold water and held it to Owen's face. On the second application he stopped screaming and after a moment, still sobbing, came to her saying, "Mummy, love me." He then allowed his mother to undress him and ten minutes later was fast asleep.

Between the eleventh and fourteenth weeks Owen had many severe temper tantrums; then their frequency diminished, and after the seventeenth week they were reported to be of rare occurrence.

As Owen became less provocative and mother less insistent on having her way, clashes between them became rarer. To illustrate:

During the thirteenth visit Owen asked for his pot and was encouraged by his mother to fetch it himself. This he did. But when mother wanted to unfasten his trousers, he resisted and moved away. She did not pursue him as she might have done at one time and was ready to carry out this task some five minutes later, when Owen declared his readiness to perform and then did so. There were many illustrations of this nature.

The relationship between Owen and his father remained a warm and affectionate one, with the special dependency slowly decreasing as he grew more confident and secure with his mother.

Owen continued to use his pot and no longer wet the bed. His appetite too was much improved, although still subject to faddy episodes which mother linked with the separation experience. He usually needed his mother to stay with him till he fell asleep. At times he would play "being in the tunnel" by sliding under the bedclothes and reappearing. At other times he insisted that she hold his hand. Mother was ambivalent about this need of her—on the one hand grateful that she was now preferred but on the other irritated to find that there was little of the evening left by the time Owen was asleep. She could only just accept that Owen needed to keep her with him until the last moment each day as a reassurance against all that he had experienced during the separation and against the daily stress of the day nursery.

Thus, toward the end of the period of systematic coverage called for by the research design, the relationship between child and mother had improved and deepened. Mother, though still ambivalent and erratic on occasions, was more adequate than could have been anticipated; and Owen, although still showing some signs of unresolved conflict, could openly express his affection for his mother. This is perhaps best represented by a direct quotation from the fieldworker's current record:

During the fifteenth week after reunion mother had just been complaining about a series of tantrums which had made her so "fed up" that she had threatened to father that she would "pack up" and send the children to an institution.

Yet while she related this with considerable feeling, her behavior toward Owen as observed was reasonably tolerant and quite affectionate; Owen in turn seemed especially content and at ease. After he had eaten biscuits much to his liking, he stretched himself with every sign of pleasure from his chair across the settee on which his mother was sitting. When by chance he kicked her, instead of scolding him, she asked, "Am I in the way?" and moved in order to make room for the child. Some time later Owen climbed on to his mother's lap, put his face to hers, kissed her, gently touched her eyes and nose. To this mother responded by asking "Is this love for Mummy?", to which Owen replied "Shesh" (Yes).

4. *Relationship of Owen and Mother to the Fieldworker throughout the Twenty Weeks.* On the day of reunion Owen maintained a neutral attitude to the fieldworker and on the ninety-minute car journey appeared almost unaware of her presence. It was the worker, however, who elicited his first laugh, following his "frozen state" after his arrival home. When she visited next day he looked up as she entered but appeared indifferent, neither smiling nor turning away. After a while he established contact with her in the same way as during the preseparation visit; by bringing his book to her and imitating the sounds of the objects. Calling her "nanny" seemed to show that he associated her with the residential nursery where he had seen her weekly; when she left he appeared to watch closely to

make sure that she had really gone, as if perhaps she raised unpleasant associations in his mind. On the fifth day after reunion, however, Owen's lack of interest lasted for only a few minutes; then he asked the fieldworker to wind up his engine and attend to him. He wanted to stand close to her in preference to his mother; he held her hand, gently picked her nails and smiled while he watched his father handling his train. When eventually he moved toward play, it was to demonstrate that he was a "bridge" connecting the two railway lines. On this occasion his "bye-bye's" to the fieldworker were cheerful.

As the friendly relationship grew, first provocative and then hostile behavior also appeared. On the eleventh day after reunion Owen climbed on to the fieldworker's lap and leaned against her, but he also smacked her playfully as if perhaps to test out her reaction.

During the sixth week after reunion, when kissing his mother good-bye, Owen spontaneously kissed the fieldworker and a week later seemed happy and at ease when left alone with her in a room. During the following visit (seventh week after reunion) Owen monopolized the fieldworker, and his play seemed largely directed toward her. He jumped and ran and let himself fall down, calling for her constant attention. He told her: "Look, I jump, I run, I fall down!" Many times he ran from the kitchen into the sitting room straight at the fieldworker, putting his arms around her and cheek close to hers. He kept hugging and kissing her, though twice his kiss turned into a bite (as had happened occasionally in the nursery). Similar behavior followed during the twelfth and thirteenth weeks after reunion. He played a game of sitting on the fieldworker's lap and suddenly dropping backward; he laughed merrily each time she pulled him up. It was over his reappearance that he rejoiced. He bit the buttons on her cardigan (in much the same way as he had done with mother previously) and pinched her arm. Initially calm and smiling, the play became wild and finally had to be controlled apparently to his relief. By the fourteenth week after reunion he did not mind remaining with the fieldworker while his mother went to the shops and his father was about the garden.

It should be noted that the development of Owen's relationship to the fieldworker anticipated and in some ways paralleled the development of his relationship to his mother. First there was an absence of affect qualitatively similar to his behavior to his mother, then the simultaneous appearance of a positive tie as well as provoca-

tive and hostile behavior. By the end of the seventeenth week his behavior had become very affectionate and trusting. As with his mother, he spontaneously caressed the fieldworker, and the provocative
and hostile elements were missing.

Mother's relationship with the fieldworker was kept within the
bounds described previously (Chapter 2). As already stated, there
was reason to think that the fieldworker's consistent support helped
mother to a greater acceptance of herself and of Owen, and enabled
her to cope with his difficult behavior in a more adequate way.

*5. A Visit to Owen's Home by Heinicke during the Seventeenth
Week after Reunion.* As required by the design, Heinicke visited
Owen in his home after he had been reunited with his parents for
sixteen weeks. Owen had not seen the male observer since the last
day of the separation.

When the observer entered, Owen stared at him with a blank expression and, after a few seconds, started biting the gun he was holding. Mother commented that Owen had not done this kind of biting
for a long time and also recalled that he had kept her at a distance
when he first came home, just as he was now doing with the observer.

Owen gradually got over his fright and began to search the observer's coat pockets as he had done in the last weeks in the nursery.
Everything was again "My" and "Mine," and when he did not have
his way, he seemed on the verge of a temper tantrum.

After about an hour, Owen invited the observer to play "golf"
with him. It was clear that he had mastered many aspects of the game
so dear to his father. Although Owen was no longer obviously
frightened of the observer, he did not like being picked up by him.
During the game he playfully kicked the observer, playfully hit mother with his fists and bit her skirt.

After the game was over and after doing "Wee-wee," Owen turned
to his favorite train game. A straight chair was laid on its back, and
Owen then put a piece of coal on the back of the chair and
pretended to light it with his mother's lighter. Then as engineer, he
sat on the edge of the chair playing "Choo-choo." (The position was
identical to the one he had assumed in sitting on the pot. Given the
context of this behavior, a connection with the various aspects of
the separation experience and particularly the train that took him
there is suggested.)

Father decided to take Owen for a walk just at the same time the observer was leaving. Mother washed his face and hands, which Owen clearly did not like. Then, when he realized that the observer was leaving the house at the same moment, Owen began to scream very loudly. Mother was puzzled by this and said that nothing similar had occurred for a long time. When the observer reassured Owen that he was not going to take him back to the nursery, Owen calmed down and gladly went on the walk, during which he especially enjoyed walking through mud puddles.

As also required by the design, Westheimer administered doll-play sessions to Owen during the sixth and sixteenth weeks after reunion; but as the results add little to what has been said, they are not included.

6. *The Two Years following the Twentieth Week after Reunion.* Although the twentieth week concluded the period of observation prescribed by the research design, Westheimer maintained some contact with the family thereafter, and brief reference to the subsequent history may be of interest. During this extension of contact, when the fieldworker's visits were irregular and infrequent, Owen maintained his attachment to her. Even after a six-month interval he greeted her with a degree of warmth which mother said he showed for no one else.

Thirty-two weeks after reunion Owen's relationship to his mother was a comfortable one. This can best be described by giving details of their interaction.

Owen, who was instructing the fieldworker on how to play golf, was not at all pleased at his mother's call for tea but cheered up when told he could have orange juice instead. He drank it very quickly and then waited impatiently for mother and the fieldworker to drink their tea and finally proclaimed, "I want you to come out now." His mother replied pleasantly, "In a little while, when we have had our tea; the tea is hot and if Mummy drank it as quickly as you drank your orange juice, she would burn her tummy." Owen laughed and contained himself, but the moment mother had finished he asked, "Will you come now?" and they went out to play together.

Later that evening Owen spontaneously kissed the fieldworker good-night but did not kiss his mother. She asked teasingly, "Don't I get a kiss?", and Owen replied, "I kissed you this morning." "Does this mean I am not getting one at night?" and Owen laughingly replied "Yes" and kissed her affectionately.

During this visit father made some observations. He considered that Owen's reactions during the previous week had shown that he had not completely got over his feelings concerning the separation. The family had traveled overnight and arrived too early at their destination and so had spent some hours at the beach before proceeding to the maternal grandmother's house. Owen had been happy there but became apprehensive the moment he realized he was to enter a strange house. He cried and seemed upset, and father had to carry him into the house and reassure him of his presence.

At this time (thirty-two weeks after reunion) Owen's temper tantrums were few, and mother hardly referred to them; they were no longer a problem.

Owen was no longer faddy about his food and was reliably clean and dry. His vocabulary had increased greatly, and he could draw with unusual skill for a child of his age. In all of this his mother took much pleasure. However, a ritual had developed around the sleeping arrangements. After watching television and finally turning off the set himself, Owen would go to his bedroom and look at his books by himself. At his call, "Mummy, I'm hiding," she had to go upstairs and find him under the bedclothes. She had to weep until he was found. Mother would then tuck him down, and holding her hand, he would quickly go to sleep.

At 3 years 9 months (sixteen months after reunion) he was in the hospital for ten days for inflammation and abcesses in both ears. According to his mother:

On admission he screamed loudly, but during the daily visit he never cried. At the end of each visiting time he asked his mother to put the bedclothes over him and tuck him in. As she walked down toward the exit, he watched her silently but always, just as she was about to pass through the doorway, he turned his face to the wall; thus, he never actually saw her leave the ward. He insisted that she should not bring toys from home—not even the favorite teddy bear which she had thought would be a comfort to him. Mother inferred that he was afraid the acceptance of his favorite toys would make the hospital stay more permanent. On return home he was very subdued, and for a few days he treated his mother as a stranger. But she thought his reaction shorter and less severe than that which followed his twelve-week separation.

Whatever other factors may have influenced his behavior, he was older on the second separation. There was also more insight in mother's attitude.

Owen was last seen by the fieldworker two years and seven months after his return from the residential nursery:

He was then a boy of 5 years, well-built and sturdy, with a pleasant expression. He had become very independent and returned home with his sister from the playing fields looking healthy and grubby. He could take a joke and happily teased his family. He talked sensibly and had a number of things to relate, and mother seemed pleased with him and also proud of him. Again he related to the fieldworker rapidly as though he knew her well and saw her frequently.

* * * * *

To anticipate once more the type of finding to be presented in later chapters, we wish to emphasize that the successive changes that took place in Owen during the separation can be linked, not only to the nature of his adaptation at the end of his eighty-one-day separation, but also to his behavior when first reunited with his parents and the series of changes that occurred subsequently.

Just as at the end of separation Owen had come to show little affection toward his father when he visited, so on the day of reunion his reaction to his mother was dull and expressionless. During his first days at home, though ready to cling to his father, he made little contact with his mother and refused most food from her.

By the end of his first week home, Owen was once more approaching his mother, and she on her part was attempting to re-establish her relationship with him. This was not easy for her, since she had ambivalent feelings about having him home again.

As mutual affection developed Owen also increasingly challenged his mother by being disobedient, messy and aggressive. On such occasions the presence of the fieldworker was of value in at least two ways. She could help mother to understand the origin of these provocations and rebuffs and thus enable her to deal with them in a firm yet affectionate way, without becoming overwhelmed by her own ambivalence. Secondly, insofar as Owen increasingly trusted the fieldworker, he could try out certain reactions toward her before directing them toward his mother.

By the ninth week after reunion mother and Owen had moved even closer together. New was Owen's tendency to bite and hit his mother. Taken together with his provocation and tempers, she found herself sorely tried; she claimed she was ready to "pack up." Nevertheless, as she repeatedly met Owen's challenges, the provocative elements diminished and the trusting affectionate ones increased.

Owen now showed signs of accelerated growth: his speech accelerated, going to the toilet was not an area of struggle, he showed signs of identifying with his father, the food fads diminished and the sleeping disturbances were no longer serious.

It is difficult to evaluate the influence on Owen's development of such factors as his illness, his mother's illness, his attendance at the day nursery and the ameliorating effect of the fieldworker's support. Without providing any conclusive evidence, it will be seen in Chapters 6 through 10, however, that an analysis of the behavior of the other children in the sample suggests that these factors are not the most important ones in accounting for Owen's behavior.

Typical Behavior during Separation

6 In the next four chapters we describe the child's development during separation and reunion. This description will be divided into two chapters dealing with typical behavior and two chapters dealing with individual differences. Thus, in this chapter we shall first describe aspects of behavior that were typical during the first twelve days of separation; namely, those features seen in almost all children. This characterization of the typical is not only of interest in its own right but also serves to introduce Chapter 7, which deals with variations in individual development during separation.

To further orient the reader, Chapter 8 describes the typical behavior seen during reunion, and Chapter 9 deals with individual differences in the development during reunion.

I. Typical Behavior during the First Twelve Days of Separation

The data to be presented on the typical sequence of behavior are derived from the systematic analysis of the clinical descriptions of each of the children recorded by Heinicke and Wolpert. We refer to the analysis of the child's total behavior into certain aspects (e.g., relation to visiting father), and how each of these aspects in turn was abstracted into a series of time periods. For example, was there a typical relationship to the visiting father during the first three days, the next nine days, etc.? (See Chapter 3 for the details of the time-period analysis.)

Given this data for each of the ten children, we can ask, for a given aspect of behavior, not only whether a phenomenon is present during a given number of days or not (e.g., whether the child's sleep was disturbed during the first three days), but also whether the incidence of the phenomena decreases, increases or remains the same for most of the children. Depending upon the nature of the judgments involved, we used Wilcoxon Matched-Pairs Signed Ranks Test and the Sign Test (Siegel, 1956) to evaluate these changes.

Just as the search for phases of development helped us to organize the case material, so it can aid us in organizing the presentation of the typical behavior seen during the separation. It will be recalled that for each of the two children described in the previous chapter there were certain days on which *several* aspects of the total behavior showed a simultaneous change. It is the fact that several aspects of the total behavior change, rather than just one aspect, that distinguishes a change of phase from a change in time period. If we now look at the points denoting change of phase for all ten children, we find that in every case there was such a major shift in development between the end of the first and the fourth day, and that, for eight of them, there was a further shift between the ninth and fifteenth day. We decided, therefore, to use the modal days of change and so to discuss the material in terms of four phases: the moment of separation, the first three days, the period from the fourth to the twelfth day and the period after the twelfth day. Although these divisions best organize the total findings, it must be emphasized that not every child nor every aspect of behavior shows a major change at each transition point, e.g., between the third and the fourth day. For this reason, some of the comparisons are most conveniently made between the first and the second weeks.

In addition to the data derived from the clinical descriptions, we have at times also presented results derived from the coded records of behavior in the Everyday Nursery Setting. The Wilcoxon Matched-Pairs Signed Ranks Test is used to evaluate the changes seen in the codings of behavior.

It can be argued that Friedman's two-way analysis of variance (Siegel, 1956) could have been used as part of our data analysis. This was in fact explored, but because the results did not add appreciably to the information to be given, they are not included.

A. The Moment of Separation

It is not possible to convey the charged atmosphere that pervades a residential nursery when a child is about to be left there. We can, however, give a summary picture and some examples of the behavior shown by the ten children under study.

As illustrated by the reaction of Josephine, the conditions immediately previous to the moment of separation are clearly important. When her father brought her to the nursery, Josephine was already crying. Although she had been carefully prepared for the event and had been taken to the nursery beforehand, the pregnant mother had been rushed to the hospital unexpectedly, and while Josephine was staying with her grandmother on the morning of admission to the nursery, a dog had scratched her. There were altogether four children, who, like Josephine, had already been separated from their mothers when they arrived at the nursery.

The other nine children showed a variety of reactions during the time shortly before the separation. Two clearly communicated their unease, as if they sensed that something painful was about to happen. Another, Gillian, had never been on the subway before and seemed to be quietly fretting. Another reaction shown by three children was to stay close to the parents. Dennis looked quite resigned and yet content while he sat on his mother's lap. Margaret too stayed close to her mother. Three other children fluctuated between staying close to their parents and exploring the environment for a while. Katie followed the nurse into the garden to look at the swing but wanted then to return to her father for a while only to venture out once more. In only one case did the child spend most of the time exploring. While the children thus seemed to sense what was about to happen, they could in most cases also deal with this unease.

This picture was drastically changed the minute the separation became more of a reality. As indicated, Josephine was already crying. Of the remaining nine, six began to cry (and the word "scream" is really more appropriate) at the exact moment that they saw the parent leaving. Thus Elizabeth began to cry as the parents left and urgently asked: "Where are you going?" She followed them so insistently that her mother had to push her back into the nursery room. Elizabeth could thus express herself verbally, but Jimmy, a young child, could in his desperation only throw himself on the floor and scream. Nor could anyone comfort him. He lay on his back sucking his bottle with his legs up as if he were a baby whose diapers were about to be changed. Between frantic sucks and cries for his mother he would sometimes writhe into a fetal position. So absorbed was he that he remained oblivious to the attacks on him of another child.

Gillian began to scream the minute the nurse tried to undress her and screamed even louder and in a desperately longing pitch when the father actually left. The same was true of Josephine. For eight of the children the crying either began or reached its highest pitch at the moment of separation.

Like Dawn, Katie failed to react to the parents' departure and also began to show unease as certain intimate routines began. When put in a bath by a friendly nurse, she said in a questioning tone "Mummy?" She wanted to have a toy telephone near her and also some chocolate. When she accidentally fell in the bathtub, she whimpered "Mummy, Mummy." As in the case of Dawn, it was not until she had been put in a crib in preparation for sleep, however, that she really began to scream and could not be consoled.

The sequence of reactions following the initial outbreak of crying differed a great deal. Two children, Josephine and Margaret, very quickly controlled their crying and Josephine even appeared happy. Every now and then she fretted without crying, however, and would say "Home, Daddy." The other children continued to cry, and some could not be comforted by anyone. For example, Jimmy screamed continuously, threw himself violently into his bed and then tried to poke out the eyes of his teddy bear. Only gradually did this teddy bear and a bottle filled with milk begin to comfort him. At this stage we can distinguish between the kind of behavior and crying which suggests control and anticipation of events, as in the case of Gillian's behavior on the subway, and the kind of desperate random movement and intense screaming illustrated by Jimmy's behavior.

Another example of desperate behavior is that of Gillian who, because she arrived in the evening, had to be put to bed right away. She insisted on keeping her coat on, clung desperately to her doll from home and cried at a frightening pitch. Since there was some response to the matron, her bed was moved into the latter's apartment. Repeatedly, she would begin to nod off from sheer fatigue only to awake screaming "Mummy." The combination of a biscuit, sucking of her coat button and perhaps sheer exhaustion finally allowed her to go to sleep.

B. The First Three Days of Separation

1. The Longing for the Parents.
Longing for the return of the parents, in the form of crying for "Mummy" and "Daddy," dominated the child's behavior during the first three days. Not that all crying

stopped after three days, but this was certainly the period of its greatest intensity.

That the longing was indeed for the parents was shown by the extreme distress after the visit of the parent which tended temporarily to disrupt such control as the child had achieved. For example, by the third day Josephine was crying relatively little, but after a visit by her father, she cried frantically and continuously for twenty minutes. Although on this occasion she recognized her father immediately and responded to him with affection, her behavior so upset him that he could not bear to visit her again.

Turning now to the coded observations. in Table 17 we present as a percentage of total activity observed in the Everyday Nursery Setting the attempts the child made to recover the parent. In the first part of the table we give the percentage of activity spent in crying for the mother and father for each of six category sampling periods during the first fourteen days. (These figures have been graphed in Figure 5.) Using the Wilcoxon Signed Ranks Test and

Figure 5.   *Showing the Crying Form of Fretting for the Parents as Per Cent of Total Activity during First Two Weeks of Separation*

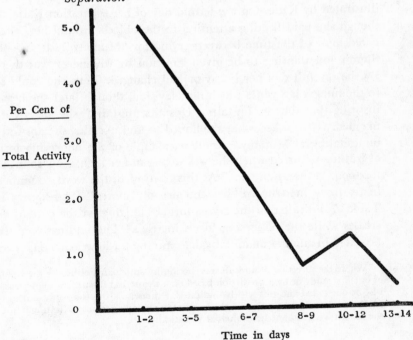

comparing the decrement in crying for the parents from days one–
two to six–seven, we obtain a P value of approximately .05.[1] The
second part of the table is designed to show, over a longer period,
how crying for the mother and father decreased and how noncrying
forms of longing for the parents increased. Because they are only
based on four cases, the figures from the fourth to the seventh weeks
are less reliable than for the first two.

Table 17.   *Showing the Fretting for the Parents as*
Percentage of Total Activity

	Days of Separation					
	1–2	*3–5*	*6–7*	*8–9*	*10–12*	*13–14*
Crying Form of Fretting for Mother and Father	5.0	3.8	2.4	.8	1.3	.4

	Weeks of Separation					
	1	*2*	*3*	*4*	*5*	*6*	*7*
Crying Form of Fretting for Mother and Father	4.4	1.0	1.9	.7	.1	.3	.1
Noncrying Form of Fretting for Mother and Father	.5	.5	.4	1.0	1.3	2.0	1.0

The shift from the crying form of fretting to a noncrying form is
illustrated by Katie. On the second day of her separation Katie, although she paid fleeting attention to the objects around her, alternated most of the time between crying for "Mummy," sucking her
thumb and wanting to be given affection by whomever was there.
By the seventh day her behavior had changed. Thus she could sit
in the nurse's lap while watching television, though later she began
insisting that they go upstairs. "Upstairs, upstairs," she angrily demanded. When asked what she hoped to find upstairs, she answered
unhesitatingly "Mummy." Another example of the noncrying form
of fretting occurred when she was sitting in her high chair shouting
for food: "More, more. . . ." As this continued, the word "mummy"
increasingly interrupted the sequence of "mores." The figures in
Table 17 indicate that the crying form of longing for the parents decreases while the noncrying forms increase.[2] The findings can also
be stated in another manner by determining for how many days each

[1] Where the direction of a result was specifically anticipated either by the results
of our first study or by a prediction based on a theoretical discussion, the test used
will be one-tailed and this will be indicated. Otherwise all tests are two-tailed.
[2] For reasons already indicated, the increase in noncrying forms of fretting beyond
the fourth week cannot be evaluated statistically.

child tended to cry for his parents; this is typically from the first to the ninth day. Similarly, we can ask whether any of the children ceased to show behavior scored in the Regain Noncry Father and Mother category toward the end of their separation; the answer is no.

2. *The Disturbance of the Child's Sleep.* Each of the ten children had difficulty in sleeping during the first nights of their stay in the residential nursery. Most of these disturbances were in the first few days; subsequently they stopped altogether or diminished greatly. The mode for the first period of sleep disturbance, the period which for every child was either the only or the worst one, was one to three days.

In descriptions of Katie and Dawn we have already emphasized how being put to bed initiates fretting. We have also seen that Gillian had a tremendous dread of going to sleep and an inevitable nodding off mingled with longing cries for "Mummy." We reported how Owen woke up in the middle of the night and called "Mummy, Daddy." Finally, certain children awoke as if terrified. For example, in the early morning hours of her second day of separation Katie suddenly awoke screaming and shouting "Mummy" and was unable to go to sleep again. She continued to cry "Mummy" all morning, and by noon her eyes were very swollen.

Thus we find that not only is the most intense fretting for the parents concomitant with the maximum sleep disturbance, but, as the examples indicate, disturbances in sleep are directly connected with longing for parents.

3. *Refusal to Participate in the Nursery Routine.* We might look at the above findings on sleep disturbances as the child's way of saying: I refuse to sleep here and want to sleep where my mummy and daddy are. Similarly the children initially refused to be undressed or dressed, refused to eat and refused to be toileted.

We have seen how Gillian refused to be undressed by the nurses. Such lack of co-operation on a specific occasion was less frequent, however, than a general refusal to be approached, picked up or comforted by them. This general refusal was, nevertheless, very short-lived; the modal length was one day. One child, Georgy, the youngest in the sample, allowed himself to be picked up immediately.

While a complete refusal to respond did not continue, specific forms of refusal did. Seven of the children at first either refused all food or certain foods; others did not refuse food but did not eat particularly well. (For one case we did not have sufficient information to make a judgment.) The modal period for the seven who refused food was one to two days. What is striking about this initial refusal is that later all children ate very well indeed, even greedily. An example is Katie, who refused all food on the first day but later became very greedy.

A similar refusal was seen in relation to toileting. Eight children specifically resisted the routine of toileting, usually by refusing to sit on the pot. Only one child complied right from the beginning. (In one case we had insufficient information.) Although wetting and soiling persisted during the first two weeks, actual resistance to toileting soon disappeared. The modal length of time for this initial resistance was one to three days.

Nevertheless, many forms of resistance to the nurses did persist. This can be seen in Table 18, where we present the frequency of resistance to demands as a percentage of the total reactions to demands. Examination of the trend reveals that the high point is during the first five days, and that it then declines, but that resistance to over one-third of demands continues.

Table 18. *Showing Frequency of Resisting the Nurses' Demands as Percentage of Total Reactions to Demands*

	Days					
	1–2	3–5	6–7	8–9	10–12	13–14
Resists Nurse	56.8	57.4	36.4	47.2	34.3	39.7

4. *Seeking a Positive Relationship with the Adults in the Nursery.* While resistance was thus the dominant response during this period, already during the first two days the children sought some type of relation with the adults in the nursery. Table 19 shows the total attempts to seek a positive relation with an adult in the nursery as a per cent of total activity scored. The specific categories making up this summary score are also given. The nature of the table as well as the results are similar to Table 4 given as part of our initial study (Heinicke, 1956, p. 135).

Table 19. *Showing Frequency of Seeking a Positive Relationship as Percentage of Total Activity*

Categories	Days					
	1–2	3–5	6–7	8–9	10–12	13–14
Seeks to Be Near Nurse and Observer	1.8	5.3	4.1	3.2	5.1	3.3
Seeks Attention from Nurse and Observer	6.3	6.9	7.5	7.0	8.1	10.9
Seeks Affection from Nurse and Observer	3.1	5.8	5.1	4.9	5.0	3.0
Sum of Above	11.2	18.0	16.7	15.1	18.2	17.2

The lowest seeking of positive relation was seen during the first two days; yet even this percentage (11.2) is quite considerable. Though the children's responses varied in nature and intensity, they had in common an effort to seek some sort of reassuring and affectionate response from the adult.

5. *The Incidence of Sucking.* While the above descriptions have emphasized the behavior patterns dominant during the first three days, other forms of behavior should also be mentioned. Even when they were stubbornly refusing all food at the regular mealtimes, children would at other times reach out to suck a bottle or a sweet. While all such sucking seemed to comfort the child, in some cases a link between the object sucked and the mother could be seen. For example, Katie spent much time sucking and biting a toy telephone. From various evidence it was clear that she realized that the real telephone served as a link to her mother; and the mother did in fact frequently call the nursery to inquire about Katie.

Much the most frequently sucked object was some part of the hand. The frequency of this as a percentage of the total activity is given in Table 20. Examination of the table reveals that over the first fourteen days, there is little change in the proportion of time spent sucking; we can add that this probably continues to be the case

Table 20. *Frequency of Thumb- and Finger-Sucking as a Percentage of Total Activity*

	Days of Separation					
	1–2	3–5	6–7	8–9	10–12	13–14
Thumb- and Finger-Sucking	2.4	2.7	2.3	2.6	2.8	3.3

in the period after the first two weeks of separation. Other behavior also commonly classified as autoerotic, such as masturbation, was observed but only infrequently.

6. *The Response to the Favorite Object from Home.* All but one of the children brought with them from home a favorite object which they had previously used to comfort themselves in times of stress. Ideally one would have liked to determine the specific meanings that the favorite object had in the life of the child, but this was not possible. Though the children continued to use these objects in the nursery, they typically abandoned them after about the first twelve days of separation and did not touch them again until the moment of reunion.

It was also found that the quality of the interaction with the favorite object differed during the course of these twelve days. During the first three, the behavior toward the object was predominantly affectionate, but after that it became ambivalent. For example, during the early days Gillian desperately clutched both her favorite rag doll and a duck, and she also had a favorite doll. When on the second day a nurse offered to hold her doll, she became extremely anxious, started to cry and could not be comforted. She stopped crying only when the nurse left her, standing in one spot, clutching her possessions. When someone approached her, she would sometimes hold out the doll, as if both to establish a contact and to keep the person at a distance.

As with Gillian, the rest of the children initially clutched and held on to their favorite object. The modal length of time that this remained the predominant response was three days. We stress predominant, because in two of the nine cases, some hostility toward the favorite object was seen from the very beginning.

7. *The Relationship with the Observer.* The children's initial reactions to the two observers, Heinicke and Wolpert, varied but were mostly positive in nature. By positive we mean specifically seeking comfort or being friendly. For example, on the second day of the separation Georgy wanted to be picked up by the observer, but when the observer refused, Georgy was content to put his head on the observer's leg. After a while he began to explore the environment but, once on his own, he suddenly began screaming and returned to the observer. An example of friendliness was the way Elizabeth, on the

second day of separation, greeted Observer Wolpert with a cheery "Hello" and then began to show her pictures. In contrast to her younger brother, Georgy, she did not at this point seem to need any physical contact.

Eight of the ten children initially had a positive relation to at least one of the observers. The modal length of time for the continuation of this positive relationship is one day. This is true for the relationship to each observer considered separately.

8. *The Expression of Hostility.* The severer forms of hostility seen later in the Everyday Nursery Setting were not observed during the first days of separation (see Table 21). They were, however, observed during the doll-play sessions which were administered at about this time—findings which will be reported in Chapter 10.

C. From the Fourth to the Twelfth Days of Separation

1. *Longing for Parents.* This phase is defined in part by a decrease in the very things we have just been emphasizing. Thus, crying for the parents decreased considerably (see Table 17). Moreover, during the second week of separation the children were less affectionate to the father when he visited and cried less when he left. (Applying the Sign Test to data derived from the time-period analysis yields a P value of .004.)

For example, when Gillian's father arrived on the eighth day of her separation, she did not seem particularly interested in him, turned her head away for a moment, quietly cried and quickly recovered. She was, however, extremely interested in the chocolate he had brought and gobbled it down. When he left, she showed little reaction and did not cry as she had previously. That she nevertheless reacted to his departure is suggested by the fact that soon afterward she cried bitterly, and no one could console her.

2. *The Decrease in Sleep Disturbance and in Resistance to the Nursery Routine.* When one compares the period under discussion with the first three days, sleeping disturbances show a pronounced decline. (Application of the Sign Test to data derived from the time-period analysis yields a P value of .002.) Similarly, the children's resistance to the nurses' demands shows a considerable decline after the first few days (see Table 18). Although this decrease is quantitatively greatest between days three–five and six–seven, comparison

of these two points does not yield a statistically reliable difference. The decrease from days one–two to thirteen–fourteen is, however, statistically reliable; applying the Wilcoxon Matched Signed Ranks Test, we obtained a P value of .01.

This phase (fourth-twelfth day) can also be characterized by the presence of certain other behavioral sequences.

3. Avoiding the Observer. Most striking of the phenomena which appeared during this time was the active avoidance of the observers. Nine of the ten children actively avoided Wolpert and eight avoided Heinicke. The modal period of time for this avoidance was from the second to the twelfth day of separation. This was true for each observer.[3] As avoidance we include all those behavioral sequences the effect of which is to avoid interaction with another person. The most obvious form of avoidance is for a child simply to run away or turn his back. A less obvious form is to bury his head in a pillow or to close his eyes. Especially dramatic were those instances where the minute the observer entered the room, the child broke into a panic of screaming. Thus the moment Heinicke entered the room on the ninth day, Josephine broke out crying and clung to a nurse. She had shown very similar reactions to Westheimer the day before and on each occasion was clearly relieved when she saw the observer leaving.

On the seventh day of his separation, Jimmy let out a scream when the observer came in and turned away from him to a nurse. Later that day he showed less panic, and when he had hurt himself, even turned to the observer; nevertheless, he immediately fled again, as if he could not for long endure any degree of closeness.

Yet it should be added that there were many moments when a child continued to seek the attention of the observers, even if at a distance. Though none of the trends in Table 19 shows a significant change, if they are analyzed separately for nurse and observer, the increase in seeking attention from the observer comes closest to being statistically significant.

4. Affectionate Relationship to Nurses. Analysis of the trend in seeking positive relations from the nurses revealed that this form of behavior was neither frequent quantitatively speaking, nor did it

---

[3] Application of the Sign Test to the period analysis indicating a shift from being friendly to avoiding the observer yields a P value of .008.

show a significant increase. Nevertheless, although attachment to substitutes was minimal, that which existed was increasingly directed to a preferred nurse rather than diffused among several. Thus, during the second week of separation, the children showed a greater tendency to prefer one nurse than they had during the first week. (Application of the Sign Test to data derived from the time-period analysis yields a P value of .008.) For example, on the first day of Gillian's separation when she wanted nothing to do with anyone, Nurse W. could not approach her. By the sixth day, however, Gillian wanted to be picked up by this same nurse and was very happy sitting in her lap. When the nurse left for a moment, Gillian first walked around in a circle and then looked in a longing manner at the door through which the nurse had departed. But it would be erroneous to give the impression that Gillian's relations with this very giving nurse were wholly affectionate, for when Nurse W. returned Gillian walked away from her.

5. *Hostile Behavior.* While the expression of affection is best studied as directed differentially toward the father, the nurse and the observer, hostility during this phase is less specifically directed. Table 21 shows the incidence of hostile behavior as a per cent of total coded behavior in the Everyday Nursery Setting. A hostile intent was inferred when the child attempted to injure something or someone; severe and mild refers to the intensity of the injury attempted. Giving someone a little push is clearly different from trying to tear out his hair. An example of severe aggression occurred on the ninth day of Katie's separation when she hit James so violently that she almost knocked him out, and Observer Wolpert had to come to his rescue. Katie then became very anxious and started to cry for her mother.

Table 21. *Showing the Frequency of Hostility as Percentage of Total Activity*

| | Days of Separation | | | | | |
	1–2	3–5	6–7	8–9	10–12	13–14
Mild Hostility	4.53	4.96	6.28	5.70	5.14	6.25
Severe Hostility	.45	.82	1.62	1.51	2.82	2.20
Total Hostility	4.98	5.78	7.88	7.21	7.96	8.45

Statistical analysis of the trend for severe hostility revealed a significant increase from days one–five to six–twelve; using the Wilcoxon Signed Ranks Test we obtain a P of .01. The trend has been plotted in Figure 6.

Figure 6. *Showing Severe Hostility as Per Cent of Total Activity during First Two Weeks of Separation*

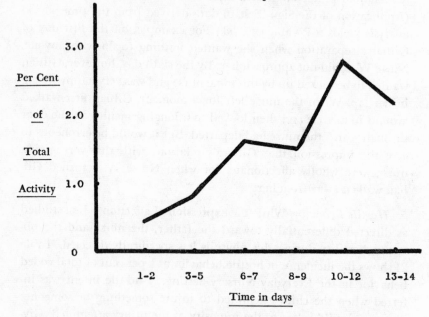

Two further considerations stress the importance of the severe outbursts noted above: the milder forms of hostility did not show a significant increase and, of the severer forms that did increase, biting was outstanding. When the severe forms of biting are expressed as a percentage of the total severe hostility, they show a significant increase from the first to the second week of separation. (Applying the Wilcoxon Signed Ranks Test, we obtain a P value of .05.)

The development of the child can be further traced by studying a number of other changes.

6. *Illness*. Eight of the children in the sample became ill at some point during their separation, and in seven of them, it began between the fourth and twelfth days. Usually the illness was some form of cold, but in three cases it was more serious. This will be discussed more fully in Chapter 10.

What may be of special interest is that the two children, Josephine and Margaret, who did not become ill were the two who achieved control of their crying immediately after the moment of separation; they are also the two who most actively avoided the observers.

7. *Eating.* In contrast to the initial refusal of food and in comparison with behavior during the rest of the first week of separation, during the second week of separation the children showed a greater interest in food, especially sweets. (Application of the Sign Test to the results of the time-period analysis yields a P value of .004.) An example is Dawn, who initially was not much interested in food. By the eighth day of her separation, however, not only did she readily eat the main course at lunch, but she had three helpings of pudding. Before she was through and with her mouth partly full she shouted "More, more, more." When the nurse finally removed her from the lunchroom, she began to cry.

8. *Breakdown in Sphincter Control.* While a breakdown in control of the anal and urethral sphincters had already begun during the first three days, it was at its most striking during the period being discussed. Only one child, Elizabeth, completely maintained her sphincter control, and she was the oldest in the sample. The remaining nine either wet or soiled or both, and for seven of them, this represented a loss compared to the control achieved previously. None of the children showed a gain in sphincter control. (Applying the Sign Test to the results of the period analysis on the sample of seven we obtain a P value of .016.) Not all of these seven children had achieved complete control before the separation, but they had achieved some measure of control and lost it again.

For example, Katie had achieved considerable control before separation. During the first two days of her separation, even though she was very reluctant to sit on the pot, she maintained that control. By the third day, however, she was wetting and soiling both during the day and at night.

9. *Decline in the Number of Different Words Used.* Another change shown by these children is a decline in the number of different words used. The demonstration of this requires a digression.

In our first study we had used as an index of speech development the sheer frequency of verbalization but had found with it no results of interest. Examination of our current data suggested that a count of the number of different words used might be a more sensitive index; Pringle and Tanner (1958) had found it to be useful in their study of children residing in a residential nursery. Among methodological points which arise in use of a word count is the question of whether two forms of the same word; e.g., "come" and "coming," are to be counted as two different words. We decided that they should be but realized also that a linguist might handle such problems in a more sophisticated manner. It is to be expected that an index of this kind would correlate with age. This was confirmed.

To compute the word-count index, data from either the everyday category observations or the doll-play protocols could be used. For purposes of the present delineation of typical responses during the first two weeks of separation, the continuous observations made in the everyday nursery situation are the more appropriate. As will be seen in Chapter 10, principal findings from these observations can be replicated using word counts derived from the doll-play.

The initial plotting of the number of different words recorded per minute of observation on each day of separation revealed an irregular curve which nevertheless declined fairly steadily from the second to the twelfth day. Using the Wilcoxon Signed Ranks Test we found that there was a significant decrease in the number of different words used when the second (.20 different words per minute) and the twelfth days (.09 different words per minute) were compared; the P value is approximately .05. We also found that the rise from the twelfth to the thirteenth day is statistically significant; the P value is approximately .05. Since the decline from the second to the twelfth day is not consistent, however, all we can conclude is that the number of different words used on the twelfth day marks a low point, and that starting with the thirteenth day, the children again used a greater number of different words. Whether the twelfth to the thirteenth day marked a transitional point could be tested by comparing the number of different words used during the first twelve days with the next four days. The value for days one–twelve is .17 and for days thirteen–sixteen is .26; applying the Wilcoxon Signed Ranks Test, the P value is approximately .05.

We conclude therefore that the separated children used fewer different words during the first twelve days of their separation than in subsequent days, and that the twelfth to the thirteenth day marks a point of transition.

That days twelve and thirteen represented a period of transition is further suggested by the fact that one particular word, "gone," was used either for the first time or most frequently at this time. The median day for the first appearance of this word was the twelfth day. "Gone" refers to things or people being gone; thus, one sometimes heard "All gone" in the context of crying for mummy. We shall later discuss these findings; most important to note is that this word was used very infrequently.

10. Relation to the Favorite Object from Home. We have noted previously that during the first three days the initial relation to the favorite toy was one of clutching and holding on, and that this changed subsequently. During the phase under discussion, eight of the nine children became ambivalent toward their favorite object. (Application of the Sign Test to the time-period analysis indicating a shift toward greater ambivalence yields a P value of .06.)

To give an example, sometimes during this period Josephine clung to her rag doll and carried it around in her teeth like a mother cat, but at other times she flung it away shouting "All gone." When on the sixth day Wolpert entered the nursery, Gillian greeted her with a forced smile and then turned away and would not look at her when approached. Shortly after this she turned to give her the Andy Pandy doll which she had been clutching. A little later she picked it up, dropped it in an aggressive way, and then picked it up again and hugged it with great affection.

11. Other Typical Responses. In the above examples, as well as in the long case illustrations, the frequency with which the children dropped things or left people only to retrieve or rejoin them later has probably become apparent. This behavior was not confined to the phase from the fourth to the twelfth day but was seen throughout the separation. Nevertheless, it was very noticeable during this phase. We have described already how Owen developed an elaborate ritual for first leaving and then rejoining the observer. Very frequent too were the constant "Bye-bye's" that could be heard as the children actively initiated a repetition of an event which had clearly been painful to them. Josephine not only avoided the observer, but when she left him would cheerfully say "Bye-bye." Sometimes, as we saw in the case of Dawn, the children greeted the observer with "Bye-bye."

Behavior entailing injury to the self and signs of both excessive gayness and sadness could also occasionally be seen during this phase. Because they were more frequently seen after the twelfth day of separation, they will be described in the next section.

Although we have described a number of common reactions and modes of coping, it should be stressed that these by no means exhaust the great variety of behavior seen. Four children were on the move constantly, as if both the searching and the activity helped them with their feelings of stress. Some clearly derived comfort from rocking themselves; yet two others preferred to remain in one spot as if this gave them security. Six children seemed almost on the verge of crying but instead continually rubbed their eyes.

II.   Typical Behavior after the First Twelve Days of Separation

The findings reported in the previous section on the typical behavior during the first twelve days could be stated with confidence because all ten children remained in the residential nursery for at least twelve days, and because their responses were in fact very homogeneous. After these first twelve days the length of time the children remained in the nursery varies considerably. Whereas five children were separated for fifteen days or less, the other five were away for seventeen, thirty-nine, forty-nine, eighty-one and one hundred and forty-one days respectively. To base our conclusions about typical behavior exclusively on the analysis of the trends shown by the second group does not seem warranted. What we can do is to describe these trends as evidenced particularly by the end of these longer separations and demonstrate that they differ from the responses shown by the children who experienced only a two-week separation. Since this comparison entails a discussion of individual differences between children and the factors that may account for them, this analysis is postponed until the next chapter.

There is, however, another analysis of typical behavior that was undertaken, and that serves as a transition from the analyses reported in this chapter and those to be reported in the next. It is made possible by the fact that every child remained in the nursery at least two days after the second visit of the father (or friend of the family), made during the second week of separation.[4] As will be seen below,

[4] Since Owen was not visited during the second week, his reactions to the visit on the sixteenth day of separation were used for this analysis.

we believe that this visit marks a transitional point in the child's development. The reactions to it can therefore be considered as indicative of trends likely to emerge in subsequent days. Because the visit typically occurred on the twelfth day of separation, and since we focus on the behavior seen in the two days *after* the visit, we have included it in this section on the typical behavior seen after the first twelve days of separation.

A. Behavior Typically Seen after the Visit of the Father on the Twelfth Day of Separation

As part of the description of the development of both Dawn and Owen we have drawn attention to the simultaneous appearance of three kinds of behavior following the visit of the father or a friend of the family. In referring to them, we shall speak of indications of *sadness and resignation*, of *excessive cheerfulness* and of *injury to the self*. Under the first heading we include the following: staring into space for long periods of time, especially if accompanied by resigned immobility, and a lack of affect; and forms of silent sadness suggested by body posture and facial expression rather than by open crying. We inferred the presence of the second when the child was excessively cheerful, and when he laughed in a context that did not seem appropriate. The third, injury to the self, included all those behaviors where the child actively injured parts of his body, whether "accidentally" or not. Falling down stairs or biting his fingernails are examples. As in all our inferences the context of the behavior was carefully taken into account.

Each of these three sorts of behavior had been observed before the twelfth day of separation, but it was not until after the visit of the parent, usually the father, during the second week of separation, that all three forms were seen simultaneously. As already noted, the median day of the parental visit during the second week of separation was the twelfth day of separation.

To determine what proportion of the children showed evidence of this development, two people independently analyzed the clinical descriptions of each child made during each of the following three periods; the two days before the visit of the parent during the second week of separation, the day of the visit and the two days after the visit. A child was judged to show the typical sequence if *all three* forms of behavior were present during the two days after the visit and not during the two days before it. The same procedure was also applied to the first visit that occurred during the first week of separation. In only four cases did the two raters disagree. A disagreement was scored when the raters disagreed on any one of the items in the trio; for example, one might note injury to the self and the other not. Re-examination of the data resulted in a set of data agreed to by both judges. Since there was an agreed judgment whether or not the trio was present before and also after the visit, and since the analysis on the ten children was carried out for both the first and second weeks of separation, we have a total of forty judgments. The results of the analysis are tabulated in Table 22.

Table 22. *Showing Presence Simultaneously of Indications of Sadness-Resignation, Excessive Cheerfulness and Injury to the Self Following the Visit of the Parent*

	Parental Visit	
	During First Week	During Second Week
Sadness-Resignation, Excessive Cheerfulness and Injury to the Self:		
Present	1	8
Absent	9	2

Examination of Table 22 reveals that indications of *sadness-resignation, excessive cheerfulness* and *injury to the self* were much more frequently present *simultaneously* in the two days following the visit during the second week of separation than they were during the first. Applying Fisher's Exact Test, we obtain a P value of approximately .005 (one-tailed).

It is of interest that for one child, Dennis, the trio appeared following only the first visit and not following the second visit of the parent; for another, Jimmy, it did not appear at all.

An example may help to clarify the above findings. Gillian had been visited by her father on the evening of the eleventh day of her separation. She had been very hesitant at first but later could approach him. The next morning she greeted Observer Heinicke with a very forced and artificial smile, then immediately became frightened, turned to the nurse for affection and remained immobile. Again allowing herself some activity, she would run away from the nurse and the observer, peep around the corner, return to the adults and then begin the sequence over again. During one of these sequences the nurse picked up another child and started swinging her in a circle. Very deliberately Gillian got in the way and was thus hit hard and knocked over. She screamed loudly until the nurse picked her up and comforted her. Suddenly the nurse had to leave. Gillian looked stunned, picked up her Andy Pandy doll, followed the nurse, clearly wanted to be picked up again and called for her daddy while throwing a kiss after the nurse. The next day Observer Wolpert recorded that Gillian for the first time greeted her with a true rather than a forced smile. It was difficult to interpret this forced smile, but it was clear that it now diminished in frequency. More impressive was the contrast between periods when she was very active and excessively cheerful, and others when she would suddenly sit immobile in one spot for ten minutes at a time staring into space. During one of the periods of activity she deliberately tore all the pages out of a book.

One further finding must be reported. We have already noted that the word "gone" was either heard for the first time or most frequently on about the twelfth day of separation. This in turn raises the question of whether the occurrence of this word is linked to the second parental visit and also to the trio of behaviors we have just discussed. Since only six children used the word "gone," our analysis is limited. It is nevertheless of interest that five of these children used the word "gone" for the first time, or most frequently, during the two days following the visit of the parent during the second week of separation.

Individual Differences in
Behavior during Separation

7 We have concentrated so far on describing the behavioral sequences which could be seen in most if not all of the children during the first two weeks of separation. The nature of our data as well as our interests suggested that an analysis of the differences in the development of the children during the separation would be a useful addition. We therefore studied these differences in development for the following three overlapping time intervals: the first week of separation, the first two weeks of separation and the last week of separation.

The most general approach was to determine what differences in development existed, how indices of such differences intercorrelate and how, in turn, such indices correlate with selected independent factors. The nature of the questions posed as well as the data available led to three different analyses. In the first section we describe such variation as existed during the first week of separation and then examine how it is related to such selected and relatively stable background factors as the previous mother-child relationship. Can individual differences in the initial reaction to separation be understood in terms of variations in the child's background and his personality?

In the second section we examine how individual differences in behavior during the first two weeks of separation relate to variations in the conditions obtaining shortly before and during the separation. Does it make a difference whether the separated child is accompanied by a sibling or not?

Finally, in the third section, we describe the variation seen during the last week of separation and relate it to such independent factors as length of separation.

180

I. Individual Differences during the First Week of Separation as Related to Background Factors

A. The Behavior during the First Week of Separation

1. Absence of Affectionate Response to the Father. In examining the various responses to the visit of the father, we found that some children were almost exclusively interested in the father as a person, expressed much affection toward him during the visit and cried a great deal when he left. At the other extreme was a child who was more interested in the sweet foods he brought than in his affection. We present the ratings and rankings in Table 23.

Table 23. *Showing Ratings and Rankings of Separated Children in Terms of a Dimension Describing the Child's Lack of Affectionate Response to the Visiting Father during the First Week of Separation*

A. Children whose predominant reaction is one of affectionate contact and fretting, but in whom there is also a little evidence of greed
1. Dawn
2. Jimmy
3. Katie
4. Josephine
5. Elizabeth
6. Georgy
7. Dennis

B. Children who do not cry during the father's visit, but in whom there is clear interest as a person, a keenness to see him, although also considerable interest in food
8. Margaret

C. Children who fret in an extreme fashion, but in whom there are also signs of lack of affectionate response to the father
9. Owen

D. Children who fret a little, but in whom there are also signs of lack of affectionate response to the father, and for whom the main interest is in the sweets he brings
10. Gillian

Examination of Table 23 reveals that the range of reactions is not very great; that is, during the first week most of the children are affectionate with their father and cry when he leaves.

2. Crying for the Parents. Even though the children's relationship to the father during the first week of separation varied little, the frequency of crying for the parents varied considerably. The index used is the same as that previously defined in Chapter 6: crying for the father and mother as a percentage of total activity coded.

3. Affectionate Relationship with the Nurses. In Table 24 we present the ratings and rankings describing the child's relationship with the nurses during the first week of separation. This dimension is designed to reflect the extent to which a child developed a relationship to the nurses in general and especially the extent of affection expressed toward one particular nurse. At one end is the child who quickly turns to the nurses and then begins to develop an affectionate relation to one or two of them, while at the other end of the dimension is the child who resists the nurse in the beginning, never shows much affection and develops no preferences.

Table 24. *Showing Ratings and Rankings of the Separated Children in Terms of a Dimension Describing the Affectionate Relationship with the Nurses during the First Week of Separation*

A. Children who resist the nurses initially, never show them affection and develop no clear-cut preference for any nurse
    1. Margaret
B. Children who resist the nurses initially and who then make contact with many nurses without preference for a particular one
    2. Elizabeth
    3. Dennis
    4. Dawn
    5. Georgy
C. Children who resist the nurses initially, then interact with many of them and even show some preference, but this is not clear-cut
    6. Josephine
    7. Jimmy
    8. Owen
D. Children who resist the nurses actively or passively in the beginning, and then begin to develop a preference for two or three nurses toward whom they also express some affection
    9. Gillian
E. Children whose predominant response is to cling to all the nurses from the beginning and who then begin to develop a preference for one or two nurses toward whom they also express some affection
    10. Katie

4. Avoidance of Observers Heinicke and Wolpert. Although during at least part of the first two weeks of separation all children avoided at least one of the observers, one child had a positive relation to both observers during the first week of separation. This then became one end of the dimension describing the relation to the observer; the consistent avoidance of both observers, with very few signs of any positive relation, became the other end. Depending on the extent of avoidance and positive relations, the other children were ranked at intermediate points. The resulting dimension is given in Table 25.

Table 25. *Showing Ratings and Rankings of Separated Children in Terms of a Dimension Describing the Child's Avoidance of Observers Heinicke and Wolpert during the First Week of Separation*

A. Children who show a positive relation to both observers
     1. Elizabeth
B. Children who avoid one observer, although not completely, and who have a positive relation with no avoidance to the other observer
     2. Dawn
     3. Georgy
     4. Dennis
C. Children whose main reaction to both observers is one of avoidance but who also show some signs of seeking positive relations
     5. Jimmy
     6. Katie
     7. Owen
     8. Gillian
     9. Josephine
D. Children who consistently avoid both observers and who show few signs of any positive relation
     10. Margaret

5. Avoidance of Observer Westheimer. To test the generality of the tendency to avoid observers, a similar dimension was developed to describe the child's reaction to Westheimer (see Table 26). Although the three observers were present with equal frequency at the moment of separation (each observed four children), Westheimer had had additional contact with all the children before the separation, while Heinicke and Wolpert had had far more contact with the child during the first week of separation. Nevertheless, rankings on the dimension relating to Heinicke and Wolpert correlate with those describing the child's relation to Westheimer to the extent of .56, which is significant at the .05 level. We conclude therefore that there is a tendency for avoidance to be a general response to the observers and not to be directed to a particular kind of observer only.

It is important to note, while Heinicke and Wolpert made systematic observations which were recorded in the presence of the child, that Westheimer did not record in the presence of the child. The avoidance therefore was not simply a function of being followed and watched.

That the avoidance was not attributable solely to the strangeness of the observer is suggested by two kinds of observation. First, there were many strangers in the nursery who took an interest in the children and whom the children did not avoid. Secondly, Westheimer had on the whole been greeted in a friendly manner by the child during her first visit to the home but, as we have seen, was for the most part either avoided or greeted initially in a subdued manner during the first week of separation.

Table 26. *Showing Ratings and Rankings of Separated Children in Terms of a Dimension Describing the Child's Avoidance of Observer Westheimer during the First Week of Separation*

A. Children whose predominant reaction to the observer is one of friendliness
> 1. Katie
> 2. Elizabeth

B. Children who are subdued at first and then accept the observer's attention rather passively
> 3. Dennis
> 4. Owen
> 5. Jimmy

C. Children who are very fretful generally and show little reaction to the observer
> 6. Georgy

D. Children whose predominant reaction to the observer is one of avoidance
> 7. Dawn
> 8. Gillian
> 9. Margaret
> 10. Josephine

6. Greed for Food. The way the children ate during the first week is shown in the ratings and rankings given in Table 27. The dimension runs from children who before the end of the week show signs of great greed to those whose reluctance to eat continued.

Table 27. *Showing Ratings and Rankings of the Separated Children in Terms of a Dimension Describing the Child's Greed for Food during the First Week of Separation*

A. Children who are reluctant to eat from the beginning and continue to be so during the first week
     1. Owen

B. Children who eat fairly well but show signs of being finicky
     2. Jimmy

C. Children who are neither reluctant nor greedy but eat normally throughout the first week
     3. Georgy
     4. Margaret
     5. Elizabeth

D. Children who, after initial reluctance, show signs of greed
     6. Dennis
     7. Gillian
     8. Josephine
     9. Dawn

E. Children who, after initial reluctance, show signs of great greed
     10. Katie

7. Sphincter Control. Similarly we ranked the children in terms of the extent of their soiling and wetting during the first week of separation. The rankings and ratings are given in Table 28.

Table 28. *Showing Ratings and Rankings of the Separated Children in Terms of a Dimension Describing Sphincter Control during the First Week of Separation*

A. Children who wear a diaper throughout the first week of separation
     1. Georgy

B. Children who wet and soil frequently and show very little control
     2. Jimmy
     3. Dawn
     4. Katie
     5. Gillian
     6. Dennis

C. Children who wet occasionally and very rarely soil
     7. Josephine
     8. Margaret

D. Children who occasionally wet but do not soil
     9. Owen

E. Children who show complete control over both sphincters
     10. Elizabeth

8. The Number of Different Words Used. To further study individual differences in the child's reaction, we also considered the variation in the number of different words used. This index has been described and used in Chapter 6 as part of the description of typical behavior. As indicated in a subsequent section it was then correlated with other indices describing the variation in reaction during the first week of separation.

9. *Expression of Severe Hostility during the First Doll Play.* In attempting to understand the possible meaning of the avoidance of the observers, we reasoned that this behavior might well be related to the expressions of severe hostility during the first doll play. Some indication of the steps in our reasoning is given below.

In previous work (Heinicke, 1956) we had noted that the separated child both seeks affection and expresses intense hostility. We assume that the emergence of such intense ambivalent feelings, and especially the hostile components, presents certain internal problems. We further assume that, primitive though the child's control mechanisms are, they do exist. During the first week of separation, when the child is trying to achieve some control over the increased hostile feelings toward the parents, to be confronted by observers who are associated with the parents (the source of frustration) may present a serious challenge to such control. The observer may well remind the child of the parents and thus activate his intense feelings. Other factors may also heighten the child's hostile feelings in the presence of the observer. The observers did not give the continuous affection that the child wanted; furthermore, they had a way of coming and then going again after a short while. Both these factors clearly could be frustrating for an already deprived child. Were the avoidance of the observers to have a defensive function in relation to the hostile feelings aroused by them, the frequent appearance of such avoidance would be accounted for. Although we do not here wish to develop these points in too extensive a theoretical direction, certain findings support the hypothesis that avoidance serves a defensive function. The difference between a subject's expressions in an everyday public situation and his expressions in a projective private situation has often been regarded as a measure of defensive operations. If in this study the child's avoidance had a specifically defensive function in relation to severe hostility, then at the height of its operation (the first week of separation), one would expect to see little severe hostility in the Everyday Nursery Setting; this was found to be the case. But, if the potential for severe hostility is present, then we might expect to observe it in the private doll-play session; in Chapter 10 we present evidence that this was so. Finally, we would expect that the greater the potential for the expression of severe hostility, the more the child would have to defend against it. A Spearman rank-order correlation of .67 between the amount of severe hostility observed during the first doll-play session and the amount of avoidance of the observers further supports the hypothesis that this avoidance has a defensive function.

Another finding supports the hypothesis that avoidance serves a defensive function. One would expect that children who at least achieve some control through the use of this defense would less frequently show their distress openly by crying for their parents. There is in fact a negative relationship between the amount of crying for the parents and the tendency to avoid Observer Westheimer; the Spearman coefficient is —.71. The relationship between the amount of crying for the parents and the avoidance of Observers Heinicke and Wolpert is also negative, but the Spearman coefficient of —.37 is not statistically significant.

B. The Intercorrelation of Behavior during the First Week of Separation

In Table 29 we present the intercorrelation of the dimensions describing the child's behavior during the first week of separation. As has already been anticipated, the children who avoided the observers most frequently also expressed the most severe hostility during their first doll-play session and cried the least for their parents.

Also noteworthy is the significant correlation between indices of the development of speech and sphincter control.

The lack of correlation in the rest of the table is particularly striking in that by the last week of separation many similarly constructed dimensions did intercorrelate to a considerably greater degree.

C. Background Factors Related to Individual Differences during the First Week of Separation

In this section we consider how variation in behavior observed during the first week of separation relates to selected background factors. Ideally these background factors would have included adequate descriptions of the child's functioning before the separation, as well as descriptions of such significant aspects of his environment as the relationship to his mother.

Table 29. *Showing Intercorrelation of Behavior Seen during First Week of Separation*

	1	2	3	4	5	6	7	8	9
1. The Avoidance of Observers Heinicke and Wolpert	——								
2. The Avoidance of Observer Westheimer	.56*	——							
3. The Expression of Severe Hostility during the First Doll Play	.67*	.74**	——						
4. The Amount of Crying for the Parents	-.37	-.71*	-.43	——					
5. The Number of Different Words Used	.04	-.30	-.12	-.21	——				
6. The Extent of Sphincter Control	.25	-.07	-.04	-.27	.76**	——			
7. The Lack of Affectionate Contact with the Father	.46	.15	-.18	-.25	.15	.46	——		
8. The Affectionate Relationship to the Nurses	.26	-.16	.08	.46	-.56*	-.32	.01	——	
9. The Greed for Food	-.02	.03	-.01	-.20	-.08	-.13	-.38	.16	——

* Significant at the .05 level
** Significant at the .01 level

The material on the child's functioning before the separation was not adequate enough to treat systematically. The relation between certain characteristics and previous experiences of the children and their reaction to separation could, however, be studied.

One would expect that the age of the child might well affect his response to separation. Within the relatively limited age range (thirteen–thirty-two months), variations in age were in fact not related to variations in the indices describing the child's reactions during the first week of separation.

One would also expect that the initial level of sphincter control and language development would be related to the child's age at separation. The level of sphincter control and the number of different words used do in fact correlate significantly with age; the Spearman coefficients are .82 and .83 respectively.

A careful check was also made as to whether the sex of the child could be related to variations in the indices describing the response to separation during the first week; no statistically significant relationships were found.

We anticipated that previous separations, especially if lengthy, might well affect the child's reactions to another separation. In our present sample, however, there was no relationship between the length of the previous separation and the initial reaction to separation. It should be noted that the previous separations are not long, and that the sample is too small to control with respect to the child's age at the time of the previous separation or the actual length of that separation.

The nature of the responses shown, as well as their intercorrelation, posed the question as to what independent factors could be related to variations found in the amount of crying for parents, the avoidance of observers and the expression of hostility in doll play. Had reliable indices been available of the child's functioning prior to separation, we would have examined them first. Because they were not, other independent factors had to be sought. As it turned out, the dimension describing *The mother's affection for and pleasure in the company of the child* was found to correlate as follows with these dimensions: —.59 with the avoidance of Observers Heinicke and Wolpert; —.19 with the avoidance of Observer Westheimer; —.28 with the expression of severe hostility during the first doll play; and .52 with amount of crying for the parents. The reader wishing to follow the steps in the reasoning that led to the computation of the above coefficients will find a partial account below.

We have suggested above (this Chapter) that the avoidance of the observer (and the associated diminished crying) could be seen as a defense against the anger felt toward the parents and is stimulated by the observer's presence. It can then be predicted that there would be a relation between the extent of this avoidance and the intensity of the hostile affects directed toward the parents before separation. In the absence of adequate observations of the child's behavior before separation, we reasoned that the intensity of these hostile affects could among other things be a function of the extent and quality of love expressed toward the child, especially by the mother.

It will be recalled that we ranked the mother on a number of dimensions. The most appropriate to our immediate task of characterizing the amount and quality of affection shown by the mother toward the child is: *The mother's affection for and pleasure in the company of the child.*

The specific prediction then would be that those children whose mothers demonstrated little affection would express more severe hostility in the doll play, more intensively avoid the observer and cry less for their parents. Although the correlation coefficients were all in the predicted direction, as we have already indicated, only those between the mother's affection for the child on the one hand, and the avoidance of Observers Heinicke and Wolpert and the crying for the parents on the other hand, were of sufficient magnitude to be near the usually accepted level of significance.

The relationship between avoidance of the observer, the absence of crying for the parents, the expression of severe hostility in the doll play and the nature of the relationship between child and parent can be seen in the case of Margaret. Her mother showed her little affection and would often become irritated with her. Feelings of ambivalence would be further heightened by the fact that the father was more solicitous toward Margaret, criticized her mother in her maternal role, but also voiced the high standards he had for Margaret. On the hypothesis advanced it follows that Margaret would be expected to avoid the observers, cry little for her parents and show hostility in doll play. The predictions are confirmed. Not only did Margaret avoid the two observers more ardently than any other child, but she was ranked high for severe hostility in the first doll play and lowest for the amount of crying. That Margaret was during the first days of the separation very sensitive to her father's demands about sphincter control can be seen in her reactions to her father's first visit to the nursery on the third day of separation. Nor is it inconsistent that such sensitivity would exist even though very little reliable control had been achieved. But before reporting this visit, we must digress to describe the first doll-play session which was administered immediately before it.

Only after very careful preparation was it possible to persuade Margaret to go with Wolpert to the room where the doll-play equipment had been set up, and once there, she behaved as if constantly ready to escape. Both her movements and her play were very controlled. In an obsessional manner she opened and closed the large brown cupboard: "I can open; I can shut." This continued for a long time until she suddenly threw it down so vigorously that it broke. She was clearly anxious but, when reassured, again threw down the pieces and then stepped on them. In quick succession she passed flatus and treated the toy bathroom sink and bathtub in the same severely hostile way. This was followed by her hitting Wolpert's white pad and by a look of misery as she did a bowel movement. As far as we know, this was the first lapse in the nursery and thus represents a break in control. Nor do we think it accidental that it was preceded by hostility to the lavatory toys and Wolpert's white pad.

Shortly after the first doll-play session, Margaret's father arrived with a friend and a great deal of fruit, mostly bananas. The minute he entered, Margaret and her older sister, Georgina, both ran up to him and embraced one of his legs while he picked up Pearl, the younger sister. They were clearly very happy to see him, and there was general excitement. Very soon after his arrival, however, Margaret looked at her father and in an inquiring voice said, "You won't smack me, Daddy?" Father looked very hurt at this suggestion as he replied, "No, I won't smack you." He then reassured both Georgina and Margaret that he loved them, but that he had to put them in the nursery until Mummy was out of the hospital. In her anxious questioning of her father, it is possible that Margaret was thinking about the loss of bowel control and the breaking of the wardrobe, and that he would "smack" her for this.

II. Individual Differences during the First Two Weeks of Separation as Related to the Conditions of Separation

In this section we examine how variations in the conditions obtaining shortly before and during the separation relate to variations in the children's behavior during the first two weeks of separation. To make this analysis possible, data on the total sample of eighteen residential children is used—the twelve[1] observed in the present study and the six in the first study (see Heinicke, 1956). This expanded sample has not been used previously and will not be used again because the information on the child's relation to observers, father and nurses was sometimes not sufficient to make the ratings and rankings of all eighteen children possible. The other behavioral dimensions

[1] It will be recalled that we studied two children in addition to the main sample of ten.

used to describe the child's reaction during the first week of separation, and the categorization of behavior in both the first and second week of separation were available, however.

The number of different conditions obtaining shortly before and during a separation, which may influence the way a child reacts, is potentially very large. On the basis both of the analyses that are possible and of our previous discussion of variables likely to be significant, we have concentrated on certain broad questions: (1) If one aspect of the separation involves the loss of the specific attachment to a significant figure, does the child's reaction vary as a function of varying amounts of contact with these significant figures? (2) If another aspect of the separation involves changes in the quality and quantity of interaction with a maternal figure, do variations in the quality and quantity of substitute care affect the child's behavior? (3) If another dimension of the separation studied here involves the shift from a familiar to an unfamiliar environment, does the child react differently if the change in the nature of the routine and environment is either striking or not so drastic? (4) Finally, how do variations in the reason for the separation affect the child's response to separation?

A. The Amount of Contact with the Parents and Siblings

We first examine how variations in the amount of contact with the parents affect the child's behavior during the first two weeks of separation. These analyses are unfortunately seriously limited by the fact that this factor varied little in this particular sample of children.

During the first two weeks of separation all eighteen children were visited by their father about once a week. Only four were visited by their mothers as well. In general these four children cried more for both mother and father than those who were not visited by their mother. (Applying the Mann-Whitney Test, we obtain a P value of approximately .05 for both the first and second week of separation.)

If the above analysis is limited, the evidence is ample that another variation in contact with significant figures, namely, the presence of the child's sibling, affects the reactions of the child during the first two weeks of separation.

Of the total sample of eighteen residential children, five were accompanied by a sibling. In four cases this sibling was one or two years older and in one case he was two years younger. In all cases a deliberate attempt was made by the nursery staff to place the children in the same room and to subject them to the same routine, thus permitting maximum companionship.

How then do the reactions of the children who were accompanied by a sibling differ from those who were not? Applying the Mann-Whitney Test we found, during the first two weeks of separation when a sibling was present, that the children cried less for their parents (P equals approximately .05), expressed severe hostility less often in doll-play during the first week of separation (P equals approximately .01) and also in the Everyday Nursery Setting during the second week (P equals approximately .01).

In other words the frequency of the reactions that are typical of children admitted to a residential nursery is diminished by the presence of a sibling.

Similar comparisons were possible for the extent of loss of sphincter control, the reduction in the number of different words used and variations in the occurrence of illness, but no differences were found. As already suggested, changes in the way that clinical impressions were recorded in the present and the first study made it impossible to compare the two subsamples on the following dimensions: the child's relation to the observer, the child's relation to the father and the child's relation to the nurses.

In order to illustrate the importance of the presence of a sibling and to show also that even so it was insufficient to comfort the child, we give excerpts from the case of Margaret. Margaret, aged 2 years 1 month, was in the nursery for seventeen days accompanied by her two sisters, 4-year-old Georgina and 1-year-old Pearl. The changes in Margaret's relationship to her siblings falls within three phases: days one–three, days four–fourteen and days fifteen–seventeen. Although concentrating on the sibling relationship, other aspects of Margaret's behavior are described to provide the necessary context.

Margaret cried very little during the first three days of separation. Instead she seemed desperately to be controlling all feeling, and despite her misery, she resisted all adults who tried to comfort her.

Margaret's resistance to friendly approaches and a feeling of family unity was no doubt enhanced when the nurse, on the first day, donned a mask and proceeded to treat Margaret's hair for nits. Her first reaction was ardent: "I don't want it"; then as the hairwashing began, she started to scream. Next her hair was cut, and a flannel placed around her head to sustain the action of the antinit solution. Her siblings were treated similarly.

On the second day of separation it became clear that all three children were reacting to the cleansing procedure. Taking the flannel off her head, Georgina threw it from her saying, "I throw you a toilet." When Margaret repeated this phrase, both sisters laughed with pleasure.

Margaret's active resistance to the nurses, and her tendency to control her feelings appeared to be supported by her relation with her two sisters, especially 4-year-old Georgina. During the first days of separation they constantly sought each other's company, talked and laughed together, and gave things to each other. They were also drawn together by a game in which Georgina encouraged Margaret to tickle her leg near the genitals, upon which they both laughed in an excited manner.

During this initial phase we could also observe Margaret's highly ambivalent behavior to her younger sister Pearl. For example on the second day of separation, Margaret was trying to poke Pearl's eyes out. When the observer intervened, Margaret became angry and explained: "Not your baby; it's my baby." Of special interest is the fact that following this behavior and its restriction, Margaret began to rock the cot in which she was standing and then to hit her head (which had been so thoroughly cleansed) against the bed. On the other hand, Margaret also kissed her "Bobo" (Pearl) and gave her much comforting attention.

A feeling of family unity was expressed in a number of ways. "She's not your sister," Margaret told the observer (Wolpert) referring to Georgina, "and not the hospital's sister." Shortly after, she added "My mummy at home." In these remarks she seemed to be telling the observer that the family was still a unit, and that the observer should not interfere.

This same tendency to hold out against the new life-setting could be seen further in Margaret's refusal to eat or to co-operate with the toileting routine. During these days apparently she simply held in her bowel movements. On the other hand she wet herself and began to play with her urine, which got her into trouble. When criticized by the nurse she protested: "My hands are clean."

During the next phase, days four–fourteen, Margaret's contact with both her sisters decreased. Interaction with Pearl stopped altogether. Although this was due partly to Pearl's own withdrawal, and the fact that they had different bedrooms, Margaret showed no desire to see her. Interaction with Georgina was reduced. This was due in large part to changes that occurred in Georgina herself. Not only did the older sister become less attentive, but she also became openly aggressive. For example, on the ninth day of separation Georgina first picked Margaret up in an affectionate motherly way and then suddenly threw her down and sat on her. Nevertheless even attention of this aggressive type tended to make Margaret more affectionate and cheerful; on occasions when Georgina was not there to attend to her, Margaret missed her and looked everywhere for her.

During the last four days of separation Margaret's typical reaction to her sister was to avoid her completely. Our hypothesis is that by physically avoiding Georgina, she was also avoiding the dangers of an aggressive interchange with Georgina. For example, when on the fourteenth day Georgina impulsively embraced her, Margaret showed no reaction. She seemed no longer to miss Georgina and made no efforts to seek her out. This avoidance was not specific to Georgina, however. During these days Margaret actively avoided all three observers and never became emotionally attached to any of the nurses.

We conclude from this description that, while the presence of siblings is initially a comfort and in particular helps to maintain the emotional ties to the family and independence of the nursery routine (see the first three days), these sibling relationships do not fully meet the needs of the child nor do they eliminate hostile impulses arising from deprivation of those needs. Thus, we would hypothesize that, as the separation continued, Margaret's defensive control, developed in relation to the hostility she felt toward her parents, was increasingly threatened by her interaction with Georgina. Just as earlier, after an open expression of ambivalence she had avoided Pearl, so later after an incident of hostility and the threat of loss of control Margaret also avoided Georgina. Difficulty

in maintaining control is, of course, further increased by the ambivalence which is a normal part of a sibling relationship.

B. The Quality and Quantity of Substitute Care

The analyses of the effects of variations in the substitute care the
children received are limited because, as previously indicated, the
care tended to be fairly similar for all. Incomplete descriptions of
the care received by the children in the first study created a further
limitation. Moreover, we are in a position to examine possible effects
during only the first two weeks of separation. If it were possible to
contrast a minimal care situation with one involving highly individualized care, and if particularly one could study the effect of such
differences over a considerable period of time, then one might well
get quite different results.

It is nevertheless of interest that such analyses as were possible revealed no significant relationship between the frequency and nature
of the nurses' care and the child's behavior. For example, a correlation of .36 was found between the frequency with which a nurse
made a positive contact with a child and the frequency with which
the child cried for his parents; this fails to reach the .05 level of significance.

The lack of significant correlation cannot be attributed to com-
bining samples differing seriously in the type of nurse care experienced by the child. Indeed, systematic comparison of the two samples
revealed that the ratio of various kinds of nurse activity to the number of child sequences observed was practically identical for the two
studies. For example, the frequency with which the nurses made a
positive contact with a child divided by the number of units scored
for a child during the first two weeks was .109 for the first study and
.104 for the second.

C. The Change from a Familiar to an Unfamiliar Environment

As we have stressed throughout the book, the children were not only
separated from their parents but were shifted from a familiar physical environment and daily routine to an unfamiliar one. That the
children were aware of these environmental differences was made
plain by their reactions to familiar objects at the moment of reunion.
The question therefore arises as to whether the reactions of the chil-

dren could vary as a function of the extent of difference between their home environment and routine and that found in the nursery.

Although it is recognized that the question of familiarity and strangeness must in part be evaluated in terms of the child's response, for the ten residential children of the present study we have sufficient information on the routine and physical environment in the child's home and in the nursery to enable us to compare children who were subjected to a large change with those subjected to a lesser one. We were able to make assessments on the following points: changes in the frequency of such things as toileting, eating, play and naps; changes in the presence of playmates, freedom to move about, frequency of outdoor play, space and furnishing of the children's rooms, the nature of the food and the availability of toys.

If we thus consider gross changes in the physical environment and routine, we find that for some children the move to the nursery represented more of a change than it did for others. We therefore ranked the children on a dimension running from considerable overall change to very little change: four children who experienced considerable change, four who experienced some change and two who experienced little change. When this ranking was compared with rankings of child behavior during separation no significant correlation was found.

D. The Reason for the Separation

The explicit reason for the separation in thirteen of the total of eighteen children placed in the residential nursery was that the mother was going to the hospital to have a baby. Of the other five, one family was homeless; in two instances the family went on a short holiday; and in two others the mother went to the hospital for treatment.

One would expect that the pregnant state of the mother might well affect certain aspects of the child's behavior during the first two weeks of separation. It is true that hostile attacks on the baby doll could often be linked to this fact (see Chapter 10), but since the separated children whose mothers were not pregnant also showed such behavior, it cannot be attributed only to the state of the mother. Furthermore, taking all the behavioral indices available on the sample of eighteen during the first two weeks of separation, no statistical-

ly significant differences were found between the children whose
mothers were pregnant and those whose mothers were not.

That none of the above indices differentiated the reactions of the
group of children whose mothers were pregnant from those who
were not, does not mean that the condition of the mother is of no
consequence. As shown in Chapter 5, Dawn's behavior during her
fifteen-day separation was very likely influenced by her knowledge
that the mother was pregnant and that the parents wanted a boy.

E. Summary of Findings on Factors Affecting Individual Differences in Behavior during the First Two Weeks of Separation

Some discussion of the findings derived in this and the previous section is necessary to place them in perspective. Certain limitations
in the analyses must be pointed out. It is very possible that certain
factors would have been shown to have an effect had the sample been
larger. For other analyses new studies would have to be conceived
and the mere increase in the size of the sample would not be sufficient. Thus, variations in the quality and quantity of interaction
with a substitute person would have to be considerable in order adequately to study their effect. Similarly, to study the relationship between the reaction to separation and such factors as the child's personality, the mother-child relationship and the pregnant state of the
mother, it would be best to maximize differences in these variables
and to remove the effect of the unfamiliar environment by studying
those situations where the child stays in his home while his mother
is away. In the present study both the homogeneity of the sample
in these respects, and the overriding effect on the child of separation
from significant figures, combined with placement in an unfamiliar
environment, makes it difficult to know what effects these variables
may have.

That much variation in the children's reactions studied here can
be related significantly to variations in the amount of contact the
child had with members of his family (the number of visits by his
mother and the presence of a sibling) is nevertheless of interest. It is
suggested that the visit and departure of the mother tended to disrupt such control over his feelings as the child had achieved and
thus to enhance the frequency of crying. By contrast, the continuous
presence of a sibling tended at first to diminish the severity of the
child's reaction, although it did not provide adequately for his needs.

The above findings also support the hypothesis that for the age group studied here, it is the loss of the specific relationship to the significant people in the child's life, particularly the mother and father, which is the most important aspect of the separation being studied here. In Chapter 12 we shall cite the literature which supports this hypothesis.

III.   Individual Differences in Behavior during the Last Week of Separation

In the same way that we described the differences in the children's reactions during the first week of separation and related them to certain independent factors, so in this section we shall repeat the analysis for the last week of separation. The status of the children at the end of separation is of interest in its own right. In addition, information about it can be used to examine the relationship between differences in that status and differences seen during the following week, namely, the first week of reunion. This will be discussed in Chapter 9.

To characterize the differences seen during the last week of separation we have used a series of dimensions very similar to those used to characterize the reaction to the first week of separation. Those describing the child's lack of affectionate contact with the father, the crying for the parents, the child's affectionate relationship to the nurses and the child's eating are almost identical. Two dimensions refer to similar areas, namely, the child's relation to the observer and the problem of sphincter control, but a change in the salient responses requires a reformulation of the points on the rating scale. Finally, two types of behavior, that involving the enactment of parental roles and that indicating possessiveness, are introduced for the first time.

A.   The Behavior during the Last Week of Separation

1. Lack of Affectionate Response to the Father. As with the dimension describing the child's relations with his father during the first week, we are once more interested in a range of responses running from a lack of affectionate response to a great deal of affectionate contact, as evidenced by the child's clinging and crying when the father left. Parallel to these responses was the child's tendency to be mainly interested either in the sweets that the father brought or in him mainly as a person. The ratings and rankings are given in Table 30.

Table 30. *Showing Ratings and Rankings of the Separated Children in Terms of a Dimension Describing the Child's Lack of Affectionate Response to the Father during the Last Week of Separation*

A. Children whose predominant reaction is one of crying and clinging, but who also show some interest in material goods the father brings
> 1. Dawn
> 2. Jimmy
> 3. Josephine

B. Children who develop some interest in the father as a source of material goods, but in whom this is no greater than their interest in the father himself
> 4. Elizabeth
> 5. Georgy
> 6. Margaret

C. Children whose relation to the father is characterized either by open hostility or *complete lack of affectionate response*, the main interest being in the material goods which he brings rather than in the father himself
> 7. Katie
> 8. Owen
> 9. Dennis
> 10. Gillian

2. Crying for the Parents. The index used to reflect the amount of crying for the parents is the same as that used to study individual differences during the first week of separation: the total amount of crying for the father and mother was divided by the total activity coded.

3. The Child's Affectionate Relationship to the Nurses. Rating and ranking the child's relationship to the nurses during the last week of separation also used the same dimension as for the first week. Once more we are interested in the intensity of affectionate relationship, and the extent to which it was directed toward one nurse who was clearly preferred by the child. The children who resisted the nurses in the beginning, never openly showed their affection and developed no preference for any one nurse even at the end of their separation, are rated as showing little attachment. The dimension is given in Table 31.

Table 31. *Showing Ratings and Rankings of the Separated Children in Terms of a Dimension Describing the Child's Affectionate Relationship with the Nurses during the Last Week of Separation*

A. Children who show neither affection nor preference for a nurse
   1. Margaret
   2. Josephine
B. Children who are friendly but show no preference for any one nurse
   3. Elizabeth
C. Children who cling to several nurses but do not develop a particular preference
   4. Jimmy
D. Children who, by the end of their separation, develop some preference for one nurse and are affectionate with her
   5. Dawn
   6. Georgy
   7. Katie
E. Children who resist the nurses actively or passively in the beginning, and then gradually develop a preference for one or, at the most, two nurses which, by the end of their separation, entails considerable affection
   8. Dennis
   9. Owen
   10. Gillian

4. The Ambivalence Expressed by the Child toward Observers Heinicke and Wolpert. In describing the child's relationship to the observer during the first week of separation, either approach or avoidance were dominant. By the end of their separation the relationship to the observer of some children could best be characterized by the open expression of ambivalence. Since we were primarily interested in the development of this ambivalence, our initial conceptualization contrasted those children who openly expressed it and those who did not—i.e., were affectionate.

Our placing the children who avoided the observer in between these extremes is explained as follows. In purely phenomenonological terms, avoidance of a person indicates more ambivalence than consistently seeking affection. Secondly, in this chapter we have shown that avoidance may well be a defense against the threat of the emergence of feelings of hate and love. Dynamically then, the child who avoids is likely to experience more ambivalence than one who seeks affection.

Thirdly, although not necessary to the formulation of the dimension, certain additional observations justified placing the children who avoid the observer between the two extremes on the dimension of the expression of ambivalence. If we study the relationship of each child to each observer, we can first single out instances where the child initially avoided the observer. As reported previously in this chapter, there are sixteen such instances out of a total of twenty possibilities (two observers times ten children). That is, in four instances the relationship could be described as consistently affectionate. If we now focus our interest on those of the sixteen instances of initial avoidance where the relationship subsequently changed—a total of nine instances—we find that in eight of them open ambivalence in relation to the observer emerged as the subsequent reaction.

By focusing then on the dimension of the extent of the openly expressed ambivalence, we rated and ranked the children as indicated in Table 32.

Table 32. *Showing Ratings and Rankings of Separated Children in Terms of a Dimension Describing the Ambivalence Expressed by the Child toward Observers Heinicke and Wolpert during the Last Week of Separation*

A. Children who are consistently *affectionate* with at least one observer
   1. Elizabeth
   2. Dawn
B. Children who *avoid* both observers
   3. Josephine
   4. Margaret
   5. Jimmy
C. Children who in relation to one or both observers express open ambivalence; i.e., simultaneously express both *affection and hostility*
   6. Georgy
   7. Dennis
   8. Katie
   9. Owen
   10. Gillian

Some evidence of the correctness of the rankings and ratings presented in Table 32 comes from the analysis of the coded records made in the Everyday Nursery Setting. If open ambivalence toward the observer replaces avoidance, and if, as we have already suggested, this ambivalence increases with length of separation, then coded records of both affectionate and hostile responses toward the observer ought to increase. That is, the results of detailed behavioral categorization ought to tally with the clinical judgments made by the observers.

In Table 33 we present the percentages respectively for the "Total Hostility to the Observers" score and total of the acts classified as "Seeks Positive Relations" for the first seven weeks of separation. Total Seeks Positive Relations includes seeking to be near the observers, seeking attention from the observers, seeking affection from the observers and following the observers. Total Hostility includes both mild and severe hostility.

Table 33. *Showing Percentages of Total Activity of Total Seeks Positive Relations and Total Hostility Directed toward Observers Heinicke and Wolpert*

| | *Weeks of Separation* | | | | | | |
	1	2	3	4	5	6	7
Total Seeks Positive Relations	7.90	10.06	14.15	19.13	19.25	20.36	24.44
Total Hostility	.29	.53	.97	5.80	6.48	9.30	9.96

We again remind the reader that by the seventh week percentages are based on only four cases. We use these percentages therefore mainly to give a general picture, rather than to provide support for a given hypothesis. We are also aware that both of the increases shown in Table 33 could simply be a function of the fact that the child who remained in the nursery for a longer period developed a relationship with the observers and thus interacted more and more with them. That an increasing proportion of all behavior should be directed toward the observers indicates the development of a relationship, but it does not explain why both the hostile and affectionate interactions should increase.

5. The Hostility Expressed by the Child in the Everyday Nursery Setting. Since the emergence of hostility is a most important reaction to separation, many findings relating to it have been examined: they are summarized in Chapter 11. Here we confine ourselves to a discussion of the index of hostility that we used in the statistical analyses referring to the end of a child's separation. Ideally, we would simply compute the Total Hostility coded during the last week of a child's separation. Unfortunately, the observations for two of the children during the last week of separation did not meet the sampling specifications outlined in Chapter 2; i.e., a minimum of three thirty-minute observations by each observer. Examination of the data revealed that this affected the stability of hostility scores based only on the last week. Therefore we extended the range of the time period covered and used the Total Hostility score expressed as a percentage of total coded behavior in the entire period following the first week of separation. We experimented with other ways of overcoming our sampling deficit, but the above best reflected the children's differential expression of hostility.

6. *Enacting Parental Behavior.* In this section we examine whether the reactions to the loss of parents include increased enacting of parental behavior. Our interest in this behavior in turn reflects the question of what types of internalization of the parental actions and expectations may be accentuated by the separation situation. We use internalization as a broad concept to include the various processes that have been designated by such concepts as incorporation, introjection and identification. See Reich (1954), Beres (1958), Sandler (1960) and Schafer (1960) for a more recent discussion of the theoretical issues involved.

Behavior was recorded both in the Doll-Play Setting and in the Everyday Nursery Setting in which the child took over certain parental roles. While some internal representation of adult behavior seems necessary to enact such sequences, they were neither frequent nor accompanied by a generalized modification of the behavior being referred to. Of those parental sequences that were seen, a punishing type of role constituted the greatest proportion. An example from Owen's doll play, administered during the period when he had developed an openly ambivalent relationship to the observer, has already been cited (see Chapter 5). After expressing the wish to get the "baby" out of the wardrobe, he suddenly exclaimed "Wee-wee, wee-wee." It was then found that he had already done a bowel movement. Although not unduly upset by this event, his feelings about it were indicated in various ways, of which the most striking was the way he took the toy toilet and spanked the mother doll with it, repeating "mack." The following aspects of this behavior should be noted. One can infer that Owen had the idea that persons get spanked when they fail to perform on the toilet. It is he who is now the punishing parent, while the mother is the bad child. Certain internalized schemata relating to the mother and himself are implied, and the force of parental authority is enacted. Yet the presence of all these did not at that moment lead to actual control of his sphincters.

Next in frequency, as observed in doll play, was a cleaning type of parental behavior. Seen only very rarely were other benign maternal sequences. Both of these, as well as an additional form of behavior modeled on the parent, are exemplified by Dennis. Two weeks before the end of his separation he was told that his mother had had a baby girl. Following this announcement he could often be seen walking around with his stomach protruding. During this period, and specifically on the forty-eighth day of separation, Dennis began a doll-play session by manipulating the toy toilet for a long time, opening and closing the lid, and putting his finger into the toilet. He spanked the toilet mildly and then put the baby into the toy bath: "Baby have bath." Following the bath, the baby was carefully bedded down in a crib and Dennis then rocked the crib. Shortly after this he became more anxious, rocked back and forth on his feet and then indicated that he wanted to have a drink of water. That is, one could infer that he wanted to be rocked and spoiled the way he had taken care of the baby. Asking for a drink of water, rocking himself either on his feet or in a chair, and the maternal type of play with the baby doll, all increased during his separation.

By contrast, aggressive attacks by Dennis on both a little girl doll and a particularly pathetic little girl in his group had been seen in the Everyday Nursery Setting on the day before the above doll play. He tried to gouge the eyes of the doll out of their sockets and hit the little girl with some scissors. The nurse quickly intervened. But later he bit this same girl and tried then to lock her up in a large doll house with the obvious intent of getting rid of her.

We are aware that the above enactment of either harsh or benign parental behavior may have many different meanings. A larger sample would be needed to clarify the issue further. But the very fact that the child enacts some form of parental behavior is in itself significant. Examination of the data revealed that such sequences occurred in at least one of the doll plays of seven of the children. For two of these children there was no change in the frequency of the behavior when the first and last doll-play sessions are compared. The remaining five all showed a greater frequency of parental behavior during the last doll play, administered at the end of the separation.

As already suggested, behavior very similar to the above was observed in the Everyday Nursery Setting, as shown by three children. Thus, often Katie behaved as if she were a punishing mother and the frequency with which she showed this type of behavior increased during her separation. On the twenty-ninth day Katie was walking around constantly repeating "Wee-wee." She carried a pan and on several occasions spanked it as if it was naughty. That this type of scolding did not actually affect her behavior is suggested by the fact that she deliberately spilled some cocoa on the floor immediately afterwards and made a terrible mess. When the nurse said "You made a mess," she repeated "Mess" but was not visibly disturbed.

The context of Katie's punitive parental behavior could be further studied on the tenth day of separation. The interplay with the observer, the nurse and a younger child highlights certain features of it. When in the playroom, Katie soon wanted to be placed in the high chair in which she had all her meals. She was looking after a teddy bear, pretending to feed him, wiping his nose and doing all this most affectionately. She asked the observer for a book, said "Thank 'oo" when it was given to her and, while looking at the book, pretended to eat. She then put the book in front of her face, said "Bye-bye," as though she were leaving the observer, then peeped out from behind the book and began to rub her eyes as if crying. Though mostly affectionate with the observer, she suddenly threw the book at her, only to urgently demand its return.

As Katie was hugging the teddy bear, Alan, a 13-month-old boy, came up to her and made a noise. She looked at him severely and said "Don't," then hit him and whispered again "Don't." As if disgusted, she turned to him and told him to "Go away." When Alan later knocked a chair over making a noise, Katie commented with a disapproving "Ooooh." At the same time she glanced at the observer as if to say "We both know how naughty he is." A possible link to her own mother-child experiences is suggested by the fact that she was now calling the observer "Mummy."

Her initial behavior on the pot an hour later also suggested an adult orientation. She willingly sat on the pot, was told by the nurse that she was a good girl and then proudly stood up announcing that she had "been." The nurse objected that she had not done anything and tried to make her sit down again, but Katie became terribly upset. Giving up, the nurse told her that if she wet herself she would be cross. She repeated after the nurse "Coss." When the nurse added "No mercy," Katie parroted "Mercy." The nurse then combed her hair, Katie clearly enjoying being made to look pretty. "Look, Mummy," she said to the observer.

She had no sooner been placed in her high chair for lunch than she also proudly displayed that she was "weeing" in her pants; she seemed delighted that she had done the "wee" on the chair.

The above behavior of the tenth day of separation was chosen because it shows Katie in a period of transition. By the fourteenth day of separation she still had not regained the level of sphincter control seen before the separation, but she was now most concerned about her lapses. Moreover, the exclusively affectionate sequences observed in relation to the teddy bear were by the thirteenth day practically nonexistent. By contrast, the sequences portraying the harsh parent increased. An example from the last week of separation is typical. Katie picked up a doll and indignantly proclaimed: "Dolly is wet." She started smacking the doll and then announced: "Dolly is crying." She kept on smacking her but then insisted: "Enough crying, enough crying."

Examination of the frequency of this behavior in each of the three children where it was observed at all in the Everyday Nursery Setting reveals that it occurred more frequently during the last week of their separation than during the first week. The findings thus parallel those of the doll play.

The interpretation of this behavior as indicating the presence of a defensive identification will be discussed further in Chapter 13. Some preliminary remarks are given below.

Our understanding of this concept follows A. Freud (1936) and Ritvo and Solnit (1958). Though the enactment of the parental roles increased, it was not new. They were part of the child's behavioral repertoire during the first part as well as before the separation. Schemata definitely related to parental behavior are internalized and include an affective aspect, whether this be sadistic or benign. As already suggested, however, the authority implied in the sadism is not associated, for example, with successful sphincter control. Similarly, the affection shown to a doll is not associated with the general ability to be affectionate to the other children. Most important, in observing such behavior one received the impression that the children, either by energetically giving love to a doll or adhering slavishly to their idea of a parental command, were desperately attempting to enhance their own feeling of being loved and approved.

7. *Concern over a Lapse in Sphincter Control.* The content of parental roles enacted suggests that the area of sphincter control and especially the concern about that control should be studied in describing the child's status at the end of his separation.

Earlier we have emphasized that from the fourth until the fourteenth day of separation the children showed a striking lack of sphincter control. Those children who remained longer than this showed some progress toward achieving complete sphincter control, but this was strikingly unstable. This very fact made it difficult to be confident of one's rating of the degree of control achieved, and we therefore concentrated on what we felt to be salient to the child's functioning at this time, namely his concern about the lapses that did occur. In Table 34 we give the results of ranking the children on the dimension of the extent of concern over a lapse in sphincter control.

Table 34. *Showing Ratings and Rankings of Separated Children in Terms of a Dimension Describing the Child's Concern over a Lapse of Sphincter Control during the Last Week of Separation*

A. Children who show no indication of concern
> 1. Elizabeth
> 2. Dawn
> 3. Jimmy
> 4. Georgy
> 5. Margaret

B. Children who show some concern over a lapse
> 6. Gillian
> 7. Katie

C. Children who show considerable concern over a lapse at the end of their separation
> 8. Josephine
> 9. Owen
> 10. Dennis

Similarly, we can make judgments of the extent of concern over sphincter lapses exhibited by each of the children in their last session of doll play. This concern was judged to be present when, in addition to the commonly recognized signs of anxiety, the child suddenly indicated that he wanted to go to the toilet. Not only was there an urgent quality to this, but the children often refused to return to the doll play.

If we relate the concern shown in doll play to that shown in the Everyday Nursery Setting we obtain the results presented in Table 35. Applying Fisher's Exact Test, we find a P value of approximately .05.

Table 35. *Showing Relation of Concern over Sphincter Lapse in Doll Play to That in the Everyday Nursery Setting*

Observation in Everyday Nursery Situation	Observation in Doll Play	
	Concern	No Concern
Concern	4	1
No Concern	0	5

Thus, the increasing concern over sphincter lapses in certain children is not confined to one situation. Before interpreting this increasing concern and related control it is necessary to present the development of the child's sphincter control during reunion. This is done in the next chapters.

8. Greed for Food. In Table 36 we have rated and ranked the children in terms of the extent of greed seen during the last week of separation, using a similar rating scale to that used for the first week of separation (see Table 27). The results indicate the much greater greed that many of the children had developed.

Table 36. *Showing Ratings and Rankings of Separated Children in Terms of a Dimension Describing the Child's Greed for Food during the Last Week of Separation*

A. Children who by the end of the separation eat well but show no signs of greed
    1. Jimmy
    2. Elizabeth

B. Children who develop definite signs of greed
    3. Dawn
    4. Georgy
    5. Margaret
    6. Josephine
    7. Dennis
    8. Gillian

C. Children who by the end of the separation develop great greed
    9. Owen
    10. Katie

9. *Signs of Possessiveness.* Consistent with the greed for food, the children also became more possessive, particularly for material things, as the period of separation lengthened. After playing briefly with the observer's keys or writing pad, Owen would claim them as "mine" to the extent that the observer found it hard to get them back. The objects involved no doubt had many different meanings; it is the quality of possessiveness, however, that we wish to emphasize. It should also be pointed out that the possessiveness was not exclusively directed to the favorite toy or presents brought by the visiting parents but extended to many material goods.

By the last week of separation three children had developed the degree of possessiveness illustrated above: all had experienced a longer separation than the others.

B. *The Intercorrelation of Behavior during the Last Week of Separation*

Examination of the various tables suggests that the eight behavioral dimensions are highly intercorrelated. The rho coefficients for seven of them are given in Table 37. Instead of determining the association between the occurrence of parental role enactments during doll play and each of these dimensions, we simply report that all four of the children who were ranked highest for ambivalence to the observer enacted the parental role during the last weeks.

Table 37. *Showing Intercorrelation of Behavior Seen during the Last Week of Separation*

Behavior Dimensions	1	2	3	4	5	6
1. The Ambivalence Expressed toward Observers Heinicke and Wolpert	——					
2. The Lack of Affectionate Contact with the Father	.82**	——				
3. The Affectionate Relationship to the Nurses	.84**	.70*	——			
4. The Hostility in the Everyday Nursery Setting	.64*	.56*	.47	——		
5. The Concern Over a Lapse in Sphincter Control	.64*	.66*	.46	.92**	——	
6. The Greed for Food	.76**	.77**	.61*	.75**	.81**	——
7. The Crying for the Parents	-.28	-.31	-.05	-.08	-.21	-.07

* Significant at the .05 level
** Significant at the .01 level

The same method was used to determine the association between ambivalence to the observer and a high degree of possessiveness. The three children who showed a specially high degree of possessiveness were among those ranked in the first four for ambivalence to the observer. (Applying Fisher's Exact Test to the resulting contingency table yields a P of .05.)

By contrast with this pattern of significant intercorrelation, the amount of crying for the parents does not correlate significantly with any of the other dimensions described. In interpreting this it must be added that by the last week of separation, both the total quantity and the range in the amount of crying for the parents was greatly diminished.

Summarizing the results of the intercorrelation of the behavioral dimensions we find that those children who by the end of their separation showed no signs of affection to their fathers, tended to express ambivalence toward the observers, became increasingly affectionate to the nurses, became greedy, showed increased concern over a lapse in sphincter control, enacted the parental role in doll play and showed a high degree of possessiveness.

In the above we have not tried to demonstrate the high degree of intercorrelation as such, but rather that certain responses do in fact cluster together. One could no doubt have developed other dimensions that would not correlate with this cluster. One could also object that the correlation might in part have been introduced by the rater who was ranking the children on all the dimensions. We shall discuss this problem in an Appendix to Chapter 9.

C. Factors Related to the Child's Status at the End of Separation

In trying to account for the differences of behavior seen at the end of separation, we have examined their relation to the various mother-child dimensions, the age of the child and the reactions seen during the first week of separation. None of these factors was associated at the usually accepted levels of significance with the findings on any of the dimensions reported.

The length of the child's separation is, however, significantly associated with all but two of the seven dimensions reported. Table 38 gives the results.

Table 38. *Showing Correlation between Length of Time Child Was Separated and Indices of His Status at the End of Separation*

Indices of Status at End of Separation	Coefficient
1. The Ambivalence Expressed toward Observers Heinicke and Wolpert	.72*
2. The Lack of Affectionate Contact with the Father	.82**
3. The Affectionate Relationship to the Nurses	.67*
4. The Hostility in the Everyday Nursery Setting	.42
5. The Concern Over a Lapse in Sphincter Control	.54*
6. The Greed for Food	.87**
7. The Amount of Crying for the Parents	−.01

* Significant at the .05 level
** Significant at the .01 level

Because the children fell into two main groups with respect to the length of their stay in the nursery, namely about two weeks and more than two weeks, it may be more accurate to use this distinction and to compare the result with those for a dichotomized form of each of the behavioral dimensions. The outcome is not very different. Applying Fisher's Exact Test to the resulting contingency tables, we find that length of separation is associated to a significant degree with six of the behavioral dimensions. The P values are as follows: relations with the observer, .005; relations with the father, .005; relations with the nurse, .005; hostility in the Everyday Nursery Setting, .05; concern over lapse in sphincter control, .05; and greed for food, .005.

Similarly we can relate length of separation to evidence of the child enacting the parental role during doll play and a high degree of possessiveness as seen in the last week or weeks of separation. The P values for the contingency tables are respectively .005 and .05. (Again, only the amount of crying is not related to length of separation.)

Once more summarizing and again slightly oversimplifying, we find that by the end of their separation those children who were separated for more than two weeks showed no signs of affection in relation to their visiting father, expressed strong ambivalence toward the observers, were generally more hostile, became more affectionate with the nurses, became greedy, were more concerned over lapses in sphincter control, more frequently enacted the parental role in doll play and showed a high degree of possessiveness. We will add to these conclusions after we have presented the findings on behavior during the reunion period and results of comparing the separated with the nonseparated children.

Typical Behavior during Reunion

8   In this and the next chapter we are concerned with the children's behavior during the period following their reunion with their parents. In this chapter we delineate reactions common to all children and in the next describe individual differences in the development during reunion.

To anticipate the latter and to provide some orientation, we have in the last chapter shown that the nature of the child's development during separation was associated with its length. Thus, the children who were separated for more than about two weeks showed a lack of affectionate response to the visiting father, developed a more positive relationship to the nurses, were openly ambivalent in relation to the observers and so forth. The questions that arise now are whether these children remain distant from their father and mother when they are again in their homes, what their further development is and whether individual variations can be understood in light of variations in development during separation. As will be seen, those children who remained in the residential nursery for more than about two weeks showed the effects of separation for a longer period than did those who had been away from home less than two weeks.

But as indicated, before describing individual variations, responses which are common to all or most children are described. This will serve as a background against which variations can be studied. Thus, certain behavior was typically seen at the moment of reunion. Applying the technique of analysis according to time periods and phases to the observations during the rest of the reunion period, we also concluded that a shift in development typically took place between the third and fourth day after reunion. Although the quality and timing of this shift was not identical for all children, generalizations could be made about a child's relationship both to his mother and to Westheimer before and after the shift. We were not able to

214

delineate as many typical forms of behavior during the period of reunion as we could for the separation; this is largely due to the children's having had very different experiences during the separation.
Proceeding to the sixteenth week of reunion, almost all children
typically avoided the nursery observer who came to visit them at
that time. To understand the implications of this reaction, as well as
for other reasons, we examine finally how the children were typically
developing after about twenty weeks of reunion.

I. Typical Behavior during the First
Three Days after Reunion

A. The Moment of Reunion

It will be recalled that it had in all cases been arranged that Westheimer should meet the parents at the nursery and drive them home.
In only one case was this not possible, and in this instance she was
replaced by Wolpert. In all cases, therefore, behavior during the actual moment of reunion and the hours after it was observed at first
hand. In seven out of the ten cases the father was not present, so that
the mother was the first to greet the child. In the remaining three,
the father and Westheimer brought the child to the mother who
was waiting for them at home or, as it happened in one case, who
was waiting in the hospital.

What then were the immediate reactions of the child to his mother? In the first study we found that five out of six children at the moment of reunion showed a negative reaction to the mother (Heinicke,
1956, p. 164). In this study, a lack of affectionate response could be
seen in all ten of them. It took two main forms.

In two instances doubt arose as to whether the child recognized
his mother. For example, when Gillian was first confronted with her
mother, she stared into space; later, when asked where her mummy
was, she turned to Westheimer.

The other reaction, that of turning or backing away, was observed
in the remaining eight cases. The child either walked away from his
mother or turned his face or back to her. Although this was similar
to the way the children avoided the observers in the nursery, in no
case did the child carry it to the point of leaving the room as often
happened with the observers.

Eight of the children either cried or came close to tears at the moment of reunion with the mother. An example is Dawn, who wanted to maintain distance, but whose mother hugged her so much that she cried. Alternating at times with the crying was another response—a blank, affectless facial expression. Owen's puzzled, dull and expressionless look is an excellent example of this. Although not as extreme as in the case of Owen, there were five other children whose facial expression was affectless upon reunion with the mother.

The reactions described were seen in relation to the mother and rarely in relation to the father. Although two of the children cried on reunion with the father, nine of the ten responded to him affectionately. For some of them reunion with the father was a happy occasion. Although one child, Owen, was at first reserved, even he never turned away from his father and was soon affectionate. In view of the failure of all ten children to respond affectionately to the mother, it is of special interest that during the first hours of reunion five of them were affectionate toward Westheimer.

One other observation applies to all the children: neither at the moment of reunion nor later did we observe any signs of regret at leaving the nurse or nursery. Although two children turned from the parent to the nurse, in each case it was short-lived, and their turning away from the parent seemed to be of more importance than turning toward the nurse.

Although detailed descriptions of the moment of reunion for Dawn and Owen have already been presented in Chapter 5, because of the great intrinsic interest of these reactions we quote from Westheimer's record of another child, Gillian:

Gillian was aged 1 year 7 months at the end of her seventy-two days' separation.

Gillian was in the nursery playing, and we watched her through the window. She seemed quite oblivious of our presence, however. For some minutes we stood there, and still she did not see us. It seemed almost incredible that though she was facing us, she was yet unaware of us. Instead, she was interested in the other children and turned to watch them. She climbed about on a little chair and never again looked in the direction of the window. When the nurse came by and realized that Gillian had not noticed us, she tapped the glass pane. Gillian looked up. On seeing her mother, however, she only stared, and she continued to stare at her without any other response for about two minutes. Then she shifted her glance toward the nurse, smiled at her, looked back at her mother and again stared at her in the same way as before. When the nurse moved away Gillian turned her head slightly to the side in a direction opposite to the one in which the nurse had disappeared. Then she turned back quickly and once again stared at her mother.

Mother then entered the nursery, went straight to Gillian and knelt down beside her. Gillian, however, made no gesture of recognition nor any other response. Instead she looked blankly at her mother apparently without any comprehension of who she was. Mother commented sadly: "She does not know me, she does not know me at all." When a little later another nurse came to dress Gillian, the child went to her very readily. Without hesitation and without looking back at her mother, Gillian left the room on the nurse's arm. In passing she looked at the fieldworker in a puzzled way.

A little later Gillian, now dressed, returned still on the nurse's arm. When the nurse tried to hand her over to her mother, Gillian refused and turned away; and she maintained her hold of the nurse. The nurse then put Gillian down on the floor, thinking that this would make a return to mother easier. But Gillian continued her hold of the nurse's hand and refused to take her mother's. Although the nurse tried repeatedly to get her to go to mother, each time Gillian turned away and clung to the nurse.

Next the nurse suggested that we should all walk along the passage, as it might then be easier for Gillian to hold her mother's hand. Gillian walked along between mother and nurse. One hand was in the nurse's, and mother tried hard to take her other one. But Gillian appeared not to notice and did not take mother's hand. At the end of the passage once again Gillian refused point blank to go to her mother.

The matron now joined the party and, with the nurse, walked downstairs with Gillian. Mother again reached for Gillian's hand, but Gillian still did not take it. Half way downstairs mother made yet another attempt, and this time Gillian did take it; but a moment later when she realized whose hand she was holding, she took it away again. Throughout this time Gillian never let go of the nurse's hand.

At the bottom of the stairs the nurse withdrew her hand and began slowly to return up the stairs. Gillian looked puzzled and bewildered. At last, however, she took her mother's hand and trotted out of the nursery at her side toward the car. Though very near to tears she tried hard not to cry, and her control did not give way until after we had reached the car. Mother entered it and the matron lifted Gillian on to her mother's lap. Then, when the door was shut, but before the fieldworker had had time to enter, Gillian suddenly broke into uncontrollable crying. This lasted for about four minutes. She sobbed and sobbed heartbrokenly. Mother kept talking to her, saying "Don't cry, Gillian, be a good girl," but Gillian did not respond and went on sobbing as before. After a while Gillian stopped crying. She lay across her mother's shoulder, still and motionless, with eyes brimming with tears and averted from her mother. Indeed only once during the whole of the journey did she look at her mother. For the rest, though mother talked to her and tried to make her feel more at ease, Gillian only stared ahead, occasionally giving the fieldworker a puzzled look. Frequently her lip quivered, especially when her mother talked to her; but she controlled herself and there were no more tears. It was a pathetic picture of a heartbroken little girl. After fifteen minutes in the car her eyes gradually began to close, and she fell asleep.

During all this time Gillian had been carrying Archy, a doll from home. Although during the last few weeks in the nursery Archy had ceased to be of importance to Gillian, now she clung to him tenaciously. While Gillian was sitting on her mother's lap in the car, mother tried to take Archy away from her, but she refused to let go. Even after she had fallen asleep, and mother tried to remove Archy in an effort to make her more comfortable, Gillian's grasp tightened, and mother desisted.

Gillian wakened when the car stopped. Since mother was unable to carry the child, the fieldworker did so. Gillian looked around and, on seeing her mother, once more broke into uncontrollable crying. After a minute or two, however, it became more controlled, and by the time we had reached the steps up to the house, her crying had stopped. Outside the front door, however, when the fieldworker gently put Gillian on the ground, she once again burst into tears. Mother tried to console her and the crying stopped again after two to three minutes. Gillian, however, was very quiet, and even in the familiar passage of her home, she looked around in bewilderment. She refused to have her coat taken off, and at the fieldworker's suggestion, mother allowed her to keep it on. She also refused to let go of Archy.

On entering the sitting room Gillian stood immobile, looking puzzled and bewildered. Uttering no sound, she stayed in this motionless state for several minutes. Mother tried hard to get her interested in something. When handed her teddy bear, Gillian took it with one hand, while with her other she continued to cling to Archy. She showed no interest in Bambi nor in the toy doll.

By now the mother was anxious for Gillian to kiss her and asked: "Give Mummy a kiss," but Gillian did not respond. Nor did she utter a word. Next she edged toward the fieldworker, who picked her up and placed her on her lap, at which Gillian seemed a little reassured. Trying desperately to get some response from the child, mother offered her a piece of bread and butter, but Gillian refused it. And when mother sought to encourage her by holding it close to her mouth, she turned away. The orange drink she refused too. Still hoping to get some acknowledgment from the child, mother kept repeating, "Where's Gillian's Mummy?", but instead Gillian only turned to the fieldworker on whose lap she still was. Mother remarked, "She thinks you are her mother," and added that Gillian evidently did not recognize her at all. Then for a long time Gillian looked round the room as though she were trying to understand where she was and why she was there.

After an interval the fieldworker tickled Gillian gently, which produced a slight suggestion of a smile. So mother repeated it, anxious that Gillian should respond to her also. This led the fieldworker to judge that it was time to leave the two together. She therefore gently removed Gillian from her lap and placed her next to her mother. For a moment Gillian's lip quivered and two big tears rolled down her face. Mother wiped them away, saying, "Don't cry, Gillian." Not a sound, however, came from the child. Mother now picked her up and carried her on her arm; though Gillian did not object she did not respond. As the fieldworker walked down the stairs, mother and Gillian watched her go. Mother remarked that it was just like the fieldworker's first visit to the house, when they had stood in a similar way. "Only," mother added, "on that occasion Gillian wanted you to go. Now she would be much happier if you could stay."

In order to study the persistence of the typical behavior, we shall examine it as it occurred during two further periods of time, namely the first three days after reunion and the next nineteen and a half weeks, making twenty weeks in all.

B. The First Three Days after Reunion

Focusing first on the child's relationship to the mother, we find that in nine cases a lack of affectionate response to her persisted in some degree throughout the first three days after reunion: this was so even though other and opposite kinds of behavior occurred as well. In five cases absence of affectionate response remained the dominant feature; there was no clinging, and the mothers characteristically complained that the children treated them like strangers. In four cases, turning away from mother alternated with episodes of clinging to her. At the end of the first day only one child, Elizabeth, responded affectionately to her mother. None of the children were at this time openly hostile toward mother.

During these days the relationship to the father was, in nine of the ten cases, an affectionate one and in four it included active clinging. Altogether, five of the ten children clung to either the father and/or mother and were afraid to be left.

None of the children expressed direct hostility toward Westheimer, but their behavior was in contrast to their initial affectionate reaction to her. Eight of them maintained some emotional distance, five by active avoidance, including one who made it clear that he was afraid that Westheimer would take him away again, and three by absence of positive affect.

To illustrate some of the above generalizations and in order to be able to follow one child in some detail, we give excerpts from the interview held in Gillian's home on the third day of reunion:

When mother opened the door to the fieldworker, she had Gillian on her arm. Gillian smiled by screwing up her eyes so that they were practically closed. She had at times done this during her stay in the nursery.

Father had been home, and as he was leaving, he hugged Gillian. She did not respond in any way; only when the door was closed after him did she look to see if he had really gone.

During the greater part of the visit Gillian was playing with her doll "Dodo." Using the same face cloth her mother had used for wiping her face, she washed the doll's face and legs. At the same time she talked to "Dodo" and hummed a little tune, giving the impression of being quite content; a little later she enjoyed playing "bee-boo" (peek-a-boo) with the fieldworker, peering around the table to see her.

At one point mother thought that Gillian needed her pot and sat her on it. Although the child did not protest, neither did she perform, and after five minutes mother took her off it.

The mother related how, after the fieldworker had left on the previous afternoon of reunion, she had found a puddle on the floor. For an hour or so following the fieldworker's departure, Gillian had remained in a bemused state but eventually had accepted some milk from her mother, though she had refused all solid food. On the second day she had refused to eat bread and butter, always enjoyed prior to the separation, but had eaten most of her dinner. She would have nothing to do with the landlady, nor would she accept chocolate from a neighbor, which mother thought was most unusual.

The mother reported that on seeing father for the first time "She looked at him very strangely, just as she did with me, and would have nothing to do with him." She would not allow him to take her on his knee, though on the second day after reunion she had not objected, even if she had not responded.

Mother herself had burst into tears after the fieldworker had left on the day of reunion. She could not bear the thought that Gillian might not want to have anything to do with her. Even after several hours at home Gillian was still "strange and unresponsive," and mother considered that she must give her time to "find herself."

On that first day Gillian was ready for bed. She allowed her mother to wash her and once in bed fell asleep almost at once. After a few hours however the child began to whimper; finally she wakened and looked about her in a bewildered manner. Mother soothed her, and eventually Gillian did go to sleep, this time more soundly.

On the second day after reunion mother considered that Gillian "has come round quite quickly" and that "she is behaving more like her usual self" again. But she would not have her mother kiss her or her father. Before the separation, "she had been a child for kissing."

It seemed that Gillian had again made some contact with her mother. She would go to her when mother called her, would allow her to attend to her and would take selected food from her. In her play too she seemed quite content. Her continuous and forced smile, however, was very marked; it seemed like a forced declaration that everything was all right.

II.   Typical Behavior from the Fourth Day to the Twentieth Week after Reunion

In contrast to the homogeneity of the children's reactions during the first two weeks of separation and the early days after reunion, in the subsequent weeks the reactions of the ten children show much variety. There was, however, certain behavior which occurred often enough to be called typical.

A. Behavior during the Whole Period

1. *Ambivalence toward Mother and Westheimer.* We have grouped together the children's reactions to these two people because in many ways they ran parallel. While qualitatively the same, the reaction to the observer was less intense than that to mother.

As previously noted, during the second and third days of reunion all but one of the children showed an absence of affectionate response to either mother and/or Westheimer. In the following weeks, eight out of the ten children at some point became openly ambivalent to the mother, being both hostile or defiant as well as affectionate to her. For five of these children the ambivalence continued for at least twelve weeks. The open ambivalence characterizes the relationship of five out of the ten children to Westheimer. Thus it can be seen that during reunion, just as during separation, there is a shift from some form of initial absence of contact to an open expression of hostility or defiance, coupled with affection. Unlike what occurred during separation, however, during the rest of the reunion period expression of hostility or defiance gradually diminished, while expression of affection became as dominant as it had been before the separation. We do not wish to imply that the avoidance of the observer early in the separation is the same thing as an absence of affectionate contact during reunion. We suggest later (Chapter 13), however, that both can be related to the problem of the expression of aggression.

2. *Relations with Father.* The children's relations with father, which during the initial period had highlighted clinging and wanting to be close to him, continued to be predominantly affectionate. Both Owen and Dawn illustrate this.

3. *Changes in Eating Behavior.* After some initial reluctance to eat (discussed below), the eating habits of nine out of the ten children returned to what they had been previous to the separation. They ate well and enjoyed most foods.

4. *Sleep Disturbance, and the Development of Sphincter Control, Speech and Identification with the Parent.* The children's development in these respects is again best characterized by a description of individual differences. (See the next chapter.) Here it suffices to say that a disturbance of sleep and progress toward complete sphincter control was seen in seven of the ten children during at least the first five weeks after reunion, and then they diminished.

Seven and eight children respectively showed a spurt in the use of language and in behavior indicative of identification with the parents. If the disturbance of sleep and progress toward complete sphincter control occurred typically in the first weeks after reunion, the spurt in the use of language and in behavior indicative of identification with the parents was more typically seen after several weeks of reunion had elapsed. Thus, five of the ten children showed *both* types of growth some time after the third week of reunion.

5. *Other Forms of Behavior.* Certain other forms of behavior are described so that comparisons with similar behavior during separation can be made. They have not been treated systematically, however, because evidence and/or variation was insufficient for them to be dealt with in this way.

Such observations as are available suggest that the child's play with favorite toys was predominantly positive, and that the incidence of illness and sucking was normal for the child. Four of the ten children showed slightly exaggerated possessiveness during the first few weeks after reunion, but this was not of the same intensity as we had observed during separation. Four others were initially sometimes sad as well as excessively cheerful. Self-injury was rarely observed.

B. *Avoidance of Observers Heinicke and Wolpert at Sixteen Weeks*

The design of the study included a visit to the home by Heinicke or Wolpert after the child had been reunited with his parents for sixteen weeks. Because the children had not seen either of the observers since leaving the nursery until this time, it is striking that all the children clearly remembered them and reacted with strong affect, and all but one made a desperate attempt to avoid them. An example will best illustrate it:

When the observer (Heinicke) approached the door of the nicely situated suburban home, he could hear Josephine, now aged 2 years 4 months, making all kinds of excited, joyous noises. As her mother opened the door, Josephine at once exclaimed "No," ran over to the staircase, sat down ejaculating another "No," and picked up the gollywog [rag doll] she had had in the nursery and threw it at the observer. Mother, observer and child then went into the garden with the intention of sitting together on a blanket. Josephine could not sit still, however, and remained excited throughout. She pulled clothes off the line and began to throw them on the grass. Though this was clearly provocative, her mother at first did nothing; the mother's tendency not to restrict her daughter was characteristic but may have been enhanced by the observer's presence and by surprise that her child should suddenly act this way.

Josephine now became even more excited. She ran about vigorously, repeatedly throwing herself into the air and landing on her bottom. She seemed to ignore any pain she inflicted on herself and to get satisfaction from her performance.

Gradually her aggression turned toward mother. She threw herself at her mother and began to bite her, first on the arm and then her necklace. Mother was again surprised by this behavior since nothing like it had occurred for some time, but she now restricted it.

Up to this point Josephine had been very afraid of the observer and assiduously avoided even his mildest approach. When the observer walked toward her a very worried look came over her face, she called "Mummy" in a crying tone and went over to her.

Although she continued to react to any approach by the observer by running away, Josephine would try to sneak up to him and to hit him on his back as long as he remained still. Sometimes she first ran away from him and then turned toward him and suddenly hit him.

Finally, while the observer sat quietly in one place, she crept close enough to cover him with a small blanket, whereupon she exclaimed "All gone" and then uncovered him again. Both this game and her running back and forth were reminiscent of the way in which, during the separation, Josephine had actively initiated many events which she had experienced passively. Mother herself remarked that the way Josephine treated the observer was quite different to the way she treated other strangers. She was surprised that Josephine should so anxiously avoid someone she had not seen for sixteen weeks.

Of particular interest is the fact that the change from avoidance of the observer to aggression is seen during one visit. Qualitatively it was very similar to the change from avoidance to ambivalence seen in relation to Westheimer at an earlier period of reunion.

The reactions of eight of the nine other children were similar to those of Josephine. Furthermore, the one exception, Dawn, is of much interest. It will be remembered that all but two of the children had avoided Observers Wolpert and Heinicke at some point during the separation. Of those two, one, Elizabeth, only avoided Heinicke and was affectionate with Wolpert, while the other, Dawn, avoided Wolpert and was consistently affectionate with Heinicke to the point of trying to follow him out of the nursery. It is, therefore, of interest that Dawn was the only child who at the sixteen-week reunion visit did not avoid Heinicke, but instead let him pick her up and even tried to follow him when he left.

It might be objected that at this visit all that is observed is simply reaction to a stranger. It is most unlikely that this was the case. First, each of the mothers reported that their children were not reacting to other unfamiliar visitors with such panic at this time. Second, it was clear from various details that the children remembered the Observers Heinicke and Wolpert. Third, the reactions of the matched nonseparated children were very different when a similar visit was made to their homes sixteen weeks after they had last seen that observer. If, for both the separated and nonseparated children, we classify the reaction as one either of approaching the observer or of avoiding him, we obtain the results given in Table 39. The two pairs of children visited by Wolpert reacted in the same way as those visited by Heinicke but have been omitted for purposes of analysis to keep the observer constant.

Table 39. *Showing Reaction of Separated and Nonseparated Children to the Visit Made by Heinicke after Sixteen Weeks of Reunion*

| Groups | Reactions to Heinicke | | |
	Approaches	Avoids	Total
Separated	1	7	8
Nonseparated	8	0	8

Applying Fisher's Exact Test we obtain a P of .005 and can conclude, therefore, that the reactions of separated children to the visit

of Heinicke sixteen weeks after reunion differ significantly from the
dominant reactions of their matched controls.

Some persisting psychological change that resulted from the experience in the nursery was thus made apparent at this visit. Since
other signs of disturbance were limited, it is possible that the panic
reaction is a specific one and confined to persons or objects specifically linked to the nursery. Even if this were so, however, it is possible that later it could lead to more serious signs of pathology were
another psychologically similar event to occur.

To attempt to explore this question further we shall look at the
development of the children approximately five months after they
had returned home. This is the point at which the systematic study
of the children ceased.

C. The Separated Children's Development Five Months after Re-
union

In Chapter 6 we described the development of the children during
separation in terms of aspects of behavior as well as of time periods.
The aspects of behavior included language development, sphincter
control, eating and the child's relationship to mother, father, siblings
and observers. Since the coverage and the time periods and qualitative descriptions for all but two of the cases were continued until the
twentieth week after reunion, this point was chosen for an assessment of the group as a whole.

First, what could be said about the child's relationships to his
mother, father and sibling after twenty weeks of reunion? And how
was he developing in his eating, sphincter control, sleeping and language? Both Heinicke and Wolpert made independent assessments
for each child in each of these areas. We asked ourselves whether the
child appeared to be progressing in a way appropriate for him.
Though the comparison was not explicit, the source of the norms
used in making these judgments was the nonseparated group.

In general our assessments revealed a favorable picture, but a few
exceptions to it were noted. Each observer thought that the doll play
of Katie reflected some residual difficulties in relation to her mother.
During the first weeks after reunion Katie had smacked her mother
and insisted "You must leave me no more." Although by the sixteenth week she was no longer doing this, in play with her doll she
was still enacting the theme. (Katie could not be assessed at twenty

weeks, so we do not know whether it would have disappeared by then.) Both Wolpert and Heinicke also agreed that Owen's bed-time ritual, still seen after twenty-two weeks of reunion, could well have been accentuated by the separation experience.

The only other signs of disturbance were evidenced in relation to Westheimer. In form they resembled the frightened avoidance of Heinicke at his visit after sixteen weeks of reunion. For example, after twenty weeks of reunion Josephine still shied away from West-heimer's car, because presumably it was linked in her mind to the fact that she rode in this car the very first time she went to the nurs-ery. Similarly, after twenty-three weeks of reunion Dennis would still not play with the doll set which Westheimer brought to the house.

Independently of Wolpert and Heinicke, Westheimer considered the data available from the period of reunion and compared them with those from the period before separation. For each child she asked herself whether he had suffered a setback in development and whether this was still in evidence twenty weeks after reunion. For five of the children, Elizabeth, Georgy, Dawn, Margaret and Gillian the answer to both questions was no.[1] In two cases, Josephine and Dennis, Westheimer pointed to the specific disturbance shown in re-lation to her but concluded that otherwise these children were de-veloping satisfactorily. In the cases of Katie and Owen, however, Westheimer judged that some setback persisted at sixteen and twenty-two weeks after reunion respectively. Like Heinicke and Wolpert, she noted especially Katie's play with her doll and Owen's bedtime ritual.

Thus the various analyses agree that after twenty weeks of re-union, five children were developing as they had before separation, one (only observed for three weeks) was developing normally at that time, two still showed a few specific fears in relation to West-heimer, and in two behavior probably due to the separation per-sisted—in one for sixteen weeks and in the other for twenty-two weeks after return home. The fact that these two children had experienced the longest periods of separation supports our hypothesis that the

---

[1] John could not be included in this analysis because he could only be observed for three weeks after reunion. At the end of that time, however, he was progressing in his development in a manner essentially similar to that seen before the sepa-ration.

longer the separation, the longer it takes the child to resume his former mode of development.

In evaluating the above conclusions as well as the analyses given below, it must be kept in mind that the supportive relationship of Miss Westheimer with each of the families may well have led to a more successful outcome than would have been the case had this support not been present.

Although not as systematic in nature as the above, further follow-up observations are presented in the Appendix at the end of this chapter.

Appendix to Chapter 8

Further Follow-up Data
on the Separated Children

Although not a formal part of the design, an effort was made to maintain contact with the ten families for at least one year and eight months after the day of reunion. This proved possible in only six cases. Statements about the children's development are further limited by the fact that the coverage after the twentieth week of reunion was not systematic, and other separations or similar traumatic events had occurred. In one instance the latter was so considerable that the child could not be included in the descriptions below. Keeping these reservations in mind but also noting that the subsample is representative of the larger sample of ten, brief statements on five of the children are given below:

1. Owen was visited at intervals until he was 5 years of age, and we have already reported as part of the case presentation in Chapter 5 how he was developing then. Of special interest is that the bedtime ritual had ceased to be a problem.

2. Similarly, Margaret was last seen when she was 5 years of age and already in school. Her mother remarked how good a child Margaret was, and how much she was enjoying school. No developmental difficulties were reported by her mother or noted by Westheimer.

3. With Dennis's family, too, contact was maintained until he was 5 years of age and ready to start school. His mother described him as physically well and full of beans; she also reported that he was continually fighting with his brother, Mathew, who was hard to manage. His refusal to play with the doll-play equipment had continued for some time but had been overcome shortly before his 4th birthday.

4. The last visit with Josephine occurred when she was $3\frac{1}{2}$ years

old. The avoidance of Westheimer seen previously was no longer there, and she even enjoyed going around the block in Westheimer's car. She attended nursery school which she enjoyed, spoke well and looked very grown-up. Though at times rough with her younger brother, this seemed within normal limits.

5. Dawn was 3 years 3 months old when last visited. She too had developed well and was speaking fluently. Though during a previous visit Dawn had clearly been upset, this was no longer the case at the final visit. Details are given in Chapter 5 as part of the case presentation.

The above findings suggest that no *obvious* and *overt* effect of the separation could be detected at a point approximately a year and eight months after the day of reunion. We wish to stress *obvious* and *overt*, since our assessments are limited for a number of reasons. We have already mentioned that these observations are not based on as frequent or as systematic a contact as those made during the five months after reunion. Nor is it possible on the basis of these observations alone to adequately assess whether or not the separation had left behind it an increased potential for emotional disturbance. It is at least possible, should these children be exposed to another separation or some other crisis, that some of them would respond in a more disturbed way than they otherwise would.

Individual Differences in Behavior
during the Period of Reunion

9 In this chapter we return to the study of individual differences. First we describe and intercorrelate a number of behavioral dimensions for each time span and then attempt to account for such variation as exists by relating it to a number of independent factors. The first time span chosen is the first week after reunion. The reason for choosing the first week instead of the previously defined time phase of the first three days is that the span of a week gave us a larger sample of behavior.

I. Individual Differences in Behavior during the First Week after Reunion

A. The Behavior during the First Week after Reunion

1. Lack of Affectionate Response to the Mother. The child's failure to respond affectionately to his mother during the first days after reunion has already been noted. It is evident in several kinds of data. The first is a relative absence of interaction: we paid special attention to whether or not the child permitted his mother to aid him in eating, going to sleep, going to the toilet, or allowed her to console him, etc. Another is in the failure either to recognize mother or to express affection to her; for example, Gillian seemed not to recognize her mother and actively refused to kiss her. Still another is in the various forms of negativism including tempers that the children showed. The dimension used in Table 40 is best clarified by saying that a spontaneous exchange of affection forms one end of it, and a lack of affectionate response the other.

Table 40. *Showing Ratings and Rankings of the Children during the First Week after Reunion in Terms of a Dimension Describing a Lack of Affectionate Response to the Mother*

A. Children who seek a great deal of affection from the mother
    1. Elizabeth
B. Children who express affection to the mother but also show their concern of losing her by following and/or clinging to her
    2. Jimmy
    3. Georgy
C. Children who show various forms of a lack of affectionate response but also show some concern about losing her by clinging and/or following her
    4. Dawn
    5. Josephine
    6. Dennis
    7. Margaret
    8. Katie
D. Children who fail to recognize their mother and show little affectionate response to her
    9. Owen
    10. Gillian

2. The Lack of Affectionate Response to Westheimer.

The extent of affectionate exchange between child and adult also guided our ratings of the children's reactions to Observer Westheimer.

Table 41. *Showing Ratings and Rankings during the First Week after Reunion in Terms of a Dimension Describing a Lack of Affectionate Response to Westheimer*

A. Children who are friendly with Westheimer
    1. Elizabeth
B. Children who are friendly to Westheimer but verbalize the fear of being separated again from their parents
    2. Margaret
C. Children who do not actively avoid Westheimer, but who show no affectionate response to her
    3. Owen
    4. Gillian
D. Children who avoid Westheimer, show signs of anxiety, but who do not cry when she enters
    5. Jimmy
    6. Dawn
    7. Georgy
E. Children who show a strong avoidance reaction which is frequently accompanied by crying
    8. Dennis
    9. Josephine
    10. Katie

Because active avoidance (of the kind seen in the nursery in relation to Heinicke and Wolpert) was the children's dominant reaction, we developed a dimension running from avoidance accompanied by crying at one end to open friendliness at the other. The
ratings and rankings are given in Table 41.

3. Reluctance to Eat. Whereas individual variations in sphincter
control, sleeping and language development are best analyzed by
using data from the first twenty weeks after reunion, such individual
variation as existed in feeding behavior was seen most clearly during
the first week after reunion. It may come as a surprise that for reunion the dimension runs from marked reluctance to eat to normal
appetite, instead of from normal appetite to great greed as it did for
separation. This is perhaps the outstanding conclusion to be drawn
from our observations. Results are given in Table 42. During the
first week after reunion eight of the children showed some reluctance
to eat; during the last week of separation six of these very children
had shown clear signs of greed. Thus there is a change from greed
to reluctance, a reluctance which is a return to the way the child
behaved during the first two days of separation.

Table 42. *Showing Ratings and Rankings of the Children during the
First Week after Reunion in Terms of a Dimension
Describing the Reluctance to Eat*

A. Children who show no particular eating difficulties
                              1. Josephine
                              2. Katie
B. Children who throughout the first week after reunion show some reluctance
    to eat
                              3. Dennis
                              4. Elizabeth
                              5. Dawn
                              6. Georgy
                              7. Jimmy
                              8. Margaret
                              9. Gillian
C. Children who throughout the first week after reunion show very little inter-
    est in food offered by the mother
                              10. Owen

An example of a child's reluctance to eat is taken from the observations of Margaret. Mother's account was that Margaret's behavior was markedly different from her preseparation behavior for
one-and-a-half days following the reunion. During this time she

would not allow mother to do anything for her. She would not take any food directly from mother, but if mother put it on the table she would eventually eat it. She could not bear to be left alone with her mother and would scream "Daddy, Daddy, Daddy," whenever he left the room. Mother reflected that this sounded as if she had beaten her all day long. After three days of reunion, mother commented that, "She now takes from me again and gives me things too."

B. Intercorrelation of Dimensions Describing Behavior during the First Week after Reunion

In Table 43 we present the rank-order coefficients resulting from the intercorrelation of the three dimensions just described.

Table 43. *Showing Intercorrelation of Dimensions Describing the Child's Behavior during the First Week after Reunion*

Dimensions	*1*	*2*	*3*
1. Lack of Affectionate Response to the Mother	——		
2. Lack of Affectionate Response to Westheimer	.09	——	
3. Reluctance to Eat	.35	-.68*	——

* Significant at the .05 level

Examination of Table 43 reveals that coefficients are low and statistically significant in only one case. Why the children who avoid the observer should show the least reluctance to eat is hard to interpret.

C. Factors Associated with the Child's Lack of Affectionate Response to His Mother

Despite the lack of correlation noted above, the dimension describing the lack of affectionate response is of such importance that it is of interest to explore what is associated with the variation in it. The differential development of the children at the end of separation is clearly one possibility. Perhaps less obvious (and in fact not previously studied) is the change in the mother's feelings and attitude to her child during the separation. To explore this, data on the development of the mother's attitude during separation are given below.

In Chapter 3 we presented a number of dimensions describing the mother's attitudes, feelings and actions before reunion. Selecting the dimension *Mother's concern about and sensitivity to the welfare of her child,* we found that in four out of ten mothers there was, by the end of separation, a marked decrease in their concern.

For example, at the beginning of her long separation from her daughter, Katie's mother was extremely upset. As she put it: "I felt my baby had died." During the early weeks she visited Katie regularly, was perceptive of changes in the child, and these distressed her deeply. After a time, however, it seemed that she could no longer face the effects of the separation on Katie and especially the failure by her daughter to show her any affection. Thus, toward the end of the twenty-week separation mother did not visit for three weeks; in explanation she remarked that she had not felt like it, and besides the weather had been bad. When it was suggested that Katie might have missed her, she shrugged her shoulders. At about this time suitable accommodation for the family was found, but mother still did not bring Katie home. She wanted to furnish and decorate the rooms first. She said that she felt she had to get herself "straight." Although some of these preparations were necessary, others could easily have been postponed. Whatever the reason may be, it was plain that at the end of the period of separation she was less sensitive to the needs of her child than she had been at its beginning.

A more detailed discussion of the change in the mother's concern will be discussed in a future publication. Here our interest is to relate the findings to the reactions of the child during the first week after reunion. The question arises as to whether the child's lack of affectionate response to his mother during the first week after reunion may be due in part to her decreased concern about and sensitivity to him.

In the following three tables, we present the results of ranking the mothers on their *Concern about and sensitivity to the welfare of their child at the beginning of separation* (Table 44), at the end of it (Table 45) and for the change that occurred (Table 46). The dimensions have been defined previously (see Chapter 3).

Table 44. *Showing Ratings and Rankings of the Mothers in Terms of Their Concern about and Sensitivity to the Welfare of Their Children at the Beginning of the Separation*

A. Mothers who show little concern about their children and tend to be concerned more about themselves
> 1. Margaret's mother
> 2. Dennis's mother
> 3. Jimmy's mother

B. Mothers who show more concern about their children than for themselves
>   4. Gillian's mother
>   5. Katie's mother
>   6. Owen's mother
>   7. Dawn's mother
>   8. Josephine's mother
>   9. Georgy's mother
>   10. Elizabeth's mother

Table 45. *Showing Ratings and Rankings of the Mothers in Terms of Their Concern about and Sensitivity to the Welfare of Their Child at the End of Separation*

A. Mothers who show little concern about their children, are remote from them, and are mainly concerned about themselves
>   1. Katie's mother
>   2. Margaret's mother

B. Mothers who are concerned about their children, but are ambivalent about having them back and indeed delay their return, frequently putting their own needs before those of the child
>   4.5. Gillian's mother
>   4.5. Owen's mother
>   4.5. Dennis's mother
>   4.5. Jimmy's mother

C. Mothers who are concerned about their children and place their needs above their own
>   7. Dawn's mother
>   8. Josephine's mother
>   9. Georgy's mother
>   10. Elizabeth's mother

Table 46. *Showing Ratings and Rankings of the Separated Mothers in Terms of the Change in Their Concern about and Sensitivity to the Welfare of Their Child*

A. Mothers who show very little or no change in their concern about their children
>   1. Elizabeth's mother
>   2. Georgy's mother
>   3. Dawn's mother
>   4. Josephine's mother
>   5. Margaret's mother

B. Mothers who show some change (i.e., decrease) in their concern about their children
>   6. Dennis's mother

C. Mothers who show considerable change (i.e., decrease) in their concern about their children
>   7. Jimmy's mother
>   8. Owen's mother
>   9. Gillian's mother
>   10. Katie's mother

Having presented the data on the mother's concern for her child during the separation and for changes in that concern, we can examine the relationship of these variables, as well as of others previously presented, to the behavior of the children during the first week after reunion. This may enable us to determine whether a lack of affectionate interaction between child and mother is a function of changes in the child, in the mother, or in both.

In Table 47 we present the results of intercorrelating the extent to which the child failed to respond affectionately to his mother after reunion, the mother's level of concern and change in concern before reunion, the child's lack of affectionate response to the visiting father at the end of separation and length of separation.

Table 47. *Showing the Intercorrelation of the Child's Lack of Affectionate Response to his Mother during the First Week after Reunion and Certain Other Dimensions*

Dimensions	1	2	3	4	5
1. Lack of Affectionate Response to His Mother in First Week after Reunion (Table 40)	——				
2. Mother's Concern about Her Child at End of Separation (Table 45)	-.62*	——			
3. Change in Mother's Concern about Her Child (Table 46)	.77**	.77**	——		
4. Lack of Affectionate Response to the Father at End of Separation (Table 30)	.77**	-.57	.62*	——	
5. Length of Separation (Table 8)	.82**	-.54	.65*	.96*	——

*Significant at the .05 level
**Significant at the .01 level

Examination of Table 47 reveals that the child's lack of affectionate response to his mother during the first week after reunion is associated particularly with a similar lack of affectionate response to the father during the last week of *separation,* and with both a low level and a decrease in mother's concern and sensitivity for her child as assessed on data obtained before reunion. Since all these dimensions correlate significantly or nearly so with length of separation, it can be stated that the longer the separation the more likely it is that not only will the child develop a tendency to be emotionally distant from his parents, but also that the mother will show less concern for and sensitivity to her child.

We conclude, therefore, that changes in both the mother and the child during separation combine to determine the manner in which they interact during the first week after reunion. By contrast, the changes in the mother's attitudes during separation are not significantly related to the child's development during the rest of the reunion. This will be discussed in the next section.

II.   Individual Differences in Behavior during the Second to Twentieth Weeks after Reunion

It has already been shown as typical that after reunion all the children initially maintained a lack of affectionate response and later became openly ambivalent toward the mother. As in other kinds of response, we observed individual variation in this instance also. In this section we describe the variation by using a series of dimensions. As before, we first present the degree to which the results intercorrelate and then present the degree to which the resulting cluster correlates with dimensions independent of it.

A.   Behavior from the Second to the Twentieth Weeks after Reunion

1. Ambivalence of Child toward Mother. Inspection of the results of the period analysis reveals that in most children hostile behavior and/or negativism emerged shortly after the time that affectionate exchanges between mother and child were resumed. In eight children hostile behavior and/or negativism was striking and lasted for a long time, but in two it did not appear at all. Hostile behavior includes such things as hitting mother and biting; negativism includes tempers and refusals, in which hostility is implied, although it is not so directly expressed. The dimension shown in Table 48 is one which attempts to capture the extent to which the child expressed both affection and hostility to the mother. The extent of the ambivalence can be conceptualized in various ways. Most meaningful to this set of data was the length of time in weeks that the ambivalent behavior persisted. The range was from zero to seventeen weeks with the median figure being nine weeks. In its emphasis on the emergence of ambivalence, the dimension described in Table 48 is similar to the one describing the child's relation to the observer during the last week of separation (Table 32).

Table 48. *Showing Ratings and Rankings of the Children in Terms of a Dimension Describing the Child's Ambivalent Behavior toward the Mother*

A. Children who seek affection, but who show no hostile behavior or negativism
   1. Elizabeth
   2. Jimmy
B. Children who, as the relationship becomes more affectionate, show some hostile behavior and negativism until the fifth week after reunion
   3. Dawn
   4. Georgy
C. Children who, as the relationship becomes more affectionate, show considerable negativism until the sixth week after reunion
   5. Margaret
D. Children who resume an affectionate relationship only gradually and with it show hostile behavior which continues for not less than twelve weeks
   6. Josephine
   7. Katie
   8. Gillian
   9. Dennis
   10. Owen

2. Ambivalence of Child toward Westheimer. It will be remembered that the child's reactions to the observer were found to be similar in a number of ways to those toward the mother. On the pattern of the dimension used for the mother, we developed another to rank-order the children's reactions to Westheimer. At one end we placed children who were not only friendly to her at once, but whose friendliness increased. At the other end are children who became affectionate only gradually and continued at times to avoid the observer, and who also expressed hostility and negativism toward her. For cases that showed neither hostile behavior nor negativism, we again made the assumption that in those who actively avoid there is greater potential for hostility than there is in those who do not. The results are given in Table 49.

3. Progress toward Sphincter Control. Turning now to other indices of behavior, we find that during the span of reunion there are changes in patterns of sphincter control, of sleeping and of language that run parallel to changes seen in the child's relation to his mother.

In describing changes in the child's sphincter control during the period of reunion, we focus on the progress he makes toward complete control. Since there was variation in the degree of control achieved by different children both before and during separation, a base line had to be established compared to which progress made during reunion could be judged. The degree of sphincter control reached in the period immediately preceding the one being considered, namely, the last week of separation, seemed most appropriate.

Table 49. *Showing Ratings and Rankings of the Children in Terms of a Dimension Describing the Child's Ambivalent Behavior toward Westheimer*

A. Children who are affectionate from the beginning, and whose friendliness increases
1. Elizabeth

B. Children who at the beginning neither avoid nor are friendly to Westheimer, but who by the third week develop a positive relation with no signs of hostility
2. Jimmy

C. Children who early in the reunion avoid or cry in the presence of Westheimer, but who by the third week develop increasingly positive relations with no signs of hostility or negativism
3. Dawn
4. Georgy
5. Katie

D. Children who at the beginning are affectionate, but who later show signs of negativism and hostility until the eleventh week after reunion
6. Margaret

E. Children who express both affection and hostility (or negativism) for not less than twelve weeks
7. Gillian
8. Owen
9. Josephine
10. Dennis

For example, by the end of separation Dennis very rarely either wet or soiled himself. He was very ashamed when he did, but despite his concern and control, the nurse felt that his achievement was not stable and was likely to break down. It is therefore not surprising that throughout the first month after reunion he refused to use the pot and fairly consistently wet and soiled his pants. After this time, however, he improved greatly, asked for the pot and was completely clean.

In Table 50 we present the ratings and rankings of the progress or regression seen during the total span of the period after reunion, taking the level of sphincter control achieved at the end of the separation as a base line.

4. Length of Time before Child Reached the Level of Sphincter Control Attained before Separation. It is of interest to compare the children not only in terms of the progress toward complete control that they were or were not making, but also in terms of the week after reunion during which they once more reached the level of control seen before separation. For example, if a child had asked before separation for his pot during the daytime even though wetting at night, then we looked for the week during reunion when this once more characterized his toileting behavior. The context of the behavior, including especially the child's feelings about his actions, was taken into account in making these comparisons. The data on which these judgments were based had been checked for reliability. The range in weeks was from the first to the fifth with the second week being the median point.

Table 50. *Showing Ratings and Rankings of the Children in Terms of a Dimension Describing the Child's Progress during Reunion toward Complete Sphincter Control*

A. Children who on reunion soil and wet, which represents considerable loss compared to control achieved at the end of separation
    1. Dennis
    2. Katie
    3. Gillian
    4. Margaret

B. Children who throughout the period of reunion show very little change in their degree of sphincter control compared to that at the end of separation
    5. Owen
    6. Josephine
    7. Elizabeth

C. Children who, although they soil and wet, show some progress compared to the complete lapse seen during separation
    8. Dawn
    9. Georgy
    10. Jimmy

5. Sleep Disturbance. During the period under discussion, seven of the ten children had noticeable difficulties falling asleep or remaining asleep. For example, Katie was terrified of being left in her crib and the only way that her parents could cope was to take her into their bed; this continued for the first month after reunion. Interestingly, even the three children who had no difficulty in these respects showed some change, inasmuch as they needed more sleep than they had before the separation. We have assigned these three children the same rank (namely, 2) and ranked the others in terms of the numbers of weeks of reunion that their sleeping difficulties persisted. The range in weeks is from zero to twenty-two with a median of four weeks.

6. *Length of Time before a Child Showed a Spurt in Language Development.* Since we have shown in the previous chapter that the number of different words used by the separated children declined during the first twelve days of separation, it is of interest to study language development during reunion.

For several children a return in use of language was seen in a striking way at the moment of reunion with the father, and it is our impression that all the children showed some improvement at this time. Margaret was a good example of this; Owen also began to talk more after he had been with his father for a while, although when he met his mother, he again became silent. In Chapter 10 we will present data that demonstrate that by six weeks after reunion the separated children were no longer at more than a minor disadvantage compared with the nonseparated children.

We also observed (and this with much greater confidence) that in a majority of children a spurt in use of language occurred some time after reunion. A spurt was judged to occur when, within an interval of about a week, the child not only used a greater number of different words but also made greater use of language to communicate his ideas and feelings. Closer examination of the timing of these spurts revealed that they often occurred either simultaneously with the high point in the child's hostile behavior to his mother or else immediately after it. Most interestingly, these spurts in use of language seemed to be accompanied by increased signs of identification with one or both parents.

For example, during her twelfth week after reunion there was a marked spurt in Gillian's use of language, and she increasingly used words to express affection for her mother. Similarly, when she swept the floor, she was clearly identifying with her mother. During this same week, moreover, she achieved complete sphincter control.

Since Gillian had expressed both hostility and affection toward her mother up to the twelfth week of reunion, these observations suggest that the longer a child takes to express ambivalent feelings toward his mother during reunion, the longer is it likely to be before he shows a spurt in his use of language.

In order to be able to test the hypothesis that these developments were related, we ranked the children in terms of the length of time in weeks before a noticeable spurt in use of language took place. The rank of ten was assigned to the child for whom this time was longest. The range is from zero weeks—i.e., no spurt—to twenty-three weeks, with a median of three weeks. Three children showed no particular spurt in language growth; as is described in the next chapter, in this regard their development was like that of the nonseparated children.

7. Length of Time before Child Showed a Spurt in Behavior Indicative of Identification. Just as most children during reunion showed spurts in their use of language, so at certain points eight of the children showed a spurt in the frequency with which they behaved like their parents. Thus, the parental role enacted became an integral part of their total behavior. For example, Owen not only imitated his father, a golfer, but in the process actually became a golfer and would try to show others how to play.

Since we have reported Katie's enactment of parental behavior during her separation and have related it to the concept of the defensive use of identifications, it may be useful to note what we consider nondefensive identification. It will be recalled that during the separation she went around spanking things, calling them dirty, but this did not greatly affect her messing. By the fifteenth week after reunion mother reported that Katie behaved like her in many ways. She would shrug her shoulders like an older person and wipe the table as clean as if her mother had done it. Although she was still scolding her doll for being messy, this behavior soon disappeared, whereas the tendency to clean like her mother did not.

Examination of the data revealed that the spurt in identification occurred at different points after reunion with different children. In the same way as for the spurt in use of language, we ranked the children in terms of the length of time (in weeks) that had elapsed before the spurt was seen. The rank of 10 was assigned to the child where the greatest number of weeks had elapsed. The range is from zero (no spurt) to thirty-four weeks, with the median at twelve weeks.

B. Intercorrelation of Dimensions Describing the Child's Behavior from the Second to the Twentieth Week after Reunion.

In Table 51 we present the rank-order correlation coefficients that result from intercorrelating results on the six dimensions used to describe the child's behavior from the second to the twentieth week after reunion. The dimension describing the length of time during which the child's ambivalence toward his mother persisted is central to the cluster.

The results of Table 51 can be summarized by saying that the children who showed ambivalent behavior toward the mother for a longer period also showed it for a longer period to the observer, made less progress in sphincter control, had a longer period of sleep disturbance and did not show a spurt in use of speech and/or of behavior indicative of identification with the parent until late in the reunion.

Table 51. *Showing Intercorrelation of Results on Dimensions Describing the Child's Behavior from the Second to the Twentieth Weeks after Reunion*

Dimensions	1	2	3	4	5	6
1. Ambivalence Shown toward Mother	——					
2. Ambivalence Shown toward Westheimer	.88**	——				
3. Progress in Sphincter Control	−.76**	−.68*	——			
4. Length of Time of Sleep Disturbance	.67*	.41	−.50	——		
5. Length of Time Before Spurt in Use of Language Occurred	.71*	.37	−.43	.72*	——	
6. Length of Time Before Spurt in Identification Behavior Occurred	.76**	.65*	−.62*	.63*	.79*	——

　*Significant at the .05 level
　**Significant at the .01 level

The relation between the various dimensions can be further specified by examining whether a given development took place before or after the ambivalence or negative behavior toward the mother was no longer prominent. Since two children showed no obvious ambivalence, the analyses were applied to the sample of eight. Although the analyses indicated that the spurt in speech development and the end of sleep disturbances occurred as frequently before as after the cessation of the obvious expression of ambivalence toward the mother, all eight children included in these analyses achieved the preseparation level of sphincter control *prior* to the cessation of this ambivalence. Similarly, the seven of these eight children who showed a spurt in behavior indicative of identification with the parents did so *after* the ambivalence had ceased. Applying the Binomial test (Siegel 1956), we obtained P values respectively of .008 and .016.

C. Factors Associated with the Length of Time a Child Shows Ambivalent Behavior to His Mother

In attempting to understand the variation in length of time that ambivalent behavior was shown to the mother, we examined a great number of variables: variations in the external circumstances of the family (e.g., housing), the nature of arrangements for the care of the child (e.g., part-time substitute care as opposed to full-time care by the mother) and the number of siblings in the home. There was enough variation in these to make analyses possible, but the results were all negative.

Since only two of the children of this sample of ten did not experience the presence of a new baby, it is not possible to check systematically whether its presence could account for the variations in reactions during reunion. There is little doubt that the children did react to the new arrival; examination of the total group and particularly those children who did not return to a new sibling, however, makes it most unlikely that this factor alone accounts for the variations seen.

The case descriptions have documented the influence of the fieldworker on the behavior of both mother and child during reunion. But though her role varied (see Chapter 4), our impression is that the degree of her influence and of resulting change did not vary greatly. Insofar as her presence was in some degree beneficial to all families, the outcome for this group is likely to be more favorable than it would be for families who have to manage by themselves. There is no reason to think, however, that any effect she may have had accounts for the great differences seen in the behavior of the children during reunion.

After inspection, the factors which appeared most promising for understanding the variations in the way the children behaved were the following: the state of the child at the end of separation (see Table 32), the mother's capacity to adapt to her child during reunion (Chapter 3) and the length of separation. Because the extent of ambivalence to Observers Heinicke and Wolpert correlates highly with all the other dimensions describing the child's state at the end of *separation,* and also because it is similar qualitatively to the child's behavior toward the mother during reunion, this dimension was chosen as an index of the child's state at the end of separation. Dimensions other than the mother's capacity to adapt to her child during reunion could have been rated, but we could not isolate any that would have been more relevant than the one chosen.

The intercorrelation of the results on the above three dimensions and that describing the ambivalence shown toward the mother during reunion are given in Table 52. Examination of the table reveals that the length of separation and the extent of ambivalence shown to the observers at the end of separation forecast about equally well the likely nature of the child's relations with his mother during the major portion of the period after reunion. Those children who at the end of their separation were showing open ambivalence to the observers were the same as those who during reunion showed the same sort of behavior toward their mothers for the longest period of time.

Although we do not wish to imply that the mother's handling is of no importance, the coefficients in Table 52 suggest that in this sample it did not play a significant part in accounting for variations in the way the child behaved toward his mother.

Table 52. *Showing Intercorrelation of the Extent of Ambivalence Seen in Relation to the Mother during Reunion and Certain Other Dimensions*

Dimensions	1	2	3	4
1. Ambivalence Shown toward Mother from Second to Twentieth Weeks after Reunion (Table 48)	——			
2. Ambivalence Shown toward Observers at End of Separation (Table 32)	.79**	——		
3. Mother's Capacity to Adapt Herself to a Disturbed Child during Reunion	–.16	.08	——	
4. Length of Separation	.75**	.72*	–.02	——

* Significant at the .05 level
** Significant at the .01 level

How is it possible, one might ask, that the mother's concern for the child, as assessed at the end of separation, is associated with the child's response during the first week after reunion, but that her capacity to adapt to a disturbed child, as assessed during the period of reunion itself, is not associated with the way he behaves toward her? The explanation lies in the fact that some of the mothers who had shown a lack of concern for their child while still separated from him became responsive to his needs once the reunion had taken place.

One can thus conclude that the changes that occur in a mother as a result of separation are usually more quickly reversed than are the changes that occur in a child. This conclusion does not rule out the possibility that in particular cases changes generated in a mother's feelings by a separation from her child are not easily reversed.

Appendix to Chapter 9

A Methodological Addendum
to Analyses Presented
in Chapters 7 and 9

It could be objected that the associations reported in Chapters 7 and 9 have been introduced into the ratings through the influence of one rater, namely, Heinicke. In rating and ranking the children his knowledge of their development during separation might have influenced the way he rated and ranked them on their behavior during reunion. For example, the correlation between ambivalence shown toward observers at the end of separation and the lack of affectionate response toward the mother during the first week after reunion that was obtained might thus be accounted for by Heinicke, who rated the children on both these dimensions.

One check on the possible bias of one observer has already been provided. Rankings of the children on the dimensions by Heinicke correlated highly with those made independently by Wolpert (see Chapter 3, Table 3).

A further check is provided by determining whether a key relationship derived by using one set of rankings (i.e., Heinicke's) can be replicated by using the other set of rankings, namely Wolpert's. The results given in Table 53 indicate that this is the case.

It can still be objected that Wolpert was also familiar with the development of the children during both separation and reunion, and that this knowledge may have enhanced the correlation found between her rankings. To check this we asked Soles to rank the children on those dimensions used in Table 53 that refer to the period of reunion before she had read the material on the child's development during separation. Her rankings of the children on the dimensions of *Lack of affectionate response to the mother during the first week after reunion* and *Ambivalence shown toward Westheimer*

from the second to the twentieth weeks after reunion correlate with
those of Wolpert to the extent of .74* and .90** respectively. For
one dimension, *Ambivalence shown toward mother from the second
to the twentieth week after reunion,* there was little correspondence;
the rank-order correlation coefficient was .34. Discussion of the difference, however, suggested that the result was not due to Wolpert's
knowledge of the children's behavior during separation having affected the way she ranked their behavior during reunion, but rather
to there having been a failure to define the dimension properly for
Soles.

Table 53. *Intercorrelation of Rankings Made for Key Dimensions
by Raters Heinicke and Wolpert*

Correlation of Dimensions	Correlation Coefficient Based on:	
	Heinicke's Rankings	Wolpert's Rankings
1. Avoidance of Observers in First Week of Separation against Ambivalence Shown toward Observers in Last Week of Separation	.38	.19
2. Ambivalence Shown toward Observers in Last Week of Separation against Lack of Affectionate Response to the Mother during the First Week after Reunion	.78**	.96*
3. Lack of Affectionate Response to the Mother during the First Week of Reunion against Ambivalence Shown toward Mother from Second to Twentieth Week after Reunion	.87*	.81*
4. Ambivalence Shown toward Mother from Second to Twentieth Week after Reunion against Ambivalence Shown toward Westheimer from the Second to Twentieth Week of Reunion	.88*	.78*

* Significant at the .05 level
** Significant at the .01 level

From this we conclude that the relationships found, particularly
those between separation and reunion, are not simply an artifact of
the way the rankings were done.

A Comparison of the Behavior of
Separated Children and of
Children Not Separated

10 Because our observations suggest that variation in a child's behavior occurs as a function both of length of stay in a residential nursery and of the amount of contact he has with members of his family, it may seem redundant to compare the reactions of the separated children with those who were not separated. Still, since some of the changes observed as a function of length of separation might be attributable to development which occurs normally, while others, such as the incidence of illness among separated children, might be no greater than among children of similar age living at home, the comparison serves a purpose. Moreover, a comparison of a completely separated group with one not separated at all enables a check to be made on the finding of the first study that separation for only eight hours a day (in a day nursery) had less effect than separation lasting twenty-four hours a day (in a residential nursery).

Comparisons that can be made between the two groups are limited. While coded records of doll play and of observations for certain behavior, for example feeding, are available for the nonseparated children, no score is available for their everyday behavior because we did not take a scoring pad into their homes.

Another limitation lies in the fact that some observations of the two groups, for example those of the child's relationship to the father, were made in such different circumstances that only rough comparisons are possible.

The type of comparison made varies, depending both on the data available and on how the difference or lack of difference between the two groups can best be demonstrated. Where behavioral dimensions are concerned, we have confined ourselves to those describing

249

the status of the separated child during the last week of separation or the second to the twentieth week after reunion and of the nonseparated child during equivalent time periods. The reasons for this are discussed in Chapter 3. In other instances it was most appropriate to compare the incidence of a specific behavior on a certain day, for example, the day when the first doll play was given.

I. The Period of Separation

A. Relations with Father and Observer

We compare the two groups of children for both of these relationships in a single section because for various reasons the data are not as adequate as we would have liked. As already suggested, observing the father-child relationship on the occasion of father's visit to a nursery is very different from observing in a home setting. Similarly, observing the child's relationship to the observer differed much in the two settings. Since it was felt that there was a limit to the number of observers that could be assimilated by the family, only one of the regular nursery observers (Heinicke or Wolpert) entered the home; in addition observations were much less frequent than for the separated children.

Nevertheless, we developed rating scales to describe the nonseparated child's relation to his father and to the observer for periods comparable to those for the separated children.

1. Lack of Affectionate Response to the Father. In Chapter 7 we reported that the longer the child remained in the residential nursery, the more likely it was that he would develop a relationship to his father characterized by a lack of affectionate response rather than by the open expression of affection.

Observation of the nonseparated children for comparable lengths of time showed no such lack of affectionate response. On the contrary, we found that all ten of the nonseparated children had warm and affectionate relationships with their father, although the degree of affection varied as is indicated by the rankings and ratings given in Table 54.

The fact that the observations of the father-child relationship for the two groups were made in such very different situations does not allow us to rank the total sample of separated and nonseparated children. Comparison of the rankings and ratings of Table 54 with those of Table 30, however, indicates that the two groups do not overlap. That is, the lack of affectionate response, interest in material goods and/or crying and clinging that occurred in the last week of separation are not observed during the comparable time-period of the nonseparated group. We conclude, therefore, that the characteristics of the separated child's relationship to his visiting father are not attributable to ordinary development nor to the fact that some separated children were observed longer than others.

Table 54. *Showing Ratings and Rankings of the Nonseparated Children in Terms of a Dimension Describing the Affection Shown toward Father*

A. Children who have a relationship with their father, but this is not very spontaneous and little time for interchange is permitted
>   1. Sally
>   2. Andrew
>   3. Anne

B. Children who have a warm and affectionate relationship with their father and enjoy having his attention
>   4. Colin
>   5. Rosemary
>   6. Helen
>   7. Jean
>   8. Ewan
>   9. Sandra

One child, Ian, could not be included in the rankings because of insufficient information.

2. Ambivalence Expressed toward Observers Heinicke and Wolpert. If we now apply this type of analysis to the nonseparated children's relationship to Observers Heinicke and Wolpert, we reach the same conclusion. We ranked and rated the ten nonseparated children in regard to the extent of ambivalence observed during the period equivalent to the separated children's last week of separation (see Table 55).

Although two children showed a mild, almost playful form of hostility, the commonest reaction to the observer was not ambivalent but is best described as friendly and even affectionate. This is in striking contrast to the avoidance of the observer or open ambivalence that characterized the separated children at the end of their separation. Thus we again conclude that these reactions are not attributable either to ordinary development or to the fact that the separated children were observed for differing lengths of time.

Table 55. *Showing Ratings and Rankings of the Nonseparated Children in Terms of a Dimension Describing Affection Shown toward Observers Heinicke and Wolpert*

A. Children who are friendly from the beginning and express affection, but who are also mildly hostile
> 1. Helen
> 2. Ewan

B. Children who are initially shy and show slight anxiety, and who later become friendly
> 3. Colin
> 4. Rosemary
> 5. Anne
> 6. Andrew
> 7. Sandra
> 8. Ian

C. Children who show some anxiety but are later friendly and affectionate to the point of wanting to remain with the observer
> 9. Jean
> 10. Sally

It is conceivable that a higher degree of ambivalence might have developed if contact between Observers Heinicke and Wolpert and the nonseparated children had been more intensive. As will be reported later, however, even when a more intense relationship between a nonseparated child and an observer (Westheimer) occurred, it was one of simple affection and not of strong ambivalence.

B. Greed for Food

In Chapter 7 we reported that the separated children became greedier, especially for sweets, the longer they stayed in the nursery. In accord with this, the first study had established that the residential children (complete separation) showed a much greater desire for candy and sweet foods than those attending a day nursery (partial separation). Children not separated at all should therefore be less greedy still.

Because the observations of how the children ate were made in similar circumstances, it is permissible to rank separated and non-separated children on the same rating scale. The results are given in Table 56. The names of the nonseparated children are italicized.

Table 56. *Showing Ratings and Rankings of the Separated and Non-separated Children in Terms of a Dimension Describing the Greed Seen at the End of the Separation Period*

A. Children who eat well, with no real feeding difficulties

5.	Ewan
6.	Andrew
5.	Jean
5.	Colin
5.	Helen
5.	Sally
5.	Anne
5.	Ian
5.	Rosemary
10.	Jimmy
11.	Elizabeth

B. Children who eat well, with reports of greed in regard to sweets

12.	Sandra

C. Children who manifest definite signs of greed

13.	Dawn
14.	Georgy
15.	Margaret
16.	Josephine
17.	Dennis
18.	Gillian

D. Children who by the end of their separation manifest great greed

19.	Owen
20.	Katie

Since there is almost no overlap, it is plainly unnecessary to apply statistical tests to these rankings. Nor is it probable that the greed observed is a function either of the way our observations were made or of ordinary development. We conclude, therefore, that children separated from parents and living in a residential nursery become more greedy than do children attending a day nursery or living at home.

C. Illness

In the first study we found that the residential nursery children more frequently developed a cold during their stay in the nursery than did the day nursery children (Heinicke, 1956, p. 145). In the present study, therefore, we classified all the children (separated and non-separated) according to whether they had a severe illness, a mild illness or remained healthy. The results are given in Table 57.

These findings can be arranged in a 2 x 2 table according to whether or not any illness occurred. Applying Fisher's Exact Test, we obtain a P value of approximately .05. This confirms that more of the separated children became ill than would be expected if they lived at home. Since the children were healthy when they entered the nursery, it is unlikely that previous ill health accounts for the finding. It should also be noted that all children left the nursery in a healthy state.

Table 57. *Showing Ratings of Separated and Nonseparated Children in Respect to Illness*

A. Children who develop a fairly serious illness which requires medical treatment

Owen
Dennis
Katie

B. Children who develop a runny nose and cold but who are not put to bed

Gillian
Jimmy
Georgy
Dawn
Elizabeth
Anne
Ian
Andrew

C. Children who do not become ill

Margaret
Josephine
Rosemary
Sandra
Sally
Helen
Colin
Ewan
Jean

D. Number of Different Words Used

In Chapter 6 we concluded that the number of different words used by the separated children was at a low point during the period from the first to the twelfth day of separation. The question we shall pose here is whether there is a similar or a different trend for the nonseparated children.

Since everyday coded observations are not available for the nonseparated children, we shall draw on the doll-play records to determine the number of different words used. As it happens, the first and second doll-play sessions were administered, on an average, on the days equivalent to the fourth and twelfth days of separation, which means that both sessions fell during the period, in the Everyday Nursery Setting, when the number of different words used was low. If the results obtained from doll-play records resemble those obtained in the Everyday Nursery Setting, we would expect the values for the separated children to be low on both occasions and to change little. By contrast we would expect the values for the nonseparated children to be higher and, if anything, to increase.

Table 58. *Mean Number of Different Words Used Per Unit of Doll Play by the Separated and Nonseparated Children Aged 18 Months or More (N Equals 7)*

Groups	Doll Play I	Doll Play II
Separated	.06	.05
		*
Nonseparated	.30	.44

Because an accurate record of the total number of minutes that a child was observed was not available for all reunion doll-play sessions, the number of different words observed in a session was this time divided by the total number of doll-play units for that session.

* Difference significant at P equals .05 or less.

The results given in Table 58 confirm these expectations. Since children below 18 months used hardly any words during doll play, we decided to confine the analysis to children 18 months or more. Therefore the sample for each of the groups was reduced to seven.

These computations show that at a point comparable to the twelfth day of separation, the nonseparated children use a significantly greater number of words than do the separated children. (Applying the Mann-Whitney U Test, a P value of .05 was obtained.) Since after the separated children had returned home this difference disappeared, we can be quite certain that it is the separation experience that is producing the effect.

E. *Breakdown in Sphincter Control Observed in the Everyday Nursery Setting*

In Chapter 7 we reported that changes in sphincter control shown by the separated children vary with length of separation. Further, we reported the findings of our first study as follows:

The residential children suffered from a greater breakdown in sphincter control. This was seen in the Everyday Nursery Setting, in the doll play and during the first week after reunion. Not only did they wet and soil more, but they more frequently resisted attempts to be toileted. While the day children also wetted a great deal at first, they rarely soiled themselves [Heinicke, 1956, p. 170].

Returning now to the present study, it is found, when children in the separated and nonseparated groups are compared, that more of the separated show a breakdown in sphincter control. A rating scale was used describing the extent of progress made toward complete sphincter control during the whole period starting with preseparation and ending when the child returns home (or the equivalent period in the nonseparated group). This means that the rating takes into account the extent of control before separation and judges progress from this base line.

It can be seen in Table 59, while all the nonseparated children made some degree of progress, that the separated children either made no progress or regressed. It is also noteworthy that even the recovery of control shown by some of the separated children toward the end of their separation was not maintained during their first week after reunion.

Table 59. *Showing Categorizations of Separated and Nonseparated Children in Terms of Extent of Progress toward Complete Sphincter Control during the Whole Period Starting with Preseparation and Ending When the Child Returns Home*

	Groups	
Categories	Nonseparated	Separated
A. Children who don't soil, wet only occasionally and who make rapid progress	5	0
B. Children who occasionally soil and wet, and who make steady progress	5	0
C. Children whose degree of control changes little during the period under consideration	0	3
D. Children who had achieved some control, lose it for a period and subsequently show some recovery	0	5
E. Children who had achieved slight control, lose it for a period, and show no recovery	0	2

F. Breakdown in Sphincter Control Observed in the Doll-Play Setting

Further confirmation of the disruption of sphincter control by separation comes from the replication of the finding of the first study that the degree of lapse in control during doll play is greater in the separated children (Heinicke, 1956, p. 157). Since in this analysis we are concerned only with the first doll-play session during separation, we can use a larger sample, namely, twelve separated children and their matched nonseparated controls. In Table 60 we give the results. If a child showed more than one of the forms of behavior listed, then he was placed in the category applicable furthest to the left in Table 60, a procedure followed also in the first study. If, as before, we compare the first two categories with the last one, making a 2 x 2 table, we obtain a P value of approximately .05. (The results for Doll Play II were similar but statistically not significant.)

Table 60. *Showing Incidence of Behavior Related to Sphincter Control during Doll Play I (N Equals 12)*

| | | | Seeks to Do | | | |
Group	Does Bowel Movement	Wets Self	Bowel Movement	Seeks to Pass Urine	Passes Flatus	No Such Behavior
Separated	5	0	0	0	1	6
Nonseparated	0	0	0	1	1	10

Thus, whether viewed in terms of regression of control or of frequency and form of lapse, the separated children manifest more disruption in sphincter control than do the nonseparated children.

By contrast, the nonseparated children showed concern with the problem of toileting and sphincter control as part of their doll play. Thus, the nonseparated children were found to play with the toy toilet more frequently than the separated.[1] The group percentages are given in Table 61. The Mann-Whitney U Test (one-tailed) (Siegel, 1956) was used in the analyses presented in Tables 61 and 62.

Of the various ways in which the nonseparated children played with the toilet, opening and closing the lid was the most frequent. That this is not a function of a general tendency to open and close

[1] Similarly, the day nursery children played more with the toy toilet than the residential nursery children (Heinicke, 1956, p. 157).

any sort of equipment frequently is shown in Table 62, where the total rate at which equipment was opened and closed is used as a base for calculating the percentages.

Table 61. *Showing Frequency of Play with Toilet as Percentage of Total Activity (N Equals 12)*

Groups	Doll Play I	Doll Play II	Doll Plays I & II
Separated	2.26	3.34	2.79
	**	*	**
Nonseparated	9.30	6.16	7.77

  * Difference significant at P equals .05 or less
 ** Difference significant at P equals .01 or less

Table 62. *Showing Frequency of Opening and Closing the Toilet as Percentage of Total Opening and Closing (N Equals 12)*

Groups	Doll Play I	Doll Play II	Doll Plays I & II
Separated	2.60	2.90	2.74
	*	**	**
Nonseparated	25.38	11.44	18.34

  * Difference significant at P equals .05 or less
 ** Difference significant at P equals .01 or less

From these analyses we conclude that in regard to sphincter control, while separated children are characterized by breakdown, nonseparated children manifest their interests by active mastery.

G. Hostile Behavior

The findings in our first study on the expression of hostility were clear-cut:

The residential children (completely separated) expressed not only a greater amount but also a more *intense* form of hostility. Furthermore, this was true both in the Nursery and in the Doll-Play Settings. While the findings on the targets of hostility were much less clear, analysis of the doll play indicated that the mother doll, certain things related to the baby, and container-like toys are the most frequent targets [Heinicke, 1956, p. 169].

Since in this study no codings of behavior in the home are available for the nonseparated children, no comparisons between the groups for behavior in this type of situation are possible. Data from doll-play sessions, however, are available for both groups of children and are reported in terms both of frequency and intensity of hostile behavior and of the objects to which it is directed.

1. Incidence and Intensity of Hostility during Doll Play. It will be recalled that data from at least four doll-play sessions are available for each child.[2] These sessions were held during the first and second weeks of separation and during the sixth and sixteenth weeks after reunion, and at comparable times for the nonseparated group. The results for sessions held during separation are presented in this section and for those held during reunion in the next one.

Whenever a child seems to intend actively to injure an object, hostility is scored, and severe and mild forms of it are distinguished. Examples of severe hostility are tearing someone's hair, biting them hard and throwing things with vehemence.

In Table 63 we present for each group the frequency with which episodes of hostile behavior occurred during each doll-play session as a percentage of the total activity scored. The asterisks between the main entries refer to the P values and indicate a significant difference; either the Mann-Whitney U Test (one-tailed) or the Wilcoxon Matched-Pairs Signed Ranks Test (one-tailed) was used for the statistical analyses.

Table 63. *Showing Frequency of Episodes of Hostile Behavior Observed in Doll-Play Sessions during the Separation Period or Its Equivalent as a Percentage of Total Activity (N Equals 9)*

Categories of Hostile Behavior	Doll-Play Session I		Doll-Play Session II
Total:			
Separated	27.9	**	19.4
	**		
Nonseparated	9.7		13.6
Mild:			
Separated	19.2	*	11.7
	**		
Nonseparated	7.9		11.5
Severe:			
Separated	8.7		7.7
	**		*
Nonseparated	1.8		2.1

* Difference significant at P equals .025 or less
** Difference significant at P equals .005 or less

[2] Since for one child a complete series of sessions could not be held, he and his matched pair are excluded. This leaves nine pairs.

As in the previous study, it is the percentage of episodes scored as severe hostility that differentiates the two groups most clearly. Thus, the separated children show a significantly greater percentage of such episodes during each of the two sessions. This is not true of episodes scored as mild hostility. The view that separation accounts for this difference is supported by the fact that during the reunion period no significant differences between separated and nonseparated groups are found.[3]

Further support for this view is provided by data on the frequency with which children in the two groups intentionally broke pieces of equipment. In the first study it was found that between them the residential nursery children (complete separation) managed to break or to destroy seven pieces of equipment, whereas the day nursery children (partial separation) showed none of this behavior (Heinicke, 1956, p. 155). In the present study the frequency with which the children in the two groups broke one or more toys is given in Table 64.

Table 64. *Showing Number of Children of Each Group Who Broke One or More Pieces of Equipment during Doll-Play Sessions I and II (N Equals 12)*

	Children Breaking One or More Toys	Children Breaking No Toys	Total Children
Separated	8	4	12
Nonseparated	1	11	12

[3] Certain other aspects of Table 63 need comment. The decrease from Session I to Session II in the percentage among the separated children of activity scored as mild hostility is unexpected. We have already noted that in the Everyday Nursery Setting the percentage of activity scored as severely hostile rises from the first five to the next six days of separation (see Chapter 6). When this rise is plotted against the decrease from Doll-Play Session I to Session II in activity scored as mildly hostile, a significant association is found: the Spearman Rank-Order Coefficient is .74, and P is less than .01.

Certain objections can be raised to the figures given in Table 63. Since Heinicke tended to code as hostile a greater (though not statistically significant) proportion of his total observations, the question arises as to whether this might account for the differences found between the separated and nonseparated groups. Insofar as Heinicke and Wolpert administered the same proportion of doll-play sessions to each group of children, however, any bias in scoring is likely to influence each group equally; the objection therefore is partially countered.

Systematic estimates of reliability would be valuable. In their absence we can determine whether a comparison using Wolpert's scores only still yields the same significant differences. Although in doing this we are reducing drastically the size of sample, it is of special note that in each of the two doll-play sessions the proportion of activity scored as severe hostility still differentiates the two groups. (P equals approximately .05 for each of the comparisons.)

It can readily be seen that once again the separated children break more toys; applying Fisher's Exact Test we obtain a P of .005. Thus, not only were the separated children more frequently scored as showing a hostile intent, but these intents more frequently ended in destruction.

2. *Objects of Hostility during Doll Play*. When compared with the findings on the incidence of hostility, the findings of the first study on the objects toward which doll-play hostility was directed were meager.

Most of the significant differences in the expression of severe hostility were found in relation to three sorts of objects: the family of dolls, things referring to the baby, and container-like objects that could be opened and closed [Heinicke, 1956, p. 153].

In this study, as in the previous one, it was only in regard to objects toward which *severe* hostility was directed that there was differentiation between the two groups of children. Objects for which differences reach significance at the usually accepted level are: the mother, the baby and the girl. Two of these had been of some consequence in the first study. Thus, the mother doll was the object toward which severe hostility was most frequently directed, while the baby was the only object toward which severe hostility was directed that differentiated the residential and day children during each of the four doll-play sessions (Heinicke, 1956, pp. 155–156).

Since hostility directed at particular dolls might at times have been merely a part of an outburst against the play equipment in general, we included in a further analysis only those instances where it was evident that the child was aware of the object he attacked. An example is when the child deliberately stepped on the mother doll after having examined it and called it "Mummy." Since the frequency of sequences in which the object of hostility is clearly identified by the child is limited, we could no longer deal with frequencies nor confine the analysis to one session. The question became: Examining both doll-play sessions, for how many children do we find a hostile sequence directed toward a clearly identified object?

Numbers of children in each group who directed hostility toward the mother doll are given in Table 65. Using Fisher's Exact Test, P is approximately .01. Thus this more detailed analysis supports the previous findings: the separated children more frequently direct hostility toward the mother doll during doll play.

Table 65. *Showing Number of Children Who Were Hostile to a Doll Clearly Identified as the Mother Doll during Doll Play I and/or II (N Equals 12)*

Groups	Hostility to Mother	No Hostility to Mother	Total Children
Separated	6	6	12
Nonseparated	0	12	12

When applied to the father doll, a similar analysis yields the same figures, though the six children showing hostility are not identical. The numbers of children who clearly identified *either* doll, father or mother, for hostile treatment are given in Table 66. (Applying Fisher's Exact Test, P value is .005.)

Table 66. *Showing Number of Children Who Were Hostile toward Dolls Clearly Identified as the Mother or Father Doll in Doll Play I and/or II (N Equals 12)*

Groups	Hostility to Mother or Father	No Hostility to Mother or Father	Total Children
Separated	8	4	12
Nonseparated	0	12	12

We have already reported that one of the other objects toward which the separated children frequently directed severe hostility was the baby. If only those instances where the doll is clearly identified as the baby are included in the analyses, we obtain the results in Table 67. The results for both Doll Plays I and II this time reach acceptable levels of significance and are therefore analyzed individually.

Table 67. *Showing Number of Children Who Were Hostile to a Doll Clearly Identified as the Baby Doll during Doll Play I (N Equals 12)*

Groups	Hostility to Baby Doll	No Hostility to Baby Doll	Total Children
Separated	7	5	12
Nonseparated	0	12	12

It can be seen that more of the separated children show this behavior: the P is approximately .005. The results for Doll Play II are similar, with a P value of approximately .025. An example is when the child takes the baby doll, puts him in and out of the large wardrobe, calls him "baby" and then suddenly throws him across the room.

II.   The Period after Reunion

A. Ambivalence toward Mother from the Second to the Twentieth Week after Reunion

In some of the previous comparisons between the separated and nonseparated groups we have hesitated to place children from both groups along the same dimension because the data for each did not seem comparable. For the mother-child relationship during reunion (or its equivalent), however, circumstances of observation were the same.

The first point to note is that the lack of affectionate response to the mother, seen to some degree in all ten separated children during the first moments or days after reunion (see Chapter 8), was not seen in any of the nonseparated children.

The second point is that during the period from the second to the twentieth week after reunion, six of the separated children behaved toward their mothers with an intensity of ambivalence seen in none of the nonseparated. Results are given in Table 68.

Table 68. *Showing Ratings Describing the Child's Ambivalent Behavior toward the Mother during the Second to the Twentieth Weeks after Reunion (or Equivalent Period)*

		Groups	
Categories		Separated	Nonseparated
A.	Children who are affectionate and show no hostile behavior or negativism	2	3
B.	Children who are affectionate and show little hostile behavior or negativism	2	7
C.	Children whose relationship is characterized by increasing affection and the simultaneous and continuous expression of open hostility or negativism	6	0

Comparing the category C with the other two in a 2 × 2 table and applying Fisher's Exact Test, we obtain a P value of approximately .01.

B. *Ambivalence toward Westheimer from the Second to Twentieth Week After Reunion*

It will be remembered (Chapter 9) that six of the ten separated children actively avoided Westheimer during the first week after reunion. None of the nonseparated children behaved in this way. Furthermore, during the period from the second to the twentieth week after reunion, five of the ten separated children expressed some form of ambivalence toward her. In Table 69 we compare the two groups in terms of the ambivalent behavior shown during this period. As before, the active avoidance is considered a defense against the emergence of ambivalence, though during reunion it no doubt also represents an anxiety that separation will occur again. Contrasting categories A and B with C and D in a 2 × 2 contingency table, and applying Fisher's Exact Test, P is less than .005. A similar result is obtained if category B is left out of the comparison.

Table 69. *Showing Ratings Describing the Child's Ambivalent Behavior toward Westheimer during the Second to the Twentieth Week after Reunion (or Equivalent Period)*

Categories	Separated	Nonseparated *
A. Children who are mainly affectionate with the observer	2	3
B. Children who are mainly affectionate but at times express some hostility or shyness	0	7
C. Children who initially avoid or cry in the observer's presence but soon become affectionate	3	0
D. Children whose relationship is characterized by increasing affection and the simultaneous and continuous expression of open hostility or negativism	5	0

C. *Progress toward Sphincter Control*

The rating scale used for comparing sphincter control in the separated and nonseparated children is the same as Table 50 in Chapter 9. This dimension measures progress toward complete sphincter control during the period from the second to the twentieth week after reunion (or its equivalent) and uses the status achieved at the end of separation as a base line.

Table 70. *Showing Ratings Describing Progress toward Complete Sphincter Control during the Period from the Second to the Twentieth Week after Reunion (or Its Equivalent)*

Categories	Separated	Nonseparated
A. Children who wet and soil, which represents a considerable loss in relation to the control previously achieved	4	0
B. Children who show little change in their sphincter control	3	0
C. Children who occasionally wet but who show progress toward complete sphincter control	3	10

When the two groups are compared in a 2 x 2 contingency table (A +B vs. C) and Fisher's Exact Test is applied, P is .005. We can conclude therefore that progress toward complete sphincter control is delayed by the separation experience.

D. Use of Language

Using the same index as was used in Table 58, Table 71 gives the findings for the number of different words used by children of the two groups, aged 18 months or over, during the reunion period (or its equivalent) and repeats the findings already presented in Table 58. In contrast to what was seen for the period of separation, no significant differences are found between the groups for either of the two doll-play sessions held during reunion.

Table 71. *Mean Number of Different Words Used Per Unit of Doll Play by the Separated and Nonseparated Children Aged 18 Months or More during Separation and after Reunion (N in Each Group Equals 7)*

	Separation		Reunion	
Groups	Doll Play I	Doll Play II	Doll Play I	Doll Play II
Separated	.06	.05 *	.39	.48
		*		
Nonseparated	.30	.44	.41	.65

* Difference significant at P equal .05 or less

Examination of the trends during separation and reunion reveals that the nonseparated children show a fairly steady rise in the number of different words they use. This is not the case for the separated children. There is a statistically significant rise (from .05 to .39) between the second doll-play session held during *separation* and the first session held after reunion. (Applying the Wilcoxon Matched Pairs Signed Rank Test, the comparison involving the separated group yields a P value of approximately .05.) For the nonseparated group there is no appreciable change between the two comparable sessions.

Although not statistically significant, another difference should be noted. In the second doll-play session after reunion, the separated children score lower than the nonseparated (.48 compared to .65), which suggests that during the sixteen weeks after reunion they did not progress as well as the nonseparated children did.

In Chapter 9, it was reported that during one of the weeks following reunion a majority of the separated children showed a spurt in their use of language. Though language growth is unlikely to be continuous even under normal circumstances, the nonseparated children were not characterized by an increase in the use of language evidenced in as short an interval as a week. Only one of the nonseparated children, Colin, showed such a similar spurt; for the other children speech development tended to be gradual. We conclude that, while the separated children no longer used significantly fewer different words during the reunion doll play than did the nonseparated children, unlike the latter they showed spurts in the use of language. For three of them this spurt occurred after the second doll play was administered, and this could account for the somewhat fewer number of different words used by the separated group of children during reunion Doll Play II (see Table 71).

E. Sleep Disturbance

Table 72 shows clearly that more of the children who had been separated had persistent sleeping difficulties during the period follow-

Table 72. *Showing Number of Children Who Had Sleeping Difficulties during the Reunion Period (or Its Equivalent) (N Equals 10)*

| | Groups | |
Category	Separated	Nonseparated
No Difficulty Recorded	3	6
Occasional Difficulties	0	3
Difficulties Persisting Longer than a Week	7	1

ing reunion (or its equivalent) than did those who had not been separated. The one child in the nonseparated group who had sleep disturbance began to sleep soundly as soon as she was moved out of her parents' bedroom. Applying Fisher's Exact Test to a 2 x 2 table comparing the first two with the last category, P is .01.

F. Acceleration in Signs of Identification

It will be recalled (Chapter 9) that after reunion many of the separated children showed a spurt in identification with one or both parents. No such spurt occurred in any of the nonseparated children. They manifested behavior suggesting identification, but it emerged gradually. Thus during the seventeenth week of the period equivalent to reunion the observer first noted that Anne pretended to pour tea for her and then handed the cup to the "visitor." At this time it was also observed that she enjoyed brushing the floor and taking the milk bottles outside. All these were activities which her mother often carried out.

G. Incidence and Intensity of Hostility during Doll Play

Results of the analysis of the episodes of hostile behavior seen during the reunion doll plays and their equivalents are given in Table 73.

Table 73. *Showing Frequency of Episodes of Hostile Behavior Observed in Doll-Play Sessions during the Reunion Period (or Its Equivalent) as a Percentage of Total Activity (N Equals 9)*

	Doll Play Held	
Categories of Hostile Behavior	Six Weeks after Reunion	Sixteen Weeks after Reunion
Total:		
Separated	7.3	4.6
Nonseparated	3.1	2.5
Mild:		
Separated	6.9	4.4
Nonseparated	2.9	2.4
Severe:		
Separated	.4	.1
Nonseparated	.1	.1

No differences of a statistically significant kind are found when separated children are compared with nonseparated. This contrasts with the differences found between the groups during separation (or its equivalent). (See Table 63.) Not only was the figure for "severe hostility" in the separated children significantly higher than it was in the nonseparated (for the second session during separation the figures are 7.7 and 2.1 respectively), but for the separated children the drop from that session to the first session during reunion (7.7 to .4) was also significant (at the .05 level); whereas for the nonseparated the drop (2.1 to .1) was not significant. (The Wilcoxon Matched Pairs Signed Ranks Test was used in these statistical analyses).[4]

H. Objects toward which Hostility Is Directed

No significant differences were found between the two groups of children.

III. Factors Other than Separation which Might Account for the Differences Found

In considering the differences of behavior found between the two groups of children, those in the residential nursery and those at home, great care must be taken to determine whether the separation is indeed the most important factor or whether other factors, possibly associated with it, are in fact more important. (The existence of this problem was broached when the two samples of separated children were compared in Chapter 4.) In this section, therefore, we consider the possible influence of certain other variables: the nature of the previous mother-child relation, the pregnant state of the mother, the age and sex of the children and the number of siblings.

A. Influence of Previous Mother-Child Relationship

In Chapter 4 it was shown that there is a difference between the separated and the nonseparated children in *The mother's affection for and pleasure in the company of the child*. The question arises, there-

---

[4] Even though not significant, the question arises why there should be any appreciable change from one session to another in the nonseparated children. Most likely it is due to a difference in scoring between Wolpert and Heinicke on the one hand and Westheimer on the other. Instead of scoring the observations on the spot, Westheimer wrote a descriptive account of the play sequence which was scored subsequently.

fore, whether such differences of behavior as are found between the two groups are a result, not of the difference in regard to separation but of the differences in this relationship.

Had we had a greater number of cases it would have been possible to have controlled for this factor before making comparisons. An alternative procedure, and the one adopted, is to eliminate the three separated children who fall at the adverse end of all the dimensions describing the mother-child relationship listed in Chapter 4, and to analyze afresh the differences between the groups using only the remaining seven children and their nonseparated controls. When this is done the two groups no longer differ significantly on any of the mother-child dimensions.

With the reduced sample of seven pairs the two groups were again compared with respect to behavior shown during both separation and reunion (or the equivalent periods). The results are all essentially the same.

Because N's are reduced, and any effect that the previous mother-child relationship might have had is lessened, it might be expected that values of P would be greater and differences therefore less often significant. This, however, is not what is found. For example, in the case of hostile behavior occurring during doll play, with one exception[5] the values of P are in fact either unchanged or smaller.

Even the results for differences in the number of words used during doll play are replicated. It will be recalled that we had already reduced the sample by confining ourselves to children aged 18 months or older; when the new criteria are applied each sample is reduced to only five cases. It is therefore especially noteworthy that when the ratios for the second session of doll play held during separation (or its equivalent) are compared, the two groups still differ significantly; applying the Mann-Whitney U Test we obtain a P value of .03.

On the basis of the above analysis, therefore, it seems clear that the nature of the previous mother-child relationship is not a major factor in accounting for the differences found between the separated and the nonseparated children.

B. The Pregnant State of the Mother

Previous analyses have already suggested that it is very unlikely that the differences reported in this chapter are simply a function of the

[5] In the case of the exception the value of P rises from .025 to .031.

fact that many of the mothers of the separated children were pregnant (see Chapter 7). The behavior which best differentiates the behavior of the separated children from that of the nonseparated children was present in the separated children whether the child's mother was pregnant or not.

C. The Age and Sex of the Children and Number of Siblings

Since the children of each group were matched for age and sex, and since the number of siblings does not differ greatly, it is unlikely that these factors account for the differences found.

We therefore conclude that the degree of separation from the parents is the single most important factor in accounting for the differences between the groups reported in this chapter.

A Summary of the Findings
on Children's Behavior during
Separation and after Reunion

11 In this chapter the findings of both the present and the first study are summarized. They are organized under the same set of headings as are used throughout the study. Under each heading are listed the main findings of this study and references are given as to where the evidence can be found. The main findings are listed chronologically from the first days of separation to the last weeks after reunion.

These findings are supplemented by those reported in the literature on separation. Since the latter is by now large, only those studies are reported that adopt the short-term longitudinal method and report direct observations of children between the ages of 3 months and 6 years. In all these studies the children had been cared for at home by a parent figure before being placed for varying periods in a residential nursery or hospital ward. Where references to studies other than the above are included, this is indicated.

The next chapter takes up in summary form some of the major factors which can be related to individual differences. In anticipation of this and as a guide to the summary, it was found that the way a child developed during both separation and reunion was determined chiefly by the length of his separation, particularly whether or not the separation lasted for longer than about two weeks. It is of course possible that in a larger sample in which cases are distributed more evenly by length of separation (within the period of one to twenty weeks), other or different points of differentiation would be found.

I. Longing for Parents

A. Longing for Parents during Separation

1. Almost all the children (nine out of ten) at some point during the

271

separation cried intensely for both parents (Chapters 6 and 7; Heinicke, 1956, p. 130).

2. In eight out of ten cases the most intense crying and/or the beginning of crying was seen at the moment of separation from the parent who brought the child to the nursery (Chapter 6).

3. During and immediately after a visit by a parent paid during the first two weeks of separation, the children cried even more than at other times. This was especially true of the few instances when the mother visited (Chapter 7; Heinicke, 1956, p. 162).

4. Children who were accompanied by a sibling cried less for their parents than those who were not (Chapter 7).

5. During the first week of separation, those children who cried the least avoided the observers the most; this was particularly true in relation to Observer Westheimer.

6. Intense crying for parents decreased markedly after the fifth day of separation but did not cease thereafter (Chapter 6; Heinicke, 1956, p. 131).

7. By contrast, fretting for parents without crying increased (Chapter 6).

B. *Longing for Parents during Reunion*

Five out of ten children cried during the first week after reunion when the mother and/or father left them or was about to leave them (Chapter 8; Heinicke, 1956, pp. 164–165).

C. *Evidence from Other Studies on Longing for Parents*

Our findings are strikingly similar to the many observations reported previously. This is particularly the case for the degree of distress shown. Writing in *War and Children*, Freud and Burlingham (1943) state that:

The personal attachment of the child to his mother which starts ... in the first year of life, comes to its full development in the second one [p. 49]. . . . . Reactions to parting at this time of life are particularly violent. The child feels suddenly deserted by all the known persons in its world to whom it has learned to attach importance. . . . Its longing for its mother becomes intolerable and throws it into states of despair which are very similar to the despair and distress shown by babies who are hungry and whose food does not appear at the accustomed time. For several hours, or even for a day or two this psychological craving of the child, the "hunger" for its mother, may override all bodily sensations [p. 50].

That the shock of parting at this stage is really serious is further proven by the observation that a number of these children fail to recognize their mothers when they are visited after they have "settled down" in their new surroundings. The mothers themselves realize that this lack of recognition is not due to any limitation of the faculty of memory as such. The same child who looks at its mother's face with stony indifference as if she were a complete stranger, will have no difficulty in recognizing lifeless objects which have belonged to its past. When taken home again it will recognize the rooms, the position of the beds, and will remember the contents of cupboards, etc.

Fathers also are treated better in this respect. The children were always more or less used to their coming and going and not dependent on them for their primitive gratifications. Consequently, parting from them is no real shock and their memory remains undisturbed. Failure to recognize the mother occurs when something has happened to the image of the mother in the child's mind, i.e., to its inner relationship to her. The mother has disappointed the child and left its longing for her unsatisfied; so it turns against her with resentment and rejects the memory of her person from its consciousness [p. 53].

On the subject of the length of time a child grieves, the authors state:

With our present experience we expect the state of homesickness to last any length of time from a few hours to several weeks or even a few months. When this period is over the child finds itself attached to new people in its new surroundings. The new ties may be less solid and more superficial than the original ones [p. 79].

An example of intense crying reported by Freud and Burlingham (1943) serves as further clarification:

There was Mary, two years and eight months old, whose mother brought the child to the nursery so that she could take up munitions work. Mary who is a gay and beautiful girl, well developed for her age, seemed at first delighted with the new experience. But when after several hours she understood that this meant separation from her mother, she broke down completely, cried incessantly and was hard to quiet [p. 132].

On the child's longing for the parents, Bowlby (1953)[1] reports as follows:

[1] Since many quotations are drawn from the work of Bowlby and Robertson, it is useful to give a description of their sample (Bowlby, 1953, p. 268): "The sample of forty-nine cases on which our observations happen to have been made is rather heterogeneous. All except three of the children were aged between 12 and 48 months at the time of separation—the exceptions were one of 4 months, one of

There were 45 children whose *initial responses* were observed: all but three
of them fretted. This was either acute, characterized by crying of varying degrees of violence, continuousness and duration, or else subdued, with whin-
ing, grizzling and generally subdued behavior. Children who could speak
cried or muttered "I want my mummy" with varying degrees of insistence.
Few can doubt that a demand for their mother's presence is the main impulse
possessing these children [pp. 268–269].

Robertson and Bowlby (1952) further concluded that the separated child "... commonly progresses through three phases of emotional response ... Protest, Despair, and Denial."[2] Though differentiating them for purposes of presentation, they say that "... it is to
be understood that in reality each merges into the next, so that a
child is often for weeks or days in a state of transition from one phase
to another." Although in their new book Robertson and Bowlby
modify and amplify their formulations of these phases, changes are
only minor, and, for historical reasons, we quote their original descriptions with only such revisions (in brackets) as have been requested by them:

1. *Protest.* In this initial phase, which may last from a few hours to seven
or eight days, the child has a strong conscious [desire for] the mother and
the expectation—based on previous experience—that she will respond to
his cries. He is acutely anxious that he has lost her, is confused and frightened
by unfamiliar surroundings, and seeks to recapture her by the full exercise
of his limited resources. He has no comprehension of his situation, and is
out of mind with fright and urgent desire for satisfactions which only
his mother can give. He will cry loudly, shake his cot, throw himself about,
and look eagerly towards any sight or sound which might prove to be the
missing mother. He may seek to cling to a nurse, perhaps the one who admitted him.

2. *Despair,* which gradually succeeds Protest, is characterized by a continuing conscious [desire for] mother coupled with increasing hopelessness. The
active physical movements have diminished or come to an end, and the crying
is now monotonous and intermittent. He is withdrawn and apathetic, makes

---

11 months, and one of 4 years 4 months. ... The situations in which these children
were observed were:

Residential Nursery	25
Fever Hospital	13
Sanatorium	9
General Hospital	2
Total	49

[2] These authors have since substituted for "Denial," the term "Detachment"
without altering the definition.

no demands on the environment and is in a state of deep mourning. This is the quiet stage known to nurses and pediatricians as the successor to Protest, and erroneously presumed to indicate a diminution of distress.

3. [Detachment] is a phase which gradually succeeds Despair, and because the child shows more interest in his surroundings it is welcomed by the staff as a sign of recovery. It is in fact a device for coping with distress of the kind known since Aesop as "sour grapes"; it would be mistaken to deem it an improvement in his state. Because the child cannot tolerate such intensity of distress he begins to make the most of his situation by repressing his feeling for his mother. In addition to his emotional [desire for] his mother he has urgent physical [desire] for food and comfort, and these he will begin to seek wherever he can find them. In the [Detachment] phase there are two types of response according to whether a substitute mother is available or not:

> a. [Detachment from mother].   The child's desire for loving care and comfort and for physical satisfactions which he cannot provide himself are so great that, if there is anyone available who has time to give him the necessary attention, he may transfer his attachments to her and adopt her as a substitute mother. As a first step he will have to deal drastically with his feeling for his own mother who has failed to meet his [desires], particularly his [desire for] her as a person to love and be loved by. In a way roughly comparable to that in which an adult may push out of mind a picture of someone who has caused gross offence, the little child may crush the picture of the mother who has (to his feeling) so cruelly abandoned him. Then he is free to seek satisfaction of his [desires] in anyone who offers some degree of substitution.

> b. [Detachment from Mother and Other Mother Figures]. If the child has no opportunity to find a human who will substitute for his mother, or if he has the experience of becoming attached to a series of people each of whom leaves and so repeats for him the pain and sense of rejection of the original loss of his mother, he will in time act as if neither mothering nor any contact with humans has much significance for him. . . . Instead he will become more and more self-centered, transferring his desires and feelings from people on to material things such as sweets, toys and food. He will no longer show upset when nurses leave. He will also cease showing feeling when his parents come and go on visiting day, and he will unwittingly cause them pain when they realize that, although he has little interest in them as particular people, he has an eager interest in the presents they bring [pp. 132–133].

In addition to this description of the general development of a child's longing for his parents, Robertson and Bowlby (1952) also comment specifically on the distinctive effects of brief and of longer separations:

With the exception of that small proportion whose apparent lack of disturbance from the very beginning of separation we know to be very unusual in
the small child in such a situation, and which was associated in some instances with a previous impairment of the capacity for attachment, all of
these children were still in some stage of Despair-[Detachment] when discharged 14 to 21 days after admission. Whatever degree of adjustment they
had appeared to have achieved as the days went by, parents' visits had almost
invariably shown to be a mere façade. On these occasions there was a break
through of intense feeling directed at the parents—especially at the mother
—in a tumultuous mixture of desire and anger. Nevertheless it was generally
true to say that, although on discharge the feeling they had for their parents
was confused and compounded of extremes of love, demand, and hostility,
a strong relationship remained. A quite different outcome was observed in
another group of children whose separations began at about the same age
but went on for very much longer. In them the phase of [Detachment] went
further, in some instances so far that all [desire for] mother or of any kind
of intimate maternal care seemed to have disappeared [p. 135].

Of the many case illustrations presented by Robertson and Bowlby
we have chosen excerpts from the case of Laura because these data
are most extensive (Robertson 1953b, 1953c). Laura was separated
from her parents for eight days while in the hospital for an operation for hernia. The beginnings of detachment referred to in the
previous quotation are recorded in the following description by
Robertson (1953b):

Each time her mother visited it took 10 to 15 minutes before Laura seemed
to recognize her properly and come out with warm feeling—as if she had
crushed out of mind the person whom she wanted most but who pained her
most. This "time-lag" was repeated in more dramatic form four months later
when she did not know her mother for two days following the five-week separation—though significantly father, who is usually of much less consequence
to the very young child, was recognized immediately [p. 8].

Elaborating on the difference in Laura's reactions to her mother
and to her father, Bowlby, Robertson and Rosenbluth (1952) write:

Laura's responses to separation from her father are very different from those
to separation from her mother, though the variables are such that it is not
easy to know the significance of these differences. In the first place she did
not ask for her father throughout the first two days, and when both her parents visited after the operation, she cried persistently for her mother, despite
her father's being nearer to her. She nevertheless held on to her father's tie
and on subsequent days asked repeatedly for him. On the other occasion
when her father visited, on the seventh day, she greeted him immediately
and there was no period of emotional freeze-up. To us it seems more proba-

ble that the intensity of her need for the father in time of illness is less great and so also is the pain of frustration. In consequence the intensity of the conflicts set up by separation from him is less.... This enables her to respond to him in a natural way. We have other examples of children who after long separation appear to have repressed all feeling for their mothers but whose relation to their father is much less impaired [p. 87].

Turning now to the work of a group of French investigators, David, Nicolas and Roudinesco (1952) classified the reactions of 12–17-months-old children who had already been separated from their families for some days into the following categories: Responses of Intense Distress, Easy Adjustment and Partial or Precarious Adjustment.

Although no statistical study was made of the relative frequencies of these differing modes of response, easy adjustment as well as manifest distress were observed in a very small number of cases (perhaps because separation had occurred already since several days). Indeed, the greater number of cases belong to the third category [p. 68].

In describing responses of intense distress, these authors write:

These children cry, moan or scream. They do not touch the toys on their beds, but completely surrender themselves to their distress and are interested in nothing.

Some calm themselves when someone is with them but start crying again when left alone.

Others, on the contrary, ignore the adults or turn away when they come to console them. They become apathetic and disinterested.

In 1955 Aubry (formerly Roudinesco) published a volume, *Maternal Deprivation*, which included a presentation and discussion of the work already referred to and also the results of a further study. In commenting on the latter Aubry writes: "The frequency of reactions of intense distress has struck us forcibly." The reason for this was that, in the second study, children between 12 and 20 months separated for the first time from their families were observed systematically during the first hours of their stay at the Vincent de Paul (Reception) Centre,[3] and for three quarters of an hour on each of the following days.

[3] This Centre is to be distinguished from the Foundation to which they were often transferred after a maximum of eight days, and in which the earlier observations had been made.

A classification of the responses of the fifty-four children observed is given below:

Acute distress with crying	34
Acute distress with apathy	8
Slight distress	12
Easy adaptation	2

It is important to note that the investigators had found that "it was not always possible to observe the actual moment of separation, for sometimes the ambulance first took the mother to the hospital and then brought the child to the Centre." This may well be of relevance for an evaluation of Aubry's conclusion that in the majority of cases "the first signs of distress do not appear at the exact moment of separation except if the cause of separation is painful in itself (sudden illness of the mother, sudden disappearance of one of the parents from the home). . . . The first signs of distress appear when the child receives attention that is usually given by his mother: undressing, bathing, putting to bed. These cause terror and tears, and then when the child finds himself alone in bed tucked up and left by the nurse who has to look after the other children, and finding everything around him unfamiliar—the room, the bed, the clothes, the other children and adults—he breaks down and distress overcomes him."

The acute distress with crying is described by Aubry as follows:

Tears are often continuous, interrupted by paroxysms and short moments of respite during which the child lies exhausted in his bed. It can last for several days; some children cried almost without interruption for six or seven days; Jean Claude, aged 16 months, who stayed one day at the Centre and 10 days at the Foundation, cried during the whole time. Usually the tears begin to space out from the third or fifth day. . . .

Most often the crying expresses despair . . . [but] sometimes despair gives place to anger. Sam, 17 months, stood in his bed, shrieking at the top of his voice without any respite and looked hostile; when he saw the observer in the distance, he went into a paroxysm of rage, shook the bars of his cot and stamped his feet. His cries became even stronger and raucous and he thrust the observer away violently.

Despair is sometimes accompanied by fear and anguish: Gabriel, 12 months, cried quietly glancing around with a frightened look. When the observer came in, he quietened, became rigid, his face became very miserable, and as the observer came near him he curled up, became distracted and suddenly shrieked with terror, putting his hands behind his back. . . .

Most of the children who do not speak show by their attitude that they are waiting and looking for their mothers. Their eyes watch the door and when it opens they start [to] come out of their apathy to examine the person who comes in. If the child is walking, he wanders sorrowfully about the room looking in the corners.

Visiting is disappointing for the parents who find their children changed, less lively and less affectionate. Most of the children were indifferent or even apathetic at the beginning of the visit and some of them cried. At the end of some time the children became more animated, and more cheerful and affectionate, but if this happened, they cried when their parents left.

Although visiting was often followed by tears and upset, it seemed to have a favorable effect on the child's behavior and adaptation: Daniel, 17 months, reacted to separation with prolonged distress, but on the 17th day he was visited by his father and foster mother. He was silent, indifferent and apathetic but a quarter of an hour after they had left he stood up in his bed smiling and chattering for the first time since his arrival.

Longing for parents is also reported by Hare (1952). She notes that four of the five two-year-old children placed in a residential nursery cried a great deal on the day of admission, and one other sobbed inconsolably for three days. Although one of them did not fret, it is important to note that his mother had deserted him on a previous occasion and he had been looked after mainly either by neighbors or in a day nursery.

None of the five children who attended nursery school whom Hare observed showed signs of acute distress, but three of them needed the reassuring presence of mother for a considerable period before they could be left on their own. This points to an important qualification of Hare's findings, namely, that the mothers of the children attending nursery school stayed until the children had become familiar with the scene.

As part of a study of the reactions of 2- to 4-year-old children to hospitalization, Prugh et al. (1953) made the following observations:

At this age level, anxiety over separation from parents was the most common manifestation and the most intense of any age level, occurring equally in both sexes and to some degree in all children. Anxiety was often associated with fear or anger at the time of departure of the parents. Constant crying, apprehensive behavior, outbursts of screaming, and acute panic when approached by an adult were frequent, together with occasional somatic concomitants of anxiety such as urinary frequency, diarrhea, vomiting, etc. Depression, at times resembling the anaclitic type described by Spitz, homesickness and withdrawal were observed in this group more than in older

children, particularly at the outset of hospitalization. The need for tangible
evidence of home and family, such as dolls, items of clothing, etc., was particularly manifest in this group, as demonstrated by the anxiety of many
children over giving them up [pp. 87–88].

Illingworth and Holt (1955) observed reactions of 181 children aged
between 1 and 14 years in the Sheffield Children's Hospital. What
is of interest here is that: "As one would expect, far more of the
younger children showed their feelings by crying than did older children. 72.6% of the 1–2-year-olds responded by crying, and 27.4% by
merely looking miserable; 52.2% of the 5–6-year-olds responded by
crying and 5.9% of the 10–14-year-olds" (p. 1260).
The authors further state that:

... whereas in the older age group only a small proportion of children
showed any disturbance after the first four days, a very high proportion of
the younger children continued to be affected after several days in hospital
and, in fact, were disturbed just as much in the third four-day period as in
the first. For instance, of the 10–14-year-old children, 25.9% were upset after
one or more visits in the first four days, as compared with 8.2% in the third
four days.... The corresponding figures for the 1–2-year-olds were 82.2%
and 100%.... In other words, they did not settle down as the days went by.
They were better during the day, but during the day a third (31.2%) were
still disturbed between the ninth and twelfth days [p. 1260].

The evidence pertaining to the longing for the parents during reunion is minimal and will be cited as part of the next section on the
relationship to the mother.

II.   The Child's Relations with His Mother

A. Relations with the Mother during Separation

Because the children for the most part had no contact with their
mothers, there is nothing to add here.

B. Relations with the Mother during Reunion

1. At the moment of reunion, all the separated children were unable
   to respond affectionately to the mother. In order of frequency,
   this took the following forms: physical avoidance, remaining present but not responding with affection, and apparent lack of recognition (Chapters 8 and 10; Heinicke, 1956, p. 165).
2. During the first week after reunion seven of ten children contin-

ued unable to make affectionate contact with mother to some degree (Chapters 8, 9 and 10; Heinicke, 1956, pp. 164–165).

3. During the early weeks after reunion all children became more affectionate toward mother than they had been at the moment of reunion. For some this took longer than for others (Chapter 9).

4. At some time during the period from the second to twentieth week after reunion, eight out of ten children went through a period of expressing some form of resistance and/or hostility toward mother, as well as becoming more affectionate toward her (Chapters 8, 9 and 10; Heinicke, 1956, pp. 166–167).

C. Evidence from Other Studies on the Child's Relations with His Mother with Special Reference to the Reunion after Separation

Since there are few findings other than those already reported on the child's relation to his mother during the period of separation, this section concentrates on the reunion period. It is often convenient to quote the literature in such a way as to include facts which, strictly speaking, are not descriptive of the mother-child relationship but are only indirectly related to it. While there is agreement regarding the frequency of a lack of affectionate response to the mother at the beginning of reunion, there is greater diversity of opinion regarding the extent to which the child clings to and follows his mother later, and also regarding the nature of other responses that appear.

Apart from the children's failure to recognize their mothers, already quoted, Freud and Burlingham (1943) have written little about the nature of the reactions occurring during reunion.

Robertson (1953) describes very varied behavior on reunion of young children whose separation from the mother had lasted from a few days to months or years. Of a series of small children discharged from the hospital or nursery fourteen to twenty-one days after admission, and "who were still in some stage of despair-[detachment]," he writes:

... although on discharge the feeling they had for their parents was confused and compounded of extremes of love, demand and hostility, a strong relationship remained. When they got home there were days, weeks, or longer of anxious behaviour in which they seemed afraid of again losing the mother. They tended to go back in their toilet training. They also had outbursts of anger against the mother, scratching and punching as if blaming her for the painful separation whose reason they could not understand. But in all the mixture of feeling there remained a strong clear need of the mother [p. 384].

Excerpts from Robertson's forthcoming full-length description of "Laura" also illustrate this:

Like most young children who return from hospital, Laura went through a period of marked anxiety and irritability. She wetted and soiled herself, and was very upset if her mother went even momentarily out of sight as if fearing she might be abandoned once more. She slept badly, and for the first few nights mother had to sleep in the same bedroom. Laura called out several times in her sleep. "Don't do it to me. I'm not a naughty girl." (Sometimes little children misconstrue being in the hospital as a punishment for being naughty.) Although she clung to her mother, she was also aggressive towards her; would suddenly punch and scratch as if blaming her for what had happened. Towards father she was consistently friendly, as she was seen to be in the film when he visited her in hospital. At this age he was of much less importance to her than mother. Mother, the one who had been closest and who had protected and cared for her in everyday life while father was at work, was therefore the one who got the brunt of her disappointment and anger over being left in hospital.

These disturbances gradually diminished; but six months later, when she got a reminder of hospital, she burst into violent tears and said angrily to her mother: "Where was you all that time?" Then she turned away from her and cried on her father's shoulder. Mother said, truly and with dismayed surprise: "She seems to blame me for something."

We cannot possibly do justice to the many detailed illustrations of reunion behavior which Bowlby and Robertson will present in a forthcoming publication. In a chapter on reunion responses they indicate that:

A failure to respond to the parents and/or rejection of them after even a brief separation are by no means uncommon. They occur much more frequently in children who are not visited and, we are inclined to believe, more readily in children under the age of three years than in those older.

This generalization is again vividly illustrated by Laura:

Four months after her eight days in hospital and when Laura was 2 years 9 months old, her mother left at short notice for the maternity hospital to have her second baby; unexpectedly, and because of complications, she was away for five weeks. Laura was cared for in the home of her maternal grandmother and during the whole time saw neither mother nor father—mother because children were not allowed to visit in the maternity hospital, and father because he judged that Laura would be too upset if she saw him. The fieldworker was not in contact with the family during the time, but it was later reported that during her first week with granny Laura had been very fretful for her mother and cried for her at night; thereafter she had been amenable and undemanding.

When mother returned from hospital she wished to have Laura home as soon as possible. She rang up granny and later spoke to Laura on the telephone. Laura was very excited to hear her mother's voice and eager to get home to her. Half-an-hour later she arrived and mother could hear her banging on the outside door and calling "Mummy, Mummy." But when the door was opened Laura looked blankly at her and exclaimed "But I want my mummy!" For the next two days she seemed not to recognize her mother and, although quite friendly, was completely detached from her. Mother was treated like a stranger to whom she had to be polite but in whom she had no emotional investment.

This was very upsetting to Mother both because of her normal expectation of being wanted by her child and because during these five weeks of separation she had developed a powerful longing for Laura. When father came home an hour or two later, Laura was mute for a few minutes. She quickly recovered and was then warmly friendly and sure of him. He had arranged to begin a holiday that day, and throughout it he and Laura had a very good relationship—in marked contrast to that with her mother who for the first two days was almost completely ignored.

Laura's parents were puzzled by the apparent nonrecognition of her mother, and wondered if she could be suffering from a partial loss of memory. So they tested her with familiar things, such as toys and household objects. Laura recognized everything shown her; she knew every nook and cranny in the home with the certainty of the bright two-year-old. Only her mother appeared unfamiliar. Every now and then Laura called her mother "Nana," her term for the grandmother, which further distressed mother. Unexpectedly there were said to have been no temper tantrums and no sleeping or eating disturbances during these two days, and when the old relationship was resumed no further upsets were reported as having occurred.

Prugh et al. (1953) report the following reactions as seen during reunion:

Behavior of an infantile or demanding nature, together with greater dependence on parents, persisted for several months in a number of children under five years of age. Wetting, soiling, and intensified pregenital gratifications, however, were ordinarily given up within three months' time.

The most common manifestations among children showing continuing disturbances were related to anxiety over separation from parents, appearing most intensely in younger children but arising also in latency children. Such anxiety was often combined with "distrust" of the parents, expressed as fear of their "leaving" again [pp. 95–96].

Aubry (1955) reports in detail the behavior on reunion of two of the children who during separation had shown "intense distress." Bernard, a 13-month-old child, had been separated from his family for twelve days because of his mother's confinement.

The return was dramatic. When the father came to fetch his son, Bernard pushed him away violently, cried and hit out whilst in his arms. He cried all the way home, and once arrived, he cried and tossed about all night so that his father could not sleep at all. The next day he repulsed his grandmother and his older brother, but then accepted them quickly. On the other hand, he showed joy at finding the neighbor's dog, and in the afternoon recognized cheerfully the observer who came to visit. The following day he went to see his mother at the maternity home. He pushed her away violently, refused to go into her arms, and the next day he cried when he saw her when she came home. At the end of 24 hours he made contact with his mother when he asked to have his pot. The following days his behavior improved progressively.

... A fortnight after his return home, Bernard recognized the observer when she visited the family, came towards her with pleasure and three times called her "Mother" (Maman). But he was still far from being adapted, and was, in fact, less well-adjusted than at the end of his stay in the Institution; his movements were nervous, his walk hesitant, his expression in repose was still tragic, and he grizzled easily and could not bear being frustrated. The parents were very upset by his hostility but were very patient and showered him with attentions as though, and quite rightly, he was a convalescent. Two months later everything was normal and there seemed to be no effects, but this long time was necessary in spite of the favourable family atmosphere, for the troubles of being separated to disappear.

III.   The Child's Relations with His Father

A. Relations with Father during Separation

1. During the first week the commonest reaction (seven out of ten) to the father when he visited was to be openly affectionate while he was there and to cry when he left (Chapters 6 and 7; Heinicke, 1956, p. 163).
2. During the second week the children were less affectionate and cried less when father left than during the first week (Chapter 6; Heinicke, 1956, pp. 163–164).
3. After the first two weeks the dominant behavior to the father when he visited was a lack of affectionate response coupled with intense interest in the sweets and presents he brought (Chapters 7 and 10; Heinicke, 1956, p. 163).

B. Relations with Father during Reunion

1. At the moment of reunion the commonest reaction to father was one of some bewilderment, but this disappeared in a matter of hours and an affectionate relationship developed (Chapter 8; Heinicke, 1956, p. 164).
2. During the first days after reunion four out of ten children clung to father and cried when he left (Chapter 8).
3. Throughout the total period after reunion only one of the ten children failed initially to respond with affection to the father and all of them quickly resumed the kind of affectionate relation seen before separation (Chapter 8).

C. Evidence from Other Studies on the Child's Relations with His Father

In the film "A Two-Year-Old Goes to the Hospital" (Robertson, 1953), it can be seen that Laura cries for her father on the third day of separation. Similarly, on the seventh day of separation she is seen to receive him without the constraint that is characteristic of her attitude toward her mother.

In regard to the shift from interest in the father to interest in sweets, Bowlby and Robertson in their forthcoming publication describe the following:

[By the seventh week of separation Paula had settled in.] She greeted her parents with smiles, was gay and agreeable during visits, and unaffected as they left. But father was disturbed by a midweek visit which he had paid by himself. Paula had refused to kiss him goodbye, and he had realized that this was because—at ward sister's request—he had withheld the little bag of sweets that had been the customary parting gift. He, eager to show affection to his little daughter and to feel it returned by her, had flared up with anxiety and resentment when he got home. He felt rejected—"It's not me she wants, it's the sweets."

IV.   The Child's Relations with Observers

A. Relations with Observers Heinicke and Wolpert during Separation

1. On the first day of separation eight out of ten children were either friendly toward or interested in Observers Heinicke or Wolpert (Chapter 6).

2. From the second to the twelfth day of separation the commonest reaction was to avoid contact with both observers (Chapters 6 and 7).
3. During the first week of separation the children, while often avoiding the observers, also frequently sought reassurance and affection from them[4] (Chapter 6; Heinicke, 1956, pp. 134–135).
4. After the first two weeks of separation the commonest reaction to the two observers was ambivalent; the children sought affection and also expressed hostility (Chapters 7 and 10).

B. *Relations with Observers Heinicke and Wolpert Sixteen Weeks after Reunion*

When confronted with one of the two observers, Heinicke, last seen in the nursery sixteen weeks previously, seven out of eight children avoided him (Chapter 8).

C. *Relations with Observer Westheimer during Separation*

During the first week of separation the children's commonest reaction to Observer Westheimer was one of avoidance or disinterest. This was in contrast to their friendly behavior toward her before the separation (Chapter 7).

D. *Relations with Observer Westheimer during Reunion*

1. During the first hours after reunion, five of the children responded to Westheimer with affection (Chapter 8).
2. Following this initial friendliness, eight out of ten children showed a lack of affectionate response to Westheimer during the first week after reunion. The commonest form this took was physical avoidance (Chapters 8, 9 and 10; Heinicke, 1956, p. 165).
3. During the early weeks following reunion, all children became more affectionate toward Westheimer. For some this took longer than for others (Chapter 9).
4. At some time during the period from the second to the twentieth week after reunion, five out of ten children went through a period of expressing some form of resistance and/or hostility to Westheimer, as well as becoming more affectionate to her (Chapters 8, 9 and 10).

---

[4] This included seeking to be picked up and held, as well as wishing to be kissed and hugged.

E. Evidence from Other Studies on the Child's Relations with Observers

Once again the findings of this study on the children's behavior toward the observers, especially their avoiding and ambivalent behavior, resemble those reported previously.

Summarizing their impressions, David, Nicolas and Roudinesco (1952) write the following about children's relation with the adults in the nursery:

In the new environment we find in most of the children on the one hand the same desperate need for an adult to be with them, but at the same time a fear of strange adults. The co-existence of these two sentiments, with the predominance or alternation of one or the other, doubtless determines the varieties of behavior which we have described [p. 72].

Two examples illustrate the way they rejected the observer:

Jean-Paul, aged 16 months, expressed it forcefully and clearly. He crawled round his cot on all fours like a fawn in a cage, crying and groaning. When the observer approached, smiling and saying hello, he flung himself flat on his bed, buried his head in the pillow and remained like this as long as anyone was near him.

Françoise developed a dislike for the observer. During her entire stay in the institution Françoise wept at the sight of the observer while at the same time she clung to a probationer nurse [p. 71].

Adding to these earlier observations, Aubry (1955) writes the following about the thirty-four children who were classified as showing "intense distress with tears":

During the first days, indifference towards adults is not rare, but more often the child refuses actively every advance from a stranger. He doubles his cries if one approaches him and either thrusts the observer away or turns from her. Sometimes his great need for motherly caresses makes him hold out his arms to the person who comes near him; if he is taken up he crouches against the person and hides his head, appearing at first to be soothed, but suddenly as he realizes that the caresses are not his mother's he begins to cry desperately and turns away. Even if the child does not cry he is not satisfied and is restless, changing his position and sighing deeply. . . .

Contact with the observer sometimes becomes gradually more positive, without setbacks. The child first accepts the adult's presence, then accepts a few advances from the adult, and little by little the first indifference, anger or fear changes. Exchanges are made, become richer, and finally a real bond is established between the observer and the child. The *eight children* who became attached to the observer made notable progress and became active during their stay in the lazaret [institution]. Five went home and three others were sent on to foster homes. This new change upset the children; one of them ceased to progress and the two others again relapsed. As we have said before, these children are susceptible to change and the least modification of their environment often results in reactions which seem to us disproportionate to the cause which provokes them.

In other cases the child remains "ambivalent." *Six children* seemed at one and the same time to desire and to doubt that the observer interested herself in them. If the child was approached he became rigid, became miserable, and often began to cry, but if the observer turned away the child leant towards her smiling, making noises. The least false step ran the risk of upsetting the child. Favourable results often were obtained if the observer sat down by the bed quite still without looking at the child and put her hand on the child's. Jean, 15 months, was crying desperately into his pillow; when the observer approached him he stopped, and became set in an attitude of defiance. At the least movement his face crumpled up in anguish. After two minutes during which the observer remained quite still, Jean timidly seized a finger, then slowly relinquished it and went to sleep peacefully. In these ambivalent cases progress is irregular and the child often relapses; some days he appears animated and plays a little with the observer, then the next day he repulses her anew and becomes apathetic again. Three of these children were transferred to foster homes and one of them was from that moment able to make real contact with the observer and to progress. The two others relapsed.

Ten children, without being ambivalent, could only make a poor superficial contact with the observer. Not one of these children could adapt himself to the institution or show normal activity after a period of acute distress.

Lastly, *three children* stayed in the institution for too short a time for their adaptation to be evaluated, while *seven* of the original 34 were never transferred from the Centre.

The reasons for variations in the capacity of a child to establish contact with the observer are as yet obscure. . . . Age and sex do not seem to be of importance.

Although there is a striking relationship between the type of adaptation a child makes in the nursery and the type of relationship he makes with the observer, the influence of this relationship on the child's reactions during his parents' visits and on his return home is [also] not clear.

We believe that the study reported here has gone some way toward clarifying these questions posed by Aubry.

In their forthcoming publication, Bowlby and Robertson record observations on the child's relation to the observer as follows:

Laura, the child who was filmed, seemed to derive much comfort from Robertson's presence in the ward throughout the day—for most of which time he sat near her cot reading, responding to her requests but never initiating an interchange. She had seen him on a visit to her home and it is possible that (like the teddy bear and blanket to which she clung) he therefore made a link with home and security. Although she did not approach him for comfort, even when up, she liked to have him near; when put on the floor she played nearby, following him like a shadow.

On the other hand, when a colleague who had no part in the project came to the ward and stood in the doorway looking in on the large number of children there, she reacted with intense anxiety.

The authors infer that their colleague was seen by Laura as a stranger with unknown intent, and that it was this that upset her. The similar reactions of Paula, a little girl of 2 years 5 months (about the same as Laura), are also explained by this inference.

Paula, seen for the first time on the second day of separation, briefly smiled at Robertson when he mentioned Mummy and Daddy, then looked anxious and slipped down out of sight beneath the covers.

Reactions similar to those seen by us in relation to the observer who visited for the first time after sixteen weeks of reunion were also observed by Robertson (1953b):

When she [Laura] was nine months home, she was left in a crèche while her parents visited an exhibition. When an official photographer appeared she became hysterical and could not be consoled for a long time. Evidently the combination of crèche and photographer reminded her of the separation experience of a year previously and she feared her parents had again abandoned her [p. 21].

Reflecting a more direct reaction to Robertson (see Bowlby and Robertson's forthcoming publication) is Paula's behavior. When he called at her home two days after her discharge he got a boisterous welcome from her brothers:

Paula seemed to share in their good spirits, and to be fully identified with my friendly welcome—she looked bright and animated and very unlike the forlorn child I had seen in hospital. But in less than half-a-minute this changed. Her face became overcast and unhappy; she ran to her mother, and when picked up hid herself in her mother's breast. Mother held her close and murmured, "You funny old thing. . . ." When her brothers left the room to play in the garden she made as if to follow, but after an anxious glance at me she changed her mind and turned back to her mother.

Twenty-five days after her return home, Robertson watched her for some time unnoticed as she played in the garden with her brothers, and confirmed the mother's report that she played actively and cheerfully.

But when she was brought in and saw me she was immediately embarrassed and apprehensive, climbed on to her mother's knee and averted a face that was overcast. She stayed thus throughout the twenty minutes of my visit.

The tension in her was so painful to watch that I suggested she might rejoin her brothers in the garden. Paula made to go, but when she saw she had to walk past me to the door she turned back to her mother. Father carried her out, and both parents afterwards commented on the "hard and fearful look" she had given me as she passed.

V.   The Favorite Object from Home

A. Behavior toward a Favorite Object during Separation

1. The median length of time during which children held on to their favorite object from home was twelve days (Chapter 6).
2. During the first three days of separation the main way of treating a favorite object was affectionate (Chapter 6).
3. From the fourth to the twelfth day, eight of the nine children who brought favorite objects from home treated them hostilely as well as affectionately (Chapter 6).
4. After the first twelve days of separation and until the day of reunion, most of the children completely ignored their previously favorite object (Chapter 6).

B. Behavior toward a Favorite Object during Reunion

During the period of reunion no particular reactions toward a favorite object were observed. Such play as was observed was mostly affectionate (Chapter 8).

C. Evidence from Other Studies Regarding the Child's Behavior toward a Favorite Object

Once again, Laura best illustrates the type of observation Robertson has recorded (see Bowlby, Robertson and Rosenbluth, 1952). She had with her in the hospital two favorite possessions—her teddy bear and an old piece of blanket which she had had since infancy and which she called her "baby."

Throughout the eight days these were her constant companions. She clung to them and cuddled them when she was alone in her cot, just before going to sleep, and also when she felt threatened—as for instance when she was visited by the surgeon. Other casual toys, such as the little bag which her mother brought on one of the visits, were treated similarly. They were clearly part and parcel of her love relationship with her mother—partly identified with herself and partly with her mother—and it was striking how she insisted that every single one of these possessions must return home with her. It is our suspicion that this strong attachment to loved toys would have faded away and been replaced by rejection of them, had this child's responses progressed to the phase of [detachment from] her mother [p. 87].

VI.   Relations with Nurses

A. Relations with Nurses during Separation

1. On the first day of separation nine of the ten children refused to have much to do with the nurses; in particular they refused to be picked up (Chapter 6; Heinicke, 1956, p. 138).
2. At the beginning of separation, the children showed much resistance to the nurses' demands and to the general routine, but as the first two weeks passed it declined. After ten to twelve days this decline is statistically significant (Chapter 6; Heinicke, 1956, p. 138).
3. During the first week of separation the children, although resistant, also frequently sought reassurance and affection from the nurses (Chapter 6; Heinicke, 1956, pp. 134-135).
4. During the second week of separation the children showed more affection to the nurses and also a greater tendency to prefer one nurse than they did during the first week (Chapter 6).
5. After the first two weeks of separation behavior toward the nurses was mainly affectionate. One or two nurses tended to be preferred, but the attachment to these substitute figures was not intense (Chapter 7; Heinicke, 1956, p. 137).
6. At the moment of reunion with the parent who came to take him home, none of the children showed more than momentary signs of wanting to stay with a nurse (Chapter 8).

B. Evidence from Other Studies on the Child's Relations with Nurses

All authors agree both that attachments to members of the staff of the nursery develop, and also that the nature of these attachments vary and affect the way a child develops.

Throughout their writings Anna Freud and Dorothy Burlingham emphasize the need that children in a nursery setting have for an emotional attachment to a parent-like figure. Convincing evidence in support comes from their experiment of dividing up some large "groups" of children into small units of three, four or five under the guidance of one young nurse or teacher who acted as their foster mother.

In all these instances the group reactions of the children quickly changed to the emotional reactions of children in a natural family setting. They formed a strong and possessive attachment to their nurse and were at the same time more exacting, but also more willing to make sacrifices for her, than they had been before. Certain steps in development which had been difficult or impossible in the group setting, as for instance habit training, were under these changed conditions easier to accomplish. The other children of the same "family" were then treated with the mixture of jealousy and toleration which is one of the characteristics of the brother-sister relationship, but this tolerance was not extended outside the family. . . . They talk about their "own" nurses as if they were precious possessions, compare them with each other or boast of them as other children do of their mothers. . . . Artificial families are usually arranged so that two nurses substitute for each other on their off-days, and children treat this substitute foster mother with a lesser degree of possessiveness but still as something of their own [A. Freud and Burlingham, 1944, pp. 53–54].

While the attachment was thus immediate and in many ways beneficial:

The reactions in the beginning were far from being exclusively happy ones. . . . The violent attachment to the mother substitutes of their own choice was anything but peaceful for the children. They clung to them full of possessiveness and anxiety when they were present, anxiously watched every one of their movements towards the door of the nursery and would burst into tears whenever they were left by them for a few minutes. . . . Luckily, this state of affairs did not last longer than two to three weeks. With the realization that their new mother-substitute really belonged to them, reappeared as often as she disappeared and had no intention to desert them altogether, the state of frenzy subsided and gave way to a quieter, more stable and comforting attachment. At the same time, the children began to develop in leaps and bounds [A. Freud and Burlingham, 1943, pp. 158-160].

Progress was particularly marked in sphincter control and use of language. Some children seemed unable to form a relationship, but even where a new attachment is possible, Freud and Burlingham (1944) conclude that:

Whatever efforts a residential nursery may make to offer "home care" to the infant, the lack in satisfaction given to these primitive desires will remain enormous. We are apt to forget it with those children who are completely under our care, i.e., homeless and motherless. It becomes obvious with all those who are visited by their mothers and go home periodically to visit their families [p. 69].

In a forthcoming publication, Bowlby and Robertson describe the separated child's initial behavior toward the nurses.

Characteristic of the child's behavior in the initial phase of fretting is unresponsiveness to the friendly advances of adults. Betty showed no interest whatever in the ministrations of the ward sister who for 20 minutes on the day of admission tried to console her with cuddles, kindly words and toys. Even on the third day staff nurse reported she had taken notice of no one. Similarly, Molly, aged 18 months, in the very different circumstances of the residential nursery, showed no particular interest in the staff during the whole of the first weeks. She then turned to nurses indiscriminately, and not until the sixth week did she begin to show preference for the nurse in whose "family" she had been placed.

Elsewhere in the text the generalization is expressed that when the residential nursery gives the child the opportunity, after he has undergone a period of being unresponsive to the nurses, he becomes increasingly oriented toward them and eventually focuses his demands and attention on one nurse.

Aubry (1955) indicates that the way that children who show intense distress with crying develop depends mostly on the quality of maternal care which can be substituted, on the possibilities open to the child to attach himself to an adult, and on the attitude of the adults who look after him. We are not told, however, how these relationships develop, nor what the reason is when they fail to do so.

VII. Hostility

A. Hostility during Separation

1. It is characteristic of the separated children that they expressed hostility in a severe form (Chapters 6, 7 and 10).
2. During the first week the separated children expressed more hostility of a severe form in the Doll-Play Setting than did the

children only partially separated or not separated at all. This difference does not hold for milder forms of hostility (Chapter 10; Heinicke, 1956, p. 154).

3. During the first week the separated children also expressed more severe hostility in the Everyday Nursery Setting, but this difference is not statistically significant (Heinicke, 1956, p. 139).

4. During the second week of separation, the separated children continued to express more severe hostility in the Doll-Play Setting than did the partially or nonseparated children. There was again no difference for the milder forms of hostility (Chapter 10; Heinicke, 1956, p. 154).

5. During the second week of separation the separated children also expressed significantly more severe hostility in the Everyday Nursery Setting (Chapter 6; Heinicke, 1956, p. 139).

6. The extent of increase in the expression of severe hostility in the Everyday Setting from the first to the second week correlates with the extent of decrease in mild hostility in the Doll-Play Setting during the same period (Chapter 10).

7. Compared to children who were accompanied by siblings, those who were not so accompanied expressed more severe hostility. During the first week this was seen in the Doll-Play Setting and during the second week in the Everyday Setting (Chapter 7).

8. During the first two weeks of separation no single object or person, except the favorite object from home, stood out especially as the recipient of hostility in the Everyday Setting (Heinicke, 1956, p. 140).

9. In the Doll-Play Setting during the same period the separated children directed their severe hostility most frequently and consistently toward the mother doll and baby doll (Chapter 10; Heinicke, 1956, p. 155).

10. The separated children more frequently bit objects during the second week than during the first week of separation (Chapter 6).

11. In the Everyday Nursery Setting the levels of both total and severe hostility observed at the end of the second week were maintained in the following weeks (Chapter 6; Heinicke 1956, p. 139). The proportion of both total and severe hostility expressed toward the observers was particularly striking (Chapter 6).

12. In the Doll-Play Setting, by contrast, the incidence of both mild and total hostility declined (Chapter 10).

B. *Hostility Following Reunion*

1. After an initial failure to respond affectionately to the mother, eight of the ten children showed some form of hostility toward her during the period from the second to the twentieth week after reunion (Chapter 9).
2. Similarly, after an initial failure to respond affectionately to Observer Westheimer, five of the ten children showed some form of hostility toward her during the second to the twentieth week of reunion (Chapter 9).
3. In doll-play sessions given at six and sixteen weeks after reunion, the separated children showed no more hostility than their nonseparated controls (Chapter 10).

C. *Evidence from Other Studies on Hostility*

Once again findings on the expression of hostility reported in the literature are highly consistent with ours.

Throughout her writings, Anna Freud (1951) stresses the important part that hostile behavior plays in the life of the separated child:

> In our Nurseries, as in other homes for homeless and motherless infants, some children were displaying an amount of aggression and destructiveness which was not only greater than anything previously known at this age but also inaccessible to the usual educational measures such as guidance, praise, punishments, etc. Senseless destruction of toys and furniture, open or surreptitious attacks on other children, biting and frequently soiling, were beyond outside control and not gradually brought under the control of the ego as is normally the case.... To test our diagnosis [that the hostility was related to missing a mother-child relationship], we ceased any attempts to combat the children's aggression directly, concentrating our efforts instead on stimulating the emotional side which had lagged behind. The results confirmed that, with the development of good object relationships, aggression became bound and its manifestations reduced to normal quantities [p. 24].

Speaking of the early weeks of separation, and once more using Laura as an example, Bowlby, Robertson and Rosenbluth (1952) note the separated child's tendency to break toys and tear books:

Laura's maltreatment of the precious hospital doll on the fourth day (a lively episode in the film) is assumed by us to be a displaced expression of her hostile feelings for her absent mother. It appears (from an analysis of the written record) that expressions of hostility increase as the days pass. Phrases beginning, "I don't like . . ." begin on the third day and are especially frequent from the fifth day onward. Hitting the doll and aggressive banging of doors when she was up are features of the fourth and successive days [pp. 87–88].

Prugh et al. (1953) report that the "Open acting-out of infantile wishes and aggressive impulses appeared most frequently in this age group [two to four years] with wild outbursts of frantic aggression and attendant guilt and anxiety. Marked inhibition of aggressive drive was observed in some children, together with the turning inward of hostility" (p. 88).

Although there is not nearly the same emphasis on hostility in her work as in the writings of Freud and Burlingham, Aubry (1955) in her discussion of the expression of feeling reports: "Sometimes despair gives place to anger. Sam, 17 months, stood in his bed, shrieking at the top of his voice without any respite, and looked hostile. . . ."

In her comparison of residential and nursery school children, Hare (1952) reports that of the five residential children three were very aggressive in play, while all five of the nursery school children showed a more normal play life.

VIII. Eating

A. Eating during Separation

1. During the first two days of separation most children (seven out of ten) refused at least some of their food (Chapter 6).
2. During the second week of separation the children showed a greater interest in food, especially sweets, than they had during the first week (Chapter 6).
3. After the first two weeks of separation most children were notably greedy, especially for sweets (Chapters 7 and 10; Heinicke, 1956, pp. 142, 163).

B. Eating Following Reunion

1. During the first week of reunion, eight of ten children refused some food (Chapters 8 and 9).

2. After the first week very few eating difficulties were observed (Chapter 8).

C. *Evidence from other Studies Regarding Eating*

Both reluctance to eat and greed are reported in the literature. The sequence of initial reluctance and subsequent greed is sometimes indicated.

Thus, Freud and Burlingham (1944) make it clear that:

... in most residential nurseries the children are "good eaters," i.e., interested in their food and enjoy it if it is good, and that eating difficulties are on the whole less prevalent than in private homes. Where abnormal reactions occur, they appear rather in the form of greed and over-eating, than in the form of inhibition, lack of appetite or refusal of food [p. 22].

In general terms these authors were impressed by ". . . a survival of oral wishes, oral greed and oral activities which seemed protracted when compared with our expectations" (A. Freud, 1951, p. 22).

The above quotations strike the main emphasis. In discussing the hours immediately after the separation, Freud and Burlingham (1943) report that: "There are some children of this age who will refuse to eat or sleep. Very many of them will refuse to be handled or comforted by strangers" (pp. 50–51).

The findings on greed and other areas of behavior noted by Robertson and Bowlby are summarized by Bowlby (1953). The following features of the period of fretting are listed:

. . . A lack of responsiveness to other people, a greedy appetite following a brief lack of it, restless nights, and a loss of control of bladder and sometimes also of bowels when these have been established [p. 269].

In another publication, Robertson (1953a) comments further on the greed seen during later weeks of separation and especially on the great interest in sweets brought by the parents. He cites the case of Barbara:

She no longer showed disturbance on her parents' weekly visits. When she saw them arrive her face lit up, not, apparently, for their own sakes but because of the diversion they brought. . . . She dug into her mother's bag and enjoyed the toys and sweets she found there; but she showed no warmer interest in her parents than in the transient nurse [p. 385].

Prugh et al. (1953) report "disturbances in feeding behavior, including anorexia, overeating, and refusal to chew food, often combined with regressive smearing of food or the demand for a return to bottle feeding ..." (p. 88).

David, Nicolas and Roudinesco (1952) suggest that:

The children's reaction to food varies both when they first arrive and during the course of their stay. Loss of appetite deserves a study to itself. Often it simply represents a way of rejecting the adult who offers the food, or a form of rebellion. Marie-Ange was on her first days, considered to be quite without appetite and was described as such by the reception centre. It was noticed, however, that she was a child who reacted in a very lively manner, who smiled at us from a distance and called to us, but who threw away all the toys she was given and hit us when we tried to attend to her. She reacted in the same way towards food: she refused it actively, turning her head away, holding her mouth tightly shut and spitting out anything that might be forced in. However, two days later when Marie-Ange had become friendly with the nurse, she ate without difficulty and with enjoyment [pp. 73–74].

The authors do more than note refusal, however:

... It is also not unusual to find excessively greedy children. One of these was René, one of the very upset children, howling inconsolably all one afternoon until meal time. He only stopped when the spoon was in his mouth and then he swallowed two large platefuls of each dish without paying any attention to the person who was feeding him [p. 74].

In a summary of this work Aubry (1955) reports in a similar way:

About half of the children ate normally. Others were difficult, some refusing to eat at all, others having special fads, such as only eating sweet things. In general the children tend to regress in their feeding habits, and to prefer liquids or sweet things. A few children ate greedily and yet others had special mannerisms while eating.

IX.   Thumb-Sucking and Finger-Sucking

A.   Thumb-Sucking and Finger-Sucking during Separation

1. There was considerable thumb- and finger-sucking during separation (Chapter 6; Heinicke, 1956, p. 140).
2. The frequency of this sucking remained fairly constant (Chapter 6; Heinicke, 1956, p. 140).

B.   Evidence from Other Studies on Thumb- and/or Finger-sucking

Most authors refer to the frequency of thumb- and/or finger-sucking. For example, A. Freud (1951) was impressed by the "... survival of oral wishes, oral greed and oral activities" in these children. ... They kept up thumb-sucking as a major autoerotic gratification ..." (p. 22).

Prugh et al. (1953) report the following about the reactions of the 2- to 4-year-old children to hospitalization:

A variety of primitive gratifications of pregenital character ... were employed to greater degree than prior to hospitalization. Thumb-sucking and rocking were common, associated with withdrawal and with masturbation in one third of the children [p. 88].

X. Sphincter Control

A. Sphincter Control during Separation

1. During the first three days of separation most children (eight out of ten) resisted all toileting (Chapter 6; Heinicke, 1956, p. 144).
2. During the fourth to the twelfth day this resistance declined; but nine out of ten children showed a breakdown in sphincter control. For seven of them this represented a loss of such control as had been achieved before separation (Chapters 6 and 10; Heinicke, 1956, pp. 143, 157).
3. The separated children were less often concerned with toilet themes in their doll play than were the nonseparated controls (Chapter 10; Heinicke, 1956, p. 157).
4. After the first two weeks of separation most of the children became increasingly concerned about lapses in sphincter control; their control increased slightly but was even then not reliable (Chapter 7).

B. Sphincter Control Following Reunion

1. During the first week following reunion the children resisted being toileted (Heinicke, 1956, p. 166).
2. Using the status achieved at the end of separation as a base line, it was noted that progress toward complete sphincter control varied a great deal in the period from the second to the twentieth week after reunion. Four of the children initially regressed, three changed little and three showed some progress (Chapters 8, 9 and 10).
3. Using the status achieved before separation the children also varied as to which week of the period following reunion they attained their previous level of sphincter control. The range was

from the first week to the fifth week with the median at the second week (Chapter 9).

4. The eight children who expressed ambivalence toward their mother all reached the level of sphincter control they were at previous to separation before the expression of this ambivalence ceased (Chapter 9).

C. Evidence Regarding Sphincter Control from Other Studies

The consistency with which all authors report a lapse in sphincter control during separation is very impressive.

Thus, A. Freud (1951) comments on the relationship between sphincter control and separation as follows:

When left by his mother in the strange environment of the Nursery, a child in the anal phase would commonly regress to the oral, a child in the phallic phase to the anal stage. These regressions were always accompanied by the loss of important ego achievements. It hardly needs mentioning that the children lost bowel and bladder control under such conditions; it is worth noting that many of those who had already learned to speak at home, lost their ability to speak [p. 25].

In regard to recovery from such regression Freud and Burlingham (1943) write:

... The wetting and dirtying which became one of the main stumbling blocks of billeting ... coincided mostly with the break in the child's attachment, and it often disappeared after a few months when the child had succeeded in forming adequate new relationships [p. 76].

It is equally well known that many children in nurseries maintain their good habits only when in contact with certain nurses and will refuse to function when helped by others [p. 21].

The findings of Bowlby and Robertson on sphincter control have already been reported. David, Nicolas and Roudinesco (1952) do not comment on this problem, but Aubry (1955) does so: "Nearly all the children soiled and did not ask for the pot."

Hare (1952) comments that wetting and soiling was the most common behavior problem seen in the separated children. Whereas four out of five of them had these difficulties frequently, only two of the five nursery school children had them and then only occasionally.

Prugh et al. (1953) report that the "regressive loss of control of bladder or bowel functions, [is] most marked in the early phases of hospitalization. Fears of the toilet or of the loss of the stool, fear of loss of control of bowel or bladder functions, as well as guilt and fear of punishment over wishes to soil or wet, were handled by mechanisms of denial, projection, and other modes of adaptation available to the child of this age (p. 88).

XI. The Use of Language

A. The Use of Language during Separation

1. During the first twelve days of separation the children used fewer different words than during the rest of the separation period (Chapters 6 and 10).
2. On the twelfth day of separation the children used the least number of different words; it was significantly smaller than on the second day of separation (Chapter 6).
3. After the twelfth day of separation the number of different words used increased. These words were, however, more difficult to understand (Chapter 6).
4. The words "gone" and "all gone" occurred most frequently when the child had been separated for about twelve days (Chapter 6).

B. The Use of Language Following Reunion

1. Those children who, before or during separation, had begun to talk showed a striking increase in the use of language at the moment of reunion, especially when with father (Chapter 9).
2. In the doll-play sessions given at the end of the sixth and sixteenth weeks of reunion, the separated children when compared to the nonseparated no longer showed a marked decrement in the number of different words used (Chapter 10).
3. Seven of ten children showed a noticeable spurt in the use of language some time during the reunion (Chapters 8, 9 and 10).
4. The time when a spurt in use of language occurred ranged from zero (no spurt) to twenty-three weeks, the median being three weeks (Chapter 9).

C. Evidence on Use of Language from Other Studies

Although the immediate effect of separation on the use of language has not frequently been studied, such findings as are reported indicate that it often suffers.

We have already quoted Anna Freud's statement that, as part of a picture of regression, many separated children "who had already learned to speak at home lost their ability to speak" (A. Freud, 1951, p. 25). Comparing the observations of children separated over a considerable period of time with observations of children in ordinary families, Freud and Burlingham (1944) come to the following conclusion:

Inquiries in other residential nurseries have confirmed the impression gained in our own. When children are home on visits, for instance at Christmas or during their mothers' holidays, they sometimes gain in speech in one or two weeks what they would have taken three months to gain in the nursery. Similarly there are many examples of children brought up at home who lose their newly acquired ability to speak during an absence of the mother. Regression of this kind is further proof of the inter-relation between contact with the mother and learning to speak [p. 19].

Comparing separated children living in institutions with children attending schools and day nurseries, Roudinesco and Appell (1951) found not only that the developmental quotient of the separated children was significantly lower, but that the greatest difference was in language comprehension (the least was in manual skill). The largest single difference was found when the nonseparated children were compared in terms of comprehension of language with those separated for one to sixteen days.

XII. Sleep

A. Sleep during Separation

1. During the first three days of separation all ten children suffered sleep disturbances, and they almost always cried for their parents when they awoke (Chapter 6).
2. After the first three days of separation sleep disturbances diminished greatly (Chapter 6).

B. Sleep during the Period Following Reunion

1. At some point during the first twenty weeks after reunion, seven of ten children had noticeable difficulty in either falling asleep or remaining asleep, or both (Chapters 8, 9 and 10).
2. The length of time that these sleeping difficulties persisted varied from one to twenty-two weeks with the median at four weeks (Chapters 8 and 9).

C. Evidence on Sleep from Other Studies

We were unable to find much in the literature on how children sleep while separated from their mothers. We have already quoted Freud and Burlingham's (1943) observation that children often refuse to eat or sleep during the first days of separation (p. 50).

In a forthcoming publication, Bowlby and Robertson have noted:

Many separated children during the phase of fretting show disturbances at nighttime, and in some instances it was these disturbances which were the chief manifestation of fretting. Wakefulness at bedtime with crying is fairly common, and many children cry on and off throughout the first few nights, often calling for their mothers, and cry again on waking. Betty and Laura both responded in this way.

Similarly, Bowlby and Robertson note that following reunion the children were upset at bedtime and woke often in the night crying.

XIII.   Illness

A. Illness during Separation

1. Between the fourth and fourteenth days of separation, eight out of ten separated children developed a cold (Chapters 6 and 10; Heinicke, 1956, p. 145).
2. Of the four children who remained in the nursery longer than two weeks, three became seriously ill for a considerable period of time; all three left the nursery in a healthy state (Chapter 10).

B. Illness Following Reunion

Little illness occurred in the separated children during the first twenty weeks after their reunion. Such illness as did occur in the separated children was not more frequent than it was in their non-separated controls (Chapter 8; Heinicke, 1956, p. 166).

C. Evidence from Other Studies on Illness

Consistent with our findings is the report by David, Nicolas and Roudinesco (1952):

Among the 20 children observed for this study . . . at one time 16 were feverish, some without any known cause, others because of diarrhea or running noses, or throat or ear infections; in three cases only, fever could be explained by the beginning of infectious illness (measles) [p. 76].

XIV.   Sadness-Resignation, Excessive Cheerfulness and Injury to Self

A. Occurrence of Sadness-Resignation, Excessive Cheerfulness and Injury to Self

1. Throughout the separation, evidence of sadness-resignation, excessive cheerfulness and injury to the self was seen (Chapter 6).
2. Evidence of the simultaneous presence of these forms of behavior was first seen after the visit by the parent or family friend during the second week of the separation (Chapter 6).

B. Occurrence of Sadness-Resignation, Excessive Cheerfulness and Injury to the Self Following Reunion

During the period of reunion, some evidence of sadness-resignation and excessive cheerfulness was seen initially but then was no longer observed. The type of self-injury seen during separation was not observed (Chapter 8).

C. Evidence from Other Studies on the Occurrence of Sadness-Resignation, Excessive Cheerfulness and Injury to the Self

Once again reports of the behavior similar to that observed in this study are to be found in the literature. To cite only a few examples, we have already noted Robertson's observations of withdrawn and apathetic behavior during the period of separation labeled "Despair." In a forthcoming publication this is contrasted both with the period of fretting that preceded it and the "settling in" that occurred later, which often included inappropriate cheerfulness:

By the seventh day Betty is reported by the nurse as "settling in." No longer was she crying inconsolably and continuously for her mother and father: instead bitter crying was interspersed with an interest in the nurses and activities going around her. Ten days later her behavior in the ward was for the most part bright and cheerful.

We have also in previous sections of this chapter noted the apathy observed in certain children by Aubry and her colleagues. We have not, however, been able to find reference to the simultaneous occurrence of sadness-resignation, excessive cheerfulness and injury to the self.

XV.   Possessiveness of Material Objects

A. Extreme Possessiveness during Separation

1. During the first two weeks of separation, signs of extreme possessiveness about material objects were rarely observed (Chapter 7).
2. Of the four children whose separation lasted longer than two
   weeks, three showed signs of extreme possessiveness (Chapter 7).

B. Extreme Possessiveness during Reunion

During the first few weeks after reunion some signs of possessiveness
were observed, but they were not of the same intensity as those observed during separation (Chapter 8).

C. Evidence of Possessiveness About Material Objects from Other Studies

A tendency for separated children to develop an intense attachment
to certain material objects has been reported by Freud and Burlingham (1943):

It is interesting to note that the affection for the parents is transferred in
many cases to material objects which have come as presents from the parents.

Hetty, two years and ten months old, had received a green knitted dress from
her mother and went on wearing it with the greatest delight. When the dress
was dirty and supposed to go to the laundry, she was upset and distressed
and refused to be comforted.

In the same manner, a little toddler in Netherhall Gardens had to go to bed
in high black shoes which his mother had brought him that day as a present
[p. 155].

Although the objects concerned may have many additional meanings, the point we wish to stress is the intensity of possessiveness that
is illustrated in the examples given above and below.

Robertson (1953b) reports an unusual degree of possessiveness
of material objects. In describing Laura's behavior as she is leaving
the hospital, he writes:

She insists on taking all her possessions home with her; even a tattered old
book she refuses to leave behind. When she dropped the book on the way
out and a nurse picked it up, she screamed in temper and snatched it away
—the fiercest feeling she showed during the whole stay [p. 6].

XVI.   Enactment of Parental Roles

A. Enactment of Parental Roles during Separation.

1. During the first two weeks of separation, behavior sequences enacting parental roles were occasionally observed. The quality and context of these suggested the defensive use of identification with parents (Chapter 7).
2. After the first two weeks of separation this type of behavior was observed more frequently (Chapter 7).

B. Enactment of Parental Roles during Reunion

1. A noticeable spurt in the amount of behavior suggesting identification with parents was shown during reunion by eight of ten children (Chapters 8 and 9).
2. The time when the spurt occurred ranged from zero (no spurt) to thirty-four weeks, with the median at twelve weeks (Chapters 8 and 9).
3. Seven of the eight children who showed a spurt in behavior suggestive of identification with the parents did so after the expression of ambivalence to the mother had ceased (Chapter 9).

In this chapter we have summarized the evidence from our own and other studies on the nature of the behavior seen when 2-year-old children are separated from their parents and placed in an institutional setting.

In the next chapter we make a similar review of findings in regard to factors which, in some part, account for variations in the children's behavior.

Factors Contributing to Variation
in Children's Behavior
during Separation and Reunion

12 In this chapter we summarize the evidence
from both the present study and other ones on some of the factors
which appear to influence the way that children behave during
separation and reunion.

Following the order of presentation in the book we first consider
factors pertaining to the child, such as his age, and those referring to
significant aspects of his environment, such as his mother's relationship to him. Then there are a number of factors which are best
thought of as conditions of the separation; the amount of contact
with his family is a good example. Finally we review the findings on
the effects of length of separation on the total experience being studied here.

I. Age at Separation

A. Evidence from This Study

Given the limited age range and small size of sample, it is perhaps
not surprising that the age of child at separation was not found to be
a significant factor. We would expect, however, that with a larger
number of children (holding constant such other factors as length
of separation) some variations in the reaction to separation even
within our age range would be found.

In order to place our work in a developmental context we have
summarized the results of a few studies of how children who are either
younger (7–12 months) or older (4–6 years) than those we studied
respond to separation. In brief, separation reactions are readily
observed during the second half of the first year of life and also during the fourth, fifth and sixth years. In general these reactions are

similar to those observed in the intervening years, but in certain respects they appear to be different.

B. Evidence from Studies of Brief Separation during the First Year of Life

Although the descriptions given by Spitz (1946) and by Schaffer and Callender (1958, 1959) of children undergoing separation during the first year of life differ in certain respects, the authors agree that reactions after about 6 months of age are different from those seen in younger ones. In his study of "anaclitic depression," Spitz (1946) sets the 6th month as the lower age limit of the appearance of the syndrome resulting from departure of the mother: "The youngest age at which the syndrome was manifested in our series was around the turn of the 6th month; the oldest was the 11th month." Similarly, Schaffer and Callender (1959) report many findings differentiating the reactions of children separated between 7 and 12 months of age from those separated at a younger age. For purposes of this brief review we concentrate on those children who were approximately 6 months or older.

Although exact comparisons are difficult, it seems that the reactions of children observed by Spitz (1946) during the second half of the first year differ in a number of respects from those that we, and others, have observed during the second and third years of life. Spitz reported that he observed:

Apprehension, sadness, weepiness.
Lack of contact, rejection of environment, withdrawal.
Retardation of development, retardation of reaction to stimuli, slowness of
    movement, dejection, stupor.
Loss of appetite, refusal to eat, loss of weight.
Insomnia [p. 316].

Only the first item—weepiness and sadness—bears close similarity to the reactions of the 2-year-old. Serious withdrawal, retardation and prolonged insomnia are not observed; older children, moreover, instead of refusing food usually become greedy. Before commenting on these differences, however, let us turn to the findings reported by Schaffer, as well as to the findings reported by both these authors, Spitz and Schaffer, on reactions to reunion.

Much of the behavior observed by Schaffer and Callender (1959) is similar to that observed by us during the second and third years of life. For example, as part of the initial reaction to loss of mother they observed a great deal of crying, negative reaction toward the observer and clinging to the mother when she visited. On the other hand, though again we must stress that the developmental changes are such that comparisons are difficult, they do not emphasize bowel upsets, they report a main tendency to refuse food rather than to be greedy and they also report a tendency to be underactive or else over-active: "Violent struggling and restlessness alternating with periods of subdued withdrawal were found in most [of these] infants" (p. 531).

Turning to a study of the reactions to reunion during the second half of the first year of life, Spitz (1946) emphasizes the dramatic recovery that occurred when a child was returned to his mother, pro-vided the separation had not continued for longer than three months:

The change in the children's observable behavior was dramatic. They sud-denly were friendly, gay, approachable. The withdrawal, the disinterest, the rejection of the outside world, the sadness, disappeared as if by magic [p. 330].

Schaffer's observations of reactions following reunion show that in the second half of the first year they are in many, though not all, respects similar to those reported in this study for children separated during the second and third years of life. On reunion, Schaffer and Callender (1959) report:

These infants cried whenever left alone by the mother, physically clung to her and refused to be put down, showed fear when approached by strangers, and were sometimes even apprehensive of such familiar figures as fathers or siblings [p. 536].

A somatic upset was found in 15 of these 27 infants, and . . . mostly took the form of a sleep upset [p. 537].

While the presence of the sleep disturbances are thus similar, am-bivalence toward mother or lapses in sphincter control after reunion are not reported. The age differences, however, make comparison difficult; it is indeed these very differences that are likely to be re-lated to variations in reactions to object loss.

From the writings of Spitz and Schaffer, therefore, it can be con-cluded that after they have reached 6 or 7 months of age, children react to being separated from the mother in a way that implies the existence of a specific relationship. They also suggest that in certain respects the reactions of children to loss of mother in the second half of the first year of life are like and in other respects unlike those seen in the second and the third year of life. More detailed comparisons and firm conclusions will, however, have to await a study that focuses systematically on such variables as the nature of care, amount of contact with parents and, especially, length of separation.

C. Evidence from Studies on Brief Separation during the Fourth to Sixth Year of Life

Since our findings are applicable to children of about 13–34 months (the age range of our sample), what can be said about the effects of separation on children aged over 3 years? David, Ancellin and Appell (1957) investigated both the initial and later reactions to brief separations of children aged between 3 years 10 months and 6 years 6 months. The method of study was in many respects similar to our own, although the setting was a holiday center rather than a residential nursery, and the separation period approximately a month.

As might be expected, a similarity was found to exist between the children of our study and this older group in the quality of certain of their responses, the most important being the degree of distress shown. To describe the initial reactions to attendance at the holiday center, the authors divide their total sample of children into three groups: those showing open distress, those showing reactions of disorientation and those showing easy initial adaptation.

Out of the fourteen children in the group sharing the infant's room we noted six cases of open distress, of which two were amongst the ten children intensively studied. In each case the distress was characterized by crying, and states of confusion, dejection, prostration and inertia, lasting several days.

These children had difficulty:

... in gaining comfort from an unknown adult, the sight of whom only served to increase their insecurity. None of them, except Simon, accepted at the beginning any form of comfort from, for example, the observers. ... It should be noted as well that all these children succeeded in emerging from their distress and that in all cases, their adaptation involved an improvement and broadening of personality.

After delineating three criteria of adaptation and describing various patterns of it, David et al. (1957) conclude:

It is noticeable that most of the children (7 out of 10) ... moved towards an improved adaptation but most did not achieve a satisfactory level until the second half of their stay and sometimes not till the last week.

On the whole, the final level of adaptation seemed to correspond in these cases more or less to the quality of their adaptation at home, except for two children in whom it was clearly superior and perhaps for a third.

Further examination of the study reveals that the 4- to 6-year old reacts to a separation of a month with distress in many ways similar to that of a 2-year-old, but that he adapts himself more readily.

This picture of adaptation during separation is supported by observations on the children's reactions during reunion. Although these authors would have preferred to carry out "a far more minutely conducted study than [they] have been able to do," it is of interest that after returning home no dramatic reaction was observed in any of the ten cases: two children had some difficulty in readjusting, however.

II.   Sex of Child

In neither this nor other studies dealing with this age group did the sex of the child account for any of the variation in reaction to separation or reunion.

III.   The Influence of Family Relationships

A. Evidence from This Study

The possible influence of family relationships on the reactions to separation and later reunion can be examined before, during and after the separation.

First, one might expect that the child's relationship to his parents before the separation might influence his reactions to separation. In Chapter 7 we have shown that the extent to which the child avoided the observers during the first week of separation was inversely related to his *mother's affection for him and her pleasure in his company*. It was thought that this might be due to some association between the child's initial reactions to separation and the level of his ambivalence toward his parents before separation. The association found was, however, statistically barely significant.

Secondly, it might be expected that changes occurring in the family, and particularly in the mother during the period of separation, might influence the child's response to reunion with the parents. In keeping with this, an association was found between a decrease in a mother's concern for and sensitivity to the welfare of her child, as observed at the beginning and end of separation, and the extent that the child lacked an affectionate response to his mother during the first week after reunion.

Finally, one might expect that variations in the mother-child relationship might influence the child's behavior in the period after reunion. The findings of Chapter 9, however, show that variations in the mother's capacity to adapt herself to a disturbed child after reunion are not associated with variations in the child's response during the period.[1]

In summary, the findings of *this study* show comparatively little connection between differences in family relationship and variations in children's response to separation and reunion. Before this conclusion can be regarded with confidence, however, there is need of a study designed specifically to vary, for example, the nature of the mother-child relationship in a sample of adequate size. Also, associations between the mother-child relationship and differential response to the separation are more likely to emerge if the child remains in the home while the mother is away. It must be remembered, moreover, that a failure to find correlations for the sample as a whole does not mean, in a given family, that the presence of a responsive mother, a jealous brother or a particularly affectionate father may not have crucial consequences.

[1] It is possible that though a single factor referring to the mother-child relationship is not significantly associated with variations in child behavior, combinations of several such factors might be. Although this study was not designed to answer such questions, and our answers can therefore at best be suggestive, we nevertheless asked whether those children who showed the greatest ambivalence toward their mothers during reunion were likely to be subject to a variety of conditions that could be experienced as a lessening of the mother's affection for them. We considered: (1) the mother's sensitivity in meeting her child's needs, and her ability to adapt to his difficulties during reunion (see definition of dimension in Chapter 3); (2) plans, even if not immediately actualized, of letting others care for her child; and (3) the extent of the mother's involvement with the new baby. We have no adequate way of weighting these factors but tried various schemes in guiding our interpretation. This analysis suggests that the five children who showed the greatest ambivalence (Table 48, Section D) were, during the first twenty weeks after reunion, no more subject to a constellation of factors likely to be experienced as a continued lessening of their mother's affection for them than were the five children who showed less ambivalence toward their mothers or none at all.

B. Evidence from Other Studies

We have been able to find little systematic evidence concerning possible effects of the previous mother-child relationship on the way a child behaves during separation. Robertson and Bowlby (1952) point out, however, that a child who is an exception to the general rule that separated children fret can often be accounted for by his having had a very unsatisfactory previous relationship with his mother:

A very small proportion of children ... were apparently unperturbed by the loss of mother and from the moment of entry into the ward were actively interested in everybody and everything around them. Investigation showed that these tended to be children whose previous experience of maternal care had been inadequate. There was for instance an illegitimate child who had lived with a series of foster-parents while his mother worked, and had perhaps, as is common in such children, already achieved such an abnormally low degree of attachment to anyone that the total change to hospital ward brought no special sense of loss; there were also one or two children who had been left in day nurseries from the early months of life and presumably also had been in lesser degree hardened against loss of mother. None of these children behaved in a way typical of the normal family child whose dependence on mother is at a peak at this age [p. 133].

It should also be pointed out that the above observation is consistent with the finding in this study of an association between the mother's affection for her child and the extent of his crying during the first week of separation. The Spearman coefficient of .52 was not quite significant at the usually accepted levels of statistical significance.

Turning then to a number of factors best thought of as conditions of the separation, we first discuss the effect of the reason for the separation.

IV. The Reason for the Separation

A. Evidence from This Study

Such analyses of the effects of the reason for the separation as were possible did not indicate that this was a major factor affecting variation in a child's response to separation. In individual instances the presence of the baby clearly made a difference, and this particularly during reunion.

Only further study can determine whether the presence or absence of a new baby has a regular and predictable effect on children's responses to separation. Again we would anticipate that a larger sample of children who are separated from their mothers but remain in the home would facilitate this further study.

B. Evidence from Other Studies

In their forthcoming volume, Bowlby and Robertson express themselves as follows in regard to the effects on behavior during reunion of the presence of a new baby:

Although the presence or not of a new baby in the home is bound to affect the behavior of the separated child on his return, we are not inclined to attach as much importance to this as some do. The disturbances which occur (during reunion) when a new baby is present are not in our experience very different from those seen when no new baby is there. It is clear to us that it is the rupture of the child's basic emotional relationship which leads to the responses which we have described and not the many conditions which tend to be associated with a separation experience, significant though these may be in other ways [extract from forthcoming publication].

V. Contact with the Family during the Separation

A. Evidence from This Study

Because all children were visited by the father and/or mother about once a week, it was not possible to study how variations in the frequency of visiting might have affected the children. We found, however, that visiting by mother and father as opposed to visits by father only tended to make a child cry more; while another form of family contact, the presence of a sibling, was associated with less crying for the parents and less hostility. The explanations advanced were that the visit of his mother when added to that of the father tends more forcefully to remind a child of his grief, while the presence of a sibling mitigates in some degree the deprivation experienced.

B. Evidence from Other Studies

Although much has been written about the importance of parental visits and the value of siblings being kept together, there are few systematic studies of the effect of these variables. As part of an effort to change the routine of a children's ward, flexible visiting hours were introduced by Prugh and his associates (1953). However, since many other changes were also made, it is difficult to determine to what extent the less severe reactions of the children were due to the more frequent visits they received.

As a special instance of contact with the family, the presence of a sibling was found in our present study to have a significant effect. The evidence in the literature on this topic is scant, but Lewis (1954) mentions that, when evaluated at the Reception Centre, those children most frequently judged to be "normal" were those who were accompanied by their siblings. She found in such cases striking evidence of the family cohesion and mutual support and loyalty.

Although the work of Pringle and Bossio (1958) deals with children of a large age range and is also a retrospective study, it is included in this review because it deals explicitly with the amount of contact that parents and relatives maintained with their children:

Three subdivisions were made: "mildly deprived, deprived, and severely deprived." Children in the first group regularly received letters and parcels, were visited and taken on outings, holidays, etc.; the second group was contacted by parents or relations only at the request of the Children's Officer; the third group had very little or no contact at all with their families since admission to the institution [p. 71].

The authors found that those children who had no contact with their parents or relatives were more seriously retarded on tests of intelligence, emotional adjustment, language development and reading comprehension than were children who had either some or regular contact.

VI.   The Nature of the Substitute Care

A. Evidence from This Study

Within the confines of this study, variations in the type of substitute care were not associated with variations in the child's behavior. We would, however, expect such an association if we were dealing with larger samples and, especially, a greater range in the nature of the substitute care.

B. Evidence from Other Studies

Two studies made in situations where the substitute care provided differed from that reported on here emphasize the importance of the quality of that care. We have already quoted from the work of Freud and Burlingham (1943, 1944) to indicate the pronounced changes for the better that took place in the children when they were assigned to the care of one nurse, despite the fact that the care they had previously received in the same institution from many nurses had in other respects been equally good.

In a carefully designed study, Rheingold (1956) demonstrated that 6-month-old children in an institution became more socially responsive when cared for largely by one person (Rheingold) than by a number of nurses (p. 45). Although the increase in social responsiveness of the children cared for by Rheingold could be seen in their relations with other adults, it was most striking in relation to Rheingold herself.

VII. Change from a Familiar to an Unfamiliar Environment

A. Evidence from This Study

The experience of the unfamiliar or strange obviously involves many things. In this study we concentrated on the gross changes in the child's routine and physical environment, but such variation in the extent of change from home to nursery environment as did exist in our sample, did not correlate with variations in child response. Since, however, all the children were moved to a new and strange environment, the above finding in itself does not rule out the importance of the unfamiliar as a factor affecting the child's response. Only a study of separation not also involving a move to a strange environment can determine what role the latter may play. Such evidence as we have from this study and from the literature suggests that being shifted to an unfamiliar environment accentuates a child's response to separation from his parents. This same evidence also indicates that merely moving a child into a strange environment does not of itself result in the kind of behavior observed in this study.

B. Evidence from Other Studies

If the question is thus posed in terms of the relative importance of two factors—a familiar or an unfamiliar environment and the presence or absence of the mother—then the following studies are relevant.

A study by Arsenian (1943) indicates that negative reactions to a strange environment are not seen when a mother figure is present. Arsenian studied the play of young children when in a strange room filled with brightly colored toys. The children were from the nursery of the Massachusetts State Reformatory for Women and ranged in age from 11.2 months to 30.1 months, an age range similar to that of the children in the present study. The reactions of the children were divided into adaptive forms, which included play, locomotion and talking, and certain more emotional reactions, including crying, thumb-sucking, fingering parts of the body, waving arms and stamping the feet.

The main comparison made by Arsenian bears clearly upon the problem of evaluating the relative importance to the child of (1) being away from mother (or familiar mother-substitute) and of (2) being in a strange situation. Sixteen children were left to play in the strange room by themselves, while another eight were allowed to have their mother or mother-substitute with them. Using a measure of security based on the reactions previously described, this author concludes:

The average security of the M-group (mother present) was greater on the first trial than the security of A-group (alone group) was on the final trials ... the immediate security of these eight children must be attributed to the presence of the familiar adult.

Arsenian further concludes:

Our generalizations derivable from the present study—and long known of nursery-school workers—is that the happiness of the child in a new situation is not guaranteed by an abundant supply of new toys. *The most certain provision that can be made for the security of young children faced with unstructured environments appears to be the presence of a familiar adult whose protective power is known* [p. 248].

In a film "Going to Hospital with Mother" (1958), Robertson further demonstrates how the continuous presence of the mother did much to alleviate the anxiety of a 2-year-old girl. Although she was under strain, neither the unfamiliar environment nor the minor surgical procedures disturbed the child unduly.

In Spitz's (1946) study of "Anaclitic Depression" the children remained in a familiar (even though institutional) environment, and the mother departed. The children's extreme reactions in this situation, and how restoration of the mother reversed them, have already been described.

Helene Deutsch's (1919) description of a 2-year-old's reaction to the loss of his nurse who, in function, had been his mother, serves to underline the importance of separation in its own right. Though remaining in his home, and though both the natural mother and a new nurse were available, this little boy responded in ways similar to the children studied here. During the first night he awoke in terror. He could hardly allow himself to fall asleep again and that night soiled himself for the first time in a year. His need for demonstrations of tenderness greatly increased, but until the ninth day after his nurse's departure he refused any offer of food.

Further study should be made of children in situations where the environment remains the same, but the mother is absent. We need to establish whether and in what degree the reactions of a 2-year-old, in his state of specific and individualized attachment, are attenuated by the familiar surroundings, and also the extent to which the care of other people is acceptable to him in his familiar environment. To what extent can other persons provide the child with gratifications associated with a given environment? To answer this requires a detailed specification of the different gratifications experienced by a given child in that environment.

VIII.   Effects of Length of Separation

A. Evidence from This Study

In Chapters 7 and 9 we described variations in the children's behavior during separation and reunion in terms of a series of ratings and rankings made for four different time spans: the first and the last week of separation, and the first and the second to twentieth weeks after reunion. The resulting rankings for each of the time spans were then intercorrelated, and in each case one dimension (set of rankings) was chosen which, both because of its correlation with the other dimensions and its theoretical relevance, best represented the resulting cluster of correlations.

Table 74 gives the further correlation of three of these key dimensions with each other and with the length of separation; it demonstrates that there is a significant association between length of separation and variations in the children's behavior both during the last week of separation and also during each of the two time spans into which reunion has been divided.[2]

Table 74. *Showing Intercorrelations of Dimensions Describing the Children's Behavior during Each of Three Periods and Length of Separation*

	1	2	3	4
1. *Last Week of Separation* Ambivalence to Observer	——			
2. *First Week of Reunion* Lack of Affectionate Response to the Mother	.78**	——		
3. *Rest of Reunion* Ambivalence to the Mother	.79**	.87**	——	
4. Length of Separation	.72*	.82**	.75**	——

  * Difference significant at P equals .05 or less
 ** Difference significant at P equals .01 or less

Taking behavior during the last week of separation as the criterion, there were many differences between children who stayed less than two weeks and those who stayed longer. Those who stayed over two weeks were more ambivalent to the observers, were generally more hostile, were less affectionate to the father on his visits, developed a stronger relationship to and a more distinct preference for certain nurses, became greedier, showed a greater concern over lapses in sphincter control, more frequently enacted the parental role in doll play and showed a high degree of possessiveness for material goods.

During reunion these same children, when compared to those separated for less than two weeks, showed an initial lack of affectionate response toward the mother, were ambivalent toward her and the observer for a longer period of time, made less progress in sphincter control, had a longer period of sleep disturbance and did not show a spurt in the use of speech and/or behavior indicative of identification with the parent until after they had been home for some time.

B. Evidence from Other Studies on the Effect of Length of Separation

Although evidence in the literature is not always consistent with

---

[2] There was no reason to expect that length of separation would be significantly associated with behavior during the first week of separation, and indeed it is not.

our findings, in general it underlines the importance of length of separation. It should be noted, however, that in examining this issue we are including one study of children younger than those in our sample, as well as other studies where separation is measured in months or years instead of in weeks.

The importance of length of separation is emphasized in several of Spitz's studies. Though dealing with a younger and probably a more deprived group, in the sense that the substitute care was not always adequate, the study written with K. Wolf (1946) is most relevant to our work. Here the children concerned lost their mothers at 6 months of age, as a result of which many of them developed symptoms such as apprehension, sadness, weepiness, lack of contact, rejection of environment, withdrawal, etc. When the mother returned, the authors report:

The change in the children's observable behavior was dramatic. They suddenly were friendly, gay, approachable. The withdrawal, the disinterest, the rejection of the outside world, the sadness, disappeared as if by magic. But over and beyond these changes most striking was the jump in the developmental quotient, within a period of twelve hours after the mother's return; in some cases, as much as 36.6 per cent higher than the previous measurement [p. 330].

Spitz and Wolf found, however, that reunion with mother did not lead to recovery when separation had continued for longer than three months.

This finding is one of the reasons why we spoke of three months as a critical period. The second reason is that in the Nursery we observed towards the end of three months the appearance of that kind of frozen, affect-impoverished expression which had strongly impressed us in Foundling Home [p. 331].

Roudinesco and Appell (1951) studied children aged between 1 and 4 years. These children were also far more deprived than those in our sample, but their findings do provide striking confirmation of the hypothesis suggested by Spitz's work, namely that the extent of the drop in developmental quotient (DQ) is a function of the length of stay in an institution. Using the Gesell Test as their measure, they found ". . . that deterioration is proportionate to the logarithm of the duration of separation." This finding applies not only to the overall DQ but to each of the subareas. These are "motor development, manual dexterity, adaptivity, expression of language, comprehension of language, and social reactions."

According to these authors, the age when separation begins is also important, mainly in its effects on the form taken by the descending curve of DQ scores. During the first eight days of separation, the scores of those separated after the age of 2 years 10 months suffer more than do those of children separated when younger. On the other hand the older children seem better able to adapt themselves so that after thirty-two days their deterioration is less rapid than it is in the younger ones.

Throughout their writing on the effects of separation, Bowlby and Robertson differentiate sharply between short- and long-stay children. In Chapter 11 we have described in some detail how these authors relate the phases of reaction to separation to the variable of length of separation. Thus, in their view the phase when a child represses the image of his mother, and also the degree to which this repression becomes consolidated, are both functions of the length of time that he is parted from her, although they hold that other variables also play a part (Bowlby, 1953, p. 270; Bowlby, 1954, p. 66).

So far we have only referred to the results of studies made on children who are actually undergoing a separation experience. Initially we intended to confine ourselves to such studies, but since length of separation has emerged as a factor central to the understanding of our findings, we are including in addition two studies which deal with the effects on later development of varying periods of stay in an institution before the age of 5.

Following earlier work by Goldfarb (1944) which had pointed to an association between the length of time spent in institutional care and later failure of foster home placement, Trasler (1960) compared the earlier history of a group of fifty-seven children who had failed at least once in their foster homes with that of eighty-one children who had settled satisfactorily.

Confining himself to a sample of children who had been admitted into public care before the age of 5 years, Trasler found a statistically significant association between frequency of failure in the first foster placement and the total length of institutional care during the first three years of life.

Trasler made a further analysis of a sample of twenty children all of whom had been removed from their first foster placement; ten of them had subsequently succeeded in a second placement, while ten had not. Those who failed in their second placement, he found, had experienced many more months of institutional care before their first placement than those who succeeded. This is all the more interesting because the two groups were carefully matched for mean age at original separation from mother, and because further analyses indicate that it is the length of time spent in an institution during the first three years rather than during later ones that is significant.

There is one study by Pringle and Bossio (1958) which fails to confirm these findings. They conclude:

Regarding the three criteria of deprivation, it was found that early first separation from the mother resulted in significantly greater ill effects on the children's development. Similarly, complete deprivation had a significantly deleterious effect. On the other hand, sheer length of institutionalization did not appear of great importance [p. 89].

This study, however, differs in material respects from those so far considered. In the first place, the indices of development used do not include success of foster placement but comprise instead the results of a great number of tests and assessments given to 8, 11 and 14-year-old children while still living in institutions.

In the second place, the criterion for age at separation (before or after 5 years of age) is a gross one and that for length of separation is calculated in an unusual way. Thus, length of separation is expressed by Pringle and Bossio (1958):

As a proportion of a child's chronological age ... thus "long-stay" children were defined as having spent more than one-third of their lives in care, while "short stays" had been away from their families for less than that time. This classification did not differentiate between continuous and intermittent periods in care, but merely indicated the total length of separation [p. 71].

Because the weight of evidence from our own and other studies points to length of separation as an important factor influencing the behavior of young children, we are inclined to conclude that the negative findings of Pringle and Bossio are to be accounted for by the particular methods of inquiry that they employed.

An Interpretation of the Findings

13 If the aim of our first study was to observe the reactions to mother-child separation more systematically than had previously been attempted, the aim of the present study was primarily to replicate and extend those findings. Though we had a number of general hypotheses in mind, no systematic or specific predictions or alternate hypotheses were formulated prior to the study. As part of our next study we shall attempt to start with specific hypotheses as suggested by our own and other findings. To aid in this task and to provide some integration of the observations presented in previous chapters, a tentative interpretation is given in the paragraphs below.

Several different theoretical frames of reference could be applied to this task of interpretation. Many authors have discussed the child's reaction to separation; a partial listing is given as part of the bibliography. Ideally one would study systematically and compare the pros and cons of the various theoretical alternatives. To do this adequately however would take us beyond the purpose of this book, which is to present some empirical findings and an interpretation of them. Furthermore, this task has recently been undertaken by Bowlby (1958, 1960a, 1960b, 1961, 1963) who, in addition, has begun to describe a theoretical schema of his own.

We are also aware that the results of the growing number of animal studies focusing on mother-child separation could be related to our findings. Again we decided that such an endeavor is beyond the scope of this volume.

At this point in our experience we prefer to do no more than apply a model which we believe offers greatest assistance in the understanding of the total set of findings. As indicated previously, we have found it useful to think of the results in relation to psychoanalytic theory, and specifically to the metapsychological points of view as formulated and revised by Rapaport (1960), and Rapaport and Gill

(1959). It must be stressed, however, that we are not attempting a complete metapsychological explanation of the phenomena we have observed. Nor do we imply that because we think our findings can be interpreted with the use of this model that the adequacy of the model is therefore demonstrated.

To apply the above model we divide the child's total development into the five phases suggested by the previous data analysis, characterize the equilibria reached in each of these five periods and attempt to show the manner in which these equilibria succeed each other. The five phases are as follows: the first three days of separation, the fourth to the twelfth day of separation, the period after the thirteenth day of separation, the first days after reunion and the second to the twentieth week after reunion. We wish to point out in particular how the continuous presence of a stress situation, i.e., separation, leads to successive efforts at adaptation and the processes by which the final mode reached is undone when the child and parent are once more reunited.

But before speaking of the functioning and the changes in functioning, we must briefly review what change in the external situation was crucial in initiating the series of equilibria.

I.   The Nature of the Traumatic Event

From a descriptive viewpoint, the 2-year-old in our study was experiencing the shift from familiar surroundings, which included the presence of both parents, to an unfamiliar nursery where the parents, of course, were not present.

Although this study was not designed to isolate definitively the relative importance to the child of the various aspects of this total event, some discussion of the question is appropriate. Study of the literature and our own observations indicates that loss of the parents and loss of the familiar environment could each be traumatic factors in their own right. Other studies, of what happens when parents depart from home, or by contrast what happens when only a change in environment occurs, are needed.

Examination of such studies as are available as well as the nature of the child's reaction to temporary placement in a residential nursery suggest that the loss of the parents and particularly the mother is of primary importance. The intense crying was mostly for the parents and began and/or reached its first peak when they left the child. The panic-like crying after the parent's departure at the end of a visit further confirmed the impression that the stress was primarily a function of their absence. The most intense aggression and longing was both defended against and expressed in relation to the parents and particularly the mother. The children initially cried desperately for their parents but also singled the mother doll out as a target of hostility. This longing and anger could eventually be expressed only indirectly—by seeking the visiting father's sweets and repressing any form of feeling toward him. That it is the absence of the parent that is crucial is further supported by our observation that none of the nonseparated children between the ages of 1 and 2 whom we observed in this study could tolerate being without his mother for any length of time, even while in his own room and playing with a friendly adult.

Furthermore, such analyses of the influence of the environment as were possible, as well as the findings of previous studies, suggest that being shifted to an unfamiliar environment accentuates the child's reactions to separation but is by itself not a sufficient factor to account for them.

Even if one accepts that loss of the parent is the principal aspect of the traumatic event studied here, the question remains as to what components of this loss are crucial. In subsequent sections we try to infer from the reactions observed how the children experienced the loss. What specific deficits the loss of the parents represented for each child can only be known through further study. Two different aspects of the general meaning of the loss can be stressed. One interpretation emphasizes the loss of the relationship to a specific mother and father, and all that this implies.

Though not easily differentiated, it may, on the other hand, be held that it is a composite of the specific functions that the parents performed that is crucial. The latter would suggest that if substitutes could adequately perform these functions, then the child would not experience stress. The most rigorous test of this expectation would be to provide such substitutes and then study the child's response.

Two findings from our own work throw some light on this matter. If the separation primarily involved the loss of a composite of functions previously performed by the parents, then even average variations in the quantity and quality of the substitute care by the nurses should have a noticeable effect on the child's response. This was not the case for the children studied here.

Another finding comes from our first study. As part of a contrast of the child's response to being placed in a day versus a residential nursery, it was determined that the quality of the nurse to child interaction was very similar in both types of situations (Heinicke, 1956, pp. 146–148). That the quality of the substitute care was similar but the reactions of the two groups of children quite different, does not support the interpretation that variations in the substitute care are crucial factors in affecting the child's level of distress.

It is our general hypothesis, therefore, that it is the loss of the specific relationship to the mother and father that constitutes the essential and most significant aspect of the traumatic event studied here. But even if this emphasis should prove mistaken, what can be examined is how the children responded to this event.

II.   The First Three Days of Separation

Separation from the parent initiates a set of changes in the child that is most readily observed in the quantity of crying. Almost all behavior was initially oriented toward the absent parents in a desperate attempt to recapture them. We wish to underline that the unavailability of the parent does not necessarily imply that the cathexis of the inner representation of that parent is also changed. Thus, during this time the reaction to the parent at a visit was affectionate, the cathexis of the inner representation was preserved, and the core of the first major adaptation was an attempt physically to bring back the object. To understand the nature of this adaptation certain further theoretical interpretations are introduced for the phase under discussion.

Descriptively such discharge of energy directed to recapturing the parents was quantitatively either slight (e.g., in the form of looking) or massive (e.g., writhing on the floor accompanied by intense crying). Some authors may feel that the concept of grief best describes the nature of this discharge, as well as the likely inner state of the child. It could be thought of as being either slight or massive.

We preferred to use a concept which included the discharge aspect, made the distinction between a slight and massive discharge and was consistent with interpretations of the child's functioning as made from a dynamic and structural point of view. Freud's concept of anxiety as redefined by Schur (1958) seemed most appropriate:

Anxiety is a reaction to a traumatic situation, or to danger, present or anticipated. In this reaction we have to distinguish between the affect anxiety, which is an ego reaction, and the discharge phenomena, which are also id manifestations[1] [pp. 217–218].

We shall assume that in the first days of his separation the child was experiencing the two types of signal as well as the traumatic form of anxiety. The latter is suggested by the extreme forms of motor and affect discharge. But it may be objected that the concept of signal anxiety is no longer applicable in a situation where the dreaded event (separation) has occurred. If, however, we conceive of the danger as involving something more than the physical separation of parent and child, then the concept may well be applicable. That is, in terms of Schur's formulation, the child is not only aware of the present danger but anticipates dangers likely to arise following the physical separation from the parents.

Freud himself explored the relation between anxiety and need satisfaction. Inquiring into what "anxiety really is," he at first suggests that manifestations of anxiety occur in situations of "missing someone who is loved and longed for ..." (Freud, 1926, p. 137). But an important addition is made in the subsequent discussion:

A moment's reflection takes us beyond this question of loss of object. The reason why the infant in arms wants to perceive the presence of the mother is only because it already knows by experience that she satisfied all its needs without delay. The situation, then, which it regards as a danger and against which it wants to be safeguarded is that of nonsatisfaction, of a *growing tension due to need*, against which it is helpless. ...

When the infant has found out by experience that an external, perceptible object can put an end to the dangerous situation which is reminiscent of birth, the content of the danger it fears is displaced from the economic situation on to the condition which determined the situation, viz., the loss of

---

[1] In a personal communication to the authors Schur has suggested the following as an elaboration of his original definition: "Anxiety is a reaction of the ego, or of its matrix (precursors) to a traumatic situation, or to danger, present or anticipated. The concomitant discharge phenomena or anxiety equivalents, even though not necessarily accompanied by conscious awareness of danger or conscious experience of anxiety, are also manifestations of changes in the id." These distinctions in turn must be seen in the context of Schur's (1960) conception of gradations of anxiety running from primary anxiety in the traumatic situation to the thought-like awareness of anticipated danger.

object. It is the absence of the mother that is now the danger; and as soon as that danger arises the infant gives the signal of anxiety, before the dreaded economic situation has set in [Freud, 1926, p. 137].

Strictly speaking, therefore, the signal type of separation anxiety can occur only before the event. But if we think of the potential dangers that are likely to follow the event of separation, then the concept of signal anxiety again becomes applicable.

By focusing on the helplessness felt by the child as a function of "growing tension due to need," we can then ask: what wishes are likely to be intensified by the separation?

There is first of all the wish to be loved. This is accentuated by the frustration of the normal and continuous interchanges of parent and child. The intense "I want Mummy" is thus the cry of a broken-hearted lover whose libidinal tensions are urgent. It is in this context that the concept of grief seems most relevant.

Much remains to be learned about the links of being loved, wishing to be loved, and the quantity and quality of the child's secondary narcissism. We would hypothesize, however, that during the second and third year of life, when the concept of self is developing at an accelerated rate (Spitz, 1957), and when the child is capable of experiencing approval and disapproval of the self, then the mother's absence intensifies the wish for this approval. Even though initially mainly resisting any intimate contact, the frequency with which a child sought some type of reassurance and affection from the adults in the nursery suggests such a need. The absence of the parents can then be thought of as the removal of the most important support of the child's secondary narcissism.

The observations during the first three days as well as throughout the separation suggest that the state of the child's narcissism is in turn intimately tied to failure or success at sphincter control. When Owen lost control on the first day, he became most concerned. Margaret did not have a bowel movement at first but held herself in for five days. When, shortly before her father's first visit, she had a bowel movement, she greeted her father with: "You are not going to spank me, are you Daddy?" Increasing concern about lapses in control as well as the verbalizations of the children tended to confirm the impression that something like the following fantasy was frequently present from the beginning of separation: "Mother left me because I was not clean."

The wish for food from the parents could also be seen. Thus the children at first refused to take food from the nurses, while only a special food or their bottle from home would quiet them. Later in the separation they were to become very greedy. Similarly the wish to be physically cared for and protected by the parents could be inferred from the way that the children at first resisted the nurses' intimate care. Later they were to become ill and demanded much attention from the nurses.

Finally, whether we view the wish to destroy as due to a defusion of instincts or as a product of frustration, insofar as it was directed to the absent love object, it would again come into conflict with the wish to be loved and would add to the "tension due to need." The same children who could very deliberately step on the mother doll during the first days did not at first express their hostility openly in the Everyday Nursery Setting. Later they could be hostile to the observer but not to the visiting father.

But the emergence of conflict and anxiety must also be considered in relation to changes in the structure of the child's personality. It is then not just a question of conflicting wishes or intensification of wishes but of a weakening and alteration of the structures through which the dynamic forces are expressed.

That the child experienced a strain on his defensive mechanisms is inferred in part from the desperate efforts made to maintain the status quo. In the first days the children were incessantly trying to bring their parents back, and through their resistance in every encounter—eating, toileting, sleeping and general handling—were saying in effect: "I don't want to have anything to do with these new people."

Other behavior could also be understood as defensive in nature and as aiding the desperate effort to maintain the current mode of adjustment. Thus, the above resistance can be related to the defensive function of the defiance frequently seen in a 2-year-old child (Gesell and Ilg, 1943; Spock, 1957). Responding to the love gained, a child usually complies with the restrictions imposed by his parents. But, as a function of the growing wish for autonomy and at moments of frustration and anger, defiant resistance to all commands and restrictions also appears. The child attempts to manipulate the adult who is associated with his anger. The most active resistance of the separated child to the commands of the adults in the nursery was seen at a time when his anger with his parents could only be expressed in the doll play. The resistance was thus not only a way of saying "I want my parents and not you," but also a way of expressing his anger with the parents and parent substitutes, controlling the latter and yet avoiding the danger of an extreme and destructive explosion.

Fitting in with the above interpretation of resistance as an active approach to a danger situation were the many occasions on which the child repeated or anticipated in an active form the events experienced passively and helplessly. This defense was clearly of major importance, and especially so during the first three days when the child was still trying to maintain active control. Having been left by his parents, the child would himself leave his favorite toy or doll, but he would make certain that he found it again. Once more, quoting Freud:

The ego, which experienced the trauma passively, now repeats it actively in a weakened version, in the hope of being able itself to direct its course [Freud, 1926, p. 167].

The control or inhibition of impulses seen at this time must also be added to the various mechanisms which the child uses to deal with his conflicts. Even so, these various efforts also frequently failed. It was during this period of desperate resistance and control that the child also most frequently woke up in terror and cried for his parents. At the point of separation, or in the first hours after it, one could see a degree of disorganization suggesting total ego regression. But this was very short-lived; the major ego regressions were to come later. Rather, it was the determination as well as the desperateness of the well-directed efforts to recapture the parents that impressed one.

This determination to recapture the parents and the lack of involvement with new adults can, of course, also be understood in light of the absorbing qualities of the state of grief. For some readers this will be an adequate interpretation of the behavior seen. Without wishing to imply that the issues relating to the concept of defense at this age (e.g., defense against external versus internal dangers) are fully clarified, we nevertheless believe that some conception of internal structure and the related concept of defense is necessary to understand fully the behavior of the children being studied here.

But whether one stresses one or the other interpretation, it is clear that the adaptive value of resistance to new adults is very limited. The 2-year-old is so dependent on the adult world, and this particularly in his need to be fed and protected physically, that the position of actively resisting and avoiding all adults is not long possible. Had the cries for the parents succeeded in bringing them back after one or two days, then they would of course have been most adaptive.

III. From the Third to the Twelfth Day of Separation

If the above mode of adaptation was not long tenable, and the resistance to new adults did in fact diminish even in the first days, one might ask what other adaptation would potentially be feasible. One solution would be quickly to drop the attachment to the parents, and then to direct the freed cathexis completely to the new adults in the nursery. Given the availability of a single affectionate mother-substitute, this could conceivably occur. In the situation of the children we studied, however, a different mode of adjustment was observed. We find that many behavioral changes occurred and that these are best drawn together by the concept of regression. If the first three days were dominated by the child's frantic efforts to bring the lost object back, in this next period the psychic energy was directed toward retrieving a lost relationship; i.e., defensively going back to an earlier phase of development.

There were first of all regressions in the child's ego functions. The following were observed: a reduced usage of words, a serious lapse in sphincter control and some breakdown in control of aggression leading to an increase in the open expression of severe hostility.[2]

In terms of an instinctual regression, there was not only a breakthrough of aggression, but also a regression to the oral phase as indicated by the increase in greed and biting.

Third, we shall think of the child's active avoidance of the observer as a sign of regression in object relations. To clarify this, a series of digressions is necessary.

It will be recalled that avoidance of the observer was typically in

---

[2] It is certainly possible to interpret this behavior as a sign of disorganization. Without excluding this possibility we believe the concept of regression more adequately integrates all the findings.

evidence during the period under discussion and did not characterize the other periods. It will also be recalled that we have previously
suggested (see Chapter 7) that the avoidance could be seen as a defensive maneuver against the felt emergence of hostile affects stimulated by the presence of the observer. We found that the more readily
a child expressed severe hostile sequences in the permissive doll-
play situation (not the Everyday Nursery Setting) the more ardently
did he avoid the observer. To avoid the stimulus, then, is a way of
bolstering the inner control of aggression.

The question arises as to why the observers should stimulate such
aggressive affects. It must be stressed again that other strangers who
came and went did not arouse such a reaction. Furthermore, during the period under discussion the nurses were no longer resisted
to the same extent. More important, resistance to the nurses in terms
of the willful "No" was qualitatively different from the panic-like
running or turning away from the observer.

It is our hypothesis that the observers were psychologically important because they were both like the parents and at the same time
very different from the parents. Though there was no evidence that
the child held the observers responsible for the separation, the child
very likely linked the parents to the observers. These associations
were probably formed as a consequence of Westheimer's visits to the
home before the separation, and/or the observer's presence both at
the moment of separation and later when the parents visited. The
nature of his (or her) street clothing (as opposed to the nurses' uni-
forms), his clear interest in him, and his coming and going in the
manner of a visitor would further enhance the child's tendency to
see the observer as a parental figure. Most important, these percep-
tions would lead the child to expect immediate positive gratification,
if not reunion, with the real parent. The searching crying of "Daddy"
as the child turned to the observer left no doubt about that.

But the child quickly realized that the observers were not parent
figures in any sense. They seldom picked up the child even though
they were friendly. They watched the child and thus performed a
role which in the past had often led to restriction as well as admiration in his life. Also they left after a short period without taking the
child with them. In brief, they did all those things which were likely
to shatter the child's hopes and further enhance his angry affects.
The observers thus tended to activate such angry feelings as were al-

ready felt toward the parents and, through the frustration of an expectation, further added to the force of these affects. Already under considerable strain in controlling the balance of excessive hostile and loving affects, the child would attempt to bolster his defenses by avoiding persons who further added to this strain. Furthermore, these efforts at control of aggression during this period coincided with the efforts to maintain a predominantly affectionate relation to the visiting parent.

But if this interpretation of the dynamic reasons for avoidance suffices, it is of interest to ask why avoidance is typically seen rather than some other type of defense. The salience of other forms of regression (libidinal and ego) suggested that the avoidance seen in relation to the observer could be viewed as a *sign* of regression in object relationships. We asked whether it could be that the child is once more reacting to strangers as he did during the second half of the first year of life. Adopting the model of regression, our observations of the nonseparated children indicated, first, that some initial shyness, followed rapidly by interest and friendliness, is the normal response of the 2-year-old to an adult if the mother is nearby. If panic-like avoidance then is not a normal response for this age group, what similar behavior can we think of that is normal for an earlier age? The eighth-month or stranger anxiety comes to mind.

The plausibility of viewing the 2-year-old's panic-like avoidance as regressively linked to the earlier form of behavior is supported by the possibility that both are reactions to the dangers of object loss. In important details the explanation of avoidance which we have given above corresponds to the theoretical account of stranger anxiety given by Spitz (1950):

We have attempted to explain this unpleasure response to the stranger's approach . . . by assuming that the child confronts the stranger's face with the memory trace of the libidinal object. On finding that the stranger is not the object, the child concludes: "This is not mother, she does not return, I have lost mother!" The stranger's face thus becomes the cue for the apperception of a rising tension between id demands and inadequate ego strength.

The id demands consist in object-libidinal strivings towards the mother, who has achieved the full status of a libidinal object by this age. These libidinal strivings are reinforced by powerful narcissistic needs. For at this age the mother has still a two-fold function: although she has already become an actual libidinal object, she is still a complementary part of the infant's immature ego [p. 143].

In the dynamic background of both phenomena, then, the following are stressed: (1) that the stranger or observer arouses the child's hope that "mother is returning," (2) that the destruction of this hope is not only a frustration in its own right but reminiscent of the affects related to separation from the mother, and (3) that both tend to be experienced as a threat to the balance between impulse expression and its control. Certain differences must also be noted. Clearly, an actual long separation is likely to lead to quantitative differences in the strength of affect. As Spitz (1950) remarks:

Eight-months' anxiety can be overcome by adequate behavior. . . . When the stranger does not present his face actively to the child the memory of this contrast will fade, the reactivated affect of anxiety will spend itself [p. 141].

By contrast, in the separated 2-year-old we not only find a more intense response, but also that nothing will stop the panic except the observer's remaining at a great distance.

Certain other differences in the two situations can be related to the greater perceptual and control functions of the 2-year-old. In his case the stimulus of a mere face or stranger is not adequate to arouse hope; now at his age only a person who is sufficiently associated with the parent will do so.

While the above interpretation of the avoidance stresses the importance of object loss, consistent with the distinction made by Benjamin and his colleagues (Benjamin, 1959, 1961, 1963; Tennes and Lampl, 1963), it is possible that this behavior was also a function of "fear of the strange as such." The avoidance could thus entail a regression to the earlier fear of the strange (about 3–5 months) as well as a regression to the stranger anxiety of the second half of the first year.

In the above then we have attempted to organize a variety of findings in terms of the concept of regression. The fact that physical illness began during this period could also be seen as a regression to a situation of being completely cared for, or at least a break in control. One could further inquire whether the break in control came first and then the illness, or vice versa. We think that very likely it was some complicated interaction of these two possibilities and certain other factors.

From the above emphasis on regression, and the implied intense and continuous cathexis of the inner representation of the parent, it also follows that the extent of the shift of cathexis from the inner representation of the parent to the inner representation of the nurse would not be great. Most of the psychic energy was at this time absorbed in an effort regressively to recapture a previously satisfactory relationship to the parents.

On the other hand, we did observe that resistance to the nurses was declining; a relationship certainly did develop. The evidence also suggests that the nurse could gratify wishes relating to feeding, being put to bed and bathing. On the other hand our discussion of the structural changes has implied that the relationship to the nurse was not sufficient adequately to deal with conflicts involving the wish to be loved, the wish to mess and the wish to destroy.

We would hypothesize that the failure to resolve these conflicts, and the associated continuing anxiety would provide the psychological force that would lead to a different adaptation. Or we can point to the inadequacy of the regressive solution in reaching any kind of equilibrium. And if these represent inner dispositions to change, it is clear that an external event, the visit of the parent or parent surrogate during the second week of separation, helped to accelerate these changes.

IV. From the Thirteenth to the Last Day of Separation

First we again remind the reader of the behavioral changes on the bases of which we are delineating this new period. Two indices of regression were on the average not seen after the twelfth day of separation: the decline in the number of different words used and the avoidance of the observer. Furthermore, two of the most *obvious* indices of the cathexis of the parents were for all practical purposes no longer seen after the twelfth day of separation: the attachment to the favorite toy from home and crying for the parents (see Chapter 6). Since we are dealing with group trends and median figures, it is important to stress that we are not saying that, exactly between the twelfth and thirteenth day, a change was seen for each child. As the case illustrations reveal, this is not so. We are dealing with general trends which express themselves slightly differently in each child.

Nor do we wish to suggest that the parental visit, which, as it happened, typically occurred on the twelfth day of separation, is responsible for the new developments. This would be contrary to our whole emphasis on the inner and continuous development of the child. For at least one constellation of behavior, however—that of the *simultaneous* presence of signs of sadness-resignation, excessive cheerfulness and injury to the self—we could say that this was very likely precipitated by the father's visit. That the words "gone" and "all gone" also characteristically appeared after this visit suggests the following interpretations.

The "gone" can be seen as a sign of the further recognition of the fact that the parents were in fact "gone"; as if the previous painful recognition had been blended with hope of a quick return, but that the arrival of the parent and his departure without him for a second time would seriously challenge the child's hope.

This type of recognition brings to mind the grief work seen as part of the mourning process in adults. Taken together with the extensive crying which had immediately preceded the appearance of "gone," one might well interpret this verbalization as an indication of reality testing. That this reality testing was in fact very limited is suggested by the infrequency of these verbalizations. Grief work involves the continuous and realistic confrontation of the painful facts.

More important, the structural context of "gone" indicates that the realistic mourning was very limited. "Gone" occurred in association with signs of sadness-resignation, excessive cheerfulness and injury to the self. This does not indicate that the psychic energy is devoted to the relinquishing of the object.[3] This interpretation is further supported by the occurrence of new structural changes involving countercathexes and considerable amounts of psychic energy. The child never stopped saying "Mummy" and "Daddy," even if this was in a subdued tone, but during the parental visit there was now no emotional contact. Rather than relinquishing the parental objects the child repressed the intense affects felt in relation to them. The intense hostility might destroy the precious object and the expression of intense affection might both overwhelm the child and once more disappoint him. That "Mummy" was in general seldom

[3] To some both these findings and the quality of the behavior described previously may suggest the concept of depression. Given both the developmental status of the children studied and the total context of their behavior, it is felt that this label is not appropriate. This is not to underestimate the possible significance for later depressions of the experiences being studied here.

mentioned by the children, and only rarely in relation to the observers, suggests that the affects in relation to her were even more strongly repressed. Simplifying, if the first adaptation stresses recapturing the object physically, and the second focuses on regressively retrieving a relationship, then the third focuses on the problem of shielding the precious object from the aggressive affects.

While repression of these affects thus engages considerable psychic energy, further energy is absorbed in a displacement of the very affects that are not expressed toward the parents. During the parental visit we could see signs of intense longing. But this was not for the parents—only for the sweet things they brought.

Similarly, the hostile affects exploded often against the children and the inanimate objects.

Both hostile and affectionate affects were also expressed toward the observers. Intense clinging alternated with vicious biting. We have previously suggested that the observers were not only like parents but in some important respects were also unlike them. They would thus be suitable objects for displacement. The children seemed to think of them as visiting parent figures and would again and again greet them with "Daddy." It seems likely then that the biting, hitting, and clinging was in fact intended for "Daddy" and what he represented.

We assume that the nature of these behaviors and the implied structural changes would not favor grief work or relinquishing the parental object. That they did occur to some extent could be inferred from the children's increasing involvement with the nurses. Improvement in sphincter control and speech may well have occurred on the basis of a transfer of some cathexis from the inner representation of the parents to representations of the nurse. But this was clearly limited. Though the quality of the speech increased, it was less distinct. Similarly, the new sphincter control was very unstable. More striking was the fact that on the day of reunion the children did not turn to the nurses.

We conclude these various arguments relating to the nature of object cathexis by emphasizing that important structural changes allowed the child to maintain most of his cathexis of the inner representation of the parents. Some of the cathexis, however, was transferred to the nurse. It remains a matter of future research whether the death of the parent would make a difference to the development discussed here. We know only that the devoted care by one nurse can make a difference (see Freud and Burlingham, 1944; Hellman, 1962). But even in her nurseries, Anna Freud observed that the adequacy of substitute care was ultimately limited. Similarly, even though the substitute nurse played an important role in the development of the child reported by Hellman, the concurrent and relatively continuous relationship to the mother makes it difficult to determine the role played by the substitute mother in the eventual normal development of this child.

In an earlier part of this discussion we stressed the dependence of the child's narcissism on the continuous and loving support of the parents. The child's feeling of well-being is highly dependent on the ever-present admiration and acknowledgment which is given in the context of basic acceptance. The parent is still the primary source of secondary narcissism. But the child is also already aware that this admiration is to some extent conditional upon his performance and competence. His narcissism is heightened when he meets the expectations of the parents. Moreover, the child has some awareness of when he has met these expectations and when not, and this in turn is related to their partial internalization.

The effort to use more words as well as the great concern about sphincter lapses seen during this time can thus be understood as a desperate effort to recapture a feeling of well-being that is associated with parental admiration. Let us consider Katie. Given her mother's pride in her ability to talk to everyone, it is not surprising that Katie copied all kinds of phrases like a parrot. Similarly, we have noted the parental role behavior enacted by the children; for example, Katie smacked her doll for wetting herself.

Yet, as noted in Chapter 7, neither the concern about having wet oneself nor the enactment of parental indignation was associated with real competence and the subsequent adult admiration that would lead to a feeling of well-being. The parrot-like speech brought the laughter of the nurses but not a truly affectionate acceptance. At best Owen's consistent "Wee-wee" confused the nurses; at worst his insistence on remaining on the pot led to a temper-loaded struggle.

It could be argued that the enactment of parental roles (for example, punishing ones) are temporary imitations of the nurses' behavior; one would not expect them to modify the behavior in question. This is unlikely as a sole explanation. The behavior was first seen before the child had had extensive contact with the nurses; it merely increased in the period under discussion. Though the nurses clearly desired the children to be clean and expressed their annoyance when they were not, they did not spank the children. The behavior was thus a product of inner forces as well as external models. Furthermore, even though such sequences as spanking the doll for wetting was not a part of integrated growth, the immediate context of the behavior suggested that the children wanted to achieve control but couldn't bring it about. Thus, we hypothesize that the enactment of these parental sequences as well as the efforts to attain competence were in the service of defense. It was a desperate effort to overcome the feeling of being unloved.

The larger context of this behavior further suggests the child's efforts at defense. To keep the angry feelings in check all affects toward the visiting father had at this time to be repressed. The obviously aggressive and/or rigid nature of both the parental role sequences and certain efforts at control further suggests that this aggressive force was being both expressed and yet contained in these sequences. Even though he knew his father was downstairs waiting to visit him, Owen insisted on remaining on his pot and exploded in a violent temper when the nurse tried to take him off it.

But, if a child is attempting to achieve a heightened state of narcissism, would not a well-established competence and associated ego identifications be a logical solution? It would seem that the tie to the nurses was not sufficiently affectionate, and that to the absent parents too aggressive, to allow for this form of identification. Not until the libidinal tie to the mother was again restored during reunion did such identifications appear.

Perhaps even more ominous for future development were the children's attempts to increase the feeling of well-being through increased oral intake and by an aggressive possessiveness toward material goods. Especially important was the fact that when the possessiveness was frustrated the child would readily lapse into a temper tantrum. We would hypothesize that the oral greed and possessiveness in general is an effort to bring about a state of well-being and contentment to substitute for the heightened state of narcissism which derives from the successful libidinal exchange with the parents. The same urgent and desperate quality that had characterized the crying for the parents now accompanied the striving for non-personal objects. More important, while the presence of the parent could in the beginning truly comfort and relax the child, the gratification by food and material goods only temporarily quelled the child's craving.

These findings and interpretations suggest an addition to our previous conclusion that structural changes permit a child both to maintain most of his cathexis of the inner representations of the parents and to shift some of it to the nurses; some of the child's psychic energy is increasingly directed toward material goods.

V. The First Days after Reunion

Just as repression of affect seen in relation to the visiting father was a key indication of the structural changes which had taken place by the end of separation, so a lack of affect when reunited with the mother is the most significant phenomenon during the first days after reunion.

That this reaction should shift so quickly from the father to the mother is not easy to interpret. We would suppose that during the separation the father was the target of the affects felt toward the mother as well as toward himself. We would further suppose that just as the child was more frustrated by the mother's absence, so his hatred as well as his longing for her would be greater. The evidence from doll play on hostility shown toward the mother doll during separation supports this hypothesis.

Insofar as the wish to destroy was thus less of a danger in relation to the father, and given the immediate pressure of needing someone to feed and physically care for him, it follows that the child should initially turn most readily to the father for that care. In terms of the child's inner equilibrium the father took the place of the nurse.

The mother's attempt to feed and dress the child was therefore resisted, not because of the continued attachment to the nurse, but because the emotional closeness to the mother might lead to an aggressive explosion.

By the end of the first week after reunion the child again permitted his mother to feed and care for him. A partial restoration of positive cathexis is implied. Moreover, the cathexis of the father had by this time probably returned to the preseparation status.

Nevertheless the cathexis of the mother had not been fully restored, and we must ask what dynamic forces and countercathexes are at work. We would hypothesize that we are once more dealing with the wish to be loved, the wish to mess and the wish to destroy. Insofar as these are repressed and can be expressed neither in direct form nor transformed but rather are subject to countercathexes, so clearly this psychic energy is not available for a full cathexis of the mother.

It is important to note, of course, that changes in the mother's capacity to express positive affect toward the child would certainly also affect the return of a mutually positive relationship. Our evidence shows, however, that she could in most cases return more quickly to the previous level of positive cathexis than could her child.

We would further assume that it was the mother's ability to meet the child with affection that provided an important incentive for him gradually to dissolve the countercathexes that had developed during the separation and to express his own intense longing for her. That is, her affectionate presence now challenges the adaptive functions of the repression of all affect.

In summary, during the first week after reunion the repression of affect in relation to the mother changes little and the cathexis seen at the end of separation for the nurse is probably transferred quickly to the father, and perhaps to some slight extent also to the mother. But what of the intense interest in food and material goods that was seen at the end of separation? If anything, after reunion the children became reluctant to eat and this was part of their general reluctance to interact with the mother. Nor did the same degree of possessiveness of material goods persist, though a certain amount was in evidence.

We would hypothesize that the mere presence of the loving mother and father in a familiar home does a great deal to restore the child's narcissism. An urgency to achieve the same state of well-being through food or material goods would thus be removed. That several children would not let their father out of their sight, and that all soon indicated their fear of the separation occurring again, certainly indicates the importance of the parents in maintaining the child's equilibrium.

If some of the pressure to heighten the narcissism was thus

removed, the initial *lack* of progress in sphincter control and speech suggests that these important areas of behavior are as yet not likely to be a source of the child's narcissistic supplies. As will be seen, not until the normal libidinal relationship with the mother has been restored could this occur.

VI.   Development from the Second to the Twentieth Week after Reunion

Rephrasing the problem posed above, how do we conceptualize the process whereby the repressed positive and negative affects toward the mother were both expressed and transformed during the reunion period?

While we have stressed the mother's outgoing affection as an important incentive and as a force tending toward disequilibrium, we would now add that the balance of permissiveness and consistent limit setting was probably also important. That is, the child was not only stimulated to return the affection, but the adequate balance of permissiveness and limitation allowed him to express the aggressive and anal derivatives without feeling that he would be swamped and/or incur a further loss of love.

Among these negative derivatives we include the stubborn defiance, the failure to achieve sphincter control and even the reluctance to speak. As instances of these derivatives were met by the mother both with continued affection and by setting limits, so the child could increasingly afford to lift the countercathexes. And as the countercathexes were loosened increment by increment, so the sheer quantity of the derivative expressions could increase.

That this process was by no means a completely smooth one is attested by the fact that it was accompanied by fairly continuous sleep disturbances. We are assuming that instability in ego structure would be particularly evident during sleep when ego control is lessened in any case.

It would appear then that the child is repeatedly testing the fantasy: "If I am dirty, destructive or defiantly independent, mother will again leave me." The challenge of this test could be seen in Mrs. C's reactions to her son's intensified provocation: "If he carries on like this, I will take him back to the nursery." The consistent support of the fieldworker no doubt helped some mothers to deal with such provocations.

The child's increasing positive cathexis of the mother could then serve as the dynamic context in which ego growth could take place. Insofar as both the child and mother took pleasure in the child's mastery, so their positive interchanges would in turn be enhanced. Improvement in toileting and sleeping tended to take place as part and parcel of the working through of ambivalent feelings. By contrast the acceleration in speech, but particularly the signs of identification with the parents, occurred after the full positive cathexis of the mother had been restored. Thus, both the quality of the behavior involved in these identifications and their dynamic and object-relationship context differentiates them from the signs of defensive identifications seen during the separation. Most important, we hypothesize that identifications emerging in the context of a libidinal tie to the mother are more likely to be integrated into the progressive development of the child and will contribute toward that development.

In evaluating the child's development, it is necessary to consider to what extent some of the aggressive affects may nevertheless be associated with these identifications. Thus, Gillian's growth accelerated on the basis of an increasingly affectionate relationship to her mother. By the fourteenth week of reunion Gillian had not only achieved complete sphincter control and shown a spurt in language development, but was also showing signs of identification with her mother. For example, during the visit made fourteen weeks after reunion Gillian first put her doll on a toy potty, would from time to time lift her and look inside the potty, and then said in a questioning manner: "Good girl, good girl." After a while she brought some face cream to the observer and said: "Nicey cream." She then brought over her mother's lipstick, and when her mother said "What do you do with it?", she put it on her lips and wanted the fieldworker to look at it and admire her.

Although these trends continued in the weeks to follow, the visit by the male observer during the sixteenth week of reunion revealed the ease with which the defensive and aggressive aspects of the above play could still be reactivated. Gillian had not seen the observer for sixteen weeks; it was clear that she immediately associated him with the nursery and avoided him like the plague. She did, however, play

with her doll, showed off her excellent command of language, and
after eating some chocolate, carefully put away the pieces of wrap-
ping. The latter behavior greatly pleased her mother.

As the observer started to leave, Gillian suddenly got out her own
pot and impulsively sat on it fully dressed. Her mother was obviously
surprised and said that she should wait. The mother also observed
that Gillian's waving was in part friendly but also a form of waving
the observer away.

This example illustrates how future separations or other stress
situations might well force the child to regress to responses seen as
part of the reactions to the initial separation under study here. Although Gillian's reactions to the observer were an exception, we cannot rule out the possibility that certain potentials for pathology remained. It is possible that for the group as a whole some of the aggressive affects were associated with the beginning of superego development. Our assessments were not accurate enough to warrant
confident interpretations, but the nature of the development was
apparently not such as to suggest obvious rigidities or lack of normal
progress.

VII.   The Relation of the Development during Separation and Reunion

In the above discussion we have attempted to follow the changes in
the adaptive equilibrium of the child who was separated from his
parents for more than two weeks. It seemed easiest to comprehend
the changes by initially confining ourselves to this group.

But having discussed the findings in this way we must now emphasize our main conclusion, namely, that the nature of the child's
adaptation at the end of the separation best predicted the nature of
his development during reunion, and that the level of that adaptation was in turn associated with the length of the child's separation.
Those children who were separated for about *two weeks* were typically still in a phase of regression in all aspects of functioning and of
very minimal cathexis of the adults in the nursery. In so far as the
conflicts relating to the absent parent could be dealt with without
involving considerable repression of affects relating to these conflicts, the child could more readily and quickly resume the previous
level of affectionate interchange with his parents as well as the de-

gree of ego development associated with such a relationship. The lack of affectionate response to the mother during reunion was short-lived, the emergence of ambivalent feelings related to the separation was minimal, and growth in such areas as sleep, sphincter control, language and identification with the parent was slowed down relatively little.

By contrast the adaptation of those children remaining *longer than two weeks* was typified by a lack of affectionate response to the visiting father. Structural changes entailing repression of affects of hate and love for the parents could be inferred, and these changes were maintained during the first weeks after reunion. Even though encouraged by the mother, the affectionate relationship to her was resumed only gradually. The expression of this affection as well as the hostile affects were both made possible and further accelerated by the easing of the countercathexes previously directed at these affects. Furthermore, it was only as these affects could be fully and repeatedly expressed, and the affectionate relationship to the mother restored, that the previous developmental progress was also restored: the growth in sphincter control, language usage and identification with the parents became noticeable, and the sleep disturbances diminished greatly. Without pretending to understand all the mechanisms involved in these changes, we believe that the above findings provide further evidence of a generalization formulated by Ritvo and Solnit (1958) as follows:

When internalization proceeds by way of a predominantly positive libidinal tie to the love object, it is more likely to proceed to completion than the internalizations that develop from a predominantly aggressive tie [p. 84].

Bibliography

Abraham, K. (1942), A short study of the development of the libido, viewed in the light of mental disorders. *Selected Papers on Psychoanalysis.* London: Hogarth Press, 1927.

Ainsworth, M. D. and Bowlby, J. (1954), Research strategy in the study of mother-child separation. *Courrier,* 4: (no. 3) 2.

Arrington, R. E. (1932), *Interrelations in the Behavior of Young Children.* New York: Columbia University Press.

Arsenian, J. (1943), Young children in an insecure situation. *J. Abnorm. Soc. Psychol.,* 38:225–249.

Aubry, J. (1955), *La Carence de Soins maternels* [Maternal Deprivation]. Paris: Presses Universitaires de France. Unpublished translation into English by Molly Townsend: Tavistock Child Development Research Unit, London, England.

Benjamin, J. D. (1959), Prediction and psychopathological theory. In: L. Jessner and E. Pavenstedt, Ed. *Dynamic Psychopathology in Childhood.* New York: Grune and Stratton, pp. 6–77.

—— (1961), Some developmental observations relating to the theory of anxiety. *J. Amer. Psychoanal. Assn.,* 9:652–688.

—— (1963), Further comments on some developmental aspects of anxiety. In: *Counterpoint,* H. S. Gaskill, Ed. New York: International Universities Press, pp. 121–153.

Beres, D. (1958), Vicissitudes of superego functions and superego precursors in childhood. *Psychoanal. Stud. Child,* 13:324–351.

Bernfeld, S. (1925), *The Psychology of the Infant.* London: Kegan Paul, 1929.

Bowlby, J. (1944), Forty-four juvenile thieves. *Int. J. Psychoanal.,* 25:1–57.

—— (1951), Maternal care and mental health. *WHO Monogr.,* No. 2.

—— (1953), Some pathological processes set in train by early mother-child separation. *J. Ment. Sci.,* 99:265–272.

—— (1954), Some pathological processes engendered by early mother-child separation. In: M. J. Senn, Ed. *Infancy and Childhood.* New York: Josiah Macy, Jr. Foundation, pp. 38–87.

—— (1958), The nature of the child's tie to the mother. *Int. J. Psychoanal.,* 39:1–24.

—— (1960a), Separation anxiety. *Int. J. Psychoanal.,* 41:1–25.

—— (1960b), Grief and mourning in infancy and early childhood. *Psychoanal. Stud. Child.,* 15:9-52.

—— (1961), Processes of mourning. *Int. J. Psychoanal.*, 42:317–340.

—— (1963), Pathological mourning and childhood mourning. *J. Amer. Psychoanal. Assn.*, 11:500–541.

——, Ainsworth, M., Boston, M., and Rosenbluth, D. (1956), The effects of mother-child separation: A follow-up study. *Brit. J. Med. Psychol.*, 29:211–247.

——, Robertson, J., and Rosenbluth, D. (1952), A two-year-old goes to the hospital. *Psychoanal. Stud. Child*, 7:82–94.

——, and ——, Forthcoming publication.

Casler, L. (1961), Maternal deprivation: A critical review of the literature. *Monogr. Soc. Res. Child Devel.*, 26, No. 2.

David, M., Ancellin, J., and Appell, G. (1957), Étude d'un groupe d'enfants ayant séjourné pendant un mois en colonie maternelle. *Information Sociales*, 8:825–893. Unpublished extracts translated into English by A. Sanders: Tavistock Child Development Research Unit, London, England.

——, Nicolas, J., and Roudinesco, J. (1952), Responses of young children to separation from their mothers: I. Observation of children ages 12–17 months recently separated from their families and living in an institution. *Courr. Cent. Int. l'Enfance*, 2 (2):66–78.

Deutsch, H. (1919), A two-year-old boy's first love comes to grief. In: *Dynamics of Psychopathology in Childhood*, L. Jessner and E. Pavenstedt, Eds. New York: Grune and Stratton, 1959.

Edelson, H. (1943), Separation anxiety in young children: A study of hospital cases. *Genet. Psychol. Monogr.*, 28:3–95.

Engel, G. L., and Reichsman, F. (1956), Spontaneous and experimentally induced depressions in an infant with a gastric fistula. *J. Amer. Psychoanal. Assn.*, 4:428–452.

Freud, A. (1936), *The Ego and the Mechanisms of Defence*. New York: International Universities Press, 1946.

—— (1951), Observations on child development. *Psychoanal. Stud. Child*, 6:18–30.

—— (1960), Discussion of Dr. John Bowlby's paper. *Psychoanal. Stud. Child*, 15:53–62.

—— (1963), Regression as a principle in mental development. *Bull. Menninger Clin.*, 27:126–139.

——, and Burlingham, D. (1943), *War and Children*. New York: Medical War Books.

——, and —— (1944), *Infants without Families*. New York: International Universities Press.

Freud, S. (1926), Inhibitions, symptoms and anxiety. *Standard Edition*, 20: 77–175. London: Hogarth Press, 1959.

Gesell, A., and Ilg, F. (1943), *Infant and Child in the Culture of Today*. New York: Harper Bros.

Gewirtz, J. (1961), A learning analysis of the effects of normal stimulation, privation and deprivation on the acquisition of social motivation and attachment. In: B. M. Foss, Ed., *Determinants of Infant Behavior*. New York: John Wiley and Sons, pp. 213–290.

Goldfarb, W. (1944), Infant rearing as a factor in foster home replacement. *Amer. J. Orthopsychiat.*, 14:162–173.

Hamilton, G. (1951), *Theory and Practice of Social Case Work*. New York: Columbia University Press.

Hare, B. (1952), A comparative study of the reactions of two-year-old children. Unpublished dissertation. University of London, Child Development Department.

Heinicke, C. M. (1953), Some antecedents and consequents of guilt and fear in young boys. Unpublished dissertation, Harvard University.

——— (1956), Some effects of separating two-year-old children from their parents: A comparative study. *Hum. Rel.*, 9:105–176.

Hellman, I. (1962), Hampstead Nursery follow-up studies: 1. Sudden separation and its effect followed over twenty years. *Psychoanal. Stud. Child*, 17:159–174.

Hollis, F. (1939), *Social Case Work in Practice*. New York: Family Welfare Assoc. of America.

Howells, J. G., and Layng, J. (1955), Separation experiences and mental health. *Lancet*, 2:285–288.

———, and ——— (1956), The effect of separation experiences on children given care away from home. *Med. Officer*, 95:345–347.

Illingworth, R. S., and Holt, K. S. (1955), Children in hospital: Some observations on their reactions with special reference to daily visiting. *Lancet*, 2:1257–1262.

Jessner, L., Blom, G., and Waldfogel, S. (1952), Emotional implications of tonsillectomy and adenoidectomy on children. *Psychoanal. Stud. Child*, 7:126–169.

———, and Kaplan, S. (1949), Reactions of children to tonsillectomy and adenoidectomy—Preliminary report. In: M. J. Senn, Ed. *Infancy and Childhood*. New York: Josiah Macy, Jr. Foundation.

Lewis, H. (1954), *Deprived Children*. Toronto: Oxford University Press.

Mahler, M. S. (1961), On sadness and grief in infancy and childhood. *Psychoanal. Stud. Child*, 16:332–351.

Pinneau, S. R. (1955), The infantile disorders of hospitalism and anaclitic depression. *Psychol. Bull.*, 52:429–462.

Pringle, K. M. L., and Bossio, V. (1958a), A study of deprived children: Part I. Intellectual, emotional, and social development. *Vita Humana*, 1 (2):65–92.

———, and ——— (1958b), A study of deprived children: Part II. Language and reading development. *Int. J. Human Develop.*, 1 (3/4):142–169.

———, and Tanner, M. (1958), The effects of early deprivation on speech development: A comparative study of four-year-olds in a Nursery School and in Residential Nurseries. *Language and Speech*, 1 (Part 4):269–287.

Prugh, D., et al. (1953), A study of the emotional reactions of children and families to hospitalization and illness. *Amer. J. Orthopsychiat.*, 23:70–106.

Rapaport, D. (1960), The structure of psychoanalytic theory. *Psychological Issues*, Monogr. 6. New York: International Universities Press.

———, and Gill, M. (1959), The points of view and assumptions of metapsychology. *Int. J. Psychoanal.*, 40:1–10.

Reich, A. (1954), Early identifications as archaic elements in the superego. *J. Amer. Psychoanal. Assn.*, 2:218–238.

Rheingold, H. (1956), The modification of social responsiveness in institutional babies. *Monogr. Soc. Res. Child Devel.*, 21, No. 63.

Richmond, M. (1917), *Social Diagnosis*. New York: Russell Sage Foundation.

Ritvo, S., and Solnit, A. J. (1958), Influences of early mother-child interaction in identification processes. *Psychoanal. Stud. Child*, 13:64–85.

Robertson, J. (1953a), Some responses of young children to loss of maternal care. *Nursing Times*, April, pp. 382–386.

——— (1953b), *A Two-Year-Old Goes to Hospital: A Guide to the Film*. London: Tavistock Publications.

Robertson, J. (1953c), *A Two-Year-Old Goes to Hospital* (film, 16 mm., sound, 45 min., in English and French). London: Tavistock Clinic; New York: New York University Film Library.

——— (1958), *Going to Hospital with Mother* (film, 16 mm., sound, 45 min., in English and French). London: Tavistock Clinic.

Robertson, J., and Bowlby, J. (1952), Responses of young children to separation from their mother. II. Observations of the sequences of response of children aged 17 to 24 months during the course of separation. *Courr. Cent. Int. l'Enfance*, 2:131–142.

Rochlin, G. (1953), Loss and restitution. *Psychoanal. Stud. Child*, 8:288–309.

——— (1961), The dread of abandonment. *Psychoanal. Stud. Child*, 16:451–469.

Roudinesco, A. J., and Appell, G. (1951), Some effects of the absence of maternal care and of institutional life on children between the ages of 1 and 4 years. *Bulletins et Mémoires de la Societé Médicale des Hôpitaux de Paris*, Extract Nos. 3 and 4.

Sandler, J. (1960), On the concept of superego. *Psychoanal. Stud. Child*, 15:128–160.

Schaeffer, E. S., and Bayley, N. (1963), Maternal behavior, child behavior, and their intercorrelations from infancy through adolescence. *Monogr. Soc. Res. Child Devel.*, 28 (No. 3).

Schafer, R. (1960), The loving and beloved superego in Freud's Structural Theory. *Psychoanal. Stud. Child*, 15:163–188.

Schaffer, H. R. (1958), Objective observations of personality development in early infancy. *Brit. J. Med. Psychol.*, 31:174–183.

———, and Callender, W. M. (1959), Psychologic effect of hospitalization in infancy. *Pediatrics*, 24:528–539.

Scharl, A. E. (1961), Regression and restitution in object loss. *Psychoanal. Stud. Child,* 16:471–479.

Schur, M. (1958), The ego and the id in anxiety. *Psychoanal. Stud. Child,* 13:190–220.

—— (1960), Discussion of Dr. John Bowlby's paper. *Psychoanal. Stud. Child,* 15:63–84.

Siegel, S. (1956), *Nonparametric Statistics for the Behavioral Sciences.* New York: McGraw-Hill.

Sofer, C. (1956), Methodology of a collaborative research project. A paper prepared for the Psychology Section of the 1956 Conference of the British Association for the Advancement of Science.

Spitz, R. A. (1945), Hospitalism: An inquiry into the genesis of psychiatric conditions in early childhood, *Psychoanal. Stud. Child,* 1:53–74.

—— (1946), Hospitalism: A follow-up report on investigation described in Vol. 1. *Psychoanal. Stud. Child,* 2:113–117.

—— (1950), Anxiety in infancy. *Int. J. Psychoanal.,* 31:138–143.

—— (1955), Reply to Pinneau. *Psychol. Bull.,* 52:453–459.

—— (1957), *No and Yes.* New York: International Universities Press.

—— (1960), Discussion of Dr. John Bowlby's paper. *Psychoanal. Stud. Child,* 15:85–94.

——, and Wolf, K. (1946), Anaclitic depression: An inquiry into the genesis of psychiatric conditions in early childhood. *Psychoanal. Stud. Child,* 2:313–342.

Spock, B. (1957), *Baby and Child Care.* New York: Giant Cardinal.

Tennes, K., and Lampl, E. (1963), Stranger and separation anxiety in infancy. Paper read at Biennial Meeting of Society for Research in Child Development.

Thompson, W. R. (1955), Early environment—its importance for later behavior. In: P. H. Hoch and J. Zubin, Eds., *Psychopathology of Childhood.* New York: Grune and Stratton, pp. 120–139.

Trasler, G. (1960), *In Place of Parents: A Study of Foster Care.* London: Routledge and Kegan Paul.

Winnicot, D. W. (1954), The depressive position in normal emotional development. *Collected Papers.* London: Tavistock, 1958.

Wright, H. F. (1960), Observational child study. In: P. H. Mussen, Ed., *Handbook of Research Methods in Child Development.* New York: John Wiley and Sons, pp. 71–139.

Yarrow, L. J. (1961), Maternal deprivation: toward an empirical and conceptual re-evaluation. *Psychol. Bull.* 58:459–490.

Name Index

Ainsworth, M. D., 1
Ancellin, J., 310
Appell, G., 302, 310, 320
Arrington, R. E., 22
Arsenian, J., 317
Aubry, J., *see* Roudinesco

Bayley, N., 56
Benjamin, J. D., 334
Beres, D., 204
Bossio, V., 315, 322
Bowlby, J., 1, 273, 274, 275, 276, 282, 285,
    288, 289, 290, 293, 295, 297, 300,
    303, 313, 314, 321, 323
Burlingham, D., 1, 272, 273, 281, 292, 293,
    296, 297, 300, 302, 303, 305, 316, 338

Callender, W. M., 308, 309

David, M., 277, 287, 298, 300, 303, 310
Deutsch, H., 318

Freud, A., 1, 207, 272, 273, 281, 292, 293,
    295, 296, 297, 298, 300, 301, 303,
    305, 316, 338
Freud, S., 327, 328, 330

Gesell, A., 329
Gill, M., 323
Goldfarb, W., 321

Hamilton, G., 25
Hare, B., 279, 296, 300
Heinicke, C. M., 1, 14, 18, 19, 20, 21, 166,
    186, 215, 253, 256, 257, 258, 260,
    261, 272, 280, 281, 284, 285, 286, 291,
    294, 296, 298, 299, 303, 326
Hellman, I., 338
Hollis, F., 25, 30
Holt, K. S., 280

Ilg, F., 329

Illingworth, R. S., 280

Lampl, E., 334
Lewis, H., 315

Nicholas, J., 277, 287, 298, 300, 303

Pringle, M. L. K., 174, 315
Prugh, D., 279, 283, 296, 297, 299, 314

Rapaport, D., 6, 323
Reich, A., 204
Rheingold, H., 316
Richmond, M., 29
Ritvo, S., 207, 345
Robertson, J., 1, 273, 274, 275, 276, 281, 282,
    285, 288, 289, 290, 293, 295, 297,
    300, 303, 304, 305, 313, 314, 317, 321
Rosenbluth, D., 276, 290, 295
Roudinesco, J., 277, 278, 284, 287, 288, 293,
    296, 298, 300, 302, 303, 304, 320

Sandler, J., 204
Schaeffer, E. S., 56
Schafer, R., 204
Schaffer, H. R., 308, 309
Schur, M., 327
Sears, P., 21
Siegel, S., 49, 160, 244
Sofer, C., 35
Solnit, A. J., 207, 345
Spitz, R., 279, 308, 309, 317, 320, 328, 333,
    334
Spock, B., 329

Tanner, M., 174
Tennes, K., 334
Trasler, G., 321

Wolf, K., 320
Wright, H. F., 14, 22

Yarrow, L., 1, 5

Subject Index